JOURNAL FOR THE STUDY OF THE NEW TESTAMENT
SUPPLEMENT SERIES
112

Sheffield Academic Press

The Temptations of Jesus in Early Christianity

Jeffrey B. Gibson

Journal for the Study of the New Testament
Supplement Series 112

Published by
Sheffield Academic Press Ltd
Mansion House
19 Kingfield Road
Sheffield, S11 9AS
England

Typeset by Sheffield Academic Press
and
Printed on acid-free paper in Great Britain
by Bookcraft
Midsomer Norton, Somerset

British Library Cataloguing in Publication Data

A catalogue record for this book is available
from the British Library

ISBN 1-85075-539-6

CONTENTS

PREFACE

The origins of this present work, a revised version of my Oxford DPhil thesis begun under the supervision of the late G.B. Caird, date back to my undergraduate days at Oxford and lay particularly in an assignment given me by John Muddiman, then my New Testament tutor (and subsequently my second thesis advisor), to see what I could make of the question of the occasion of the Epistle to the Hebrews. At the time of the assignment I had never read the Epistle, let alone any of the secondary literature dealing with it or the discussions of its background in the standard New Testament 'Introductions'. So I had no predispositions toward a particular answer on the question at hand nor any knowledge of what scholarship had argued on this matter. All I knew was that, because of the silence of the Epistle itself on the matter of why it was written and the absence of any reliable external information or tradition which might provide clues in this regard, an attempt at determining what had been the occasion of the Epistle would involve a process of inference, working backwards from those passages that seemed to speak, if only indirectly, of the situation in which the Epistle's readers found themselves, to the situation itself. So, primed and ready to discover or be struck by just such passages, I began to read the work. I did not have to read long before they began to appear.

I found from the beginning of the second chapter onwards, and then piled closely one upon another, passages which seemed worthy of note: verses speaking of the possibility of the readers 'drifting away' (παραρρέω) through disobedience (παρακοή) to what had been revealed to them of God's ways in his Son (2.1, cf. 3-5; 3.12-13; 4.1-2) as well as of the necessity of holding fast (κατέχω/κρατέω) and remaining steadfast in faithfulness to an 'assurance' (ὑπόστασις), a 'confidence' (παρρησία), a 'hope' (ἐλπίς) and an original 'confession' (ὁμολογία) to which they had some time ago committed themselves even though a present crisis, a painful and trying 'time of need', seemed to throw doubt on the validity of these things (3.6, 14-15; 4.14).

Then I came to Heb. 4.15—a passage which, along with 2.17, not only says that *because* of their 'confidence' and their faithfulness the readers of Hebrews were, at the time of the Epistle's writing, undergoing temptations (πειρασμοί), but which has as a basic assumption the conviction that these temptations were in essence the same as those which both the author and readers of Hebrews knew the earthly Jesus to have experienced. And I paused. Bells were ringing. What came to mind as I read this verse and its counterpart was a particular passage from John Howard Yoder's *The Politics of Jesus* (Grand Rapids: Eerdmans, 1972), which I had only recently (and, as I later thought, serendipitously) read:

> Being human, Jesus must have been subject somehow or other to the testings of pride, envy, anger, sloth, avarice, gluttony, and lust. But it does not enter into the concerns of the Gospel writer to give us any information about any struggles he may have had with their attraction. The one temptation the man Jesus faced—and faced again and again—as a constitutive element of his public ministry, was the temptation to exercise social responsibility, in the interest of justified revolution, through the use of available violent methods. Social withdrawal was no temptation for him; that option...was excluded at the outset. Any alliance with the Sadducean establishment in the exercise of *conservative* social responsibility...was likewise excluded at the outset. We understand Jesus only if we can empathize with...the self-evident, axiomatic, sweeping rejection of both quietism and establishment responsibility, and the difficult, constantly reopened, genuinely attractive option of the crusade (*Politics of Jesus*, p. 98).

Accepting without question the truth of Yoder's dual thesis—that within the Early Church there was a unified conception of the nature and content of Jesus' temptations, and that this conception centered in the idea that the only point over which Jesus was ever thought to have been tempted was whether he was going to be a warrior king who would liberate his people from oppression through violence—I placed this alongside Heb. 4.17 and came up with a sort of exegetical syllogism:

> The author of Hebrews viewed the temptations of Jesus as the epitome of what his readers were undergoing.

> The author of Hebrews knew that Jesus' temptations involved whether or not, in the name of God and in pursuit of God's purposes, Jesus would engage in or advocate a holy war against his people Israel's oppressors.

> Therefore, the temptations that the readers of Hebrews faced were, likewise, to join with theocratically motivated, violent revolutionary forces to defeat Israel's enemies.

Having reached this conclusion, naturally the next step was to ask *when* within the first century CE, and *in what particular historical circumstances*, would Christians have found themselves faced with, let alone be attracted to, such an option? Josephus and his *Jewish War*, which I had also recently been reading, provided the answer: *during the years 66–70 CE in the revolt and subsequent war of the Jews against Rome.* Here erupts a particular cause—the establishment of God's sovereignty in Zion—to which any Christian, let alone the readers of Hebrews, would be mightily drawn. Here Christians were caught up in a moving appeal, at times enforced with less than salutary means of persuasion, to band together with their religious compatriots in active service to their ancestral faith. Here, especially in the initial stages of the war (which saw such things as the unexpected rout at the foot of the Temple and the eventual defeat of the legions of the Roman Legate, Cestius Gallus, the appointment and installation of a new High Priest untainted by collaboration with Rome, and the purification and rededication of the Temple), insurgent Jewish nationalists, using treachery and violence, had seemingly begun to achieve the very thing which the Sons of the Covenant had been promised and for which all pious Jews had long hoped: the liberation of Israel. And given the successes enjoyed by these nationalists in their military campaigns against the superior might of Rome, here, too, was apparent proof that the means and methods these men employed to attain their ends actually enjoyed divine approval.

Surely, I concluded, the revolt against Rome was the historical background against which Hebrews was written, and the probability of its readers being caught up in the revolt's allurement, with all it seemed to promise them, was to be perceived as the occasion that prompted Hebrews' author to take pen in hand. After all, I thought, did not the author's exhortations to hold on to what he and his readers had been taught were God's ways (3.12; 6.4-6, 11-12), to side with the Christian's new High Priest (4.14; 10.19-25), to rally round their better altar (13.10), and to move outside the 'camp' of Israel (Jerusalem) (13.13), come more brilliantly and vibrantly alive under this particular assumption as to when and why the Epistle was written than under any other? And did not his apparent repudiations of the current Jewish high priesthood and sacrificial practices (e.g. 9.11-14; 10.1-18) have an especial fit with the ideology of the revolt, where these institutions, used as butresses of, and symbols for, its revolutionary program, turned the Temple into a hotbed of revolutionary nationalism, a 'den of robbers', instead of a house of prayer for all nations?

And so, in the white heat of an enthusiasm brought on by the certainty that I and I alone had found the key to an interpretative door which generations of scholars had failed to unlock, I placed my views on paper.

My tutor, however, quickly pulled me up short when I presented my thesis to him. Not only did he point out, by drawing my attention to the work of Alexander Nairne (especially his *The Epistle of Priesthood* [Edinburgh: T. & T. Clark, 1913] and *The Epistle to the Hebrews* [Cambridge: Cambridge University Press, 1921]), that my reconstruction of the occasion of the Hebrews was hardly original or new; he also noted that however interesting and provocative my contention might be, it was both fundamentally unsubstantiated and logically flawed. I had begged the question, assuming as true the very thing I needed to make my case, namely, that there was indeed within the early Church a unified conception of the nature and content of Jesus' temptations. It may very well have been so, though he doubted it. After all, when one looks at Gospel temptation stories and takes into account all of the variations that are displayed there, not only intratextually but among parallel reports of the same temptation story, regarding the circumstances and occasions in which Jesus' temptations are said to occur and the interlocutors who initiate them, is there not at least a *prima facie* case for the perception in the early church that Jesus underwent many types of temptations involving a gamut of concerns? But in any event, he noted, until I demonstrated through analysis and solid exegesis the truth of my assumption, I had no secure grounds either for using it as a major premise in my larger argument or for appealing to it as evidence supporting the conclusion about Hebrews that I had drawn.

I accepted these remarks as they were intended—as a challenge rather than as a rebuke, and I became determined to prove, when circumstances afforded themselves, both Yoder and myself correct. What follows is a contribution towards doing so.

The present work would never have seen completion without the help of many others. Thanks are due especially to Paul Griffiths, Trevor Williams, Richard Pervo, Robert Jewett, Don Wendland, Richard Stegner, Ed Sanders, Lincoln Hurst, Colin Brown, Robert Morgan, and, of course, to John Muddiman, not only for generously giving of their limited time to read the work and offer extensive comments on its various drafts, but for their continued encouragement, especially during the many times when I was less than enthused about continuing the project.

I must also express my gratitude to the Trustees of the Hall-Houghton Studentship in the Greek New Testament, Oxford, for electing me to the Studentship in 1982 and for providing me with funds for maintenance and research. I hope what they find here justifies the confidence they once placed in me so long ago.

Thanks are also due to to Keith Burton for his patience in instructing me in the ways and means of word processing and the intricacies of the electronic *TLG*, to Denny Laub and David Himrod for supplying me with books, to Mdm. Angelique von Rosenberg for her able assistance in guiding me through the German literature, and to C. Rowland and D.R. Catchpole, my DPhil thesis examiners, for pointing out to me in a lively and rewarding discussion where I might anticipate critical attack should the thesis ever be published unaltered. And my editor at Sheffield Academic Press, Webb Mealy, deserves special commendation for his hard work in preparing this study for publication.

Much of what constitutes Chapter 2 has already appeared as 'Jesus' Wilderness Temptation according to Mark', *JSNT* 53 (1994), pp. 3-34. A large portion of an earler draft of Chapter 5 was published as 'Jesus' Refusal to Produce a "Sign" (Mk 8.11-13)', *JSNT* 38 (1990), pp. 37-66. I wish to thank the editors of that journal, C.M. Tuckett and Francis Watson, for their comments and suggestions on matters of presentation and argumentation, many of which have been incorporated into the present work.

I should like to dedicate this book to two men, both of whom have in their respective ways been my guiding lights: my father, Regis E. Gibson, whose continuing refrain, until a particularly debilitating stroke took away his ability to make it, was 'How long does it take to write a thesis?' He prompted me more (and in more ways) than he knows. And to George Bradford Caird, late Dean Irelands Professor of Biblical Interpretation at the University of Oxford, sorely missed, under whom the work which forms the basis of this book was begun. I regret not having completed it before his passing. Flights of angels sing thee to thy rest.

ABBREVIATIONS

ASV	American Standard Version
ATR	*Anglican Theological Review*
BAGD	W. Bauer, W.F. Arndt, F.W. Gingrich and F.W. Danker, *Greek–English Lexicon of the New Testament and other Early Christian Literature*
BDF	F. Blass, A. Debrunner and R.W. Funk, *A Greek Grammar of the New Testament and other Early Christian Literature*
Bib	*Biblica*
BibRes	*Biblical Research*
BibSac	*Bibliotheca Sacra*
BT	*The Bible Translator*
BJRL	*Bulletin of the John Rylands University Library of Manchester*
BR	*Bible Review*
BTB	*Biblical Theology Bulletin*
BZ	*Biblische Zeitschrift*
Cath	*Catholica*
CBQ	*Catholic Biblical Quarterly*
CBrugTomL	*Collationes brugenses*
Con	*Concilium*
CrQ	*Crozier Quarterly*
EDNT	*Exegetical Dictionary of the New Testament*
EstBíb	*Estudia Bíblica*
ETL	*Ephemerides Theologicae Lovanienses*
EvQ	*Evangelical Quarterly*
EvT	*Evangelische Theologie*
ExpTim	*Expository Times*
GKC	*Gesenius' Hebrew Grammar*, ed. E. Kautzch, trans. A.E. Cowley
HNT	Handbuch zum Neuen Testament
HTR	*Harvard Theological Review*
HUCA	*Hebrew Union College Annual*
IB	*Interpreter's Bible*
IDB	*Interpreter's Dictionary of the Bible*
IDBSup	*Interpreter's Dictionary of the Bible, Supplemantary Volume*
Int	*Interpretation*
ISBE	*International Standard Bible Encyclopedia*, rev. edn
JB	Jerusalem Bible

JBL	*Journal of Biblical Literature*
JBLMS	*Journal of Biblical Literature*, Monograph Series
JBR	*Journal of Bible and Religion*
JETS	*Journal of the Evangelical Theological Society*
JJS	*Journal of Jewish Studies*
JQR	*Jewish Quarterly Review*
JR	*Journal of Religion*
JSNT	*Journal for the Study of the New Testament*
JSNTSup	*Journal for the Study of the New Testament*, Supplement Series
JTS	*Journal of Theological Studies*
KJV	King James ('Authorized') Version
LB	*Linguistica Biblica*
LCL	Loeb Classical Library
NAB	New American Bible
NASB	New American Standard Bible
NEB	New English Bible
NIDNTT	*New International Dictionary of New Testament Theology*
NIV	New International Version
NovT	*Novum Testamentum*
NovTSup	*Novum Testamentum* Supplements
NTS	*New Testament Studies*
OTP	J.H. Charlesworth (ed.), *The Old Testament Pseudepigrapha* (2 vols.)
RB	*Revue Biblique*
RevExp	*Review and Expositer*
RNT	Regensberger Neues Testament
RSV	Revised Standard Version
RTR	*Reformed Theological Review*
RV	Revised Version
SBLMS	Society of Biblical Literature Monograph Series
SBLSP	Society of Biblical Literature Seminar Papers
SE	*Studia Evangelica* I, II, III (= TU 73 [1959], 87 [1964], 88 [1964], etc.)
SJT	*Scottish Journal of Theology*
StBib	*Studia Biblica*
Str–B	H. Strack and P. Billerbeck, *Kommentar zum Neuen Testament aus Talmud und Midrasch*
TDNT	*Theological Dictionary of the New Testament*
TEV	Today's English Version (The Good News Bible)
THAT	*Theologisches Handwörterbuch zum Alten Testament*
THKNT	Theologischer Handkommentar zum Neuen Testament
ThWAT	*Theologisches Wörterbuch zum Alten Testament*
TLG	*Thesaurus Linguae Grecae*
TLZ	*Theologische Literaturzeitung*
TS	*Theological Studies*

TZ	*Theologische Zeitschrift*
USQR	*Union Seminary Quarterly Review*
VC	*Vigiliae Christianae*
VD	*Verbum Domine*
VT	*Vetus Testamentum*
ZNW	*Zeitschrift für die neutestamenliche Wissenschaft*
ZST	*Zeitschrift für systematische Theologie*
ZTK	*Zeitschrift für Theologie und Kirche*

INTRODUCTION

> Then Jesus was led up by the Spirit into the wilderness to be tempted by the devil.

> The Pharisees came and began to argue with him, seeking from him a 'sign' from heaven, tempting him.

> And...a lawyer stood up to 'put him to the test'...

> But knowing their hypocrisy, he said to them, 'Why do you tempt me?'

According to the Synoptic tradition an important (indeed, perhaps the most characteristic) feature of Jesus' life lay in the experience which the ancient Greek speaking world termed πειρασμός, 'temptation'. This is clear if only from the frequency with which reports concerning Jesus' subjection to such an experience appear in the tradition. We find notices, for instance, in Luke and Matthew and Mark that Jesus underwent 'temptation' in the wilderness immediately after his Baptism,[1] on account of a demand made by his opponents for a 'sign from heaven',[2] in the challenge about paying taxes to the Roman Emperor,[3] and before his arrest in Gethsemane.[4] Mark and Matthew both note that Jesus was 'tempted' when confronted with the so-called 'Confession' of Peter at Caesarea Philippi[5] and in the question of the Pharisees concerning the legitimacy of divorce.[6] Matthew reports that a Pharisee's question concerning the 'greatest' of the commandments of the Mosaic Law was an occasion of 'temptation' for Jesus,[7] and Luke recounts that Jesus was 'tempted' by a lawyer's demand to know Jesus' idea of the requirements for inheriting eternal life.[8] Moreover, Luke records that Jesus

1. See Mt. 4.2; Mk 1.13; Lk. 4.2, 13.
2. See Mt. 16.1-14; Mk 8.11-13; Lk. 11.16, 29-32.
3. See Mt. 22.17-18; Mk 12.15; Lk. 20.23 A D.
4. See Mt. 26.36-46, cf. v. 41; Mk 14.32-42, cp. v. 38; Lk. 22.40-46, cp. v. 46.
5. See Mk 8.27-33; Mt. 16.13-23.
6. See Mk 10.2; Mt. 19.3.
7. Mt. 21.35.
8. Lk. 10.25.

himself designated the course of his ministry specifically as a series of 'temptations'.[9]

But it is not only in the Synoptic tradition that Jesus' life is viewed as one typified by continued subjection to experiences of πειρασμός. A 'Johannine' tradition found at Jn 7.53–8.11 in D E (F) G K M U G II 28 700 892 *al* (but also after Lk. 21.38 in f^{13})—a story of Jesus being 'tempted' by a question on the legitimacy of stoning a woman caught in the act of adultery—evinces this perception, as does a story found partially preserved in *Egerton Papyrus 2* (Fragment 2 recto).[10] And this is especially the case in the Epistle to the Hebrews. For as such important texts as Heb. 2.17-18 and 4.15 show, the author of that Epistle works from a fundamental historical and theological understanding which holds 'temptation' to have been *the* essential and defining characteristic of Jesus' earthly existence.[11]

Given this, it seems clear that there was a widespread—perhaps universal—discernment within the early Church that the life of Jesus was primarily a life under 'temptation'.

But what, according to the literary witness, was the early Church's understanding of *the nature and content* of these experiences? Further, was it variform or uniform? Did the early Church—or even any given evangelist—hold the view that Jesus was 'tempted' in a variety of ways over a full range of issues? Or was their position in this regard that his 'temptations' were always of one type and involving only one particular concern?

These are no idle questions. Their answer, especially if the latter possibility is the case, has important ramifications. Would not proof of a uniform conception of the nature and content of Jesus πειρασμοί lead us to a new or clearer view of how the early Church perceived the exigencies of its Lord's mission and message? Would it not provide us with fresh or deeper insights into such prominent New Testament themes as Sonship, obedience, faithfulness or discipleship? And would it

---

9.   Lk. 22.28.

10.   On the questions of the date, authorship and canonicity of the pericope *de Adultera*, see R.E. Brown, *The Gospel according to John (i–xii)* (Garden City: Doubleday, 1966), pp. 335-36. For the text of *Egerton Papyrus 2* Fragment 2 recto— a fragment of a story concerning Jesus being 'tempted' by a question on the legitimacy of paying taxes to the Emperor—as well as for a discussion of such questions as its date and its literary relationship to the Synoptic Tradition's versions of the Tax Question 'temptation', see below, Chapter 9.

11.   On this, see H. Seesemann, 'πεῖρα, κτλ.', *TDNT*, VI, p. 33.

not open up new possibilities for establishing the occasion of those New Testament writings, such as the Gospel of Mark or even the Epistle to the Hebrews, where notice of, and appeal to, the example of Jesus in 'temptation' appears as a prominent feature?[12]

12. The reconstruction of the occasion of the Epistle to the Hebrews is complicated by two facts. First, there is a conspicuous absence of any authoritative external tradition speaking reliably on the question of the epistle's origins; secondly, the epistle itself says nothing directly in this regard. The task of establishing the epistle's occasion is, therefore, of necessity a matter of (a) selecting those passages in the epistle which seem to be specifically addressed to the contingencies of the situation in which the epistle's readers found themselves, then (b) quarrying from them by inference the information about the readers' situation which they hold, and then finally (c) coordinating the information thus gained into a hypothesis which seems best to account for it. So the question that presses upon us is: of all the many and varied passages in the epistle addressed to the situation of its readers that hold promise for furnishing information vital to establishing the epistle's occasion, *which should be selected to be quarried*?

A strong case can be made for those passages which deal with Jesus' 'temptations', i.e., Heb. 2.18 and 4.15. Being paraenetic in form, they are addressed directly to the situation in which the readers of the epistle were involved, and, more significantly, they presuppose an exact parallelism between what they relate about Jesus on the one hand and what they have to say about the epistle's readers on the other (on this, see F. Laub, *Bekenntnis und Auslegung: Die Paranetische Funktion der Christologie im Hebraerbrief* [Regensburg: Pustet, 1980], pp. 109-12). Indeed, the very reason that the references to Jesus' experiences of being 'tempted' are employed in the epistle is that in the mind of Hebrews' author these experiences are thought to be not only analogous to, but identical with, those which his readers were undergoing. Accordingly, discovering the occasion of the Epistle to the Hebrews is a matter of unpacking the particular conception of the content of Jesus' 'temptations' that the author of the Epistle had in mind.

Unfortunately, however, the author of Hebrews does not make explicit his conception of the content of Jesus' 'temptations'. He states directly nothing in relation to precisely how, or over what issue, he thought Jesus to have been 'tempted'. (The statement in Heb. 2.18 that Jesus πέπονθεν αὐτὸς πειρασθείς indicates that Jesus' 'temptations' were thought by both Hebrews' author and readers alike as something which came upon Jesus in his sufferings. But which sufferings are in view are not, here at least, immediately apparent.) Therefore, by virtue of the fact of its author's silence—a silence due, surely, to the fact that the author could assume that his readers shared his particular conception of the content of Jesus' 'temptations' and not to the author or his readers having no such conception—the very passages which could lead to establishing the reader's situation are prevented from doing so.

But if the early Church held and maintained a consistent and unified view of the nature and content of Jesus' 'temptations', the silence of the author of Hebrews

There are, therefore, compelling reasons for determining whether or not this fact can indeed be established. The remaining question is, then, How would one go about demonstrating that it was so? Surely, determining whether or not the early Church's view of the nature and content of Jesus' temptations was uniform involves taking the following steps:

1.   investigating the extant accounts portraying Jesus as subject to πειρασμός that from a source-critical or literary point of view are the oldest of these accounts and independent of one another, and determining what they each have to say regarding the issue at hand;

2.   moving on, with the same goal in mind, to an investigation of those 'temptation' stories which are adaptations of the more original accounts;

3.   comparing the results of the second step with those of the first.

If all three steps are carried out, then several things will have been determined: *first*, just what the early Church understood as the particular concern(s) over which Jesus had been 'tempted'; *secondly*, how frequently or infrequently any particular conception of the content of those 'temptations' was entertained; and, *thirdly*, which (if any) of the earlier conceptions—whatever they might have been—about the nature and content of Jesus' 'temptations' were preserved relatively intact, and which were substantially altered as stories of Jesus' subjection to πειρασμός were passed on and adapted in the tradition.

The present study represents a contribution towards the attainment of these goals. In the following pages I shall be concerned with carrying out only the first of the three investigative steps outlined above. The material that qualifies as this step's appropriate subject matter is, I believe, *in*

---

concerning his conception of the content of Jesus' 'temptations' may not be, to put it colloquially, as 'deafening' as it might otherwise seem; and rather than being disqualified as ultimately useless for determining the Epistle's occasion, the passages in Hebrews which deal with Jesus' 'temptations' may in the end prove immensely helpful. For if the Church's view of the nature and content of Jesus' 'temptations' was unified, then we would have good reason to assume both that the author of Hebrews had this view in mind when he refers to the fact that Jesus was 'tempted' and that the readers of the epistle would have thought along these lines when the example of Jesus under 'temptation' was brought before them, both author and readers having no other view of the content of Jesus' 'temptations' available to them to draw upon or inform their imaginations.

itself sufficiently extensive, and the tasks at hand in examining it sufficiently engaging, that to go beyond it to the 'secondary' material and carry out steps two and three would prove too ambitious within the confines of a single study.

Accordingly, it is necessary for me to note which of the various 'temptation' stories I regard as literarily independent and, from a source-critical point of view, the oldest and most original—and which, therefore, will stand as the 'touchstones' of my analysis. These are the following:[13]

1.   The Markan account of Jesus' 'temptation' in the wilderness (Mk 1.9-13).[14]

13. As should be evident from my lists of 'primary' and 'secondary' 'temptation' traditions, I assume here, when dealing with the Synoptic manifestations of 'temptation of Jesus' traditions, the solution to the Synoptic Problem generally known as 'a modified Two-Source hypothesis'. Despite spirited challenges made to this solution by W.R. Farmer (*The Synoptic Problem* [Macon, GA: Mercer University Press, 1964]; *idem*, 'A "Skeleton in the Closet" of Gospel Research', *BR* 9 [1961], pp. 18-42) and more recently by E.P. Sanders and M. Davies (*Studying the Synoptic Gospels* [London: SCM Press, 1989], pp. 51-122) and M.D. Goulder (*Luke: A New Paradigm* [JSNTSup, 20; Sheffield: JSOT Press, 1993]), I am still persuaded that the authors of the Gospels of Matthew and Luke, while making use of material peculiar to themselves, each independently knew and used both the Gospel of Mark as well as another common source which can be reconstructed out of the text of Matthew and Luke as the postulated collection of material known as 'Q'.

On the Synoptic Problem itself and the variety of solutions that have been advanced in attempts to solve it, see W.G. Kümmel, *Introduction to the New Testament* (London: SCM Press, 1975), pp. 38-80. For a full description and defence of the 'modified Two Source hypothesis', see J.A. Fitzmyer, 'The Priority of Mark and the "Q" Source in Luke', in *Jesus and Man's Hope* (ed. D.G. Miller; 2 vols.; Pittsburgh: Pickwick Press, 1971), I, pp. 131-70, now reprinted in Fitzmyer, *To Advance the Gospel* (New York: Crossroads, 1981), pp. 3-40. See also Fitzmyer's elaboration of this position, with special attention to Luke's dependence on Mark and Q in his *The Gospel according to Luke, 1–9* (Garden City: Doubleday, 1981), pp. 63-106. For the classic statement of the 'Two Document Hypothesis'—the hypothesis of which my position regarding the solution of the Synoptic Problem is a modification, see B.H. Streeter, *The Four Gospels* (London: Macmillan, 1924).

14. On this as the proper extent of the Markan version of the tradition of Jesus' Wilderness 'temptation', see below, pp. 24-31.

2.   The Markan account of Jesus' experience of being 'tempted' when confronted with a demand for a ' "sign" from heaven' (Mk 8.1-13).[15]

3.   The Markan account of Jesus' experience of being 'tempted' at Caesarea Philippi (Mk 8.27-33).

4.   The Markan account of Jesus being 'tempted' when asked about the legitimacy of divorce (Mk 10.1-12).

5.   The Markan account of Jesus being 'tempted' when asked about the legitimacy of paying taxes to the Roman Emperor (Mk 12.13-17).

6.   The Markan account of Jesus in Gethsemane (Mk 14.32-42).

7.   The 'Q' version of the tradition of Jesus' 'temptation' in the wilderness (Mt. 4.1-11//Lk. 4.1-13).

8.   The 'Q' version of the tradition of the demand for a 'sign' (Mt. 12.38-39//Lk. 11.16, 29).[16]

9.   The Lukan account of Jesus' experience of being 'tempted' when confronted with a question on the requirements of inheriting eternal life (Lk. 10.25-26), which I take to be derived from Q.

10.   The Lukan report of Jesus' testimony that his ministry was conducted in the face of 'temptations' (Lk. 22.28).

11.   The 'Johannine' story of Jesus' being 'tempted' when confronted with the question on stoning a woman caught in the act of adultery (Jn 7.53–8.11).

The versions of the various narrative traditions concerned with Jesus' 'temptations' which I consider to be secondary to, and literary adaptations of, older, more original traditions—and which, therefore, I will not investigate here—are the following:

1.   The Matthean version of the tradition of Jesus' 'temptation' in the wilderness (Mt. 4.1-11).

2.   The Lukan version of Jesus' 'temptation' in the wilderness (Lk. 4.1-13).

---

15. On this as the proper extent of the Markan version of the 'sign' demand tradition, see below, pp. 124-27.

16. As we will see, the Q account of the Demand for a 'sign' actually extends beyond Mt. 12.38-39//Lk. 11.16, 29 and includes not only Mt. 12.40-41//Lk. 11.30-32 but much of Mt. 12.22-37//Lk. 11.14-28 as well. This, along with the fact that the Q account is a '"temptation" tradition', will be shown below in Chapters 4 and 5.

3.   The Matthean version of the account of Jesus' 'temptation' in the demand for a '"sign" from heaven' (Mt. 16.1-2a, 4).

4.   The Lukan version of the account of Jesus' 'temptation' in the demand for a '"sign" from heaven' (Lk. 11.16, 29-32).

5.   The Matthean version of the account of Jesus' 'temptation' when faced with Peter's 'confession' at Caesarea Philippi (Mt. 16.13-23).

6.   The Matthean version of the account of Jesus' 'temptation' in the question on the legitimacy of divorce (Mt. 19.1-12).

7.   The Matthean and Lukan accounts of Jesus' 'temptation' by the question concerning the legitimacy of paying taxes to Caesar (Mt. 22.15-22; Lk. 20.20-26 A D).

8.   The Matthean account of Jesus' being 'tempted' when confronted with the question of the 'greatest commandment' (Mt. 23.34-40).

9.   The Matthean version of the tradition of Jesus' 'temptation' in Gethsemane (Mt. 26.36-46).

10.   The Lukan account of Jesus in Gethsemane (Lk. 22.40-46).

11.   The *Egerton Papyrus* account of Jesus being 'tempted' by the question on the legitimacy of paying taxes to Caesar (Fragment 2 recto).

As the reader turns to the table of contents or moves through the text of this study, two things will stand out. First, I have devoted a disproportionate amount of space to my analysis and discussion of the Markan versions of the traditions of Jesus' Wilderness and 'Demand for a Sign' 'temptations' relative to that given over to the versions of the other 'temptation' traditions examined here. The main reason for this is that here in particular, certainly more so than with any of the other versions of the 'temptation' traditions I investigate, my conclusions on what is being said are not only *new* but, as we will see, *in diametrical opposition to what has previously been advanced by others on these matters*. When one finds oneself not only arguing *for* a view which seems never (or only rarely and without much fervour) to have been put forward, but also arguing *against* virtually all other interpretations, let alone 'standard' and widely accepted ones, a lengthy discussion is inevitable.

Secondly, I have provided a tradition history of each of the versions of the 'temptation' traditions I investigate. At first glance, this might seem puzzling. Why, if I am principally trying to determine what a given *canonical* text has to say regarding the nature and content of the 'temptation' experience it recounts, should I be at all concerned with determining whether or not that text had a *Vorlage*, let alone trying to outline it if it existed, or establish whether and to what extent it has been redacted? The answer lies in the fact that if we are to ascertain whether or not there was within the early Church a unitary view of Jesus' πειρασμοί, then we must know not only what evidence the 'primary' traditions provide on this matter *when compared with one another*, but also in what way these traditions *individually within themselves*, that is, within their own respective 'trajectories', serve to confirm or disconfirm the likelihood of a unitary view. Tracing the history of the development of each 'primary' tradition is, therefore, a necessity.

I trust my efforts will be seen as worthwhile.

Chapter 1

THE TRADITION OF JESUS' WILDERNESS TEMPTATION: THE ACCOUNTS AND THEIR RELATIONSHIP

The tradition that at the beginning of his ministry Jesus experienced temptation during a sojourn in the wilderness is recounted by each of the three Synoptic evangelists. Critical scholarship has demonstrated that the Markan version of this tradition is not only more primitive than that of both Matthew and Luke, but is to some extent their literary source.[1] In light of this it might be thought that an investigation of the tradition of Jesus' Wilderness temptation that seeks, as I do here, to examine the development of that tradition in early Christianity involves then only a comparison of the accounts in Matthew and Luke with the account in Mark. But matters are not this simple. For literary and source-critical studies of the three Synoptic versions of the Wilderness temptation tradition also reveal that the Matthean and Lukan versions of that tradition were not dependent upon Mark alone, but upon another, non-Markan version of that tradition as well, a version that most likely came from the Synoptic source Q.[2] Accordingly, any sound investigation of

---

1. On this, see for instance, R. Bultmann, *The History of the Synoptic Tradition* (Oxford: Basil Blackwell, 1963), pp. 254-56; R. Schnackenburg, 'Der Sinn der Versuchung Jesu bei den Synoptikern', *TQ* 132 (1952), pp. 297-326, esp. pp. 300-305; P. Pokorny, 'The Temptation Stories and their Intention', *NTS* 20 (1973–74), pp. 115-27, esp. pp. 115-17; J.A. Fitzmyer, *The Gospel according to Luke, 1–9* (New York: Doubleday, 1981), pp. 506-507; R.H. Gundry, *Matthew: A Commentary on his Literary and Theological Art* (Grand Rapids: Eerdmans, 1982), pp. 53-54; V. Taylor, *The Gospel according to St Mark* (London: Macmillan, 1955), pp. 162-63.

2. Bultmann, *History*, p. 256; Schnackenburg, 'Der Sinn', p. 305; Pokorny, 'The Temptation Stories', p. 117; Fitzmyer, *Luke 1–9*, p. 507; Gundry, *Matthew*, p. 54; Taylor, *Mark*, p. 163; P. Hoffmann, 'Die Versuchungsgeschichte in der Logienquelle: Zur Auseinandersetzung der Judenchristen mit dem politischen Messianismus', *BZ* 13 (1969), pp. 207-23, esp. p. 207; E. Lohmeyer, 'Die

the Wilderness temptation tradition must begin with the question of the relationship between the Markan and Q versions of that tradition before it can proceed any further. And this, of course, involves a comparison of texts. But what precisely is the text of Mark's version of the tradition? Where in the Gospel does it actually begin and end? And what is the text of the Q version of this tradition? What was its original extent and wording? It with these questions that my study of the tradition of Jesus' Wilderness temptation begins.

The Extent of Mark's Version of the Wilderness Temptation

It is generally assumed that Mark's Wilderness temptation story is limited to vv. 12-13 of the first chapter of his Gospel. This stands out, for instance, when one turns to the commentaries. There these verses are regularly treated separately from Mk 1.9-11 on the one hand and Mk 1.14-15 on the other.[3] It is also clear from the fact that traditionally editors of critical editions of the Greek text of Mark have placed breaks before and after these verses, signaling a judgment that these verses are not integrally part of what comes before or after them,[4] and that

---

Versuchung Jesu', *ZSTh* 14 (1937), pp. 619-50 reprinted in *Urchristliche Mystik* (Darmstadt: Wissenschaftliche Buchgesellschaft, 1958), pp. 83-122; E. Best, *The Temptation and the Passion: The Markan Soteriology* (Cambridge: Cambridge University Press, 1965), p. 3; M. Dibelius, *From Tradition to Gospel* (New York: Charles Scribners' Sons, 1933), p. 275; B. Easton, *The Gospel according to St Luke* (Edinburgh: T. & T. Clark, 1926), pp. 48-49; A. Harnack, *The Sayings of Jesus: The Second Source of St Matthew and St Luke* (London: Williams & Norgate, 1908), p. 44; P. Ketter, *Die Versuchung Jesu nach dem Berichte der Synoptiker* (Münster: Aschendorff, 1918); H. Mahnke, *Der Versuchungsgeschichte im Rahmen der synoptische Evangelien* (Frankfurt: Lang, 1978), pp. 183-90; J.H. Marshall, *Commentary on Luke* (Grand Rapids: Eerdmans, 1978), p. 166; A. Polag, *Fragmenta Q: Textheft zur Logienquelle* (Neukirchen–Vluyn: Neukirchener Verlag, 1979), pp. 30-32; S. Schultz, *Q, Die Spruchquelle der Evangelisten* (Zürich: Theologische Verlag, 1972), p. 177; B. Weiss, *Die Quellen des Lukasevangeliums* (Stuttgart: J.G. Cotta, 1907), p. 102.

3. Cf., e.g., Taylor, *Mark*, p. 162; W.L. Lane, *The Gospel according to Mark* (Grand Rapids: Eerdmans, 1974), p. 53.

4. This is the case in, e.g., the editions of Westcott and Hort, A. Souter, Tischendorf, J.M.S. Baljon (*Novum Testamentum Graece* [Gronigen: J.B. Woltes, 1898]), C. Wordsworth (*The New Testament of our Lord and Saviour Jesus Christ in the Original Greek* [London: Rivingtons, 1881]), R.G.V. Tasker, Nestle–Aland[26], and UBS[3]. Mk 1.9-11 and 12-13 are, however, placed together as a unit by

translators of Mark frequently render Mk 1.12-13 as a paragraph.[5]

Now, I think that the assumption is correct with regard to where in Mark the Wilderness temptation story *ends*. With Mk 1.14-15 there is a radical shift in scene and perspective from that which precedes these verses. Jesus is in Galilee, not the wilderness. He is presented in action, and not, as in vv. 12 and 13, being acted upon. Moreover, the phrase with which these verses begin (μετὰ δὲ τὸ παραδοθῆναι, κτλ.) is disjunctive.[6] So, given these and other considerations,[7] it seems certain that in Mark there is a clear break in the Gospel's narrative line between Mk 1.13 and Mk 1.14-15.

But is this assumption correct with regard to where in Mark the story *begins*? To my mind several considerations make it certain that it is not, and that, quite to the contrary, the Markan account of Jesus' Wilderness temptation should be seen as beginning at Mk 1.9 and including within its compass the account of Jesus' Baptism (Mk 1.9-11).[8] These considerations are the following: first, that despite any impression they might give to the contrary Mk 1.9-11 and Mk 1.12-13 are not individual pericopae, let alone ones that have a secondary literary connection with one another; secondly, the notable extent to which Mk 1.12-13 and Mk 1.9-11 are related to one another in terms of vocabulary and narrative style; and thirdly, the meaning καὶ εὐθύς bears at Mk 1.12.

The Formal Unity of Mark 1.9-13

While Mark's account of Jesus' Baptism is often read as a self-contained and well rounded narrative, literary (narrative) criticism and form-critical

---

F.H.A. Scrivener (*Novum Testamentum* [New York: Henry Holt, 1887]) and A. Merk (*Novum Testamentum Graece et Latine* [Rome: Pontifical Biblical Institute, 1951]).

5. See, for instance, the KJV, RV, NAS, RSV, JB, NEB, NAB, TEV, NIV, Goodspeed, and the translation of the Gospel of Mark by D. Rhoads and D. Mitchie in their *Mark as Story* (Philadelphia: Fortress Press, 1982), pp. 7-34, esp. p. 8.

6. On this, W. Marxsen, *Mark the Evangelist* (Nashville: Abingdon, 1969), pp. 38-39; K.L. Schmidt, *Der Rahmen der Geschichte Jesu* (Berlin: Trowitzch & Sohn, 1919), p. 34.

7. For instance, the fact that Mk 1.14-15 is quite different form-critically from what most immediately precedes it. On this, see F. Mussner, 'Gottesherrschaft und Sendung Jesu nach Markus 1,14f.', in Mussner (ed.), *Prasentia Salutis* (Düsseldorf: Patmos, 1967), pp. 81-98, esp. pp. 90-91.

8. That 'The Baptism of Jesus' is adequate as a name for Mk 1.9-11 is doubtful since so much more than Jesus' baptism is described there. But I use it here since it is these verses' conventional designation.

analysis of the account show it to be neither a literary whole nor an example of any formal literary category. As a story Mk 1.9-11 is deficient. It has no real ending.[9] As a pericope, it defies formal classification. To be sure, classification has been attempted. But the fact that Bultmann calls it a 'faith-legend',[10] while Dibelius calls it a 'Myth',[11] and Taylor names it a 'Story about Jesus'[12] only indicates that it has no discernible or discoverable form. For on the one hand, none of the designations used by these form critics actually indicates a narrative form.[13] And, on the other, the fact that so many form critics can describe the material in Mk 1.9-11 in so many varying ways means that the structure of the material is neither evident nor recognizable.[14]

By form-critical and literary-critical standards, Mk 1.12-13 is, like Mk 1.9-11, also both truncated and categorically indefinable. As a story, it is too brief, even by Markan criteria, to be aesthetically satisfying.

9. Taylor, *Mark*, p. 158.
10. Bultmann, *History*, p. 248.
11. Dibelius, *Formation*, p. 271.
12. Taylor, *Mark*, p. 158.
13. Taylor, *Mark*, p. 158. See also Taylor's note on the 'form', or, rather, the lack of it, of 'Stories about Jesus' at pp. 80-81.
14. In his major study of these verses, F. Lentzen-Deis (*Die Taufe Jesu nach den Synoptikern: Literarkritische und gattungsgeschichtliche Untersuchungen* [Frankfort am Main: Knecht, 1970] has classified Mk 1.9-11 as a *Deute-Vision*, an 'interpretative vision'. The form has the following elements: (a) angels are seen and they make a proclamation consisting of a title attributed to the recipient of the revelation; (b) a justification of the title.

There are, however, several difficulties with this view. While Lentzen-Deis has made an admirable case for the existence of this particular literary form, he has not shown that it was known or used in the first century CE. His exemplars of the *Deute-Vision* are primarily two texts from the Neophiti Targum on Genesis (*Targ. Neof. Gen.* 22.10; 28.12). They are, therefore, relatively late, at least in their present form. So the assumption that the tradition embodied within them dates back to Mark's time, let alone that it would have been known to and used by Mark, is somewhat precarious. Moreover, despite some formal similarities of Mk 1.9-11 with the Targummic texts, there seems to be too little in common between the Markan story and the *Deute-Vision* stories, whatever their date might be, to assume literary dependence of the former on the latter. Substantial components of Mk 1.9-11—the opening of the heavens, the descent of the Spirit like a dove—are without parallel, while the vision of the angels, a key element of the *Deute-Vision*, does not figure in the verses from Mark. On this, see L. Sabourin, *The Gospel according to St Matthew* (Bombay: St Paul Publications, 1982), pp. 282-84.

More important, it is incomplete in that it leaves the identity of its protagonist unspecified.[15] Formally, it is unclassifiable. Dibelius says as much when he declares that it is a 'note' mentioning but not elaborating Jesus' temptation, a piece of tradition that gave occasion to Matthew and Luke to narrate a dialogue between Jesus and Satan in their respective parallels to Mk 1.12-13.[16] Bultmann thinks that it may belong either to the category of 'nature myth of the kind that tells of Marduk's fight with the dragon of chaos or that of "Temptations of Holy Men" who are put to the test (by evil) and emerge victorious', but he prescinds from making a decision one way or the other on the grounds that Mk 1.12-13 is 'rudimentary'.[17] So he, too, if only tacitly, acknowledges that the material has no recognizable structure, or that what structure it may have does not resemble that of any fixed literary type. And Taylor follows suit in labeling Mk 1.12-13 another 'Story about Jesus'.[18]

When, however, we read Mk 1.9-12 as the preface to Mk 1.12-13, or, conversely, Mk 1.12-13 as the continuation of the narrative line begun in Mk 1.9-12, the result is a well rounded narrative that is not only aesthetically pleasing and rhetorically complete. It also names its protagonist, and has a clear beginning, middle and end. Moreover, the narrative is also one whose form is strikingly parallel to that of the stories in biblical and non-biblical traditions dealing with religious figures who, like Jesus, are put to the test.[19]

15. The story consistently refers to its protagonist only by means of the third person masculine pronoun, recounting that 'he', not 'Jesus', was driven into the wilderness, was tempted by Satan, was 'with' the 'wild beasts', and was served by angels (αὐτόν, αὐτός, αὐτός, αὐτόν respectively).

16. Dibelius, *Formation*, p. 274.

17. Bultmann, *History*, p. 253.

18. Taylor, *Mark*, p. 81.

19. On this, see H.A. Kelly, 'The Devil in the Desert', *CBQ* 26 (1964), pp. 190-220, esp. pp. 198-202. See also, M.E. Andrews, 'PEIRASMOS—A Study in Form Criticism', *ATR* 24 (1942), pp. 229-44.

Among the Biblical traditions concerning the temptations of holy men by Evil, to which Mk 1.9-13 finds material and formal parallels, are Job 1–2, Sir. 44.19-20, *Jub.* 17.1–18.13; 19.1-9, *Apoc. Abr.* 12.1–14.14, and *b. Sanh.* 89b.

Among the non-biblical traditions of the temptations of holy men by evil to which Mk 1.9-13 is parallel in form and substance, see the story of the temptation of Buddha by Mara (Canto 11 of *The Legend of Buddha Shakyamuni*) and the story of Zarathustra's confrontation with Angra Mainyu (*Vendidad* 19.5-10).

The Verbal and Stylistic Similarities of Mark 1.9-11 and Mark 1.12-13
Mk 1.12-13 and 9-11 are related to one another in terms of vocabulary
and narrative style. Both sets of verses are rife with what J.M. Robinson
terms 'cosmic language'.[20] The absolute τὸ πνεῦμα of v. 10, which is,
notably, rare in Mark,[21] also appears in v. 12. A description of the action
of the Spirit upon Jesus is a prominent feature of both sets of verses.
Indeed, the action of the Spirit mentioned in v. 12 is that which was
begun in v. 10.[22] The object of the verb in v. 12, αὐτόν, refers to the
subject of the verb in v. 10, Ἰησοῦς, and derives its sense from that
referent. The sentence structure evident in vv. 10 and 11a—(καί) +
subject + verb (a structure which, incidentally, does not represent
Mark's usual style[23])—is repeated in v. 12. All this indicates that Mk
1.9-11 and Mk 1.12-13 are to be regarded not as separate and unrelated
pericopes, but as complementary and necessary narrative elements of a
single story.

The Link Provided by καὶ εὐθύς *at Mark 1.12*
Mk 1.12 begins with the expression καὶ εὐθύς. In Mark's Gospel this
expression—'and immediately'—is sometimes found employed with a
purely stylistic function, as a verbal link indicating only a literary and not
an essential or intrinsic connection between the material which it joins.[24]

Despite their differences, what all of these traditions have in common with one
another is that they are each set out according to a basic structure of (1) the
call/commission of the holy man or an announcement by heavenly powers of whom
the holy man is 'thought to be'; (2) a notice or depiction of his subjection to
temptation.

On the similarity between the story of Buddha's temptation and that of Jesus in the
Markan temptation story, see J. Aufhauser, *Buddha und Jesus* (Kl. Texte, 157; Bonn:
A. Marcus & E. Weber, 1926), pp. 24-29. On the similarities between Zarathustra's
temptation and the Markan temptation story, see H.P. Houghton, 'On the
Temptations of Christ and Zarathustra', *ATR* 26 (1944–45), pp. 166-75.

20. J.M. Robinson, *The Problem of History in Mark* (London: SCM Press,
1957), pp. 26, 28.

21. Taylor, *Mark*, p. 160.

22. Lane, *Mark*, 59.

23. M. Zerwick, *Untersuchungen zum Markus-Stil: Ein Beitrag zur stilistichen
Durcharbeitung des Neuen Testaments* (Rome: Pontifical Biblical Institute, 1937),
pp. 75-81.

24. J. Sundwall, *Die Zusammensetzung des Markusevangeliums* (Acta
Academiae Abensis, Humanitaniora, IX; Åbo: Åbo Akadamie, 1934]), pp. 1-86, esp.
pp. 7-8; D. Daube, *The Sudden in the Scripture* (Leiden: Brill, 1964), pp. 46-60.

But in other instances, including Mk 1.12, its function is to signify a temporal or, more precisely, an inferential link, emphasizing a more radical and necessary connection between the material that precedes and follows it.[25] Accordingly, appearing at the beginning of Mk 1.12, the expression καὶ εὐθύς has the effect of presenting Jesus' Wilderness temptation as the corollary and consequence of something which transpired in an immediately antecedent experience. And since in the present context this experience is Jesus' Baptism, then in Mark's Gospel, Jesus' Wilderness temptation is not presented as something separate or distinct from that experience, or portrayed as an event only sequentially but not essentially related to it. On the contrary, the temptation is united with it. With καὶ εὐθύς, Mk 1.12-13 appears as the inescapable conclusion of, and the organic sequel to, Mk 1.9-11.[26]

In view of these considerations, it is inadmissible to assume that in his Gospel Mark's story of Jesus' Wilderness temptation is, or was intended by Mark to be seen as, limited only to Mk 1.12-13. Rather, given all that I have noted above, it seems clear that the story begins at least at Mk 1.9 and that vv. 9-13 are to be taken together as a single unit, a narrative whole.[27]

25. Daube, *The Sudden*, p. 47; Marksen, *Mark*, p. 38; A. Stock, *The Method and Message of Mark* (Wilmington: Michael Glazier, 1989), p. 55.

26. Taylor, *Mark*, pp. 158, 163; Lane, *Mark*, p. 59; E.J. Pryke, *Redactional Style in the Markan Gospel* (Cambridge: Cambridge University Press, 1978), pp. 91-92; J.D. Kingsbury, *The Christology of Mark's Gospel* (Philadelphia: Fortress Press, 1983), p. 63.

If, as many have argued, the appearance here of καὶ εὐθύς is due to Mark, then there can be no doubt that, at least as far as Mark was concerned, Mk 1.12-13 and Mk 1.9-11 belong together as a narrative unit. For on these grounds he actually took pains to ensure that his readers would see the one set of verses as belonging structurally and thematically with the other. There is some doubt, however, whether the phrase is redactional. On this, see below, p. 45.

27. Taylor, *Mark*, pp. 158, 162-63; Robinson, *Problem of History*, pp. 26-28; C.R. Kazmierski, *Jesus, The Son of God: A Study of the Markan Tradition and its Redaction by the Evangelist* (Wurzburg: Echter Verlag, 1979), pp. 63-64; J. Gnilka, *Das Evangelium nach Markus*, I (Zürich: Benzinger, 1978), p. 56; R.A. Guelich, *Mark 1–8:26* (Dallas: Word Books, 1989), pp. 5, 37.

There is one more consideration which, at first glance, seems to lend additional credence to this view: if we assume that in the Gospel of Mark Mk 1.9-11 is a pericope that is complete in and of itself and therefore separate from, rather than an integral part of, what follows it (i.e. Mk 1.12-13), then we must also assume that in recording these verses *as such* Mark has violated his own peculiar literary and

Just how, if in any way at all, this affects the exegesis of Mark's version of this temptation tradition is a question that certainly must be addressed. But since at the moment we are still concerned with the issue of the relationship of the two primary versions of the Wilderness temptation tradition, I will forestall attempting to do this until I deal with another issue, namely, determining the full extent and original text of the Q version of the tradition.

The Extent of the Q Version of the Wilderness Temptation

The extent of the main body of the Q version of the tradition of Jesus' Wilderness temptation is not disputed. Its basic profile is clear: (a) a notice of the temptation's instigation, setting, perpetrator and duration (Mt. 4.1-2//Lk. 4.1-2) followed by (b) a relatively lengthy tripartite dialogue between Jesus and the Devil (ὁ διάβολος) in which the the Devil confronts Jesus in the wilderness, then on the wing of the Temple, and then on a mountain from which Jesus can see all the Kingdoms of the world and their glory, and then petitions him to procure bread from stones, to throw himself down from a dangerous height, to acknowldege the Devil as ruler of the kingdoms of the world (Mt. 4.3-10//Lk. 4.3-12), and then (c) a conclusion noting the Devil's departure (Mt. 4.11// Lk. 4.13). What *is* in question, however, in determining the full extent of the Q version of the tradition of Jesus' Wilderness temptation, is whether or not that version was, as in Mark, immediately preceded by, and included material dealing with, Jesus' Baptism. Scholars are divided on this issue. Those who believe that it was so preceded, B.H. Streeter,[28]

narrative techniques of ending stories—especially stories he has taken up from the tradition—with some sense of closure (Mk 16.8 notwithstanding. But see N.R. Peterson, 'When is the End not the End? Literary Reflections on the Ending of Mark's Narrative', *Int* 34 [1980] pp. 151-66). As Taylor has noted (*Mark*, p. 158), no other Markan pericope ends as abruptly as does Mk 1.9-11. On the other hand, if we assume that Mk 1.9-11 is only the first part of a larger pericope, one which ends at v. 13, then no such problem arises. The narrative line begun in vv. 9-11 then ends in a more characteristically Markan way (Taylor, *Mark*, p. 80). But the validity of the consideration is dependent upon granting Mark more responsibility for the composition of Mk 1.9-11 and 12-13 than is usually thought to be warranted. On the various scholarly proposals for what is traditional and what is redactional in these verses, see below.

28. Streeter, 'The Original Extent of Q', in W. Sanday (ed.), *Oxford Studies in the Synoptic Problem* (Oxford: Clarendon Press, 1911), pp. 184-208, esp. p. 187;

A. Harnack,[29] and others,[30] are convinced of this fact by the following considerations:
First, in Mt. 3.13-17//Lk. 3.21-22 there are several agreements between Matthew and Luke against Mark (see below). These agreements seem to give grounds for positing a Q *Vorlage* for Mt. 3.13-17// Lk. 3.21-22. Secondly, in its use of historic presents in narrative (cf. Mt. 3.13// Lk. 3.21) Mt. 3.13-17//Lk. 3.21-22 is stylistically uncharacteristic of either Matthew or Luke. It is, however, of a piece in this regard with Mt. 4.1-11//Lk. 4.1-13 (cf. Mt. 4.5//Lk. 4.9; Mt. 4.8b//Lk. 4.5; Mt. 4.11// Lk. 4.13).[31]

Thirdly, accepting the originality of the 'Western' reading of Lk. 3.22 (σὺ εἶ ὁ υἱός μου, ἐγὼ σήμερον γεγέννηκά σε), Luke renders the wording of the heavenly voice differently from what he found in Mark (σὺ εἶ ὁ υἱός μου ὁ ἀγαπητός, ἐν σοὶ εὐδόκησα). This cannot be explained by the supposition that Luke intentionally, and on his own authority, altered the tradition which lay before him in Mark, for 'he could not but have found the version [he uses] inconvenient, after what he had narrated in chapters i. and ii';[32] rather it is to be allowed, for on the hypothesis that a Baptismal voice worded wholly according to

idem, The Four Gospels (London: Macmillan, 1924), p. 188.

29. *The Sayings of Jesus: The Second Source of St Matthew and St Luke* (London: Williams & Norgate, 1908), pp. 310-13.

30. J.D. Crossan, *In Fragments: The Aphorisms of Jesus* (San Francisco: Harper & Row, 1983), p. 342; W. Grundmann, *Das Evangelium nach Lukas* (THKNT, 3; Berlin: Evangelische Verlagsanstalt, 10th edn, 1984), pp. 106-107; P. Hoffmann, *Studien zur Theologie der Logienquelle* (Münster: Aschendorf, 1975), p. 4; A.M. Hunter, *The Works and Words of Jesus* (London: SCM Press, 1950), p. 132; U. Luz, 'Q4', *SBLSP* (1984), p. 376; I.H. Marshall, *Commentary on Luke* (Grand Rapids: Eerdmans, 1978), p. 152; A. Polag, *Fragmenta Q: Textheft zur Logienquelle* (Neukirchen–Vluyn: Neukirchener Verlag, 1979), pp. 30-31; W. Schmithals, *Das Evangelium nach Lukas* (Zürich: Theologischer Verlag, 1980), p. 54; H. Schurmann, *Das Lukasevangelium* (Freiburg: Herder & Herder, 1969), pp. 197, 218; E. Schweizer, 'υἱός', *TDNT*, VIII, p. 377 n. 314; *idem, The Good News according to Matthew* (Atlanta: John Knox, 1975), p. 58; P. Vassiliadis, 'The Nature and Extent of the Q Document', *NovT* 20 (1978), p. 73.

31. W.C. Allen, *A Critical and Exegetical Commentary on the Gospel according to S. Matthew* (Edinburgh: T. & T. Clark, 1909), p. 31, cp. pp. xx, lxxxvi; *idem*, 'The Book of Sayings Used by the Editor of the First Gospel', in *Oxford Studies in the Synoptic Problem*, p. 274.

32. Harnack, *Sayings*, p. 313.

Ps. 2.7 existed in Q, it makes sense that Luke, knowing it, felt compelled, as was his usual practice when dealing with overlaps of Mark and Q, to use it in preference to the Markan text.[33]

Finally, in the Q version of the tradition of Jesus' Wilderness temptation the presupposition and ground of that temptation is that Jesus has been declared and commissioned to be υἱός τοῦ θεοῦ (cf. Mt. 4.3// Lk. 4.3; Mt. 4.5//Lk. 4.9).[34] This makes it likely that some account of this event would have preceded the story of the Wilderness temptation.[35]

But those who do not believe that Q contained an account of Jesus' Baptism[36] point out (1) that the Matthew–Luke agreements against Mark in Mt. 3.13-17//Lk. 3.21-22 are either too slight in extent to posit a Q *Vorlage*,[37] or readily explainable as redactional,[38] (2) that the use of the historic present in Mt. 3.13//Lk. 3.21, though unusual, is still redactional,[39] (3) that the Western text of Lk. 3.22, even if the original reading of Luke, scarcely proves anything about Q,[40] and (4) that the title 'Son of God' in Mt. 4.1-11//Lk. 4.1-13 does not require an explanatory narrative any more than does the title 'Son of Man', which is by far

33. Harnack, *Sayings*, p. 313; Streeter, 'Original Extent of Q', p. 187.

34. This is apparent in the Devil's couching his address to Jesus as υἱὸς τοῦ θεοῦ within the phrase εἰ...εἰ, which, as we will see below in Chapter 3, p. 98, is an acknowledgment that Jesus has been called to the office of 'Son'.

35. Marshall, *Luke*, p. 152; Schmithals, *Lukas*, p. 54; Schurmann, *Lukasevagelium*, p. 197; Schweizer, 'υἱός', p. 377; *idem, Matthew*, p. 58; G.S. Stanton, 'On the Christology of Q', in B. Lindars and S. Smalley (eds.), *Christ and the Spirit: Essays in Honour of C.F.D. Moule* (Cambridge: Cambridge University Press, 1973), p. 35; D.R. Catchpole, 'The Beginning of Q', *NTS* 38 (1992), pp. 205-221, esp. p. 218.

36. B.S. Easton, *The Gospel according to St Luke* (New York: Charles Scribners' Sons, 1926), pp. xiii, xviii; Fitzmyer, *Luke 1–9*, p. 479; J.C. Hawkins, *Horae Synopticae* (Oxford: Clarendon Press, 1909), p. 109; J.S. Kloppenborg, *The Formation of Q: Trajectories in Ancient Wisdom Collections* (Philadelphia: Fortress Press, 1987), pp. 84-85; W.L. Knox, *The Sources of the Synoptic Gospels* (Cambridge: Cambridge University Press, 1957), II, p. 4; T.W. Manson, *The Sayings of Jesus* (London: SCM Press, 1937), p. 41.

37. Fitzmyer, *Luke 1–9*, p. 479; G.O. Williams, 'The Baptism in Luke's Gospel', *JTS* 45 (1944), pp. 31-38.

38. Kloppenborg, *Formation of Q*, pp. 85-86 n. 157.

39. Gundry, *Matthew*, p. 49.

40. Kloppenborg, *Formation of Q*, p. 85; Vassiliadis, 'Nature and Extent of Q', p. 69.

the more common title for Jesus in Q.[41]

To my mind, it is clear that the respective critiques of the arguments from the use of the historic present and the existence of the Western text of Lk. 3.22 are sound. But the view that the extent of Matthew–Luke agreements is slight seems hardly justifiable. On the contrary, the extent of the agreement is actually fairly broad. Both Matthew and Luke use a participial form of 'to baptize' against Mark's finite form of the verb. Both use a form ἀνοίγω in their respective parallels to Mk 1.10 and agree in saying 'the heavens were opened' (ἠνεῴχθησαν [αὐτῷ] οἱ οὐρανοί, Mt. 3.15; ἀνεῳχθῆναι τὸν οὐρανόν, Lk. 3.21) over against Mark's 'He saw the heavens torn asunder' (σχιζόμενους). Both have ἐπ' αὐτόν in the description of the Spirit's descent upon Jesus against Mark's use of εἰς αὐτόν. And both place καταβαῖνω before ὡς (ὡσεὶ) περιστεράν instead of after this phrase as Mark does.[42] Nor is the view that these agreements are only redactional ultimately convincing. Only some of them can be explained away in this manner.

Similarly, the argument for the existence in Q of a narrative explaining why Jesus is called 'Son of God' in Mt. 4.1-11//Lk. 4.1-13 cannot be dismissed on the grounds that we find no narrative in Q grounding its 'Son of Man' Christology. *Why should we?* According to Q the office of 'Son of Man' is not something to which Jesus was appointed. It is something Jesus by himself assumes. But the office of 'Son of God' comes to Jesus from outside himself and is something to which he is called.

So in the end, the case for an account of Jesus' Baptism in Q is strong. But what then did it look like? A full reconstruction is beyond our grasp. But certainly it contained four elements: (1) a notice of Jesus coming to be baptized, (2) a notice of the heavens opening using the verb ἀνοίγω, (3) a description of the Spirit descending 'upon' Jesus which used the preposition ἐπ', and (4) a notice of God declaring Jesus υἱὸς τοῦ θεοῦ.[43] Moreover, the wording of this last element almost certainly contained the pronoun μου and possibly also the phrase ὁ ἀγαπητός.[44]

---

41. Kloppenborg, *Formation of Q*, p. 85.

42. Cf. Jacobson, 'Wisdom Christology', p. 35; Schurmann, *Lukasevangelium*, I, p. 197 n. 70; Marshall, *Luke*, p. 152.

43. Stanton, 'Christology of Q', p. 35.

44. M. Albertz, *Die synoptischen Streitgesprache: Ein Beitrag zur Formgeschichte des Urchristentums* (Berlin: Trowitzsch & Sohn, 1921), p. 165. See

To establish the remainder of the text of the Q version of the tradition of Jesus' Wilderness temptation, it is necessary to do three things: first, identify and eliminate from Mt. 4.1-11 and Lk. 4.1-13 respectively the elements presently within these texts which are taken over from Mk 1.9-13; second, to compare with one another the 'stripped down' versions of Mt. 4.1-11 and Lk. 4.1-13, outlining the manner in which these texts now diverge from one another; and then, third, to examine these divergencies in light of the editorial tendencies, stylistic and linguistic habits, and theological phrases known to be peculiar to each evangelist.

This work has already been undertaken by a number of scholars including A. Harnack,[45] S. Schulz,[46] P. Hoffmann,[47] A. Polag,[48] D. Zeller,[49] W. Schenk,[50] and most recently by L. Vaage.[51] A comparison and correlation of their endeavors (which in the end differ from one another only slightly)[52] reveals that the text of the Q account of Jesus' Wilderness temptation (excluding the verses recounting Jesus' Baptism) most probably ran along the following lines:

ὁ Ἰησοῦς δὲ ἀνήχθη ὑπὸ τοῦ πνεύματος ἐν τῇ ἐρήμῳ πειρασθῆναι ὑπὸ τοῦ διαβόλου. καὶ νηστεύσας ἡμέρας τεσσεράκοντα καὶ νύκτας τεσσεράκοντα, ὕστερον ἐπείνασεν.

εἶπεν δὲ αὐτῷ ὁ διάβολος· εἰ υἱὸς εἶ τοῦ θεοῦ, εἰπὲ ἵνα οἱ λίθοι οὗτοι ἄρτοι γένωνται. καὶ ἀποκριθεὶς εἶπεν ὁ Ἰησοῦς· γέγραπται ὅτι οὐκ ἐπ' ἄρτῳ μόνῳ ζήσεται ὁ ἄνθρωπος.

also P.G. Bretcher, *The Temptation of Jesus in Matthew* (DTh thesis, Concordia Seminary, St Louis; 1966), pp. 162-82. While both Albertz and Bretcher agree in seeing the heavenly voice addressing Jesus as ὁ υἱὸς ὁ ἀγαπητός, they differ with respect to the question of whether the 'Baptismal word' itself was cast, as in Mk 1.11, in terms of a direct address to Jesus (σὺ εἶ) or, as in Mt 3.17, as a public proclamation (οὗτός ἐστιν). Bretcher opts for the latter view because he sees the Old Testament root of the heavenly voice to be not the Ps. 2 but Exod. 4.22.

45.   Harnack, *Sayings of Jesus*, pp. 41-48.
46.   Schulz, *Q*, pp. 177-81.
47.   'Versuchungsgeschicte', pp. 208-209.
48.   Polag, *Fragmenta Q*, pp. 30-32.
49.   'Versuchungsgeschicte Jesu', pp. 61-62.
50.   *Synopse zur Redenquelle der Evangelisten: Q Synopse und Reconstruction in deutscher Übersetzung mit kurzen Erlauterungen* (Düsseldorf: Patmos Verlag, 1981).
51.   'Q 4', in *SBLSP* (1984), pp. 346-73.
52.   For a notation of the main differences, see Vaage, 'Q 4', *passim*.

τότε παραλαμβάνει αὐτὸν ὁ διάβολος εἰς 'Ιερουσαλὴμ καὶ
ἔστησεν αὐτὸν ἐπὶ τὸ πτερύγιον τοῦ ἱεροῦ
καὶ εἶπεν αὐτῷ· εἰ υἱὸς εἶ τοῦ θεοῦ,
βάλε σεαυτὸν κάτω· γέγραπται γὰρ ὅτι τοῖς ἀγγέλοις αὐτοῦ
ἐντελεῖται περὶ σοῦ καὶ ἐπὶ χειρῶν ἀροῦσίν σε, μήποτε προσκόψῃς
πρὸς λίθον τὸν πόδα σου.
καὶ ἀποκριθεὶς εἶπεν [ἔφη] αὐτῷ ὁ 'Ιησοῦς·
[πάλιν] γέγραπται· οὐκ ἐκπειράσεις κύριον τὸν θεόν σου.

καὶ πάλιν παραλαμβάνει αὐτὸν ὁ διάβολος εἰς ὄρος ὑψηλὸν καὶ
δείκνυσιν αὐτῷ πάσας τὰς βασιλείας τοῦ κόσμου καὶ τὴν δόξαν
αὐτῶν καὶ εἶπεν αὐτῷ·
ταῦτά σοι πάντα δώσω, ἐὰν προσκυνήσῃς μοι.
καὶ ἀποκριθεὶς εἶπεν αὐτῷ [λέγει αὐτῷ] ὁ 'Ιησοῦς.
γέγραπται· κύριον τὸν θεόν σου προσκυνήσεις καὶ αὐτῷ μόνῳ
λατρεύσεις.

The Relationship between the Two Versions of the Tradition

A comparison of the Q version of the tradition of Jesus' Wilderness
temptation with that of Mark shows that they have four points in
common: (1) Jesus' possession by the Holy Spirit, (2) the influence of a
demonic figure, (3) the naming of the scene of the events as ἡ ἔρημος,
and (4) the giving of the duration of the experience as forty days. There
is, then, between the two versions not some small similarity in detail, but
a degree of overlap sufficient to justify the assertion that Mk 1.9-13 and
the Q story of Jesus' Wilderness temptation are in some way connected.
But in what way? There are three possibilities: first, the Q story is drawn
from Mark; second, the Markan story is drawn from Q; and, third, both
versions are dependent on a common tradition or represent independent,
overlapping traditions.

The first possibility, though supported by Wellhausen,[53] and to some
extent by Bultmann,[54] is not very plausible. To accept it involves holding
improbable views on the date of Q, not to mention that of Mark. And
even should it be the case, we would still be left with the question of the

---

53. J. Wellhausen, *Einleitung in die drie ersten Evangelisten* (Berlin: Druck &
Verlag von George Reimer, 1905), pp. 73-74.
54. *History*, pp. 253-54. See also A. Fridrichsen, 'Le problème du miracle dans le
Christianisme primitif' (dissertation, Paris, 1925), pp. 89-90, 123 n. 30, who thinks
that Q's third (mountain) incident of temptation derives from the Markan version of
the Wilderness temptation tradition, albeit a mutilated version of it.

origin, source and tradition history of the material in the Q story which is evidently non-Markan.

The second possibility has several arguments in its favour. First, Mark's version of the tradition of Jesus' Wilderness temptation is brief, at least compared to the Q account, and reads as though it were a mere fragment or a summary of a longer account.[55] Secondly, the thematic background of the Markan version is the same as that of Q, Deuteronomy 6–8.[56] Thirdly, there appears to be a trace of the Q version of the tradition in Mark's account: Mt. 4.6//Lk. 4.10-11 and its quotation of Psalm 91, which speaks of the lion, adder and dragon (i.e. θηρία; cf. Ps. 91.13), stands behind the reference in Mk 1.13 to Jesus' being with 'wild beasts'.[57]

None of these arguments, however, stands up to scrutiny. As I will show below, the view that Mark's version of the Wilderness temptation tradition reads like a fragment of, or a brief summary based on, a longer version of the temptation story and not like an account complete in and of itself is highly questionable. Not only does this view assume without proof, and through a dubious process of thinking, that the Markan version is too spare to be anything but a fragment or an epitome, but it also does not take Mark seriously enough on his own terms.[58] The fact that the thematic background of the Markan version of the tradition is, like that of the Q account, Deuteronomy 6–8 is by no means certain,[59] and even should this be the case,[60] it need hardly imply that in this instance Mark was drawing on Q. The thematic overlap could just as easily be explained by Mark and Q *independently* drawing on a common source

55. Streeter, 'St Mark's Knowledge of Q', in *Oxford Studies in the Synoptic Problem*, pp. 167-83, esp. p. 168; J. Weiss, *Das Markusevangelium* (Göttingen: Vandenhoeck & Ruprecht, 1912), p. 75. See also J. Dupont, 'L'arrière-fond biblique du récit des tentations de Jésus', *NTS* 3 (1956–57), pp. 287-304, esp. pp. 298-99; A. Feuillet, 'L'episode de la tentation d'après l'Evangile selon Saint Marc (1,12-13)', *EstBíb* 19 (1960), pp. 49-73.

56. On Deut. 6–8 as the background to the Q version of Jesus' Wilderness temptation, see below, pp. 85-87.

57. Dupont, 'L'arrière-fond', pp. 288, 294-95. B.W. Bacon, *The Gospel of Mark: Its Composition and Date* (New Haven: Yale University Press, 1925), pp. 156-57.

58. On this, see below, pp. 52-53.

59. Cf. Pokorny, 'The Temptation Stories', pp. 117, 120-22.

60. As will be seen below, I assume it actually is.

in which Deuteronomy 6–8 figured prominently.[61] Finally, it is difficult to see how Mark's notice of Jesus' being with the 'wild beasts' can be taken as a reference to Mt. 4.6//Lk. 4.10-11 and its quotation of Psalm 91 since the reference in Psalm 91 to 'beasts' is in a verse of the Psalm not given by Q and nowhere implied in the Q account. The only way to maintain Mark's dependence on Q here is to conjecture along with B.W. Bacon[62] that Mark inferred the latter detail from Q by extending the quotation from the Psalm, which in Q is limited to v. 12, to the following verse. But as T.E. Floyd Honey asks, can we seriously imagine Mark knowing Q and then 'giving such prominence to a detail which he had only inferred from Q, while omitting all reference to the significant words which prompted the inference?'[63]

But quite apart from the absence of any positive evidence on its behalf, the view of Markan dependence upon the Q version of the Wilderness temptation tradition should be rejected for two other reasons. First, it fails to account for the differences between the two versions in the ordering of, and the emphasis placed upon, certain of the details common to them both. If Mark had known Q, would we not expect him either (a) to recount that the temptation of Jesus was at the end of the forty days of Jesus' Wilderness sojourn (cf. Mt. 4.2//Lk. 4.2) and not, as he does, as something continuous through that period (cf. Mk 1.13a), or (b) to have Jesus denounce the ministrations of angels as an option he must reject (cf. Mt. 4.6-7//Lk. 4.9-12) instead of having Jesus accept it (cf. Mk 1.13a), or (c) to note that the purveyor or perpetrator of Jesus' temptation was 'the Devil' (ὁ διάβολος, cf. Mt. 4.3//Lk. 4.3; Mt. 4.5, 8; Lk. 4.6; Mt. 4.11//Lk.4:13) and not Satan (Σατανᾶς, Mk 1.13a)? Secondly, it raises more questions than it resolves. Why, for instance, does Mark not mention the detail, so prominent in Q as the fundamental presupposition of the Wilderness temptation, that before Jesus encountered the devil he ate nothing and was hungry? And why did Mark not reproduce the threefold disputation between Jesus and the devil? If, as J. Weiss suggests,[64] it was because he was averse to recording Jesus'

---

61. G.D. Castor, 'The Relation of Mark to the Source Q', *JBL* 31 (1912), pp. 82-91, esp. p. 85.

62. Bacon, *Mark*, pp. 156-57.

63. T.E. Floyd-Honey, 'Did Mark Use Q?' *JBL* 62 (1943), pp. 319-31, esp. p. 321; Castor, 'Relation of Mark', p. 85; cf. also Pokorny, 'Temptation Stories', pp. 116-17.

64. J. Weiss, *Das älteste Evangelium*, pp. 133-34. Cf. also R.H. Lightfoot, *The*

temptation in any detail, then why does he take the time elsewhere in his Gospel not only to transmit but also to add detail to other 'testing of Jesus' traditions?[65] If, as Rawlinson maintains,[66] it was because Mark assumed his readers already knew the Q story and that, therefore, it would be redundant to relate it in its entirety, why then do we not find Mark feeling the same way about, and dealing similarly with, the Beelzebul controversy (Mk 3.22-32; Mt. 12.22-32//Lk. 11.14-23), or the story of the sending out of the disciples (Mk 6.7-11; Mt. 10.1-16// Lk. 9.1-5, 10.1-12), or the parable of the Mustard Seed (Mk 4.30-32; Mt. 13.30-32//Lk. 13.18-19), and other passages he relates which can also be found in Q?[67] If, as Streeter contends,[68] it was because he felt that the details and outline of the story were intrinsically uninteresting, and that, in the interest of getting as quickly as possible to his own special matter, they could be glossed over, then why would Mark go on to make Jesus' conflict with Satanic forces and his triumph over the great Adversary one of his Gospel's prominent themes?[69]

In light of all of this, it seems impossible to think that the Markan version of the tradition of Jesus' Wilderness temptation is an extract from, a summary of, or in any other way dependent upon, the version found in Q.[70]

What, then, of the third possibility, that is, that Mk 1.9-13 and the Q story of the Wilderness temptation represent separate but overlapping accounts that ultimately go back to a common source? This, surely,

---

Gospel Message of St Mark (Oxford: Clarendon Press, 1950), pp. 17-18; U. Mauser, *Christ in the Wilderness* (London: SCM Press, 1963), p. 100; Lane, *Mark*, pp. 60-61; F.W. Danker, 'The Demonic Secret in Mark: A Re-Examination of the Cry of Dereliction (15:34)', *ZNW* 61 (1970), pp. 48-69, esp. 60-61.

65. Taylor, *Mark*, p. 163. On the number of 'temptation' traditions Mark employs and the additions he makes to them, see the relevant sections in the subsequent chapters.

66. A.E.J. Rawlinson, *The Gospel according to Mark* (London: Methuen, 1947), p. 12.

67. Castor, 'Relation of Mark', pp. 83-89.

68. Streeter, 'St Mark's Knowledge', p. 168.

69. Taylor, *Mark*, p. 163; Cf. also M. Goguel, *L'Evangile de Marc* (Paris: E. Leroux, 1909), p. 54.

70. J. Moffatt, *Introduction to the Literature of the New Testament* (Edinburgh: T. & T. Clark, 3rd edn, 1918), p. 219; B.H. Throckmorton, 'Did Mark Know Q?', *JBL* 67 (1948), p. 319; Castor, 'The Relation of Mark', p. 85; Floyd-Honey, 'Did Mark Use Q?', p. 321; Pokorny, 'The Temptation Stories', p. 117.

must be the case. For it, and it alone, best accounts not only for the similarities between the two versions, but also for their differences.

Accordingly, my investigation of the tradition of Jesus' Wilderness temptation will proceed under the assumption that its Markan version is independent of that of Q.[71]

---

71. Best, *The Temptation and the Passion*, p. 3; Pokorny, 'The Temptation Stories', p. 117; Taylor, *Mark*, p. 163; E. Lohmeyer, *Das Evangelium des Markus* (Göttingen: Vandenhoeck & Ruprecht, 1963), p. 28; E. Haenchen, *Der Weg Jesu: Eine Erklärung des Markus-Evangeliums und der kanonischen Parallelen* (Berlin: Alfred Töpelmann, 1966), p. 64-65.

Chapter 2

MARK'S ACCOUNT OF JESUS' WILDERNESS TEMPTATION

1. *The Tradition History of the Account*

Commentators are in little doubt that Mark's story of Jesus' Wilderness temptation does not originate with the evangelist but is derived from, and is largely dependent for both its form and substance on, an older pre-Markan tradition.[1] The question still remains, however, as to how much, if in any way at all, the present Markan story differs from the tradition that it is based upon. Is there any evidence of Mark's editorial or compositional hand within Mk 1.9-13? To this question we now turn.

My methodology for ascertaining whether the present text of Mk 1.9-13 differs in content and wording from that of the tradition which Mark took up as the basis of his version of the story of Jesus' Wilderness temptation will be to apply to each of these verses comprising the Markan account the particular stylistic, linguistic, and thematic or literary tests developed by R.H. Stein and others especially for the purpose of laying bare Markan redactional activity. As these tests direct one to do, I will ask of each of these verses whether its vocabulary is specifically Markan, whether it is written in Markan style, and whether it contains or displays any of Mark's known, peculiar theological or literary themes.[2] If, in respect of a given verse, any or all of these questions are answered

---

1. See, for instance, R. Bultmann, *The History of the Synoptic Tradition* (Oxford: Basil Blackwell, 1963), p. 253; V. Taylor, *The Gospel according to St Mark* (London: Macmillan, 1955), p. 163; R.A. Guelich, *Mark 1–8:26* (Dallas: Word, 1988), p. 37.

2. On this methodology as the proper 'tool' for ascertaining not only whether a given verse in Mark's Gospel is Markan but also the extent to which a verse in Mark possess Markan or pre-Markan material, see R.H. Stein, 'The "Redactionsgeschichtlich" Investigation of a Markan Seam (Mc 1:21f.)', *ZNW* 61 (1970), pp. 70-83.

negatively, then there will be reason to suspect that the verse in question is pre-Markan or contains pre-Markan material.

Tradition and Redaction in Mark 1.9

Verse 9 is presently composed of four elements: (a) an introductory formula (καὶ ἐγένετο), (b) an indication of time (ἐν ἐκείναις ταῖς ἡμέραις) interwoven into the introductory formula, (c) a notice about Jesus, specifying both that he 'came' as well as the point of origin of his 'coming' (ἦλθεν Ἰησοῦς ἀπὸ Ναζερέτ τῆς Γαλιλαίας), and (d) a notice that Jesus underwent the baptism of John (καὶ ἐβαπτίσθη εἰς τὸν Ἰορδάνην ὑπὸ Ἰωάννου).

There is no reason to suspect that the introductory formula, element (a), is not traditional. It is not Markan stylistically, and all of the other instances of its relatively few appearances in Mark's Gospel (2.15; 2.23 and 4.4) are derived from the tradition.[3]

The time reference, element (b)—a Hebraism[4] found often in the Hebrew Scriptures and the LXX to signify that a period of time is divinely inaugurated—also seems to be traditional. True, in at least one of the times (i.e. Mk 4.35) Mark employs the expression, or something similar to it (e.g. αἱ ἐκείναι ἡμέραι), the phrase is secondary to its context.[5] And Mark's inserting it here at Mk 1.9 would certainly serve his interest, already made plain in Mk 1.1-8, in drawing attention to the fact that God stands behind the events narrated in Mk 1.9-13. But in the majority of instances of its appearance in Mark the phrase is not redactional, but taken over from the tradition.[6] And the idea that God stood behind the events of Mk 1.9-13 is not a Markan invention, but a presupposition of the text Mark was working from as the basis for his Temptation story.

The traditional nature of element (c), the notice of Jesus' 'coming' from Nazareth of Galilee,[7] is, for the most part, not suspect. Its style and

---

3. Bultmann, *History*, p. 340; C.R. Kazmierski, *Jesus, The Son of God: A Study of the Markan Tradition and its Redaction by the Evangelist* (Wurzburg: Echter Verlag, 1979), p. 32.

4. E. Lohmeyer, *Das Evangelium des Markus* (Göttingen: Vandenhoeck & Ruprecht, 1963), p. 20 n. 4.

5. Bultmann, *History*, p. 340; Kazmierski, *Jesus, The Son of God*, p. 33.

6. Kazmierski, *Jesus, The Son of God*, p. 33.

7. Some debate exists over whether Ναζαρέτ modifies Ἰησοῦς or ἦλθεν. But that the latter option is the case in Mk 1.9 and, consequently, that the text says that

vocabulary are not particularly Markan, and few scholars have seen there any other evidence of Mark's hand. Gnilka[8] and Marxsen,[9] however, argue that the phrase τῆς Γαλιλαίας in this element is a secondary Markan addition. It reflects, they say, a peculiar and notable Markan theme, an interest in Galilee. That Mark has an interest in Galilee seems clear.[10] But that the appearance here of the phrase τῆς Γαλιλαίας is due to this interest begs the question. In fact, as Kazmierski notes,[11] its presence here is most probably due to a concern to add the name of the region to that of a town so little known as Nazareth, thus making Jesus' point of origin less obscure than it would otherwise have been. And this is not necessarily a Markan interest. Indeed,

> there is no compelling reason to attribute the phrase [τῆς Γαλιλαίας] to Mark since as likely as not it could have been part of the tradition long before, especially if the pericope as a whole is of early origin.[12]

Accordingly, it seems reasonable to conclude that none of element (c) comes from Mark; rather, it comes from Mark's *Vorlage.*

The traditional nature of element (d), the notice of Jesus being baptized, cannot be questioned. No trace of Mark's hand can be found there. Moreover, the notice is presupposed in v. 10, so it, or something very much like it, must have stood in Mark's *Vorlage.*[13]

Since, then, we find little, if anything, in v. 9 that decisively and unambiguously reflects Markan style, Markan vocabulary, or any particular peculiar Markan theme, the text and wording of the whole of v. 9 is to be judged pre-Markan.

Jesus came *from* Nazareth rather than that Jesus from (of) Nazareth *came* is now accepted by the majority of commentators. On this see Kazmierski, *Jesus, The Son of God*, p. 34; Guelich, *Mark 1–8:26*, p. 31.

8.   J. Gnilka, *Das Evangelium nach Markus (Mk. 1–8:26)* (Zürich: Neukirchener Verlag, 1978), p. 49.

9.   W. Marxsen, *Mark the Evangelist* (Nashville: Abingdon, 1969), pp. 54-56.

10.   On this, see Marxsen, *Mark*, pp. 54-111; R.H. Lightfoot, *Locality and Doctrine in the Gospels* (New York: Harper & Brothers, 1938); and E. Lohmeyer, *Galiläa und Jerusalem* (Göttingen: Vandenhoeck & Ruprecht, 1936).

11.   *Jesus, The Son of God*, pp. 34-35.

12.   *Jesus, The Son of God*, p. 35.

13.   Kazmierski, *Jesus, The Son of God*, p. 35.

Tradition and Redaction in Mark 1.10

Verse 10 is composed of (a) a notice stating that Jesus was a recipient of, and privy to, certain special apocalyptic events (εἶδεν σχιζομένους τοὺς οὐρανοὺς καὶ τὸ πνεῦμα ὡς περιστερὰν καταβαῖνον εἰς αὐτόν)[14] and (b) a time reference indicating when in relation to Jesus' submission to John's baptism these events occurred (καὶ εὐθὺς ἀναβαίνων ἐκ τοῦ ὕδατος). The only portions of these notices which have any claim to be Markan are the use of εἰς instead of ἐν to designate place, and the phrase καὶ εὐθύς. εἰς in place of ἐν is found frequently in Mark,[15] and εὐθύς, 'suddenly', is a Markan favourite.[16] But εἰς for locative ἐν is not peculiar to Mark. On the contrary, as C.H. Turner has shown,[17] it is a common Hellenistic usage, and therefore its appearance here cannot be taken as evidence of Markan redaction. And the fact that Mark favours a word cannot automatically be taken to mean that its appearance in any given instance of its usage is secondary to its context. For if Mark found in traditional material words he favoured, he would hardly be loath to reproduce them. Now, εὐθύς is demonstrably traditional in the miracle stories[18] as well as in other places in the Gospel. And so Guelich's observation, that 'despite the frequency [of εὐθύς] in Mark, one must use caution before assigning the term to Markan redaction',[19] should be taken to heart here.

There is, therefore, no reason to believe that Mk 1.10 now differs from the tradition that it is based upon.

Tradition and Redaction in Mark 1.11

Verse 11 consists of two elements: (a) a notice that after (καί) seeing the sky rent and the Spirit of God[20] descending upon him [Jesus],[21] a

---

14. On the nature of these events, see below, pp. 70-71.

15. Taylor, *Mark*, p. 44.

16. It appears some 26 times.

17. C.H. Turner, 'Markan Usage: Notes Critical and Exegetical on the Second Gospel', *JTS* 26 (1924–25), pp. 14-20.

18. G. Theissen, *The Miracle Stories of the Gospel Tradition* (Philadelphia: Fortress Press, 1983), p. 199.

19. *Mark 1–8:26*, p. 30 note c. See also F. Hahn, *The Titles of Jesus in Christology* (London: Lutterworth, 1969), p. 337; J. Weiss, "ΕΥΘΥΣ bei Markus', *ZNW* 2 (1910), pp. 124-33.

20. That 'the Spirit' is the Spirit of God, see E. Schweizer, 'πνεῦμα', *TDNT*, VI, p. 400.

21. *Contra* Bultmann, *History*, p. 247; Hahn, *Titles of Jesus*, pp. 293, 324 n. 95,

heavenly voice spoke to Jesus (φωνὴ ἐγένετο ἐκ τῶν οὐρανῶν), and (b) a description of what the voice said (σὺ εἶ ὁ υἱός μου ὁ ἀγαπητός, ἐν σοὶ εὐδόκησα) which is cast in the form of an appointment oracle.[22] There is no reason to doubt the traditional nature of the first element of this verse. Nothing of its vocabulary or style is Markan. On the contrary, several of its distinctive features such as the absolute use of τὸ πνεῦμα and a sentence structure of καί + subject + verb are distinctly unMarkan.[23] But according to some scholars, there is reason to doubt that the second of the verse's elements is traditional, at least in its entirety. Dalman,[24] Bousset,[25] Jeremias,[26] Cullmann[27] and Fuller[28] have posited that 'my son' (υἱός μου) modifies an earlier, ambiguous 'my servant'/'my child' (παῖς μου), and, therefore, that the text of Mark's *Vorlage* here read σὺ εἶ ὁ παῖς μου ὁ ἀγαπητός, ἐν σοὶ εὐδόκησα. However, as I.H. Marshall has shown,[29] the evidence for this view is not strong and the arguments that these scholars have adduced on its behalf are not compelling. But even if the view were true, it would not necessarily mean that the text noted above was the text that Mark read in his *Vorlage* of this element. An exchange of υἱός for παῖς could have taken place in the tradition before this text came to Mark. So in the absence of any hard evidence that such an exchange was *due* to Mark, let alone that it actually occurred, we should assume that its present

338-39, 344 n. 39 and others who render εἰς as 'into'. On this, see J.D. Kingsbury, *The Christology of Mark* (Philadelphia: Fortress Press, 1983), pp. 62-63.

22. On this, see below, p. 70.

23. On this, see M. Zerwick, *Untersuchungen sum Markus-Stil: Ein Beitrag zur stilistichen Durcharbeitung des Neuen Testaments* (Rome: Pontifical Biblical Institute, 1937), pp. 75-81.

24. Dalman, *The Words of Jesus Considered in the Light of Post-Biblical Jewish Writings and the Aramaic Language* (Edinburgh: T. & T. Clark, 1902), pp. 276-80.

25. W. Bousset, *Kyrios Christos: A History of Belief in Christ from the Beginnings of Christianity to Irenaeus* (Nashville: Abingdon, 1970), pp. 97-98.

26. J. Jeremias, *Abba: Studien zur neutestamentlichen Theologie und Zeitgeschichte* (Göttingen: Vandenhoeck & Ruprecht, 1966), pp. 191-98; *idem*, 'παῖς θεοῦ', *TDNT*, V, pp. 701-702.

27. O. Cullmann, *The Christology of the New Testament* (Philadelphia: Westminster Press, 1963), p. 66.

28. R. Fuller, *The Foundations of New Testament Christology* (New York: Charles Scribner & Sons, 1965), pp. 169-70.

29. I.H. Marshall, 'Son of God or Servant of Yahweh?—A Reconsideration of Mark 1.11', *NTS* 15 (1968–69), pp. 326-36.

form is traditional and faithfully represents what Mark himself read when he took the text up for his own use.

Tradition and Redaction in Mark 1.12

Can any evidence for Mark's redactional or compositional hand be found within this verse? Most commentators would say *no*, that it is in its entirety traditional. But Gnilka argues that save for the phrase καὶ εὐθύς, all of Mk 1.12, the statement about Jesus being driven into the wilderness by the Spirit, was *not* present in the original text of Mk 1.9-12. It is, he says, a transitional verse composed by Mark from the absolute use of 'the Spirit' in 1.10.[30] But the suggestion that Mark's *Vorlage* did not contain v. 12 cannot, however, be accepted. As we have seen above, the syntax of the language employed in v. 12, that is, (καί) + subject + verb, is not Markan. Nor is the use, found there, of the absolute τὸ πνεῦμα. So there seems little in the way of linguistic or stylistic grounds for claiming the verse to be a Markan composition. Moreover, one must reckon with the fact that Mk 1.12 has an almost exact parallel in the Q form of the tradition of Jesus' Wilderness temptation, a tradition which, as we have seen, is independent of Mark. In light of this, we must conclude that the verse not only stood in Mark's *Vorlage* but originally read much as we read it now.

Tradition and Redaction in Mark 1.13

The only serious challenge to the wholly traditional nature of this verse is that of Bultmann. In his view, Mark's *Vorlage* did not contain the phrase πειραζόμενος ὑπὸ τοῦ Σατανᾶ. This, he argues was something Mark added to it.[31] Now it should be noted that the reason Bultmann makes this claim has nothing to do with form-critical, linguistic or stylistic considerations. Rather, it is that he believes the material Mark had in front of him, while *possibly* a story which belongs to the type of 'the "Temptations of Holy Men" who are put to the test (by evil) and emerge victorious',[32] was more likely originally to have been a 'representation of Jesus as Paradisal Man, or as a saint who lived once more with the beasts, with whom mankind has lived in enmity ever

---

30. Gnilka, *Markus*, I, p. 56.

31. Bultmann, *History*, pp. 253-54. Here Bultmann is following what he calls a 'tempting' (!) suggestion of N. Freese, 'Die Versuchung Jesus nach den Synoptiker' (Dissertation, Halle, 1922).

32. Bultmann, *History*, p. 253.

since the Fall'.[33] This view rests, however, on the assumptions, first, that the background of the statement about Jesus being μετὰ τῶν θηρίων (cf. v. 13)—which, according to Bultmann, the material that Mark employed as the basis of Mk 1.9-13 already contained—indicates peaceful coexistence and a restored harmony between Jesus and the beasts of which it speaks, and, secondly, that the motif embodied in the phrase is drawn from the theology of *Urzeit–Endzeit* speculations and typologies current in first-century Judaism and Christianity. But as I will show below, these assumptions are wholly unfounded. And if so, then so also is the view derived from it. Moreover, as Gnilka has pointed out, there are no form-critical or literary reasons to say that the phrase πειραζόμενος ὑπο τοῦ Σατανᾶ was not original to Mark's *Vorlage*.[34] So we find here, too, that the whole of the text of v. 13 as it presently stands in Mark should be taken as traditional.

Conclusions: Tradition and Redaction in Mark 1.9-13

Throughout this section I have been trying to determine how much, if in any way at all, Mark has modified the *Vorlage* upon which his story of Jesus' Wilderness temptation is built and from which it was derived. The question posed was: Is there any evidence of Mark's editorial or compositional hand within Mk 1.9-13. After examining these verses, we have seen that the answer is *no*. Mark has made no substantial changes in the form or wording of the material he here employs, nor has he added anything to it. Accordingly, I will proceed with my investigation of Mark's version of the tradition of Jesus' Wilderness temptation under the assumption that what now appears in Mk 1.9-13 represents unmodified, traditional, pre-Markan material.

2. *The Nature, Content and Outcome of Jesus' Wilderness Temptation according to Mark*

I turn now to the question of what Mark has to say regarding the nature, content, and outcome of Jesus' Wilderness temptation. In doing so I am fully aware that to many this is a profitless undertaking. For according to the consensus of critical scholarship it is a *given* that the Markan story of Jesus' Wilderness temptation contains no information whatsoever concerning either the nature and content of this temptation

---

33. Bultmann, *History*, p. 254.
34. Gnilka, *Markus*, I, p. 56.

or its outcome.[35] *Mark, it is continually reported, was satisfied when handing on the tradition only to assert* that *Jesus was tempted and no more*.[36] But is this actually the case? Is Mark's version of Jesus' Wilderness temptation really, as most scholars say, only a bare statement of fact? In answering this question, let us examine just what underlies this view and how scholars have arrived at it.

Given the certainty with which it is put forth, its durability as a critical

35.   A representative statement of this position is the assertion of E. Best that 'the account of the Temptation in Mark is bare of details. Not only are we not told in what way Jesus was tempted but we are not even told the outcome of the Temptation' (*The Temptation and the Passion*, p. 4). In his revised version of this work (Cambridge: Cambridge University Press, 1991), p. xviii, Best reiterates this point of view. See also his *Mark: The Gospel as Story* (Edinburgh: T. & T. Clark, 1983), pp. 57, 73.

This view has also been reaffirmed by K.W. Chase in the most recent thoroughgoing study of all of the Synoptic stories of the temptations of Jesus. Cf. Chase, 'The Synoptic Πειρασμοί of Jesus: Their Christological Significance' (unpublished ThD Dissertation, New Orleans Baptist Theological Seminary, 1989), p. 15: 'There is no indication of the precise nature or content of the temptation...[and] Mark gives no explicit statement of the outcome of the temptation'.

36.   See Best, *The Temptation and the Passion*, p. 3. As I have already noted above (pp. 39-40), various explanations have been offered for this. One, given by V. Taylor (*Mark*, p. 163), E. Lohmeyer (*Markus*, p. 28), and E. Haenchen (*Der Weg Jesu: Eine Erklärung des Markus-Evangeliums und der kanonischen Parallelen* [Berlin: Töpelmann, 1966], pp. 64-65) is that Mark did not know anything with regard to the Wilderness temptation except the fact that Jesus was tempted there by Satan. Another, advanced by A.E.J. Rawlinson (*The Gospel according to St Mark* [London: Methuen, 1925], p. 12) is that Mark was quite aware of a more detailed story, but presuming a similar knowledge on the part of his audience, assumed he need not relate it in detail and abridged it accordingly. Yet another, supported by J. Weiss (*Das älteste Evangelium* [Göttingen: Vandenhoeck & Ruprecht, 1903], pp. 133-34), R.H. Lightfoot (*The Gospel Message of St Mark* [Oxford: Clarendon Press, 1950], pp. 17-18), U. Mauser (*Christ in the Wilderness* [London: SCM Press, 1963], p. 100), W.L. Lane (*The Gospel according to Mark* [Grand Rapids: Eerdmans, 1974], pp. 60-61) and F. Danker ('The Demonic Secret in Mark: A Re-Examination of the Cry of Dereliction (Mk. 15:34)', *ZNW* 61 (1970), pp. 48-69, esp. pp. 60-61), among others, is that, again, Mark knew a lengthier temptation tradition than what he produces in his prologue, but for theological reasons or in pursuit of redactional concerns related the details of this tradition elsewhere in or throughout his Gospel. Notably, behind every one of these necessarily speculative explanations lies the assumption that the Wilderness temptation story itself contains no information concerning the nature or content of the temptation or its outcome.

commonplace,[37] as well as the number and the weight of the names of scholars who hold it,[38] one would expect this contention to be grounded

37.   It was, for instance, already a prominent fixture in the scholarly exegesis of the Wilderness temptation tradition of the early nineteenth century. Cf., e.g., W.M.L. de Wette, *Kurtzgefasstes exegetisches Handbuch zum Neuen Testament* (3 vols.; Leipzig: Weidmann'sche Buchhandlung, 1836–48), I, 2.5.33; F. Schleiermacher, *Über den Schriften des Lukas: Kritischer Versuch* (8th edn, Berlin: Druck & Verlag von G. Reimer, 1817), pp. 59-60; and D.F. Strauss, *Das Leben Jesu, kritisch bearbeitet* (Berlin: Verlag von C.F. Osiander, 1835–36), I, p. 400.

38.   Besides those named in notes 35 and 36 above, the proponents include, but are not limited to, W.C. Allen (*The Gospel according to Saint Mark* [London: Macmillan, 1915], pp. 56-57), H. Anderson (*The Gospel of Mark* [London: Oliphants, 1976], pp. 80-81), B.W. Bacon (*The Gospel of Mark: Its Composition and Date* [New Haven: Yale University Press, 1925], pp. 156-57), H. Balmforth (*The Gospel according to Saint Luke* [Oxford: Clarendon Press, 1930], p. 138); C.K. Barrett, *The Holy Spirit in the Gospel Tradition* [London: SPCK, 1947], pp. 49, 51), F.W. Beare (*The Earliest Records of Jesus* [Nashville: Abingdon, 1962], p. 42), J.W. Bowman (*The Gospel of Mark* [Leiden: Brill, 1965], p. 109), A.W.F. Blunt (*The Gospel according to Saint Mark* [Oxford: Clarendon Press, 1929], p. 139), R.E. Brown ('Incidents that are Units in the Synoptic Gospels but Dispersed in St John', *CBQ* 23 [1961], p. 155), A.B. Bruce ('The Synoptic Gospels', in *The Expositor's Greek Testament* [London: Hodder & Stoughton, 1897], I, pp. 343-44), R. Bultmann (*History*, p. 254), T.A. Burkill (*Mysterious Revelation* [Ithaca, NY: Cornell University Press, 1963], p. 21), P. Carrington (*According to Mark* [Cambridge: Cambridge University Press, 1960], p. 41), G.D. Castor ('The Relation of Mark to the Source Q', *JBL* 31 [1912], pp. 82-91, esp. p. 85), M. Dibelius (*From Tradition to Gospel* [New York: Charles Scribner & Sons, 1933], p. 274), J. Dupont ('L'arrière-fond biblique du récit des tentations de Jésus', *NTS* 3 [1956–57], pp. 287-304, esp. pp. 294-95), A. Edersheim (*The Life and Times of Jesus Messiah* [London: Longman & Green, 1883], p. 207), T.E. Floyd-Honey ('Did Mark Use Q?', *JBL* 63 [1943], pp. 319-31, esp. p. 320), W.J. Foxell (*The Temptations of Jesus: A Study* [London: SPCK, 1920], p. 9), J. Gnilka (*Markus*, I, p. 55), F.W. Green (*The Gospel according to Saint Matthew* [Oxford: Clarendon Press, 1936], p. 118), E.P. Gould (*A Critical and Exegetical Commentary on the Gospel according to Saint Mark* [Edinburgh: T. & T. Clark, 1896], p. 12), F.C. Grant ('The Gospel according to St Mark: Introduction and Exegesis', *IB*, VII, pp. 664-65), R.A. Guelich (*Mark 1:8-26*, p. 37), R.H. Gundry (*Matthew: A Commentary on his Literary and Theological Art* [Grand Rapids: Eerdmans, 1982], p. 54), F. Hahn (*The Titles of Jesus in Christology*, p. 340), J. Hargreaves (*A Guide to St Mark's Gospel* [London: SPCK, 1965], p. 14), A. Harnack (*The Sayings of Jesus: The Second Source of St Matthew and St Luke* [London: Williams & Norgate, 1908], p. 196 n. 1), D. Hill (*The Gospel of Matthew* [London: Oliphants, 1972], p. 99), W.H. Harrington

in a full-scale and often iterated exegetical analysis of the Markan passage. One could also expect that this exegesis, when carried out, would

(*Mark* [Wilmington: Michael Glazier, 1979], p. 8), D.C. Hester ('Luke 4:1-13', *Int* 31 [1977], pp. 53-59, esp. pp. 53-54), M.D. Hooker [London: A. & C. Black, 1991], p. 49), A.M. Hunter (*The Gospel according to St Mark* [London: SCM, 1948], p. 29; *idem, The Works and Words of Jesus* [London: SCM Press, 1950], p. 38), J. Jeremias (*New Testament Theology: The Proclamation of Jesus* [New York: Charles Scribner & Sons, 1971], pp. 68-69), S.E. Johnson (*The Gospel of Mark* [London: A. & C. Black, 1969], p. 41; *idem*, 'The Gospel according to St Matthew: Introduction and Exegesis', *IB*, VII, p. 237), E. Klostermann (*Das Markusevangelium* [Tübingen: J.C.B. Mohr (Paul Sielbeck), 1950], p. 9), M.-J. Lagrange (*The Gospel according to Saint Mark* [London: Burns, Oates & Washbourne, 1930], pp. 6-7), W. Lowrie (*Jesus According to St Mark* [London: Longmanns, Green & Co., 1929], pp. 30-31), W.K. Lowther-Clarke ('The Gospel according to Mark', in *Concise Bible Commentary* [London: SPCK, 1952], p. 694), H.E. Luccock ('The Gospel according to St Mark: Exposition', *IB*, VII, p. 654, and *Footprints of the Son of Man as Traced by Saint Mark* [New York: Thomas Whittaker, 1886], p. 26), D. Luhrmann (*Das Markusevangelium* [HZNT, 3; Tübingen: J.C.B. Mohr (Paul Sielbeck), 1987], p. 39), E.J. Mally ('The Gospel according to Mark', in R.E. Brown, J.A. Fitzmyer and R. Murphy (eds.), *The Jerome Biblical Commentary* [Englewood Cliffs: Prentice–Hall, 1968], II, p. 25), C.S. Mann (*Mark* [Garden City: Doubleday, 1986], pp. 202-203), J. Moffat (*Introduction to the Literature of the New Testament* [Edinburgh: T. & T. Clark, 3rd edn, 1918], p. 219), C.F.D. Moule (*The Gospel according to Mark* [Cambridge: Cambridge University Press, 1965], p. 11), D.E. Nineham (*The Gospel of St Mark* [New York: Penguin, 1963], p. 63), T.H. Robinson (*The Gospel of Matthew* [London: Hodder & Stoughton, 1928], p. 19), L. Sabourin (*The Gospel according to St Matthew* [Bombay: St Paul Publications, 1982], I, p. 297), J. Schmid (*Das Evangelium nach Markus* [Regensburg: Pustet, 1963], p. 26), J. Schniewind (*Das Evangelium nach Markus* [Göttingen: Vandenhoeck & Ruprecht, 1963], pp. 48-49), E. Schweizer (*The Good News according to Matthew* [Richmond, VA: John Knox, 1975], p. 58; *idem, The Good News according to Mark* [Richmond, VA: John Knox , 1970], pp. 42-43), K. Stendahl ('Matthew', in M. Black and H.H. Rowley [eds.], *Peake's Commentary on the Bible* [London: Nelson & Sons, 1962], p. 773), A. Stock (*The Method and Message of Mark* [Wilmington: Michael Glazier, 1989], p. 56; B.H. Streeter ('St Mark's Knowledge of Q' in W. Sanday [ed.], *Oxford Studies in the Synoptic Problem* [Oxford: Clarendon Press, 1911), p. 168; *idem, The Four Gospels* [London: Macmillan, 1924], pp. 187-88), J.M. Thompson (*Jesus according to St Mark* [London: Methuen, 1910], p. 42), R.C. Trench (*Studies in the Gospels* [London: Macmillan, 1867], pp. 1, 9), E. Trocmé (*The Formation of the Gospel according to Mark* [Philadelphia: Westminster Press, 1963], pp. 159-60), B.H. Throckmorton ('Did Mark Know Q?', *JBL* 67 [1948], p. 324), H. Wansbrough ('St Mark', in R.G. Fuller, L. Johnson and C. Kearnes (eds.), *A New Catholic Commentary on Holy*

be careful to focus exclusively on Mark's text, examining the story in light of the literary and *religionsgeschictlich* background that its context, its form, and its constituent and peculiar elements would suggest belongs to it. But surprisingly, *this is not the case*. So far as I am able to discern from a review of the relevant literature, the contention now under consideration is rarely exegetically defended; and when it is, it is never grounded in exegesis limited solely to the Markan story itself. Rather, the contention seems to be something that is drawn specifically, and solely, from a certain process of thought, often unconsciously carried out, the steps of which run as follows:

1. Mark's is not the only account of Jesus' Wilderness temptation extant in the canonical Gospel tradition. Both Matthew and Luke have parallel accounts of this event (Mt. 4.1-11; Lk 4.1-13).
2. The Markan Wilderness temptation story is devoid of many of the details which the parallel Matthean and Lukan Wilderness temptation stories possess.
3. It is only in these non-Markan details that the information concerning both the outcome and the nature and content of Jesus' Wilderness temptation resides.
4. A Wilderness temptation account devoid of these details does not, indeed cannot, reveal the manner in which, and the issue over which Jesus was on this occasion tempted or how successfully he withstood the temptation.

It should be immediately apparent that this process of thought is logically deficient. It engages in *petitio principii*, assuming in the third element of its logical chain the very thing that needs to be proved for its fourth element (and any conclusion based upon it) to be true. Now, to be sure, it is indisputable that the Matthean and Lukan accounts of Jesus' Wilderness temptation are more detailed than their Markan counterpart. No trace, for instance, of the elaborate dialogue between Jesus

Scripture [London: Nelson, 1969], p. 959), B. Weiss (*Das Markusevangelium und seine Synoptischen Parallelen* [Berlin: Wilheim Hertz, 1872], p. 51), J. Wellhausen (*Einleitung in die drie ersten Evangelisten* [Berlin: George Reimer, 1905], pp. 73-74), W.W. Wessel ('Mark', in F.E. Gaebelein [ed.], *The Expositor's Bible Commentary* [Grand Rapids: Zondervan, 1984], VI, p. 623), R. McL. Wilson ('Mark', in M. Black and H.H. Rowley (eds.), *Peake's Commentary on the Bible* [London: Nelson & Sons, 1962], p. 800).

and the Devil which appears in both Mt. 4.1-11 and Lk. 4.1-13 can be found in Mark. Nor can it be denied that the extra non-Markan details of these accounts contain information pertinent to outlining the nature, content and outcome of Jesus' Wilderness temptation. But is it really the case that it is *only* in these extra non-Markan details that such information resides? Are not the details of the Markan version of the Wilderness temptation tradition, however comparatively few they may be, sufficiently resonant *in themselves* to give the information purportedly not contained there? Has not an unwarranted and methodologically unsound concentration on what is *not* in Mark effectively forestalled this question from being asked, let alone answered? It would seem, then, that until these questions are posed and answered, we will not know whether or not the view that the Markan story is silent on the matters of the nature, content, and outcome of Jesus' Wilderness temptation is tenable.

And so it is now necessary to remove the Markan version of the tradition from the shadow cast upon it by that of Matthew and Luke and to examine its details afresh, on their own terms, and from within the standpoint provided by the particular religious and cultural milieu in which Mark and his audience lived and moved, to see whether or not, once left to themselves, these details actually have a voice. It is to this examination that I now turn.

The Nature of Jesus' Wilderness Temptation according to Mark
To determine whether Mark gave explicit information within Mk 1.9-13 concerning the nature of the temptation that he there recounts Jesus as experiencing, I will follow what seems to be the most natural course of action, namely, to turn first to the section of the Markan story where the most explicit notice that Jesus was tempted appears, that is, Mk 1.13a, and to examine it in light of the question of what Mark would have thought he was saying, and what his audience would have taken him to have said, when he recounted, and his audience read or heard, each of its constituent details, given the conceptual heritage and mind-set that he and his audience as Christians were likely to have had. Then I will examine in some detail both the notice in Mk 1.12 concerning Jesus' being led into the wilderness by the Spirit and the notice of Mk 1.13b concerning a relationship between Jesus, 'wild beasts' and angels with the same question in mind.

καὶ ἦν ἐν τῇ ἐρήμῳ τεσσεράκοντα ἡμέρας πειραζόμενος ὑπὸ τοῦ Σατανᾶ (Mk 1.13a)

Mk 1.13a is composed of four separate (though inter-related) notices: (1) that Jesus experienced temptation, (2) that Jesus' temptation had a particular perpetrator, (3) that the temptation had a particular setting or locale, and (4) that the temptation had a particular duration. Let us consider each of these notices in turn to see what information, if any, they contain regarding the nature of the event they deal with.

Jesus Tempted. In Mk 1.13a the idea that Jesus was tempted is expressed by Mark through the use of the word πειραζόμενος, the present passive participle of the verb πειράζω. Literally, the participle stands for the phrase, 'being tried'. What, if anything, does this phrase tell us about the nature of the event of which it speaks? I have noted above that for the preponderance of scholars the answer to this question is 'nothing at all'. To them the phrase is in itself so brief and spare that it is not capable of being anything other than a simple assertion, a statement of fact. But to my mind this view has two serious difficulties. The first is that *it equates brevity with vacuity.* The second is that it assumes that for Mark and for his readers the participle πειραζόμενος, even when used, as here, with reference to a person, was *in no way connotative*, that in their minds the phrase construed from πειραζόμενος did not bear any meaning or semantic range beyond its literal sense and conjured up for them no image or set of associations.

But this assumption is untenable. The verb πειράζω, an Ionic and *koine* form of the predominantly Attic πειράω, 'to try',[39] and the root of the participle used in Mk 1.13a, was not, in Mark's time, a new or unfamiliar word. It is attested in secular Greek as early as Homer (*Od.* 9.281; 16.319; 23.114), and from the fifth century BCE to the second century CE it is employed some 60 times by a variety of other Classical and Hellenistic writers.[40] It appears some thirty times in the Septuagint translation of the Hebrew Scriptures,[41] where, in all but two

---

39. On this, see BDF, §101.
40. See the Appendix: Instances of the Verb πειράζω in Classical and Hellenistic Greek.
41. Gen. 22.1; Exod. 15.25; 16.4; 17.2, 7; 20.20; Num. 14.22; Deut. 4.34; 8.2 (accepting here the reading of Alexandrinus and Vaticanus against that of Sinaiticus which has ἐκπειράζω); 13.3(4); 33.8; Judg. 2.22; 3.1, 4; 6.39; 1 Kgs 10.1; 2 Chron. 9.1; 32.31; Ps. 25(26).2; 34(35).18; 77(78).41, 56; 94(95).9; 105(106).14; Eccl. 2.1; 7.24(23); Isa. 7.12; Dan. 1.12, 14; 12.10.

instances, it is a translation equivalent of the piel of *nasah*,[42] 'to try', 'to prove',[43] 16 times in the Apocrypha of the Septuagint,[44] 6 times in the extant fragments of the non-Septuagintal Greek versions of the Hebrew Scriptures,[45] and 6 times in the Greek Pseudepigrapha.[46] Moreover, *it was an essential part of the vocabulary of early Christianity.*[47]

42. The two exceptions are Ps. 34(35).16 and Dan. 12.10, where there is no underlying Hebrew text.

43. On the range of meanings with which *nasah* is used in the Hebrew Scriptures, see A. Helfmeyer, '*nissah, massot, massah*', *ThWAT*, V, pp. 473-87; G. Gerleman, '*nsh*, versuchen', *THAT*, V, pp. 69-71; B. Gerhardsson, *The Testing of God's Son (Matt. 4:1-11 and Par.)* (Lund: Gleerup, 1966), pp. 25-35.

44. Wis. 1.2; 2.17, 24; 3.5; 11.9; 12.26; Sir. 4.17; 13.11; 18.23; 31(34).10; 37.27; 39.4; Tob. 12.14; Jdt. 8.12, 25, 26.

For all of the instances of the use of πειράζω in Wisdom, Tobit and Judith there is, of course, no Hebrew equivalent. In Sir. 4.17; 13.11; 37.27 πειράζω is used as the translation equivalent of *nasah*. (On this, see Hatch and Redpath, *Concordance to the Septuagint* [Oxford: Clarendon Press, 1906], III, p. 188). *nasah* presumably underlies πειράζω in Sir. 18.23; 31(34).10; 39.4 as well, but we lack the Hebrew text for these verses. On the Hebrew text of Sirach, see I. Levi, *The Hebrew Text of Ben Sirah* (Oxford: Clarendon Press, 1904); A. DiLella, *The Wisdom of Ben Sira* (Garden City: Doubleday, 1966).

45. Aquila, Deut. 28.56; Symmachus, Gen. 44.15; Deut. 33.8; Mal. 3.10; Theodotion, Dan. 1.12, 14. Each of these instances have Hebrew equivalents. In Aquila, Deut. 28.56, Symmachus, Deut. 33.8 and Theodotion, Dan. 1.12, 14 it is *nasah*, in Symmachus Gen. 44.15 it is *naḥaš*, and in Symmachus, Mal. 3.10 it is *baḥan*.

46. 4 Macc. 9.7; 15.16; *T. Dan* 1.3; *Sedr.* 8.5; in a fragment of a Greek version of *Jub.* 10.9 and in Aristeas the Exegete, 'Life of Job' (preserved by Eusebius in *Praef. Ev.* 9.25.1-4). With the exception of the instance in the fragment from *Jubilees*, there are here, too, as in the use of πειράζω in the Apocrypha, no Hebrew equivalents.

47. πειράζω appears a total of 68 times in Christian literature written before the end of the second century CE: 23 times in the New Testament writings (Mk 1.13; 8.11; 10.2; 12.15; Mt. 4.1, 3; 16.1; 19.3; 22.18; 22.35; Lk. 4.2; 11.16; Jn 6.6; 8.6; Acts 5.9; 9.26; 15.10; 15.26 [D E]; 16.7; 24.26; 1 Cor. 7.5; 10.9, 13; 2 Cor. 13.5; Gal. 6.1; 1 Thess. 3.5 [2×]; Heb. 2.18; 3.9; 4.15; 11.17, 39; Jas 1.13 [3×], 14; Rev. 2.2, 10; 3.10), twice in Hermas (*Sim.* 7.1; 8.2.7), once in the Ignatian Epistles (*Magn.* 7.1; cp. also *Phil.* 9.1-3 [3×]; 11.1 [once along with one instance of ἐκπειράζω and one of ἀπείραστον], but the spurious nature and relatively late date of this work has long been known]), once in *Egerton Papyrus 2* (Fragment 2 recto, lines 43-59), twice in the Gospel of Thomas (Logion 91, where the verb is included in Greek in the Coptic text), once in the *Acts of the Christian Martyrs* (*Mart. Carp.* 19.2), seven times in *The Acts of John* (40.1; 88.3; 90.22 [along with ἀπείραστον] in the primary text [cf. M. Bonnet, *Acta Apostolorum Apocrypha* (Leipzig:

Given this, Mark and his readers would not only have been acquainted with the word, they would have been familiar with the contexts in which it was used, its range of signification, and the associations that were attached to it and to its derivatives. *The question, then, is not whether* πειραζόμενος *in Mk 1.13a would have been connotative, but what connotations it was known to have.*

What, then, did πειραζόμενος, 'being tried', connote? The evidence indicates that it was basically the idea of being *probed and 'put to the proof'*, that is, 'tested' *to ascertain or to demonstrate trustworthiness.*[48] And when the participle—indeed, any form of πειράζω—was used, as in Mk 1.13a, with reference to a person, its connotation was even more specific: *being probed and proved, often through hardship and adversity, in order to determine the extent of one's worthiness to be entrusted with, or the degree of one's loyalty or devotion to, a given commission*

Mendellssohn, 1898)] and 10.13; 57.5-6 [3× along with ἀπείραστον] in the Recension [also in Bonnet (1898)], twice in Justin's *Dialogue with Trypho* (103.6; 125.4; cf. also Ps. Justin *Expositio rectae fidei* 388.C.8), 17 times in the works of Clement of Alexandria (*Protrepticus* 9.84.3; 10.95.2; *Paedagogus* 1.8.62; *Stromata* 2.20.103; 3.6.51; 3.12.80; 3.15.96; 4.4.13 [2×]; 4.12.85 [2×]; 4.16.104 [2×]; 7.3.20; 7.12.74; *Ecolgae propheticae* 53.2.3; *Excerpta ex Theodoto* 1.5.4) and twelve times in the Clementine literature (*Hom. 2* 43.1; *Hom. 3* 39.5 [3×]; 43.2; 55.2-3 [3×]; *Hom. 12* 29.4; *Hom. 16* 13.4-5 [4×]. Cp. also *Epitome Prior* 37.14 [2×]; 41.2 and *Epitome Altera* 37.15 [2×]; 41.2; 96.18, but these instances need not be taken into account here since they are essentially reduplications of several of the instances of πειράζω in the *Homilies*. Moreover, the works they appear in date from after the second century CE.

On πειράζω as a vital part of the vocabulary of early Christianity, see Korn, *ΠΕΙΡΑΣΜΟΣ*, pp. 76-88; Seesemann, 'πεῖρα, κτλ.', *TDNT*, VI, p. 28; S. Brown, *Apostasy and Perseverance in the Theology of Luke* (Rome: Pontifical Biblical Institute, 1969), pp. 20-35; Wellhausen, *Einleitung*, pp. 33-34.

48. J. Korn, *ΠΕΙΡΑΣΜΟΣ: Die Versuchung des Glaubigen in der greischischen Bible* (Stuttgart: Kohlhammer, 1937), pp. 8-19, 24-26; B. Gerhardsson, *Testing of God's Son*, pp. 25-26. See also B. Van Iersel, *The Bible on the Temptations of Man* (DePere, WI: St Norbert Abbey Press, 1966), pp. 1-6. That the specific connotation of 'testing' and 'proving' is inextricably linked with πειράζω is brought out clearly by the fact that in both secular and biblical Greek the synonyms of the verb are πυρόω, [ἐξ-]ατάξεω and δοκιμάζω. On this, see Brown, *Apostasy and Perseverance in the Theology of Luke* (Rome: Pontifical Biblical Institute, 1969), p. 20; *idem*, 'Deliverance from the Crucible: Some Further Reflections on 1 QH III.1-18', *NTS* 14 (1967–68), pp. 247-59, esp. p. 258; Seesemann, 'πεῖρα, κτλ.', p. 29. See also R.C. Trench, *Synonyms of the New Testament* (London: Macmillan, 12th edn, 1894), §lxxiv.

and its constraints.[49] So 'central'[50] was this connotation to this usage of the participle and its root, that the statement that someone was πειραζόμενος could not be made without communicating the idea that this person was undergoing an experience in which character or fidelity was being 'put to the proof'.[51] One only need look at such New Testament passages as Lk. 4.2; Heb. 2.18; 11.17 and Jas 1.13 where πειραζόμενος is used as it is in Mk 1.13a (i.e. relatively, if not wholly, 'unmarked'[52] and with respect to a person) to see that this is so.

In light of this, it is unreasonable and unwarranted to assume that the notice at Mk 1.13a of Jesus being tempted originally gave no information concerning the nature of that temptation. On the contrary, since in Mark's time and among those schooled in the biblical tradition (as Mark and presumably his intended audience were) the notice's wording was extremely evocative and bore a specific set of associations, we should actually assume that in Mark's eyes, and in those of his intended audience, this notice, even brief as it is, actually spoke volumes on the issue and signified that the temptation was a trial of Jesus' faithfulness.[53]

---

49. Korn, *ΠΕΙΡΑΣΜΟΣ*, pp. 18-20, 24-48, 87-88; Gerhardsson, *The Testing of God's Son*, pp. 26-27. That this is the case is clear from the fact that in both secular and biblical Greek the terminology used to speak of persons who have been 'tempted/tried' is confined to such words as δοκιμή/δόκιμος/ἀδόκιμος, τέλειος, πίστος and the virtues necessary to withstand being 'tempted/tried' are ὑπομονή and πίστις. On this, see Brown, *Apostasy and Perseverance*, pp. 29-36.

It might be argued that πειραζόμενος also connoted the idea of '(something or someone) being *attempted*', since in biblical and non-biblical literature the root verb πειράζω is on occasion also used with the sense of 'to try to do something', 'to venture', 'to make an attempt' (cf., e.g., Deut. 4.34; Acts 9.26; Polybius, *Histories* 2.6.9; 8.4.7; 30.23.2). But since, as BAGD, p. 640a notes and a careful review of the evidence shows, this sense appears *only when the root is used intransitively or with reference to a verbal object*, πειραζόμενος connoting 'being attempted' does not seem possible, let alone syntactically likely.

50. On the concept of 'central and peripheral' senses of words, see C.R. Taber, 'Semantics', *IDB*, V, p. 803.

51. Cf. F.J.A. Hort, *The Epistle of St James* (London: Macmillan, 1909), p. 4. Cf. also Korn, *ΠΕΙΡΑΣΜΟΣ*, pp. 18-20, 44-48.

52. By 'ummarked' I mean having little or no contextual clues which might indicate in which of its possible senses a word or a statement is being used. On this, see Taber, 'Semantics', pp. 802-803.

53. Korn, *ΠΕΙΡΑΣΜΟΣ*, p. 77; Cranfield, *The Gospel according to Saint Mark* (Cambridge: Cambridge University Press, 1963), p. 58; B.H. Branscomb, *The Gospel of Mark* (London: Hodder & Stoughton, 1937), pp. 20-21.

The Perpetrator of the Temptation. The temptation that Jesus is said to experience in Mk 1.9-13 is designated by Mark at v. 13a as coming to him through a personal figure, Satan (πειραζόμενος ὑπὸ τοῦ Σατανᾶ).[54] If we are to accept the contention that Mark says nothing within his temptation story concerning the nature of Jesus' temptation, we have to assume that this detail would have had no particular significance for Mark and his original audience. But this is hardly likely. Indeed, when the detail is set against the background of contemporary belief regarding who Satan was and the activities he was thought to engage in, it is obvious that it must give information on the nature of Jesus' Wilderness temptation.

The figure whom Mark designates as the perpetrator of Jesus' Wilderness temptation, whether called Satan or one of a host of other names,[55] was not an 'unknown quantity'. On the contrary, in Mark's time and in the thought world which Mark and his audience shared, Satan's identity and the activities characteristic of him were both well-defined and widely known. He was regarded primarily as the Accuser or, more specifically, as the Evil Adversary,[56] and this in two ways. First, in the sense that he was thought of as standing in opposition to God, seeking to frustrate God's work by leading his elect astray and destroying the relationship between God and humankind;[57] secondly, in that he (Satan) was known to be one whose primary function was the proving of the faith and steadfastness, not of people in general, but of the pious.[58] This first way

---

54.   That ὁ Σατανᾶς is here at Mk 1.13a a proper name, not a common noun, and denotes a particular being, a distinct personality, see Taylor, *Mark*, p. 164.

55.   E.g. Belial, Beliar, Beelzebul, Mastema, Sammael, the Angel of Lawlessness, the Angel of Death, ἀντίδικος, ὁ διάβολος, ὁ ἐχθρός, ὁ πειράζων, ἄρχον τοῦ κόσμου τούτου, etc.

56.   On this, see W. Foerster, 'διάβολος', *TDNT*, II, pp. 75-81.

57.   See W. Foerster, 'Σατανᾶς', *TDNT*, VII (1971), p. 160; B. Noack, *Satanas und Soteria: Untersuchungen zur neutestamentlichen Dämonologie* (Copenhagen: G.E.C. Gads, 1948), pp. 83-86.

58.   See G.B. Caird, *Principalities and Powers: A Study in Pauline Theology* (Oxford: Clarendon Press, 1956), pp. 31-39; W. Foerster and G. von Rad, 'διάβολος', *TDNT*, II, pp. 69-80; T.H. Gaster, 'Satan', *IDB*, IV, pp. 224-28; R.H. Hiers, 'Satan, Demons, and the Kingdom of God', *SJT* 27 (1974), pp. 35-47, esp. p. 41; H.A. Kelly, 'The Devil in the Desert', pp. 202-13; T. Ling, *The Significance of Satan: New Testament Demonology and its Contemporary Significance* (London: SPCK, 1961), pp. 61-64. Satan does not 'tempt/test' non-believers because they are already under his power. On this, see K.G. Kuhn, 'New

of viewing Satan as Adversary is clear, for instance, in the Damascus Document, where Satan (here under the name Belial) is presented as the bane of the people of Israel, attempting repeatedly to make them stumble in her obedience to God:

> And in all those years Belial shall be unleashed against Israel;
> as God said by the hand of the prophet Isaiah, son of Amos,
> 'Terror and pit and snare are upon thee, O inhabitants of the land'.
> The explanation of this (is that) these are Belial's three nets of which
> Levi, son of Jacob, spoke, by which he (Belial) ensnared Israel,
> and which he set [be]fore them as three sorts of righteousness:
> the first is lust,
> the second is riches,
> (and) the third is defilement of the Sanctuary.
> Whoever escapes this is caught by that,
> and whoever escapes that one is caught by this.[59]

The conception of Satan as Adversary of the elect is also clear in such texts as 1QS 3.21-25; *Jub.* 10.8; Mt. 16.25; Mk 4.15; 8.33, 1 Thess. 2.18; 2 Cor. 12.7; 1 Pet. 5.8; Rev. 2.10, 12; 12.17; 13.7.

The second way of viewing Satan as Adversary is clear, for instance, not only in the prologue of the book of Job and the traditions that are derived from it,[60] but also in the scene in the *Book of Jubilees* in which Satan (here called Mastema[61]) is portrayed as the one who instigates the supreme testing of Abraham (i.e. the sacrifice of Isaac) to see if Abraham would remain constant in his faithfulness (17.16; cf. 18.12).[62] It is clear also and especially in *b. Sanh.* 89b (an important text which will be examined in more detail in the next chapter), and in the *Martyrdom of Isaiah*, where Satan (again under the name Belial[63]) stands behind a

---

Light on Temptation, Sin, and Flesh in the New Testament', in K. Stendahl (ed.), *The Scrolls and the New Testament* (New York: Charles Scribner & Sons, 1957), pp. 94-113, esp. p. 95.

59.   CD A 4.12-19 as given by A. Dupont-Sommer in *Essene Writings from Qumran* (Oxford: Oxford University Press, 1961), p. 128.

60.   E.g. *T. Job*, esp. chs. 23–26.

61.   On the meaning of the word *mastema* and its philological relation with *satan*, see Gaster, 'Satan', p. 225.

62.   Cf. also 10.8-9 in the surviving fragment of the Greek text of *Jubilees*, where, in a slight departure from what we find in the Ethiopc text, Satan, called here ὁ διάβολος, is presented as one who 'tests' faithfulness.

63.   Beliar, Sammael and Satan seem to be used interchangeably in this work, cf. Kelley, 'The Devil in the Desert', p. 211 n. 57.

series of attempts and inducements to persuade Isaiah (who, on account of 'the worship of Satan and his wantonness' in the Temple, has renounced and fled from Jerusalem) to return to the Holy City and take up a place of prominence there (cf. *Mart. Isa.* 5), as well as in such texts as *1 En.* 40.7, *Jub.* 1.20; 48.15, 18; *Apoc. Zeph.* 4.2; 10.5; *Apoc. Abr.* 13, *Ass. of Mos.* 17–18; 1 Thess. 3.5 (under the title ὁ πειράζων); Mt. 4.1-11; Lk. 4.1-13. Most importantly, it is the view of Satan which Mark himself holds.[64]

Given this, it seems impossible to think that when Mark employed a statement about Jesus being tempted ὑπὸ τοῦ Σατανᾶ, he (Mark) could be taken as saying nothing with regard to the nature of the temptation to which that statement refers. A temptation designated as one perpetrated by Satan was by definition a 'testing' of faithfulness to God.

Accordingly, when Mark relates in Mk 1.13a that Jesus was 'being tried by Satan' he is doing—and would have been taken by his audience as doing—far more than stating a fact. He is conveying information to his audience on the nature of that trial: that it was an experience in which Jesus' religious fidelity was put to the test.[65]

The Locale of the Temptation. As noted above, another detail that Mark gives within v. 13a regarding Jesus' post-baptismal temptation is that this temptation had a specific locale, 'the wilderness' (ἡ ἔρημος) (cf. also Mk 1.12). What purpose, if any, did giving this detail serve? To answer this question, we must determine what meaning both the term ἔρημος and the phrase 'in the wilderness' would have had for Mark and his audience.

In Mark's time the substantive ἔρημος could mean *any* location normally devoid of human inhabitants or any lonely, desolate, even dangerous place.[66] But it often had another, more specific meaning. Under the influence of its usage in the LXX, where it stands consistently for the definite *midbar*, ἔρημος with the article came to designate the

---

64. This seems clear from the fact that at Mk 8.27-33, the story of Peter's 'Confession', Mark has Jesus call Peter Satan when Peter inadvertently puts Jesus to the test over his (Jesus') willingness to 'think the things of God' and not 'the things of men' regarding the way that his Messiahship should be fleshed out. On this, see below, Chapter 7.

65. Cranfield, *Mark*, p. 58; R. Schnackenburg, 'Der Sinn der Versuchung Jesu bei den Synoptikern', *TQ* 132 (1952), pp. 297-326, esp. p. 310.

66. See, e.g., R. Kittel, 'ἔρημος', *TDNT*, II, p. 644.

wilderness of Israel's post-Exodus sojourn.[67] In contemporary belief this ἔρημος was regarded as the locus where certain divine actions, typified by those displayed by God towards the Israelites during the time of their wilderness wanderings, would be experienced anew.[68] Accordingly, in early Judaism and early Christianity ἡ ἔρημος sometimes signifies a place of judgment and renewal.[69] It also denotes a place of deliverance, redemption and divine aid.[70] But more predominantly—and often concurrently with these other perspectives—ἡ ἔρημος specifically signifies a place of 'testing', particularly the 'testing' of covenant loyalty, of one's dedication to be obedient to God.[71] Indeed, as U. Mauser and W.R. Stegner have shown,[72] there existed in the first century such a

67. R.W. Funk, 'The Wilderness', *JBL* 78 (1959), pp. 206-207. According to Funk, a lonely or uninhabited region is signified in the LXX and the New Testament by anarthrous ἔρημος, ἔρημος as an adjective (usually in conjunction with τόπος, cf. Mk 1.35, 45; 6.31, 32, 35) or the diminutive of ἔρημος (cf. Mk 8.4, ἐρημία).

68. Funk, 'The Wilderness', pp. 209-14; Mauser, *Christ in the Wilderness*, pp. 53-76. See also W. Schmauch, 'In der Wuste: Beobachtungen zur Raumbeziehung des Glaubens im NT', in *Memoriam Ernst Lohmeyer* (Stuttgart: Evangelisches Verlag, 1951), pp. 19-50.

69. Cf. *1 En.* 28.1; 29.1; *Mart. of Isa.* 2.8-12; *2 Bar.* 13.10, and to some extent, though rooted in Isa. 40.3 rather than Hosea, 1QS 8.13-16. See also *Peṣ. R.* 13, 55a.

70. In support of this, see the references in Josephus to revolutionary or apocalyptic leaders who induced various groups to go with them into the wilderness by the promise that, once there, 'signs of freedom' or 'redemption' would be given (*Ant.* 20.167 = *War* 2.622, cf. Acts 21.38; *War* 2.259 = *Ant.* 20.188). Cf. also *Ant.* 20.97.99; *War* 6.351; 7.438. On the Rabbinic subscription to this aspect of wilderness typology, see R. Kittel, 'ἔρημος', p. 646. Cf. also 1QS 9.19.

71. This belief in the wilderness as predominantly the place of 'religious' 'testing', that is, a 'testing of faithfulness', is explicitly emphasized in the writings of the Qumran community where virtually every reference to 'going into the wilderness' is inextricably bound up with the idea of being put to the test over one's faithfulness to God. It also implicitly underlies the rabbinic belief that the wilderness was a favourite haunt of Satan and his demonic forces (cf. *Str–B*, IV, pp. 515-16). Certainly New Testament authors understood the wilderness in this manner. According to Matthew, for instance, when Jesus is led into ἡ ἔρημος (Mt. 4.1) it is expressly to be put to the test (πειράσθηναι, infinitive of purpose). On this, see P. Bonnard, 'La Signification du désert selon le-Nouveau Testament. Essai sur l'interprétation théologique, par l'Eglise primitive, d'un concept historico-géographique', in J.-J. von Allem (ed.), *Hommage et Reconnaissance: Recueil de Travaux publiés a l'occasion du soixantiéme anniversaire de Karl Barth* (Paris: Neuchâtel & Niestlé, 1946), pp. 9-18.

72. Mauser, *Christ in the Wilderness*, p. 99; W.R. Stegner, 'Wilderness and

strong correlation between the concept denoted by the phrase ἡ ἔρημος and that of 'testing' of obedience, that it was then conventional to regard being in the ἔρημος as synonymous with being subjected to a 'trial of faithfulness'. This is particularly true of ἡ ἔρημος when reference to it is accompanied by themes of being led there under divine direction and of being constrained by God to remain there for a fixed period of time.[73] In Mark's time, then, to say that one was in the ἔρημος (i.e. the 'wilderness' of the Exodus) was a kind of 'shorthand' way of saying that one's faithfulness was being 'put to the test'.

Now, it is clear that, according to Mark, the ἔρημος in which Jesus experiences temptation is not just *any* wilderness. It is *the* wilderness, the scene of Israel's post-Exodus wanderings. There are three reasons for saying this. In the first place, the word ἔρημος in Mk 1.13 is accompanied by the definite article. Secondly, according to Mark, πειρασμός takes place there. And thirdly, Mark designates the location of Jesus' temptation experience as the lower Jordan valley,[74] the area which in contemporary thought was regarded as the setting of the latter half of the book of Exodus and of Leviticus, Numbers and Deuteronomy.[75] Accordingly, when Mark says that Jesus experienced temptation ἐν τῇ ἐρήμῳ, Mark does more than simply locate Jesus' temptation. Using geography to serve a theological interest, he says something very concrete about that temptation's nature, namely, that it involved a proving of Jesus' devotion to God.

The Duration of the Temptation. At Mk 1.13a Mark specifies that Jesus was tempted 'for forty days' (τεσσεράκοντα ἡμέρας). What, if anything, was this time reference intended to convey? There are three possibilities. First, if it is a simple and literal chronological statement, then, by its use, Mark would be noting the fact that Jesus' temptation took

Testing in the Scrolls and in Matthew 4:1-11', *BR* 12 (1967), pp. 18-27, esp. pp. 22-23, 26.

    73.   Stegner, 'Wilderness and Testing', p. 23.

    74.   It might be objected that in light of Mk 1.2-4 the primary association of ἡ ἔρημος in Mark—or at least in Mk 1.13—is with the wilderness of eschatological judgment and redemption. But since Jesus is already in this wilderness on the eve of his temptation (cf. Mk 1.9), the wilderness into which he is driven (presumably further) by the Spirit (Mk 1.12), and in which he is compelled to stay, must be somewhat different. On this, see H.B. Swete, *The Gospel according to St Mark* (London: Macmillan, 1905), p. 11, and E. Klostermann, *Markusevangelium*, p. 13.

    75.   Funk, 'The Wilderness', pp. 209, 214.

place over a specific period of time.[76] Secondly, it could be conveying the idea that Jesus' temptation, whatever its nature, was complete and exhaustive, since in biblical thought forty is not always chronological but schematic, and is often associated with long periods of human endurance.[77] Thirdly, it could be intended to highlight the temptation as typological, that is, as corresponding to a prototype from the Old Testament—specifically the temptation which the wilderness generation endured—since in Mark's time the number forty evoked memories of important events in salvation history, particularly Israel's Wilderness temptations.[78]

This last possibility is surely the case, since in its context (i.e. in association with ἡ ἔρημος and πειράζω) the phrase τεσσαράκοντα ἡμέρας clearly brings to mind Deut. 8.2-4 where Israel is instructed to remember 'all the way which the Lord your God has led you in the wilderness (ἐν τῇ ἐρήμῳ), that he might afflict you and tempt you (ἐκπειράσῃ σε)...these forty years (τεσσαράκοντα ἔτη)' (cf. also Deut. 29.2-5).[79]

Now it should be noted that in Deut. 8.2 the temptation, which is, according to Mark, the prototype of Jesus' Wilderness experience,[80] carries the explicit purpose of discovering whether Israel would keep God's commandments or not (εἰ φυλάξῃ τὰς ἐντολὰς αὐτοῦ ἢ οὔ).

---

76. For a similar usage, see Acts 4.22.

77. H. Balz, 'τεσσεράκοντα, κτλ.', *TDNT*, VIII, p. 137.

78. Balz, 'τεσσεράκοντα', pp. 136, 138.

79. Such Scholars as Kittel ('ἔρημος', p. 645) and Cranfield (*Mark*, p. 57) deny that the reference to forty days in Mk 1.13a is meant to recall Deut. 8.2-4 and its recapitulation of Israel's experience of forty years of wilderness 'temptation/testing'. To their minds, the parallel of days to years is too inexact. But such a view neglects the fact that the emphasis in both Mark and in Deuteronomy is not upon the actual span of time elapsed but on the point that the respective spans are fixed and for a purpose. It also fails to see that already in the Pentateuch itself (e.g. in Num. 14.34) forty years and forty days can be corresponding periods (on this, see Gerhardsson, *Testing of God's Son*, pp. 42-44). Furthermore, as A. Meyer has observed ('Die evangelischen Berichte über die Versuchung Christi', in A. Meyer (ed.), *Festgabe H. Blümner übericht zum 9, August 1914 von Freunden und Schülern* [Zürich: Berichthaus, 1914], p. 447), since the period in question is associated with an individual and not a people, days instead of years are more appropriate if the purpose for which the period has been fixed is to be achieved.

80. Balz, 'τεσσεράκοντα', p. 138; Schnackenburg, 'Der Sinn', p. 306-307; A. Feuillet, 'L'episode de la tentation d'après l'Evangile selon Saint Marc (1,12-13)', *EstBíb* 19 (1960), pp. 49-73, esp. p. 58.

Accordingly, when Mark says that Jesus was tempted τεσσαράκοντα ἡμέρας, he is making a statement concerning the nature of that temptation, namely, that it was a 'probing', a 'test' and involved a proving of Jesus' faithfulness and devotion to God.

If these observations are correct, then in Mk 1.13a Mark was hardly silent with regard to the question of the nature of Jesus' Wilderness temptation. On the contrary, he there spoke quite openly and plainly on the matter and revealed, in no uncertain terms and in a variety of ways, that Jesus' temptation was a 'testing', cut from the same cloth as the Israelites' when God tempted them in the wilderness, or Job's or Isaiah's or that of the Abraham of *Jubilees* when faced by Satan, a testing whose purpose was to reveal the depths of Jesus' fidelity to God.

But Mk 1.13a is not the only place within Mk 1.9-13 that Mark makes and gives voice to this point. He does so in v. 12 and in v. 13b as well.

καὶ εὐθὺς τὸ πνεῦμα αὐτὸν ἐκβάλλει εἰς τὴν ἔρημον (Mk 1.12).

In this notice Mark designates Jesus' Wilderness temptation as an experience both that Jesus was constrained to undergo and that occurred under the direction and agency of God.[81] 'The Spirit' which is said here to 'drive' (ἐκβάλλω) Jesus into the wilderness, the place of temptation, is, of course, the Spirit of God. The activity in which it here engages (i.e. expulsion) is the exercise of a type of power used to bring divine purposes to fulfilment.[82] Accordingly, in saying that 'the Spirit' forces or, more literally, impels Jesus into his Wilderness temptation, Mark in effect says that this temptation is willed by God, indeed, that God is its ultimate author.[83] Now, as Mark and his audience will have known, given their religious and conceptual heritage, 'God-authored' or divinely-willed temptations are 'testings' of faithfulness.[84] So in saying that Jesus' Wilderness temptation is willed by God, Mark is saying that it is a proving of Jesus' fidelity. Here too, then, in the notice of the Spirit driving Jesus into the wilderness, Mark gives information on the nature of Jesus' Wilderness temptation.

---

81. Rawlinson, *Mark*, p. 12; Schweizer, *Mark*, p. 42; L.W. Hurtado, *Mark* (San Francisco: Harper & Row, 1983), p. 6.

82. On this, see Schweizer, 'πνεῦμα, κτλ.', *TDNT*, VII, p. 398.

83. Kingsbury, *Christology of Mark's Gospel*, p. 68.

84. On this, see Gerhardsson, *Testing of God's Son*, pp. 27-28; Seesemann, 'πεῖρα, κτλ.', pp. 25-26.

καὶ ἦν μετὰ τῶν θηρίων, καὶ οἱ ἄγγελοι διηκόνουν αὐτῷ (Mk 1.13b).

In this verse Mark relates that attendant to his wilderness sojourn Jesus was in the presence of 'wild beasts' and was 'served' by angels.[85] Was this statement made in order to reveal something about the nature of Jesus' Wilderness temptation? The answer to this question depends entirely upon how this statement is explained. There are, I think, three possibilities:

The first is that the statement was meant simply as *a pictorial description of the desolation and danger of the landscape in which Jesus found himself*. In saying that Jesus was with beasts and angels, Mark was only emphasizing the loneliness of Jesus' ordeal and (perhaps) his heroism in facing it.[86] He has no human companions in his struggle. But, given that (1) the context of the verse abounds with theological and religious ideas and (2) that each of the other images that appear there seem allusory, this interpretation of Mk 1.13b seems far too prosaic to be given much credence.

Another suggestion, championed by J. Jeremias[87] and others,[88] is that the statement is *a reminiscence of the friendly relations between Adam and the beasts in the Garden of Eden before the fall*, and is grounded in the expectation, adumbrated in Isa. 11.6-9 and Hos. 2.18 [20], that in the last days peace would again prevail between human beings and animals. In saying that 'wild beasts' were 'with' Jesus after his temptation and that angels then 'served' him, Mark's intention, they argue, was to present Jesus as a second Adam and to say that in Jesus and his activity 'the gate of Paradise is again opened'.[89] Now it should be noted that this suggestion is grounded in two assumptions. The first is that

85. On the nature of this 'being with' and of this 'service', see below.

86. Cf. Cranfield, *Mark*, p. 59; Lagrange, *Mark*, p. 6.

87. Jeremias, "Ἀδάμ', *TDNT*, I, pp. 141-43; *idem*, 'Nachwort zum Artikel von H.-G. Leder', *ZNW* 54 (1963), pp. 278-79; *idem, New Testament Theology*, pp. 69-70.

88. Balz, 'τεσσεράκοντα', pp. 138-39; Klostermann, *Markusevangelium*, p. 31; Schniewind, *Das Evangelium nach Markus*, p. 49; U. Holmeister, '"Jesus lebte mit den wilden Tieren", Mk. 1:13', in *Vom Worte des Lebens, Festschrift für M. Meinertz* (Münster, 1951), pp. 85-92; W.A. Schulze, 'Der Heilige und die wilden Tiere. Zur Exegese von Mc. 1,13b', *ZNW* 46 (1955), pp. 280-83.

89. Jeremias, *New Testament Theology*, p. 70. See also Pesch, *Markusevagelium*, I, p. 96; Schulze, 'Der Heilige und die wilden Tiere', pp. 280-83; Taylor, *Mark*, p. 164.

the 'with' (μετά) in the phrase 'with the wild beasts' denotes close communion.[90] The second is that the 'service' (διακονέω) rendered to Jesus by the angels is 'table-service'.[91] This is the type of service which, according to Jeremias, Jewish tradition thought of as bringing sustenance to Adam when he was in Paradise.[92] But both of these assumptions are highly dubious. For μετά here, in light of its coupling with ἦν, seems to signify dominion and mastery rather than communion.[93] And with regard to διακονέω in the Markan story, nothing in either its immediate context or its usage elsewhere by Mark (save for Mk 1.31) suggests that 'to give table-service' (i.e. 'to feed') is the meaning that the verb is meant to have in Mk 1.13b.[94] But even if these assumptions were correct, there are still several considerations which stand against taking Mk 1.13b as emphasizing a Jesus–Adam typology. First, as Lohmeyer has demonstrated,[95] in Mk 1.13b the 'wild beasts' and angels stand over against one another. So, while either the reference to the beasts *or* the reference to the angels might be intended as an allusion to

90.   Jeremias, *New Testament Theology*, p. 69; Cf. also Guelich, *Mark 1–8:26*, p. 39. On the meanings of μετά with the genitive, see BDF, §227.

91.   Jeremias, *New Testament Theology*, p. 70.

92.   Jeremias, ''Αδάμ', *TDNT*, I, p. 141; *New Testament Theology*, p. 70.

93.   Scholars such as Jeremias, who argue for μετά meaning 'communion' in Mk 1.13, while seemingly having Markan usage on their side (but cf. Mk 8.38; 14.32 where μετά signifies mastery over), nonetheless ignore the significance of the construction in which the preposition is found (i.e. ἦν μετά). In the LXX, μετά with some form (especially ἦν) of the imperfect of εἰμί is used in many of its instances to signify the subordination of one man or group to another, and bears or implies the specific meaning 'to be under the (military) command of' (cf. Gen. 8.1; 34.5; Num. 14.23; Judg. 14.11; 1 Sam. 13.2; 14.21, 23; 22.2; 2 Sam. 3.22; 23.9; 1 Kgs 11.40; 2 Kgs 25.25; 1 Chron. 11.13; Neh. 2.12; Jer. 33.24; 48.2; Est. 2.20; 1 Esdras 8.62; cf. also the use of a form of the present of εἰμί with μετά in Gen. 44.18; Num. 14.23; 1 Sam. 14.21; Neh. 2.12; Zeph. 2.15).

On μετά in Mk 1.13 as meaning 'mastery over' not 'in communion with', see E. Fascher, 'Jesus und die Tiere', *TLZ* 90 (1965), cols. 561-70; M. Sabbe, 'De tentatione in deserto', *CBrugTomL* 50 (1954), p. 466 n. 30. See also Holmeister, ' "Jesus lebte" ', p. 87; Schulze, 'Der Heilige und die wilden Tiere', p. 282.

94.   Best, *The Temptation and the Passion*, pp. 9-10. Indeed, if the other instances of the use of διακονέω by Mark (cf. Mk 9.35; 10.43; 15.41 and most notably Mk 10.45) show us anything about Mark's concerns and his understanding of the meaning of διακονέω, it is that for him the verb is meant to be seen primarily as bearing the meaning 'to render the sort of service a client owes a king'.

95.   Lohmeyer, *Markus*, p. 27.

the idea of paradise, *both* references cannot be intended as such; and therefore an explanation of Mk 1.13b wholly in terms of a *Urzeit–Endzeit*/Paradise typology is incomplete and inadequate. Secondly, in Mark's time θηρία normally suggested evil rather than good, fierceness and opposition rather than docility and co-operation.[96] Thirdly, the theme or portrayal of Jesus as a second Adam plays no real part in Mark's Christolgy nor, indeed, is it ever hinted at elsewhere in his Gospel. Why would Mark make this comparison in the first place if he never intended to employ or exploit it again? Fourthly, as E. Best has pointed out, to assume that in Mk 1.13b Mark is drawing a parallel between Jesus and Adam, one must ignore or downplay the fact that the parallelism is not very exact: Jesus was in the desert, whereas Adam was in the Garden.[97] And finally, despite Jeremias' claim to the contrary, in Jewish tradition of Mark's time, there is no great emphasis placed upon either the presence of 'wild beasts' with Adam or angels ministering to him.[98] So the explanation of Mk 1.13b as a *Paradiesesgeschichte* does not seem credible.

The third possibility is that Mk 1.13b is an *allusion to the particular catenation of ideas embodied in such writings as Ps. 91.11-13, T. Iss. 7.7, T. Benj. 5.2 and T. Naph. 8.4.* Ps. 91.11-13 (LXX) reads:

> For [God] shall give his angels charge concerning you,
> to keep you in all of your ways.
> They shall bear you up on their hands,
> lest at any time you dash your foot against a stone.
> You shall tread on the asp and the basilisk:
> and you shall trample on the lion and the dragon.

Testament of Issachar 7.7 reads:

> If you do these as well [i.e. acts of piety and trust in God, cf. 7.1-6],
> my children,
> Every spirit of Beliar will flee from you,
> And no act of human evil will have power over you.
> Every wild creature you shall subdue,
> so long as you have the God of heaven with you,
> and walk with all mankind in sincerity of heart.

---

96. Best, *The Temptation and the Passion*, pp. 8-9. See also, F.C. Grant, *The Earliest Gospel* (Nashville: Abingdon, 1943), p. 77.

97. Best, *The Temptation and the Passion*, p. 8.

98. H.-G. Leder, 'Sünderfallerzählung und Versuchungs-geschichte: Zur Interpretation von Mc. 1:12f.', *ZNW* 54 (1963), pp. 188-216, esp. pp. 203-206.

Testament of Benjamin 5.2 reads:

> If you continue to do good,
> even the unclean spirits will flee from you
> and wild animals will fear you.

Testament of Napthali 8.4, 6 reads:

> If you achieve good, my children, men and angels will bless you;
> and God will be glorified through you among the gentiles.
> The devil will flee from you;
> wild animals will be afraid of you, and the angels will stand by you.
> The one who does not good, men and angels will curse,
> and God will be dishonored among the gentiles because of him;
> and the devil will inhabit him, and the Lord will hate him.

This third possibility must surely be the case. For in the first place, the parallelism between the appearance of the combination of 'beasts' and angels and the devil (or demons) in both Mark and these other writings is too close and curious to be accidental.[99] And secondly, in both contexts 'beasts' and angels stand over against one another.

It should be noted, then, that in Psalm 91 and the *Testaments of the Twelve Patriarchs* two ideas stand out. The first is that those who are confronted by 'beasts' and angels stand in a covenant relationship with God.[100] The second is that the manner in which those so confronted are 'with' the 'beasts' and angels is something that is wholly determined by *whether or not they are faithful under trial to God's covenant and obey its demands*. In Psalm 91 the angels protect, and the 'beasts' (and demons) are subject to, those who, despite the danger and distress brought on by trusting God, still cling to him in love. In the *Testament of Naphtali* it is promised, on the one hand, that the angels will bless and cleave to, and the 'beasts' (and demons) fear, those who imitate the example of the Patriarch's devotion and 'work that which is good', but that, on the other, the angels will curse and the 'beasts' (and the Devil) will master the sons of the covenant who turn their backs on God and,

---

99. On the dependence of the Markan reference upon Ps. 91, see F. Spitta, 'Betrage zur Erklärung der Synoptiker', *ZNW* 5 (1904), pp. 325-26; Dupont, 'L'arrière-fond', pp. 298, 294-95. For a contrary view, see P. Pokorny, 'The Temptation Stories and their Intention', *NTS* 20 (1973–74), pp. 115-27, esp. pp. 116-17. The case for the dependence of the Markan reference on the *Testament of Napthali* has been argued by Feuillet, 'L'episode…selon St. Marc', pp. 72-73.

100. Cf. Ps. 91.2, 14. In the *Testament of the Twelve Patriarchs* they are the sons of noted Patriarchs and therefore Israelites, i.e., sons of the Covenant.

in spite of clear directives to the contrary, 'do that which is evil'.[101] In other words, *the conceptual background to the theme of being 'with' 'beasts' and angels is the idea of 'testing' and especially 'testing of faithfulness and obedience to covenantal obligations'*. Accordingly, in describing Jesus as being 'with' 'beasts' and angels consequent to his Wilderness temptation, Mark is saying something about that temptation, namely, that it involved proving whether or not Jesus would be faithful and obedient to God.

Conclusions: The Nature of Jesus' Wilderness Temptation according to Mark. Given all that has been shown above, it can hardly be the case that Mk 1.9-13 says nothing with regard to the nature of the temptation that Jesus is there said to have experienced, and that in the end these verses embody only a statement of the fact that in the wilderness Jesus was tempted. On the contrary, within these verses—particularly in the explicit notice of Jesus' temptation (Mk 1.13a), in the description of Jesus under the influence of the Spirit (Mk 1.12), and in the notice of Jesus 'with' 'beasts' and angels (Mk 1.13b)—Mark carefully and repeatedly emphasizes that the nature of Jesus' Wilderness temptation involved a trial which was meant to determine whether or not Jesus would be faithful to God.

But does Mark here also reveal anything concerning the content of that temptation? Or is he, as is usually contended, silent on this matter? This is the question to which I now turn.

---

101. The theme of the mastery of, or subjection to, the 'beasts' appears not only in Ps. 91, and the texts of the *Testaments* already cited. It is, notably, also a constituent element of the Deuteronomic 'wilderness "testing" of God's Son' tradition. We read, for instance, in Deut. 32.19-24 of God sending 'beasts' (LXX: θηρία) to devour the Israelites when, contrary to his commandments, they sacrificed to *sedîm* (LXX: demons) which are no gods. As the immediately preceding passage (Deut. 32.8-13) notes, this event took place specifically during the wilderness period, the time when God was intent to lead, care for, and engage in the disciplining instruction (LXX: ἐπαίδευσεν) of Israel, his begotten (cf. v. 18). Significantly, in each of these passages the theme is also intimately connected with a call for covenant faithfulness (cp. *T. Iss.* 7.6; *T. Benj.* 4.5; Deut. 32.46-47).

Accordingly, this repeated association of the imagery of 'beasts' and the charge to 'do good' and 'love the Lord' indicates that in the first century, and indeed earlier, the conjunction of the ideas of being 'with' wild 'beasts' and covenant faithfulness was a firmly established *topos*.

The Content of Jesus' Wilderness Temptation according to Mark
I have demonstrated above that in Mk 1.9-13 Mark was quite explicit in noting that Jesus' Wilderness temptation involved a trial of his (Jesus') devotion and faithfulness to God. But how, according to Mark, was Jesus to show these attributes? What were the demands from God to which Jesus had to prove himself loyal? In other words, what, if anything at all, does Mark present as the *content* of Jesus' Wilderness temptation? And does he do this within the confines of the Wilderness temptation story?

To determine this it seems most natural to turn to the earlier portion of Mk 1.9-11, especially vv. 10-11, and examine what Mark says there. The main reason for saying this is that Mark himself, in his reproduction (or addition) of εὐθύς in Mk 1.12a,[102] encourages us to do so. In reproducing (or adding) this word, Mark envisions and presents what he narrates as taking place in Mk 1.12-13 as the corollary and consequence of that which is said to occur in the verses immediately preceding the adverb.[103] What, then, according to Mark, takes place there?

In Mk 1.10-11 Jesus experiences two revelatory events, one visual and one auditory.[104] The visual event, the descent of the Spirit (τὸ πνεῦμα) upon Jesus,[105] represents God's empowering of Jesus for ministry.[106] The second, auditory event—a voice from heaven cast in the form of an initiation and ordination oracle[107] and directed to Jesus, declaring to

---

102. On the question of whether εὐθύς here is a redactional addition by Mark to his *Vorlage*, see above, p. 45. If it is not, that is, if εὐθύς is original to Mark's source, then Mark, in reproducing the word, agrees that it should stand and operate, as it does, as a pointer within the text that the temptation is the corollary of the baptism. On the function of the phrase within Mk 1.9-11, see above, pp. 30-31.

103. Cf. Daube, *The Sudden in the Scripture* (Leiden: Brill, 1964), p. 47; Lane, *Mark*, p. 59; Mann, *Mark*, p. 202; Pesch, *Markusevangelium*, I, p. 94.

104. Kingsbury, *The Christology of Mark's Gospel*, p. 61.

105. Again, that εἰς here has the meaning 'upon' and not 'into', as, for instance, Hahn maintains (*Titles of Jesus*, pp. 338-39, 344 n. 39), see Kingsbury, *Christology of Mark's Gospel*, pp. 62-63. See also Pesch, *Das Markusevangelium*, I, p. 91.

106. J.M. Robinson, *The Problem of History in Mark* (London: SCM Press, 1957), p. 29; Kingsbury, *Christology of Mark's Gospel*, p. 64; Lentzen-Deis, *Die Tauffe Jesu nach den Synoptikern: Literarkritische und gattungsgeschichtliche Untersuchungen* (Frankfort am Main: Knecht, 1970), p. 278.

107. On this, see M. Dibelius, *From Tradition to Gospel* (New York: Charles Scribner & Sons, 1933), p. 272; Bultmann, *History*, p. 248 n. 1; G. Schrenk, 'εὐδοκέω, εὐδοκία', *TDNT*, II, pp. 738-51, esp. p. 740. On the form and function of the initiation/ordination formula itself, see H. Gunkel, *The Psalms: A Form*

Jesus, σὺ εἶ ὁ υἱός μου ὁ ἀγαπητός, ἐν σοὶ εὐδόκησα—represents God himself[108] speaking to Jesus, predicating who he 'thinks' Jesus is.[109] When we ask what purpose Mark had in mind in attributing this experience to Jesus, it was at the very least to depict Jesus' being called, commissioned and empowered by God to a certain status and, with it, a mission.[110] *But it was also to make known to the readers of the Gospel the 'marching orders' Jesus received from God regarding the nature and direction of the mission, that is, the principles upon which that mission was to be fleshed out and acted upon, the particular demands to which God wanted Jesus to show himself obedient if Jesus was faithfully to live out his divine appointment.*[111] For implicit within a call to a status and a mission such as that found in Mk 1.11 are the expectations of the one issuing it on how the appointment which the call effectuates is to be carried out and accomplished.[112] So if we wish to know what Mark presented within Mk 1.9-13 as the content of Jesus' Wilderness temptation, that is, the particular demands from God to which Jesus, when confronted by Satan, was to show himself loyal, we must determine the particular status and the mission that, according to Mark, Jesus was called to when God spoke to him at his baptism.

What, then, *is* that status and its attendant mission? Knowing this is a matter of knowing precisely *who* it is that, according to Mark, Jesus is called to be when addressed by God as ὁ υἱός μου ὁ ἀγαπητός, ἐν σοὶ εὐδόκησα. Of the many answers commentators have given to this question,[113] surely the correct one is that advanced and advocated by

---

Critical Introduction (Philadelphia: Fortress Press, 1967), p. 7.

108. That the voice is the direct voice of God and not, as is usually maintained, the *bath-qol*, the so-called 'daughter of the voice', see Kazmierski, *Jesus, the Son of God*, pp. 36-37. See also Kingsbury, *Christology of Mark's Gospel*, p. 65; Lohmeyer, *Markus*, p. 24; H. Traub, 'οὐρανός', *TDNT*, V, p. 530.

109. Kingsbury, *Christology of Mark's Gospel*, p. 66; Gnilka, *Markus*, I, p. 53; E. Norden, *Agnostos Theos* (Leipzig: Teubner, 1913), pp. 177-78.

110. On this, see R.C. Tannehill, 'The Gospel of Mark as Narrative Christology', *Semeia* 16 (1979), pp. 57-98, esp. p. 61.

111. Tannehill, 'Gospel of Mark', p. 90 n. 2.

112. On the appointment oracle as something which not only calls the one addressed by it to a role but also makes known to the recipient how it is expected to be carried it out, see S. Mowinckel, *He That Cometh* (Oxford: Basil Blackwell, 1965), pp. 37-38; *idem*, *The Psalms in Israel's Worship* (Oxford: Basil Blackwell, 1967), p. 65.

113. It has been held that the voice speaks of Jesus: (1) solely as The Davidic King

V. Taylor,[114] W. Lane[115] and J.D. Kingsbury,[116] among others:[117] that the heavenly voice declares Jesus to be at once (1) the anointed *King of Israel*, the figure who is to establish and implement the sovereign authority of God over a rebellious world by rescuing and permanently delivering those willing to submit to this authority from those forces

(cf. J.D.G. Dunn, *Jesus and the Spirit* [London: SCM Press, 1975], pp. 27, 65, 366 n. 72, 378 n. 122; Gould, *Mark*, p. 12; R.H. Gundry, *The Use of the Old Testament in St Matthew's Gospel* [Leiden: Brill, 1967], p. 112; E. Lovestram, *Son and Saviour: A Study of Acts 13,32-37: With an Appendix: Son of God in the Synoptic Gospels* [Lund: Gleerup, 1961], pp. 97-101; E. Schweizer, 'υἱός', *TDNT*, VIII, pp. 340-99; H. Weinel, *Biblische Theologie des Neuen Testaments* [Tübingen: Mohr, 1928], p. 170); (2) solely as the Servant of God (cf. G. Dalman, *The Words of Jesus* [Edinburgh: T.& T. Clark, 1902], pp. 227-28; W. Boussett, *Kyrios Christos* [Nashville: Abingdon, 1970], pp. 97-98; O. Cullmann, *Baptism in the New Testament* [London: SCM Press, 1950], pp. 16-18, *idem*, *The Christology of the New Testament* [Philadelphia: Westminster Press, 1963], p. 66; J. Jeremias, *Abba: Studien zur neuetestamentlichen Theologie und Zeitgeschichte* [Göttingen: Vandenhoeck & Ruprecht, 1966], pp. 191-98; *idem*, 'παῖς θεοῦ', *TDNT*, V, pp. 701-702; Cranfield, *Mark*, pp. 55-56; Gnilka, *Markus*, I, p. 50; R.H. Fuller, *The Mission and Achievement of Jesus* [London: SCM Press, 1954], pp. 86-88; *idem*, *The Foundations of New Testament Christology* [New York: Charles Scribner & Sons, 1965], pp. 169-70; C. Maurer, 'Knecht Gottes und Sohn Gottes im Passionsbericht des Markusevangeliums', *ZTK* 50 [1953], pp. 1-38; R. Schnackenburg, *The Gospel according to Mark* [New York: Herder & Herder, 1971], pp. 10-11); (3) solely or predominantly as Isaac (cf. G. Vermes, 'Redemption and Genesis XXII', in *Scripture and Tradition in Judaism* [Leiden: Brill, 1961], pp. 193-227, esp. pp. 204-11; A. Gabour, 'Deux Fils uniques: Isaac et Jésus; Connexions vetero testamentaries de Mc 1,11', *StEv* 4 [1968], pp. 198-204; A. Richardson, *The Theology of the New Testament* [London: SCM Press, 1958], p. 180; C.H. Turner, 'HO HUIOS MOU HO AGAPETOS', *JTS* 27 [1926], pp. 113-29; W.R. Stenger, 'The Baptism of Jesus: A Story Modeled on the Binding of Isaac', *BR* [1985], pp. 36-46; J.E. Wood, 'Isaac Typology in the New Testament', *NTS* 14 [1967–68], pp. 583-589, esp. p. 586); or (4) as Israel (A. Feuillett, 'Le Baptême de Jésus d'après L'Evangile selon Saint Marc [1,9-11]', *CBQ* 21 [1959], pp. 468-90, esp. pp. 473-74; M. Hooker, *Jesus and the Servant* [London: SPCK, 1959], pp. 68-73; *idem*, *The Gospel according to Mark* [London: A. & C. Black, 1991], p. 48).

114. Taylor, *Mark*, p. 162.

115. *Mark*, p. 57.

116. Kingsbury, *Christology of Mark's Gospel*, p. 65.

117. Anderson, *Mark*, pp. 78-80 (guardedly); Hurtado, *Mark*, p. 6; Mann, *Mark*, p. 201; Marshall, 'Son of God or Servant of Yahweh?', p. 335; Nineham, *Mark*, p. 62; Rawlinson, *Mark*, p. 10; Schweizer, *Mark*, p. 37 (guardedly); Swete, *Mark*, p. 10.

hostile to God and his saving purpose;[118] (2) the *Isaianic Servant of the Lord* (παῖς θεοῦ/'*ebed yhwh*), the figure dominating the so-called 'Servant Songs' in Isaiah 40–55,[119] who is divinely elected and empowered to bring glorly to God by establishing God's justice on earth, first, in releasing Israel from bondage and re-establising the covenant that God had made with his people, and second, in leading other nations to acknowledge Yahweh (cf. e.g. Isa. 49.6); this figure accomplishes his task not through conquest and domination, but by voluntarily passing through a vale of suffering, bearing humiliation and defeat (cf. Isa. 42.2-3; 53.3-12);[120] and (3) *Isaak*, the beloved of Abraham, the Virtuous and Obedient One, the Lamb, who is to offer himself willingly as a sacrifice to atone for the sins of human beings. Several considerations make this clear.

First, the wording of the voice is grounded in imagery linked with these three particular figures. The phrase σὺ εἶ ὁ υἱός μου ὁ ἀγαπητός, ἐν σοὶ εὐδόκησα employs language associated with specific beloved 'sons',[121] namely, the anointed King[122] and Isaac,[123] while ἐν σοὶ

118. On this as the task of Israel's King/Messiah, see Cullmann, *Christology*, pp. 113-17.

119. On these, see C.R. North, *The Suffering Servant in Deutero-Isaiah* (Oxford: Oxford University Press, 1948), pp. 117-38.

120. On this as the task of the Isaianic παῖς θεοῦ, see Cullmann, *Christology*, p. 53.

121. I assume here, following G.D. Kilpatrick ('The Order of some Noun and Adjective Phrases in the New Testament', *NovT* 5 [1962], pp. 111-14) and others (e.g. Best, *Temptation*, p. 148 n. 3, 169-70; Kazmierski, *Jesus, the Son of God*, pp. 53-54; Lane, *Mark*, pp. 58 n. 65; Schweizer, 'υἱός', p. 367 n. 235; Stegner, 'Baptism', p. 42; Swete, *Mark*, p. 10; Wood, 'Isaac Typology', p. 586), that ὁ ἀγαπητός is used adjectivally in Mk 1.11b and, therefore, that the heavenly voice addresses Jesus as 'my beloved Son', not 'my Son, the Beloved'.

122. On the King as a 'beloved son', see Schweizer, 'υἱός', p. 368; Gundry, *The Use of the Old Testament in St Matthew's Gospel*, p. 112; L. Cerfaux, 'Les sources scripturaires de Mt.', *ETL* 31 (1955), pp. 335-36.

123. One of the strongest points in favour of seeing an identification in Mk 1.11b of Jesus with Isaac, particularly Isaac the sacrificial victim, is that there is a striking linguistic parallel between the Markan text and several verses in the story of the sacrifice of Isaac in Gen. 22:

λαβὲ τὸν υἱόν σου τὸν ἀγαπητόν, ὃν ἠγάπησας, τὸν Ισαακ...(v. 2)
οὐκ ἐφείσω τοῦ υἱοῦ σου τοῦ ἀγαπητοῦ δι' ἐμέ (v. 12)
οὐκ ἐφείσω τοῦ υἱοῦ σου τοῦ ἀγαπητοῦ δι' ἐμέ...(v. 16)

εὐδόκησα employs language associated with the Servant[124] and possibly Isaac.[125]

As Kazmierski (*Jesus, the Son of God*, p. 55), Marshall ('Son of God', p. 334 [guardedly]), A. Richardson (*Theology of the New Testament* [London: SCM Press, 1958], p. 180), Turner ('HO HUIOS MOU HO AGAPETOS', pp. 123-24) and Vermes ('Redemption and Genesis XXII', pp. 222-23) note, the verbal and stylistic correspondence between Mark's phrase and the way Isaac is referred to by God in Gen. 22 is too exact to be anything other than an allusion to the Genesis text.

For the latest discussion and defense of the claim that Mk 1.11b identifies Jesus with Isaac, see Guelich, *Mark*, pp. 33-34.

That a reference within the voice to Isaac would also be taken, let alone intended, as a reference to Isaac *as willing victim and atoning sacrifice* assumes, of course, that this was the way in which Isaac was viewed by first-century Jews and Christians. For the evidence in favour of this, see E. Best, *Tempation*, pp. 169-72; R.J. Daly, 'Soteriological Significance', pp. 69-71; A. Gabour, 'Deux Fils uniques', pp. 198-204; G. Vermes, 'Redemption and Genesis XXII', pp. 204-11; Wood, 'Isaac Typology', p. 586.

124. A number of scholars, especially M.D. Hooker (*Jesus and the Servant*, pp. 71-72, *idem*, *St Mark*, p. 48), have argued strongly against the view that Mk 1.11c is drawn from Isa. 42.1. Their primary objection to this view is the fact that the wording of Mk 1.11c is significantly different from that of the Isaian text in either its Hebrew or any of its Greek forms. But even if this objection is valid, this does not mean that at Mk 1.11c Jesus is not addressed as the Servant, for, as B.D. Chilton has argued recently (*A Galiean Rabbi and his Bible* [Wilmington: Michael Glazier, 1984], pp. 129-31), the background of Mk 1.11c may very well be the 'I am well pleased' passages of the Isaiah Targum (e.g. 41.8-9; 43.10, 20; 44.1-12), passages which in the Targum are connected with the Servant of God. There, Chilton notes, we find not only the precise phrase that appears in Mk 1.11c (cf. 41.8-9; 43.10, 20; 44.1-2), but also, as in the beginning of the Markan verse, the use of the phrase in a solemn address (41.8, 9) and an identification of the recipient of the phrase with the Messiah (43.10). In other words,

> we have in the Targum alone an idiom which corresponds to the expression of the Baptismal voice, and which has a range of associations—the direct address of 41:8, 9, the references to…the messiah in 43:1—which suits the usage of the expression by the voice in the narrative of Jesus' Baptism (p. 130).

Now, according to Chilton, the tradition embodied in these passages pre-dates both the Targum and Mark. So what appears in these Targum passages reflects an interpretation of Isaiah, *as well as a way of alluding to the biblical text of Isa. 42.1*, that was fixed and conventional early in the first century. Given this, it is reasonable to conclude that whether or not Mk 1.11c is drawn directly from Isa. 42.1, the heavenly voice is still using language and imagery associated with the figure of the Servant.

The second reason arises from the fact that the declaration made by God at Jesus' Baptism is repeated two more times in Mark's Gospel and in each instance the intent to portray Jesus as King of Israel, Suffering Servant, and Sacrificial Victim is central. The first instance of the repetition of the Baptismal declaration occurs at the climax of the story of Jesus' Transfiguration (Mk 9.2-8) when God proclaims to Peter, James, and John that Jesus is his 'beloved Son' (καὶ ἐγένετο φωνὴ ἐκ τῆς νεφέλης· οὗτός ἐστιν ὁ υἱός μου ὁ ἀγαπητός, v. 7). Why, according to Mark, does God do this? It is because Jesus has just shown that he has accepted suffering and self-sacrifice as his destiny as Messiah, and, despite inducements to the contrary, he will not be swayed from this path (cf. Mk 8.27–9.1).[126] The second instance occurs at the climax of the story of Jesus' Crucifixion (Mk 15.16-40) when a Roman soldier, the captain of Jesus' execution detail, exclaims that Jesus was indeed the Son of God (ὁ κεντυρίων…εἶπεν· ἀληθῶς οὗτος ὁ ἄνθρωπος υἱὸς θεοῦ ἦν, Mk 15.39b).[127] Why should the soldier make this remark? According to Mark it is because he saw both the manner of Jesus' dying and the circumstances surrounding his death (ἰδὼν…ὁ παρεστηκὼς ἐξ ἐναντίας αὐτοῦ ὅτι οὕτως ἐξέπνευσεν δέ).[128] The manner of Jesus'

Assuming the truth of Chilton's view regarding the date of these passages, it seems clear that in Mk 1.11c Jesus is addressed as God's Servant.

125. Daly ('Soteriological Significance', pp. 69-70), Lentzen-Deis (*Taufe Jesu*, pp. 239-40) and Stegner ('Baptism', pp. 42-43) all claim that the words ἐν σοὶ εὐδόκησα in Mk 1.11c are an echo of the heavenly voice in the Targumic story of the Binding of Isaac (*Targ.* Gen. 22), a voice that applies the term *yaḥida* (= εὐδοκέω) to Isaac and therefore speaks of him, as the voice in Mk 1.11b does of Jesus, in terms of Isaac being the object of God's elective pleasure.

Now, there is certainly a close correspondence between the wording and theme of Mk 1.11c and that of the divine address to Isaac in the Targum on Gen. 22. But given the relatively late date of the Targum, this cannot be taken as indicating that the Markan phrase is an actual echo of that Targumic passage. Might we not assume, however, despite this, and despite the lack of hard evidence in its favour, that the phrase is still a reference to Isaac on the grounds that the Targum's identification of Isaac as one who is the object of God's elective pleasure probably reflects not a new idea, but an earlier and traditional designation for him?

126. On this, see Schweizer, *Mark*, p. 182. Cf. also T.H. Weeden, *Mark: Traditions in Conflict* (Philadelphia: Fortress Press, 1971), p. 53.

127. That this, and not 'this man was *a* Son of God' is the correct rendering of this phrase, is maintained by E.C. Colwell, 'A Definite Rule for the Use of the Article in the Greek New Testament', *JBL* 52 (1933), pp. 12-21.

128. On this, see Kingsbury, *Christology of Mark's Gospel*, p. 129; cf. also

dying is his engagement as the Christ, the King of Israel, in a resolute passiveness in the face of derision (15.29; cp. 14.65; 15.15-20), a refusal to escape or mitigate the sufferings appointed for him (15.23), the willing endurance of desolating torments, a dedicated obedience to a divine command that one should save one's life by losing it (15.29-32), and a continuing trust in an apparently absent God (15.34).[129] In other words, the manner of Jesus Messiah's death is, among other things, that of the Servant of Isaiah.[130] And the circumstances surrounding Jesus' death center in the machinations of the husbandmen of the vineyard of Israel to do away with the one who, like Isaac, is υἱὸς ἀγαπητός. If, then, the repetitions of the Baptismal voice designate Jesus as King of Israel, Servant and Sacrificial victim, *we can be certain that that passage which they echo does so as well.*

Thirdly, Mark strives to portray Jesus as one who knows that the con-straining force behind his ministry, empowering and guiding it from the start, is a specific divine commission to be a Messiah who is to suffer and die at the hands of human beings and serve humankind by giving his life as a ransom for many. This is most clear, for instance, in Mk 8.31 when Mark has Jesus note that suffering and dying is something that he 'must' (δεῖ) do to fulfil his appointment as God's anointed and accomplish his commission to establish the reign of God, as well as in Mk 10.45, where Mark has Jesus, speaking as God's anointed vice-regent, declare that a mission involving serving, not being served, giving up his life, not taking that of others, and ransoming the 'many' is the end for which he, the one destined to inherit 'royal splendor' (δόξα, cf. Mk 10.37)[131] and sovereignty as King,[132] actually 'came'.[133] It would be unusual for Mark to present Jesus in this way unless, in his eyes, Jesus had actually, at the outset of his ministry, been commissioned to

the remarks in Bultmann, *History*, pp. 273-74.

129. Kingsbury, *Christology of Mark's Gospel*, pp. 130-31.

130. Maurer, 'Knecht Gottes und Sohn Gottes', pp. 1-38.

131. See the similar use to which the word is put in Lk. 4.6.

132. As the Matthean parallel to Mk 10.37 shows, the term δόξα is here synonymous with both 'kingdom' and 'sovereignty'. On the meaning of the term here, see J. Muddiman, 'The Glory of Jesus, Mark 10:37', in L.D. Hurst and N.T. Wright (eds.), *The Glory of Christ in the New Testament: Studies in Christology in Memory of George Bradford Caird* (Oxford: Clarendon Press, 1987), pp. 51-58.

133. On δεῖ and ἐξῆλθον as indicating divine necessity, determination and constraint, see, respectively, Lane, *Mark*, p. 294 n. 72, and Schniewind, *Markus*, pp. 52-53.

be King of Israel, Servant, and Sacrificial Victim.

The final, and I think decisive, reason is the fact that at Mk 10.32-45, the story of the Request of James and John, Mark not only has Jesus declare that he has been called and appointed by God to exercise divine sovereignty through a ministry of service and a giving up of his life (Mk 10.45); he also has Jesus designate that call and appointment as something which is grounded in his (Jesus') Baptism (cf. Mk 10.38, 39). Jesus' conviction that as Messiah he must serve rather than be served, and give his life as a 'ransom' is, Mark has Jesus say, the specific and inescapable requirement and constraint of τὸ βάπτισμα ὃ ἐγὼ βαπτίζομαι.[134] And if it is the requirement and constraint of his Jordan experience, then it is the exigency of the voice which came to him then and interpreted the significance of that experience.

In light of these considerations we may conclude that, according to Mark, what the voice at Jesus' Baptism is intent to declare is that Jesus is Israel's anointed king and God's Messiah, charged with attaining victory over the forces of evil, *and* the Beloved, the one destined for death, *and* the Servant who heals his people and brings justice to the nations by submitting to, rather than inflicting, persecution and suffering. This being the case, then the mission predicated of Jesus by the voice is to establish God's sovereignty over the world not by royal activity of conquest, domination, and suppression of Israel's enemies (as in Ps. 2), but through self-sacrifice, endurance of persecution, and the giving up, not the taking, of life in the service of 'the many'.

What, then, is the significance of this finding? I have shown above that in Mark's eyes Jesus' temptation in the wilderness centers in Jesus showing himself faithful and obedient to the form and the requirements of the destiny that is his in light of the status and mission that God attributes to him with the words σὺ εἶ ὁ υἱός μου ὁ ἀγαπητός, ἐν σοὶ εὐδόκησα. I have also shown that uncovering what Mark says regarding the content of Jesus' Wilderness temptation is, then, a matter of being clear on Mark's presentation of that destiny, which, in turn, is a matter of discovering who, according to Mark, the heavenly voice says Jesus is and calls him to be. Accordingly, the finding that for Mark the identity appointed to Jesus with the words σὺ εἶ ὁ υἱός μου...is that of the divine Son who is King of Israel *in so far as* he is The Servant, and

---

134. On this, see Cullmann, *Baptism in the New Testament*, p. 19; *idem*, *Christology*, p. 67; G. Delling, 'ΒΑΠΤΙΣΜΑ ΒΑΠΤΙΖΘΕΝΑΙ', *NovT* 2 (1957), pp. 95-97.

Isaac, the Willing Sacrifice, allows us to see clearly not only what, in Mark's presentation of things, the form and exigencies of that destiny were, but also what for him formed its ground or content. In light of what has been outlined above, this is *whether Jesus will willingly submit himself in obedience to the aspect of the divine counsel which ordains suffering and death rather than conquest and the taking of life as the means by which the Son is to accomplish his work.* And, notably, all of this is revealed within the confines of Mk 1.9-13.

It is hardly the case, then, that the Markan version of the tradition of Jesus' Wilderness temptation says nothing about the content of that temptation. On the contrary, not only is it not mute on this matter, but what it says is astoundingly clear.

The Outcome of Jesus' Wilderness Temptation according to Mark
But can the same thing be said with regard to the question of the reputed silence of the Markan story on the outcome of Jesus' temptation? Does the story, when allowed to speak for itself, also disclose whether or not Jesus proved himself worthy of his particular commission? The answer to this question can be found, I think, in Mk 1.13b— the notice about Jesus, 'beasts', and angels—especially after three things about this notice are clarified. These three things are: (1) the nature of the relationship of Jesus to the 'beasts'; (2) the meaning of the fact that angels 'serve' Jesus; and (3) how, according to Mark, the events recounted in Mk 1.13b are related to the events narrated in Mk 1.12-13a, especially the event of the temptation.

Jesus and the 'Wild Beasts'. According to Mark, while Jesus was in the wilderness, he 'was with' (ἦν μετά) 'wild beasts'. What does this signify? To answer this we must take into account two facts. First, as noted above, in the biblical tradition and in Mark 'wild beasts' (θηρία) are hostile creatures and are presented as such in Mk 1.13b. They are congruent with Satan. They are denizens of the wilderness. They stand over against the angels who in this verse are said to be on Jesus' side.[135] Secondly, as LXX usage indicates, the phrase ἦν μετά designates a type of accompaniment in which there is subordination of one to another.[136]

---

135. Cf. Best, *Temptation*, pp. 8-9; Kelly, 'The Devil in the Desert', pp. 191-95; Lane, *Mark*, p. 61; Lohmeyer, *Markus*, p. 27; Marxsen, *Mark*, p. 27; Mauser, *Christ in the Wilderness*, pp. 100-101.

136. On this, see above, n. 93. That Mark intended ἦν μετά in Mk 1.13 to be taken

In light of these facts, there is nothing to suggest that in Mark's eyes the relationship in Mk 1.13b between Jesus and the beasts of the wilderness is one of peace and harmony. Rather it is one in which Jesus stands over the beasts as their master and Lord. Jesus' being 'with' the beasts means that he has somehow subdued them.[137]

Jesus and the Angels. In Mk 1.13b the relationship between Jesus and the angels is quite vividly depicted. The angels 'serve' (διακονέω) him. What is the meaning of this? It is, clearly, that the angels are subordinate to Jesus. For however one renders the verb—whether with the sense of 'to bring food to',[138] or, as is more likely, 'to offer care and support to'[139]—the activity that the angels are here said to engage in is what a slave renders to a master.[140] So, in saying that in the wilderness Jesus was being 'served' by angels, Mark portrays Jesus as one whom the angels have found worthy of their fealty.[141]

But when, according to Mark, did beasts and angels subjugate themselves to Jesus, and why? The answer to this turns on Mark's understanding of the relationship of the events recounted in Mk 1.13b with those recorded in Mk 1.12-13a.

Mark 1.13b and Mark 1.12-13a. It is often suggested that the events in Mk 1.13b and in Mk 1.12-13a are in Mark's mind contiguous: Jesus' being 'with' the 'beasts' and his being 'served' by angels transpire at the same time as Jesus' expulsion into the wilderness by the Spirit, his sojourn there, and his testing by Satan.[142] But this cannot be the case. The καί which begins Mk 1.13b and links this text with Mk 1.12-13a, having no explicit temporal reference following it, is *concessive not*

to signify 'mastery over' or 'subordination of one to another' is supported by the fact that each time he uses the phrase (albeit variants of it) elsewhere in his Gospel (i.e. Mk 3.14; 5.18; 14.67), he employs it with this meaning.

137. Holmeister, '"Jesus lebte"', pp. 89-92. See also M. Sabbe, 'De tentatione in deserto', *CBrugTomL* 50 (1954), p. 466 n. 30.

138. So, e.g., Feuillet, 'L'episode...selon Saint Marc', p. 66; Jeremias, *New Testament Theology*, p. 70; H.W. Beyer, 'διακονέω, κτλ.', *TDNT*, II, p. 85.

139. So Best, *The Temptation and the Passion*, pp. 9-10.

140. On the meaning of διακονέω in Mark, see above, note .

141. Schniewind, *Markus*, p. 47; cf. Heb. 1.6.

142. Anderson, *Mark*, p. 82; Branscomb, *Mark*, p. 21; Lane, *Mark*, p. 62; Mauser, *Christ in the Wilderness*, p. 101.

co-ordinating.[143] It bears the sense of 'and so' and thus designates Jesus' being 'with' the 'beasts' and his attendance by angels as events which are not only subsequent to but, importantly, *the consequence of his temptation*.

This, for my purposes, is of no small moment. Recall that part of the background of Mark's Wilderness temptation story is the viewpoint presented in the *Testaments of Issachar, Benjamin* and *Naphtali*, that one's relationship to hostile creatures on the one hand and angels on the other depends on how one adheres to God's commissions and commands. In these Testaments the precondition both of (a) one's ability to master beasts and of (b) the attainment of the ministration of angels is *'tested' and approved faithfulness to God's commands*. It is when a son of the covenant 'works good' (see, e.g., the *Testament of Naphtali* 8.4), that is, remains obedient to God, when obedience seems costly or imprudent, that

> Both men and angels shall bless you:
> And God shall be glorified among the Gentiles through you,
> And the devil shall flee from you,
> And the wild beasts shall fear you,
> And the Lord shall love you,
> And the angels cleave to you (8.4).

Accordingly, with this presupposition as its background, Mark's report that after and as a result of being tempted, Jesus had beasts and angels subjugating themselves to him is *both a declaration by Mark that Jesus' Wilderness temptation had an outcome and the disclosing of his view concerning what that outcome was*.

We may conclude, then, that Mark's story of Jesus Wilderness 'testing' is not silent with regard to the question of the result of that temptation.[144] For, given the significance of what is said in Mk 1.13b and how the events reported there are related by Mark to the events in Mk 1.12-13a, the story makes abundantly clear that in the wilderness Jesus successfully resisted the efforts of Satan to sway him from his divinely appointed path and proved himself loyal and obedient to the commission he received at his Baptism.[145]

---

143. On this, see *BAGD*, p. 227.

144. Cranfield, *Mark*, p. 60.

145. This conclusion is supported by the fact that in Mk 1.14-15, Jesus' first public appearance in Galilee, that is, immediately after the episode of Baptism-'testing', Mark presents Jesus as the εὐαγγελιστής, the one authorized to preach the

Summary and Conclusions

The primary focus of the preceding pages has been the question of whether the Markan version of the tradition of Jesus' Wilderness temptation is, as most scholars contend, only a spare statement of fact, asserting no more than *that* at the beginning of his ministry Jesus was tempted, and containing no information concerning either the nature and content of that temptation or its outcome. The evidence uncovered in the course of examining the Markan account shows that the critical consensus in this regard is both ill-founded and incorrect. Mark *has* something to say on all of these matters and he says it quite plainly within the confines of his account: the temptation was a 'testing' of Jesus' obedience to God. It centers in whether Jesus was willing to accept, as he is constrained by God to do, suffering and death as the path to which, as Messiah, he must adhere. And in this temptation Jesus showed himself faithful to the commission entrusted to him. It has been through a conspicuous failure both to examine the details of Mark's story on their own terms and to listen to what they say with first-century ears that scholars have failed to note all of this. All the while, the real question that should have been posed when asking whether in Mk 1.9-11 Mark spoke on these matters is not 'Why did Mark not say more?' but 'What more did Mark really need to say?'.

3. *Has Mark Changed the Tradition?*

We have seen that from a history of traditions point of view Mark's story of Jesus's Wilderness temptation is secondary. It is based upon, and developed out of, a more primitive traditional story of Jesus being confronted by Satan. Given this, it must be asked if Mark's view of the nature and content of Jesus' Wilderness temptation is also secondary. Does Mark convey in Mk 1.9-13 something different from what is propounded in this regard in the material from which his story is derived? Or does he merely take up and reproduce the original

---

good news of God's victory and the dawning of his Kingdom and empowered to bring the content of his message about. Such authority would hardly be granted to one not worthy of it. So the description of Jesus as the one who comes from the wilderness into Galilee with the εὐαγγέλιον is built upon the presupposition that there was not only an outcome to his Wilderness experience, but that it was a successful one. On this, see L.J. Keck, 'The Introduction to Mark's Gospel', *NTS* 12 (1966), pp. 361-62.

tradition's understanding of these matters? To answer this, we must first know (a) whether or not the original tradition assumes, as does Mk 1.9-13, that the event of which it speaks was one where Jesus was subjected to 'testing', and, more precisely, to a 'testing of his faithfulness and obedience', and, if so, (b) whether the tradition also assumes that the content of this temptation involved an invitation to Jesus to reject suffering and engage in triumphalism.

That the tradition upon which Mark based Mk 1.9-13 intended to recount Jesus being subjected to a 'testing of faithfulness' seems certain. As in Mk 1.9-13 the temptation it speaks of is divinely directed, perpetrated by the supreme 'tempter' Satan, and occurs in a place known in Judaism and Christianity as a site of such 'testing'.

It also seems certain that the tradition underlying Mk 1.9-13 assumed, as does Mark, that the content of the 'testing' of Jesus centered in an invitation to deny that service to those not of Israel and, suffering as opposed to subjugation of Israel's enemies and triumphalism, was the divinely appointed means by which God's sovereignty was to be established in the world. For here, too, we find Jesus anointed with God's Spirit and addressed by a divinely authored ordination oracle and therefore being called by God to a status and a mission. Here, too, the mission and status that Jesus is called to is that of the anointed 'Beloved Son' and 'one who pleases God', which, as we have seen above, given the resonance of these appellations, involved attempting to attain and exercise God's sovereignty over the world by serving, not being served, suffering rather than making others suffer, and giving up one's life for, rather than taking the lives of, Israel's enemies.

In his account of Jesus' Wilderness temptation, therefore, Mark does not convey something different with respect to the nature and content of that temptation from what lay before him in the tradition. His presentation of these matters is identical with that of the materials upon which he is here dependent.

Chapter 3

JESUS' WILDERNESS TEMPTATION ACCORDING TO Q

Preliminary Considerations

The Contents, Form and Background of the Q Account
As we have seen above, the Q version of the tradition of Jesus' Wilderness temptation consists of two basic elements: (1) a brief notice of a call and commissioning of Jesus (Mt. 3.13, 16-17//Lk. 3.21-22) and (2) a longer narrative concerned with elucidating in some detail the temptation event (Mt. 4.1-11//Lk. 4.1-13). The narrative consists of three episodes of temptation (Mt. 4.3-4//Lk. 4.3-4, 9-12, 5-8), each cast in the form of a dialogue, which are framed by (a) an introductory notice (Mt. 4.1-2//Lk. 4.1-2) depicting Jesus both being led by God's Spirit into the wilderness to experience a πειρασμός carried out by (ὑπό) 'the Devil' (ὁ διάβολος) (Mt. 4.1//Lk.4.1-2) and being divinely impelled to fast and experience 'hunger' (Mt. 4.1//Lk. 4.2); and (b) a conclusion (Mt. 4.11//Lk. 4.13) depicting the Devil's departure. The episodes of temptation have a common pattern: (1) a notice of locale (the wilderness, the 'wing' of the temple, a mountain top, respectively),[1] (2) a challenge to Jesus from the Devil (to procure 'bread', to leap from the 'wing' of the Temple, to acknowledge the Devil as the ruler of the Kingdoms of the world) which, save in the third episode, is prefaced by and

---

1. As is evident, I assume here the originality of Matthew's presentation of the order in which the confrontations between Jesus and the Devil were presented in Q. On this, see, among others, J. Fitzmyer, *The Gospel according to Luke I–IX* (Garden City: Doubleday, 1981), pp. 507-508; H. Mahnke, *Die Versuchungsgeschichte im Rahmen der Synoptischen Evangelien* (Frankfurt: Lang, 1978), pp. 170-82. For analysis of the strengths of the arguments usually put forward in defense of the originality of the Matthean order, see T.R. Donaldson, *Jesus on the Mountain: A Study in Matthean Theology* (Sheffield: JSOT Press, 1985), pp. 88-90. It should be noted that nothing in the arguments below would be affected if the Matthean order were secondary to that of Luke.

predicated on the statement εἰ υἱὸς εἶ τοῦ θεοῦ (frequently translated 'if you are the Son of God') and constructed on the basis of imperatives (εἰπέ, βάλε), and (3) a reply from Jesus which he introduces with γέγραπται ('it is written') and which is derived verbatim from the LXX^A of Deuteronomy (cp. Mt. 4.4//Lk. 4.4 with Deut. 8.3; Mt. 4.7// Lk. 4.12 with Deut. 6.13; Mt. 4.10//Lk. 4.8 with Deut. 6.16). Moreover, in each episode of temptation the replies function as the points towards which the thrust of the episode's dialogue necessarily moves, thus providing an essential key for understanding both the intent behind each of the Devil's challenges and the substance of the temptations which they represent.

It is often claimed that form-critically, the closest parallels to the Q temptation story are to be found in the accounts of disputations over the Law or the interpretation of Scripture in Haggadic midrash.[2] This is true so far as one's focus is limited primarily to the section of the story devoted to the episodes of temptation themselves, where the Devil challenges Jesus and Jesus responds with Scriptural quotations (i.e. Mt. 4.3-10//Lk. 4.3-12). But when we take the story in its entirety and consider form-critically and from a literary-critical and thematic point of view, the shape given it both by the notice of the Baptism (Mt. 3.13, 16-17// Lk. 3.21-22) and by the frame of Mt. 4.1-2, 11//Lk. 4.1-2, 13, then the story's closest and most complementary parallels are those stories in biblical and related literature given over to portraying a 'servant of God' or the pious person subjected to trials in order to determine or display the nature and extent of his or her faithfulness, prime examples of which are Genesis 22 (the testing of Abraham by God), Deuteronomy 6–8 (the testing of Israel), Job 1–3 (the temptation of Job), Wis. 2.12-24 (the righteous man/'son of God' [ὁ δίκαιος υἱὸς θεοῦ]), *T. Abr.* 12–13; *t. Sanh.* 89b, *Gen. R.* 56.4, *Jub.* 17 (temptations of Abraham by Azazel, Satan, Sammael and God, respectively), *T. Job* (of Job by Satan), and *Martyrdom of Isaiah* 5 (temptation of Isaiah by Mastema).[3]

---

2.   Cf. R. Bultmann, *The History of the Synoptic Tradition* (Oxford: Basil Blackwell, 1963), p. 254; E. Percy, *Die Botschaft Jesu* (Lund: Gleerup, 1953), p. 17; W.D. Davies and D.C. Allinson, *Matthew* (Edinburgh: T. & T. Clark, 1988), I, p. 352; Donaldson, *Jesus on the Mountain*, p. 90.

3.   For a full listing and discussion of these Pseudepigrapical and Rabbinic stories along with their biblical antecedents, see J.H. Korn, *ΠΕΙΡΑΣΜΟΣ: Die Versuchung des Gläubigen in der greischischen Bibel* (Stuttgart: W. Kohlhammer, 1937), pp. 48-76. One should also consult the non-biblical examples of this type such

The question then arises: Which, if any, of these stories forms the background and model of the Q temptation story or provides its interpretative key? J. Dupont,[4] B. Gerhardsson,[5] G.P. Thompson[6] and others have made the case that the background and model of the Q temptation story is to be sought in the account of the temptation of Israel in the wilderness as this is outlined in Deuteronomy 6–8. Among the considerations which these scholars note as supporting this conclusion are:

1. the basic themes of the Deuteronomic story (i.e. being led by the God, the wilderness, 'hunger', temptation/testing of God's Son, the necessity of obedience to God's word) are repeated and are given places of prominence in the Q account;

2. the wording of the introduction of the Q account (i.e. Mt. 4.1-2//Lk. 4.1-2) is reminiscent of that of Deut. 8.2 both in the Hebrew and LXX versions of that text;

3. Jesus' temptations are parallel with those to which Israel was subjected according to Deuteronomy 6–8;

4. all of Jesus' responses to the Devil's petitions are derived from this unit of the Deuteronomic text (Deut. 8.2-3; 6.16; 6.13); and

5. the fact that though they appear in Q in reverse order from their sequence in Deuteronomy 6–8, Jesus' quotations from this passage nevertheless correspond to the order of the events to which they refer as recorded in the Old Testament (the provision of manna in the wilderness [Exod. 16], the testing at Massah [Exod. 17], the worship of the golden calf [Exod. 32] or, as I think more likely, the story of how Israel succumbed to fear when hearing the report of the men who had been sent into Canaan to 'spy out' the land [Num. 13.25-33]) and thus,

as *Samyutta-Nikaya* 2.10 (text in J. Aufhauser, *Buddah und Jesus in ihren Paralleltexten* [Bonn: A. Marcus & E. Weber, 1926], pp. 27-28) and Vendidad 19.1, where Gautama Buddha and Zarathustra respectively are the servants of God in question.

4.   J. Dupont, 'L'arrière-fond biblique du récit des tentations de Jesus', *NTS* 3 (1956–57), pp. 287-88.

5.   B. Gerhardsson, *The Testing of God's Son (Matt. 4:1-11 & Par)* (Lund: C.W.K. Gleerup, 1966).

6.   G.P. Thompson, 'Called—Proved—Obedient: A Study in the Baptism and Temptation Narratives of Matthew and Luke', *JTS* ns 11 (1960), pp. 1-12.

to use Dupont's words, the quotations seem to portray Jesus' experience as a 'résume de l'historie de sa traverée du désert'.[7] This view is, however, not without its detractors. Its validity has been challenged on the grounds that despite all Mt. 4.1-3//Lk. 4.1-3 and the story of Israel's Wilderness temptation in Deuteronomy 6–8 have in common, there are three points at which the two accounts differ so significantly that the Israel–Jesus identification seems difficult to maintain: (1) in Deuteronomy 6–8 Israel is tested by *God*, whereas in Mt. 4.1-11//Lk. 4.1-13 Jesus' πειρασμός is carried out by the Devil; (2) Israel was in the wilderness for forty years whereas Jesus is described as being there forty days; and (3) in substance the temptations of Jesus are different from the temptations of Israel in the wilderness in that Jesus' temptations are addressed to a 'son' depicted as having the power to perform miracles, and they center on whether or not he would exploit that power for his own benefit, while Israel's temptations are addressed to a 'son' who has no such powers and bear only on Israel's faith and confidence in its God.

But none of these objections have any real weight. Given the import of the notice of the Spirit's activity in Mt. 4.1//Lk. 4.1-2, there is no doubt that in Q Jesus' πειρασμός, though noted as carried out by the Devil, is thought of as originating with, or determined by God, or as under God's direction.[8] Nor, as we have already seen when dealing with the meaning of 'forty days' in Mk 1.13, is there any real discrepancy between forty years and forty days.[9] Finally, as we will see presently, the main assumption of the third objection—the presupposition that Jesus is depicted in Mt. 4.1-11//Lk. 4.1-13 as one having the power to work miracles—has no grounding in the text.[10]

In light of this it seems clear that the Q account of Jesus' Wilderness

---

7.   Dupont, 'L'arrière-fond biblique', p. 292.

8.   On this, see F.C. Grant, *An Introduction to New Testament Thought* (New York: Abingdon Press, 1950), p. 208; E. Lohmeyer, *Das Evangelium des Matthäus* (Göttingen: Vandenhoeck & Ruprecht, 1956), p. 57; K.H. Rengsdorf, *Das Evangelium nach Lukas* (Göttingen: Vandenhoeck & Ruprecht, 1937), p. 52; and especially E. Fascher, *Jesus und der Satan* (Halle: Max Niemeyer Verlag, 1949), p. 31.

9.   See above, p. 63. The lack of discrepancy has recently been upheld by W.L. Kyne, *A Christology of Solidarity: Jesus as the Representative of his People in Matthew* (Lanham, MD: University Press of America, 1991), p. 30.

10.   See below, pp. 99-100.

temptation is intent to present Jesus' experience specifically in parallelism with, indeed, as the *recapitulation of*, the temptation which Israel,
God's firstborn and υἱός, was subjected to during *its* wilderness wanderings, as this was recounted in Deuteronomy 6–8.

Before we turn to the attempt to determine what is said in the Q
version of Jesus' Wilderness temptation concerning the nature and
content that temptation, we must, however, for reasons to be discussed
presently, ask whether the Q story is a unitary composition.

Independent Traditions or an Original Unity?

A number of scholars, among them, notably, J. Jeremias and E.
Lohmeyer, argue that the three specific episodes of the Devil confronting and petitioning Jesus which now comprise the bulk of the Q
Wilderness temptation story did not originally form a unity. Rather, the
episodes of temptation over bread and temptation on the 'wing' of the
Temple originated together quite apart from, and circulated for a time in
the early Church independently of, the episode of the temptation on the
mountain.[11] The evidence which they bring forward in support of this
contention is as follows.

1. The version of the tradition of Jesus' Wilderness temptation
   apparently preserved in the Gospel to the Hebrews[12] seems to
   know only of Jesus' temptation on a high mountain.[13]
2. The episodes of temptation involving bread and at the Temple
   each center precisely in an explicit challenge of the Devil to
   Jesus as 'Son of God', whereas the temptation on the mountain has no such direct diabolic address or challenge to Jesus.
   The formal similarity between the episodes of the temptation
   over bread and the temptation at the Temple on the one hand
   and their formal dissimilarity with the form of the episode of
   temptation on the mountain on the other, suggests that the

11. J. Jeremias, *New Testament Theology. I. The Proclamation of Jesus* (New
York: Charles Scribner & Sons, 1971), pp. 71-72; E. Lohmeyer, 'Die Versuchung
Jesu', *ZST* 14 (1937), pp. 619-50, esp. p. 622 (reprinted in *Urchristliche Mystic*
[Darmstadt: Wissenschaftliche Buchgesellschaft, 1958], pp. 83-122).

12. As Jeremias himself admits (*New Testament Theology*, p. 71 n. 1), there is
some possibility that this text might refer to the story of the transfiguration, not the
episode of temptation on a mountain.

13. Jeremias, *New Testament Theology*, p. 71; Lohmeyer, 'Versuchung Jesu',
p. 622.

episodes of the bread and Temple 'temptations' were formed independently of the mountain episode and transmitted originally as a pair in a self-contained unit to which the episode on the mountain was only eventually added.[14]

3. The assumption of an origin and transmission of a story of temptation on a mountain originally independent of a story of a bread–Temple temptation accounts for the varying place which the Temple temptation episode now has in the respective Matthean and Lukan versions of the Wilderness temptation tradition. Luke's record of the Temple episode occurring after the episode of temptation on a mountain, and not, as in Matthew, after the episode of temptation over bread, is due to simple displacement caused by the insertion of the mountain temptation story (presumably by a pre-Lukan editor) into an originally unified bread–Temple temptation story.[15]

If this contention is true, my task of determining the view(s) of the early Church concerning the nature and content of Jesus' temptations is enlarged: *there would be two (i.e. Mt. 4.3-4; 5-7//Lk. 4.3-4; 9-12 and Mt. 4.8-10//Lk. 4.5-8), not one (Mt. 4.1-11//Lk. 4.1-13) independent versions of the Wilderness temptation tradition left to investigate.* But the contention hardly seems credible. The evidence adduced in its support forcibly resists being impressed into the particular service that the advocates of the 'two Q versions' view would have it perform. Let us see how this is so, taking the arguments in the reverse order in which I have outlined them above.

1. *Two traditions as the explanation of the differences between Matthew and Luke as to the order of the episodes of temptation.* There main difficulty with this view is that, while 'solving' one problem, the solution creates others. To hold that the differences in the Lukan and Matthean sequence of the 'temptations' is due to a pre-Lukan editor inserting the story of the mountain temptation into an already existing bread–Temple temptation story necessarily entails the view that at some

14. Lohmeyer, 'Versuchung Jesu', p. 622; cf. also Bultmann, *History*, p. 256; M. Dibelius, *From Tradition to Gospel* (New York: Charles Scribner & Sons, 1935), p. 275; M.-J. Lagrange, *L'Evangile selon Saint Matthieu* (Paris: Gabalda, 1948), p. 60; A. Farrer, *The Triple Victory: Christ's Temptations according to Matthew* (London: Faith Press, 1965), p. 64.

15. Jeremias, *New Testament Theology*, p. 71.

point before Matthew took up and used the 'present' Q version of the Wilderness temptation tradition (i.e. one with three episodes of temptation), there was also a pre-Matthean editor who, like the pre-Lukan editor, was familiar with both sets of traditions, and who also felt moved to join together the story of the mountain temptation and the bread–Temple temptation story yet saw some necessity of operating differently from the purported pre-Lukan editor, and attached the mountain story to the end of the episode of temptation at the Temple rather than in between the bread–Temple temptation story's two constituent episodes. For unless we see Matthew dependent upon Luke here, *or fortuitously adding the mountain temptation episode himself*, there is otherwise no reason to see why the tradition which Matthew reproduces at Mt. 3.13, (16-17, 4.1-11) would agree with that now behind Lk. 3.21-22, 4.11-13 in having all three of that tradition's episodes of temptation. It might just as easily have happened that Matthew's version of the tradition would have contained only Mt. (3.13, 16-17) 4.3-4, 5-7//Lk. (3.21-22) 4.3-4, 9-12. But this view not only complicates the generally accepted theory of synoptic relationships by unnecessarily multiplying synoptic sources and streams of tradition; it also ignores the simpler and more likely explanation that the variance between Matthew and Luke in the sequence of the episodes of temptation is due to the redactional activities of one or the other of the evangelists.[16]

2. *The formal dissimilarity between the bread–Temple temptation story and the story of the mountain temptation.* The problem with this bit of evidence is that the formal dissimilarity between the first two temptations is more apparent than real. While the episode of the temptation on the mountain admittedly contains no diabolic address or challenge comparable with that found in the episodes of temptation over bread or at the Temple, the presumption that Jesus is 'Son of God', and is specifically tempted as such, is still a fundamental presupposition of the mountain temptation story. For as Jesus' response to the Devil at Mt. 4.10//Lk. 4.8 shows, the background of this episode is Deut. 6.13, a text whose theme is how God's Son, Israel—commissioned to conquer the peoples of Canaan, but faced with evidence that obedience to God will hinder and not help them, indeed, cause them to fail, in this enterprise—must not think that following other gods will give it its only

16. On this, see Fitzmeyer, *Luke I–IX*, pp. 507-508.

real chance of accomplishing this end. Furthermore, the Devil's actions of showing Jesus all the kingdoms of the earth and their glory (cf. Mt. 4.8//Lk. 4.5, δείκνυσιν αὐτῷ πάσας τὰς βασιλείας τοῦ κόσμου καὶ τὴν δόξαν αὐτῶν) and offering to convey them immediately to Jesus (cf. Mt. 4.9//Lk. 4.7, ταῦτά σοι πάντα δώσω) are grounded in the idea of Jesus as Son. For, as D. Daube has demonstrated,[17] these actions presuppose that the kingdoms and their glory—things which the contextualizing passage in Deuteronomy delimit as bequeathed to Israel/God's son—rightfully belong to Jesus'.[18] The formal disharmony between the episodes of 'bread' and Temple temptation on the one hand and the episode of temptation on a mountain on the others is, therefore, not as great as is usually thought, and is certainly not sufficient to warrant the view that the mountain temptation episode is as something so formally distinct from the others that it must have originally been a tradition developed and passed on independently of the them. And if these slight differences are to be taken as indicating formal disharmony, then one must argue for the original independence of the bread and Temple episodes as well, for despite their undeniable similarities, there is also a strong indication—most notably in the absence in the 'bread' episode of a long Old Testament quotation by the Devil, which is so prominent a part of the Temple episode—that the formal correspondence between the two episodes is by no means as complete as the advocates of the separate traditions contention take it to be.[19]

17. Daube, *Studies in Biblical Law* (Cambridge: Cambridge University Press, 1947), pp. 24-39, esp. pp. 35-36.

18. It has been argued by P. Doble ('The Temptations', *ExpTim* 72 [1961–62], p. 92) that Q's description of the Devil showing Jesus 'the kingdoms of the world and their glory' and the wording of the Devil's offer to give them to Jesus (ταῦτά σοι πάντα δώσω) are drawn primarily from Ps. 2.7-8 LXX where Yahweh proclaims the king to be his Son and specifically instructs him to 'Ask of me and I will give to you the nations of the earth for your inheritance and the ends of the earth for your possession' (αἴτησαι παρ' ἐμοῦ, καὶ δώσω σοι ἔθνη τὴν κληρονομίαν σου καὶ τὴν κατάσχεσίν σου τὰ πέρατα τῆς γῆς). If so, then, despite the absence in the mountain temptation episode of the υἱός statement so prominent in the others, there is additional evidence that Jesus is portrayed and approached there as 'Son'.

19. Donaldson, *Jesus on the Mountain*, p. 89. There is also an apparent absence in the 'bread' episode of a description of the Devil taking Jesus anywhere, a description which, notably, *both* the Temple and mountain temptation episodes possess.

3. *The 'witness' of the Gospel to the Hebrews*. The claim that the temptation tradition preserved in the *Gospel to the Hebrews* provides evidence for an originally independent mountain temptation story simply cannot be substantiated. The *Gospel* is preserved for us only in fragments.[20] Consequently, we have no way of knowing for certain that the *Gospel* preserved and reproduced *only* a story of a mountain temptation. It is perfectly conceivable that the *Gospel to the Hebrews* actually contained a longer temptation account of which the fragment that has come down to us was only a small part. Indeed, this seems a relatively likely possibility when we consider (a) the apparent tendency of the *Gospel* to amplify traditions otherwise known to us from the Synoptic gospels and to preserve possibly authentic dominical *logia* and traditional narrative material not found in the canonical Gospels, and (b) the fact, recorded by Nicephorus,[21] that the *Gospel* in its original form comprised 2200 lines (i.e. only 300 fewer than the canonical Matthew).[22] But, more importantly, even if the *Gospel to the Hebrews* reproduced in its account of Jesus' pre-ministry temptation *only* a temptation on a mountain, this fact could not be pressed as evidence for the original independence of a mountain temptation tradition from the bread–Temple tradition. For we would still not be certain that the temptation story as it is reproduced in the *Gospel to the Hebrews* represents the full extent of the tradition as it came to the *Gospel's* author. The appearance there of only the mountain temptation could be due not so much to the fact that the author knew only of this tradition, but to the fact that he possessed a longer account and chose deliberately to use only a portion of it. Therefore, without corroborative evidence both that the *Gospel to the Hebrews* knew only a mountain temptation tradition and that the tradition itself came to the Gospel's author only in something similar to its present form, the claim that the *Gospel to the Hebrews* provides evidence for an originally independent mountain temptation tradition is an empty assertion which, like many arguments from silence, has little to commend its acceptance.

---

20. See P. Vielhauller, 'The Gospel to the Hebrews', in E. Hennecke, *New Testament Apocrypha*, I (ed. W. Schneemelcher; Philadelphia: Westminster Press, 1963), pp. 158-65.
21. Vielhauller, 'The Gospel to the Hebrews', p. 159.
22. Vielhauller, 'The Gospel to the Hebrews', p. 159.

It appears, in summary, that there are radical weaknesses in the evidence reputedly showing that the bread–Temple and the mountain temptation stories arose and circulated independently of one another. Refusing to bear the weight put upon it, the contention that Mt. 4.1-11//Lk. 4.1-13 is made up of two originally independent traditions shows itself to be highly questionable.

There are, moreover, other considerations to take into account when assessing the credibility of the independent traditions thesis. The contention does nothing to clarify why each of the respective temptation scenes should come to end with a quotation not only from the book of Deuteronomy, but from the same self-contained section of that book. Nor does it explain adequately the manifest thematic, conceptual and organic unity which the three temptation scenes possess with both the temptation story's present 'introduction' (including Mt. 3.13, 16-17// Lk. 3.21-22) and with each other by virtue of such quotations.[23] The individual quotations are embedded too deeply within the theology and structure of each of the temptation scenes to be considered secondary additions. Not only do they provide the essential key to the meaning of each temptation, but (as already noted), from a form-critical point of view, they are the point towards which the thrust of the dialogues in the temptation scenes necessarily move.[24] Furthermore, the unity that the quotations exhibit both with the 'introduction' to the temptation story and with each other is too great to have come about, as the 'independent traditions' contention must assume, by happy accident.

In other words, in light of (a) the lack of relevant or convincing evidence or cogent arguments in favour of the contention that two originally separate traditions stand behind the Q Wilderness temptation story, and (b) the unified background in Deuteronomy of each of the Q story's three scenes, it seems certain that the basic narrative underlying Mt. 3.13, 16-17; 4.1-11//Lk. 3.21-22; 4.1-13 was from its inception a unified construction.

---

23. On this, see Fitzmyer, *Luke 1–9*, p. 508; I.H. Marshall, *Commentary on Luke* (Grand Rapids: Eerdmans, 1978), p. 167; Dupont, 'L'arrière-fond biblique', pp. 286-91.

24. Bultmann, *History*, pp. 271-75; E. Schweizer, *The Good News according to Matthew* (Atlanta: John Knox Press, 1975), p. 58; H. Seesemann, 'πεῖρα, κτλ.', *TDNT*, VI, pp. 34-36.

A Vorlage?

It may, I think, be taken as certain that the first element of Q's version of the tradition of Jesus' Wilderness temptation, that is, the brief notice now standing behind Mt. 3.13, 16-17//Lk. 3.21-22 of a call and commissioning of Jesus to the office and duties of 'Son',[25] is not something created or composed by the editor of Q *de novo*, but is, rather, a piece of traditional material that has been taken up in Q and reproduced substantially unaltered. The existence elsewhere in the Synoptic tradition (i.e. at Mk 1.9-11) of an independent and, from a traditions-history point of view, primitive parallel to the Q notice of Jesus' call and commissioning[26] testifies to its traditional nature. So the question of a *Vorlage* for this portion of the Q story may be answered in the affirmative.

But what about the second element of the Q story, that is, the longer narrative standing behind Mt. 4.1-11//Lk. 4.1-13 which is concerned with elucidating the temptation event? Is its substance and/or its form derived from primitive tradition? The answer is both yes and no. There is good reason to suspect that the narrative *theme* of the Mt. 4.1-11// Lk. 4.1-13—Jesus being subjected to a pre-ministry πειρασμός carried out by the Devil—is not original to Q, but has been taken up by Q from an early, pre-Q, even possibly pre-Easter, tradition. For, as the evidence of Mk 3.27//Lk. 11.21-22//Mt. 12.29 (the parable/saying concerning the strong men dueling in which, as Jeremias notes, Jesus publicly 'alludes directly to a victory over Satan that has preceded his own [public] activity'[27]) indicates, (1) the theme is not only ancient, belonging to the earliest layer of the Synoptic tradition and perhaps stemming from Jesus himself,[28] and (2) was known to, preserved by, and transmitted within the early Church apart from the other vehicle in which the theme was

---

25. For my reconstruction of the text of this notice along with a defense of the view that it was part of Q, let alone part of the temptation story, see above, Chapter 1, p. 35.

26. On the independence of Mk 1.9-11, as well as the tradition behind it, from its parallel in Q, see above, Chapter 1, pp. 37-41.

27. *New Testament Theology*, p. 73. See also E. Best, *The Temptation and the Passion: The Markan Soteriology* (Cambridge: Cambridge University Press, 1965), pp. 11-15.

28. The antiquity and even the authenticity of the parable/saying is guaranteed by the fact that there is a degree of tension between the theology expressed within it, namely, that Jesus has overcome Satan before his ministry and apart from his crucifixion and resurrection, and that of the *early church*, which saw Jesus as vanquisher of Satan by virtue of these latter events.

also (albeit more fully and specifically) recounted (i.e. a *story* of Jesus' Wilderness temptation such as that found in Mk 1.9-13 or Mt. 4.1-11// Lk. 4.1-13), but (3) was also known to Q in this form. But the reasons adduced above in support of the contention that the story presently found within Mt. 4.1-11//Lk. 4.1-13 was not built up from separate, originally independent traditions indicate that there is no reason to suspect that Mt. 4.1-11//Lk. 4.1-13 is developed from, let alone a secondary expansion of, a pre-Q, traditional *narrative*. On the contrary, given how well each of its individual elements are integrated with one another, the *story* of the tripartite confrontation between Jesus and the Devil found now within Mt. 4.1-11//Lk. 4.1-13 must be taken as an original composition, created 'at one go' in its present form.[29] Whether or not this composition is by the original editor(s) or compiler(s) of Q or, as some suggest, was composed by someone originally standing outside of the Q circle (and therefore is material that is a late addition to Q),[30] the evidence strongly suggests that the bulk of Mt. 4.1-11//Lk 4.1-13 probably had no narrative *Vorlage*.

In light of this conclusion, we will not need, then, as with the Markan version of the tradition of Jesus' Wilderness temptation, to attempt to determine whether or not the Q story differs conceptually in any way from the tradition upon which it is based, at least with respect to the question of the *content* of Jesus' Wilderness temptation. For the dominical saying from which the theme (but not the substance) of Mt. 4.1-11//Lk. 4.1-13 seems to spring alludes only to *the fact of* a pre-ministry temptation by Satan (albeit one that was successfully met and involved a 'testing' of faithfulness, given the perpetrator of the πειρασμός), and not to that temptation's *content*. So, just as *how* Q narrates the content of Jesus Wilderness temptation (a midrashic dialogue, in three parts, grounded in themes from Deuteronomy) stems from Q itself, so also

29. Gerhardsson, *The Testing of God's Son*, p. 16.

30. On this, see, e.g., Kloppenborg, *The Formation of Q*, pp. 247-48. The view that the Q Wilderness temptation story is a late addition to Q has recently been strongly challenged by C.M. Tuckett ('The Temptation Narrative in Q', in F. Van Segbroeck, C.M. Tuckett, G. Van Belle and J. Verheyden [eds.], *The Four Gospels 1992: Festschrift Frans Neieynck* [3 vols.; Leuven: Leuven University Press, 1992], I, pp. 479-507), who demonstrates the thematic and conceptual links that exist between Mt. 4.1-11//Lk. 4.1-13 and other sections of Q which are not regarded by Q specialists as late.

what Q actually says on this matter is from a literary point of view original to Q.

2. *The Nature, Content, and Outcome of Jesus' Wilderness Temptation in Q*

The Nature of the Temptation according to Q

I have shown above that in the Markan version of the tradition of Jesus' Wilderness temptation the nature of that temptation involved a 'testing' of Jesus' faithfulness to God. Now we must determine whether or not this is also the case in the Q version of that tradition. There are at least four things that indicate that it is:

First, as in Mark, the temptation is identified as initiated by God, through the agency of his Spirit.[31] As we have seen, temptations initiated by God are temptations of faithfulness.

Secondly, the temptation is said to be carried out by ὁ διάβολος, the Devil. As we have also seen when dealing with the Markan Wilderness temptation story, the Devil is a figure whose primary function is to put the faithfulness of the pious to the proof.

Thirdly, as has been shown above, the Q temptation story has been shaped so as to have Deuteronomy 6–8 as its primary background. With this, Jesus' temptation is presented as a recapitulation of God's previous temptation of another of his Sons, the Exodus generation, *a temptation which was undertaken specifically to reveal whether or not that Son would keep the commandments God had given him.*[32]

Finally, Jesus' responses to the Devil's prompting all have to do with the necessity of his single-minded devotion to the will and ways of God. These responses would hardly be appropriate unless at issue in his temptation was his dedication to remaining faithful and obedient to 'the things of God'.

But if for Q the nature of Jesus' Wilderness temptation involves whether or not Jesus will be faithful and obedient to God, what does

---

31. Cf. n. , above. See also, Fitzmyer, *Luke 1–9*, p. 516; C.K. Barrett, *The Holy Spirit in the Gospel Tradition* (London: SPCK, 1947), p. 47; E. Schweizer, 'πνεῦμα, κτλ.', *TDNT*, VI, p. 398.

32. Gerhardsson, *Testing*, pp. 27-28; Thompson, 'Called—Proved—Obedient', p. 2; Schweizer, *Matthew*, p. 58. J. Schniewind, *Das Evangelium nach Matthäus* (Göttingen: Vandenhoeck & Ruprecht, 1964), p. 27.

showing this faithfulness and obedience centre in? What, according to Q, is the content of this temptation?

The Content of Jesus' Temptation according to Q

As we have seen, in Q's presentation of the tradition of Jesus' Wilderness temptation, the particular πειρασμός Jesus is there said to encounter occurs when the Devil (ὁ διάβολος) confronts a 'hungered' Jesus, first in the wilderness, then on the 'wing' of the Temple, and finally on a mountaintop where Jesus can see all that the Devil possesses. The Devil presses upon him three specific petitions: to procure bread from stones (Mt. 4.3//Lk. 4.3), to throw himself down from the 'wing' of the Temple (Mt. 4.5//Lk. 4.9), and to recognize his temper as ruler of the kingdoms of the world (Mt. 4.8-9//Lk. 4.6-7). Accordingly, a proper understanding of Q's view of the content of the Wilderness temptation depends upon gaining certainty of just what, according to Q, the Devil, in doing these things, is up to. What, in confronting and petitioning Jesus as he does, is the Devil actually trying to get Jesus to do?

This question is usually answered in one (or in a combination) of three ways: (1) the Devil is trying to get Jesus to prove *to himself*, through performing a miracle, the reality of his divine sonship; (2) the Devil is trying to get Jesus to perform a *Schauwunder*, and more particularly one that would instantly be recognizable and accepted as a phenomenon authenticating a claim to Messiahship; in this case Jesus would be proving the reality of his sonship *to others*; or (3) the Devil is trying to get Jesus to chose a way of being God's Son that is not God's way— each of the petitions representing 'false' Messianic paths—and thus inadvertently presses Jesus to work out and establish for himself the pattern of his sonship.[33]

---

33. There is, of course, yet another answer, the favourite of the Church Fathers, but also found frequently in more modern literature (on this, see P.G. Bratcher, 'The Temptation of Jesus in Matthew' [doctoral dissertation, Concordia Seminary, St Louis, 1966], pp. 5-6, 52-65) that the petitions are to be seen in terms of the Devil attempting to get Jesus to succumb to such things as 'the lust of the flesh, the lust of the eyes, and the pride of life' (cf. 1 Jn 2.16). But I have not taken this 'moralistic' view into account here because it relies too heavily on a questionable and, as C.F.D. Moule has demonstrated ('An Unresolved Problem in the Temptation Clause in the Lord's Prayer', *RTR* 33 [1974], pp. 65-75), a relatively modern and unbiblical interpretation of πειρασμός as 'seduction' or 'enticement to evil'. The answer cannot be seriously considered as something that Q might have intended.

Are any of these answers correct? I think not. Q, I believe, has something quite different in mind, namely, that the Devil is attempting to get Jesus *to deny the God-givenness of a particular pattern of sonship* with which Jesus is *already* familiar and to which he has already been called—a pattern characterized by peaceableness in the face of hostility and by a demonstration of love and concern for the enemy.

To see that this is so, it is helpful to first point out the inadequacies of the traditional answers to the question of what, according to Q, the Devil is up to.

The Traditional Answers
a. *An attempt to get Jesus to prove to himself the reality of his Sonship.* In the history of the interpretation of the temptation story, the view that the Devil is trying in his petitions to get Jesus to prove to himself through miracle that he really is God's Son has been both durable and popular. It appears as the preferred position of the Antiochene school of exegesis as represented by Theodore of Mopseutsia,[34] and it can be found mooted frequently throughout post-Reformation and modern exegesis.[35] It is, after all, so its advocates maintain, the most natural

---

34. Cf. *On the Incarnation of the Son of God* 13. That this view appears in patristic exegesis both no earlier than Theodore and, until after Luther, nowhere else outside of the Antiochene school, is due to the fact that the Antiochenes were the first and only commentators before the Reformation to approach the temptation story from the perspective of Jesus rather than the Devil. As K.P. Köppen, in his review of trends in the interpretation of the story of Jesus Wilderness temptation from the second to the sixteenth century (*Die Auslegung der Versuchungsgerichte unter besonderer Berücksichtigung der Alten Kirche* [Tübingen: Mohr, 1961], has demonstrated, until the Reformation, exposition of the temptation story was on the whole governed by the supposition both that the story proceeded from the Devil's point of view and that the temptation occurs because the Devil is uncertain as to Jesus' identity. He tempted Jesus in order to discover Jesus' true nature. Cf., e.g., Clement of Alexandria, *Eclogae propheticae* 53.2.3 'The Devil knew that the Lord was coming; but that it was Jesus he did not know. That is why he tempted him, to find out.' On this as the common view of the Fathers (save, perhaps, for Origen), see M. Steiner, *La tentation de Jésus dans l'inteprétation patristique de Saint Justin à Origine* (Paris: J. Gabalda, 1962), p. 100.

35. We find the view propounded in the seventeenth century, for instance, by Joahann Gerhard (*Annotationes Posthumae in Evangelium Matthaei* [Jena: Georg Sengenwald, 1663], pp. 204-205) and George Cailixt (*Quator Evangelicorum Scriptorum Concordia et Explicicatio* [Helmstadt: Henningus Mullerus, 1663) in the eighteenth (at least with respect to the first of the Devil's petitions) by Matthew Henry, and in the nineteenth by R.C. Trench (*Studies in the Gospels* [London:

reading of the text. Does not the Devil solicit Jesus to perform mighty acts? Does he not begin his petitions with the phrase '*if* you are the son of God' (εἰ υἱὸς εἶ τοῦ θεοῦ, cf. Mt. 4.3, 6//Lk. 4.3, 9)? And is this not strong evidence that the dominant motif of the temptation story is Jesus' own doubts about the *fact* of his Messiahship?[36]

The answer, of course, is no. In the first place, as many grammarians have pointed out, the actual sense of εἰ in the phrase εἰ υἱὸς εἶ τοῦ θεοῦ is 'since', not 'if'.[37] Consequently, what the Devil is doing in prefacing his petitions in this way is not raising a question but expressing a concession.[38] He is, in effect, acknowledging the truth of a state of affairs to which, at the outset of his petitions, both he and Jesus are privy, namely, that Jesus actually is 'God's Son'.[39]

Secondly, despite a widely held assumption to the contrary,[40] there is

Macmillan, 3rd edn, 1874], p. 31), A. Plummer (*The Gospel according to S. Luke* [Edinburgh: T. & T. Clark, 1896], p. 109) and A.C.A. Hall (*Christ's Temptations and Ours* [New York: Longmans, Green & Co., 1897], *ad. loc.*). Twentieth-century proponents include A.H. McNeil (*The Gospel according to St Matthew* [London: Macmillan, 1915], pp. 37, 38), E.S. Jones ('The Temptation Narrative', *RevExp* 53 [1956] pp. 303-13, esp. pp. 308-10), A.R.C. Leaney (*The Gospel according to St Luke* [London: A. & C. Black, 1958], p. 115), A.B. Taylor ('Decision in the Desert: The Temptation of Jesus in the Light of Deuteronomy', *Int* 15 [1960], pp. 300-309), P. Doble ('The Temptations', pp. 91-93), W. Powell ('The Temptations', *ExpTim* 72 [1961], p. 248), and J.A.T. Robinson ('The Temptations', in *Twelve New Testament Studies* [London: SCM Press, 1962], pp. 53-60).

36. On this, see Doble, 'The Temptations', pp. 91-93.

37. See, e.g., A.T. Robertson, *A Grammar of the Greek New Testament in the Light of Historical Research* (Nashville: Broadman Press, 1917), p. 1009. See also *BAGD*, p. 189.

38. On this, see R. Holst, 'The Temptation of Jesus: If thou art the Son of God', *ExpTim* 82 (1971), pp. 334-44.

39. Holst, 'The Temptation of Jesus', p. 344. See also J. Reuman, *Jesus in the Church's Gospels* (Philadelphia: Fortress Press, 1968), p. 291.

40. Cf., e.g., W.C. Allen (*The Gospel according to S. Matthew* [Edinburgh: T. & T. Clark, 1907], p. 31): 'The Tempter implied that Sonship involved the power to work miracles'; E. Schweizer ('υἱός, κτλ.', *TDNT*, VIII, p. 377): 'Satan's questions presuppose a tradition in which the Son of God manifests himself primarily by his mighty acts'; J.S. Kloppenborg (*The Formation of Q: Trajectories in Ancient Wisdom Collections* [Philadelphia: Fortress Press, 1987], p. 253): 'Throughout [Mt. 4.1-11//Lk. 4.1-13], the assumption is that Jesus *can* perform miracles should he wish to do so'. See also, M. Albertz, *Die Synoptischen Streigesprache: Ein Beitrag zur Formengeschichte des Urchristentums* (Berlin: Trowitzche & Sohn, 1921), pp. 42-43.

nothing within the story that indicates either the presupposition and use here by Q (even if only to argue against it) of a tradition which pictured the Son of God as a bearer of miraculous power, or a perception on either Jesus' or the Devil's part that Jesus should perform a miracle, *let alone that he even has the power to do so*.[41] For the Devil's petition about bread (εἰπὲ ἵνα οἱ λίθοι οὗτοι ἄρτοι γένωνται, which, given its wording, should be construed along the lines of 'give the command [to God] so that he will provide bread', and not '[you youself] turn these stones into bread'),[42] together with the presupposition of the petition given on the 'wing' of the Temple (i.e. the theology of Ps. 91, with its promise to the God-fearer of angelic guardianship against evil and 'scourges', long life and rescue from harm), and, most importantly,

---

41. On this, see Bretcher, *Temptation of Jesus*, pp. 183-86.

42. Compare the wording of the petition with that of Mt. 20.21 (ὁ δὲ εἶπεν αὐτῇ, Τί θέλεις; λέγει αὐτῷ, Εἰπὲ ἵνα καθίσωσιν οὗτοι οἱ δύο υἱοί μου εἷς ἐκ δεξιῶν σου καὶ εἷς ἐξ εὐωνύμων σου ἐν τῇ βασιλείᾳ σου), where, as in Mt. 4.3//Lk. 4.3, Jesus is petitioned (but this time by the mother of the sons James and John, the sons of Zebedee, cf. v. 20) to utter a word of power (εἰπέ). Here the presupposition behind the petition is clearly not that Jesus has powers of his own to grant what is asked of him, but that, given his status as 'Son of the Living God' (cf. Mt. 16.16), he can give a command that will (must?) be honoured by God. See also Lk. 9.45, a petition to Jesus from the sons of Zebedee to command that 'fire from heaven' come down on certain villages of Samaria (θέλεις εἴπωμεν πῦρ καταβῆναι ἀπὸ τοῦ οὐρανοῦ καὶ ἀναλῶσαι αὐτούς), which, as Kyne notes (*A Christology of Solidarity*, p. 33), is not only cast in a construction similar to that of the Devil's petition in Q 4.3, but also carries with it the idea 'that the "command" could only be accomplished though the power of God'.

Moreover, the rendering of the Devil's challenge as 'give the command (to God) so that he will provide bread', and not '(you [Jesus] yourself) turn these stones into bread' seems to be demanded not just by the wording in which the petition is cast, but also by the theological context in which (as Jesus' response at Mt. 4.4//Lk. 4.4 suggests) the petition is to be set and interpreted, namely, the ideas about 'bread' and Sonship delineated in Deut. 8. In this passage there is no question of the Son of God, Israel, having the power himself to produce 'bread', let alone whether he can or should use it if he were so inclined. Rather, the issue expounded is the Son's covenantal right to have God produce 'bread' for him, and whether or not it is correct for the Son/Israel, when under hardship, to then *demand* that God fulfil his obligations in this matter.

For an argument to the effect that it would still be illegitimate to see any presupposition of Jesus as a miracle worker lying in or behind the Devil's first petition *even if* the petition is to be taken as an proposal to Jesus directly that he, not God, perform a miraculous act, see Bretcher, *The Temptation of Jesus*, pp. 186-88.

Jesus' replies to these petitions, show that what is thought here to belong to the Son is not the power to work miracles, but the right *to divine protection*.[43]

In light of these considerations, it is difficult to see how, according to Q, getting Jesus to prove to *himself* through miracle that he is indeed God's Son could be the intention lying behind the Devil's petitions.

But let us grant for the moment that εἰ *is* used within the temptation story by Q with the meaning of 'if', that the Devil's petitions indicate the presupposition and use here of a tradition in which the υἱὸς τοῦ θεοῦ is defined as a miracle working man of God, and that in saying εἰ υἱὸς εἶ τοῦ θεοῦ to Jesus, the Devil is hoping to move Jesus to question his status as God's Son. Can we then say, as the advocates of this view insist, that the issue of doubt on the part of Jesus (and the inadmissability of resolving it miraculously) is the temptation story's sole or dominant motif?

Again the answer must be no. It is difficult to see how the issue of the reality of Jesus' sonship, let alone of having it proven by miracle, comes into play in the episode of the temptation story where, in exchange for his conveyance of the world's kingdoms and their glory, the Devil demands recognition that he is ruler of the world (Mt. 4.9-10//Lk. 4.6-7). What within this episode indicates, even implicitly, that Jesus doubts that he is υἱὸς τοῦ θεοῦ or that the Devil is attempting to engender in Jesus this doubt?[44] On the contrary, the reality of Jesus' sonship seems to be the petition's basic presupposition. And how could receiving rulership of the kingdoms of the world from *the Devil* stand as proof to Jesus of the fact that he was *God's* Son, even should he here have doubts about his status?

In the end, then, the view that the Devil is attempting to get Jesus to prove to himself the reality of his divine sonship has little to say for itself even as a partial explanation of how the petitions are to be understood.

b. *An attempt to get Jesus to prove to others the reality of his Sonship.*
What, then, of the second view, that by urging Jesus to procure bread,

43. This was noted more than one hundred years ago by A.L. Williams and B.C. Caffin (*St Matthew* [2 vols.; Pulpit Commentary; New York: Funk & Wagnalls, 1892], I, p. 105], though, save for Bretcher (*Temptation of Jesus*, pp. 70, 183-86), their contention seems largely to have been ignored.

44. The Devil's remark εἰ υἱὸς εἶ τοῦ θεοῦ is conspicuously absent at the beginning of this episode.

leap off the 'wing' of the Temple, and offer fealty to one other than God, the Devil is trying to get Jesus to prove *to others* through spectacular display that he is truly υἱὸς τοῦ θεοῦ? Despite the fact that it, too, has had a long history of acceptance and that the names of its advocates are many and weighty,[45] this view is, I think, no more acceptable as an explanation of what the Devil is up to with his petitions than the view we just considered. In the first place, like that view, the 'proof *to others*' contention also assumes that, according to Q, the context in which the Devil approaches Jesus is both one of doubt about the reality of Jesus' divine status (though this time on the part of co-religionists whom Jesus is likely to encounter) as well as one in which Jesus is viewed as able to work miracles if he so desires.[46] But as I have already noted, these assumptions are highly questionable and have no grounding in the text of the Q story.

But even if these objections were to be set aside, there are still others that render the 'proof to others' view untenable. Telling here is the fact that there is nothing in the story to indicate the assumption that, should Jesus accede to the Devil's demands, his accessions, whatever they might represent, *would be witnessed by others*. Nowhere within the story, in either its narrative elements or in the exchanges of dialogue between the Devil and Jesus, is there mention of spectators.[47] Now since public witness is a key element in the form 'demonstrative miracle', the fact that the public is not mentioned here indicates that demonstration or authentication of identity to others is not at issue.[48]

---

45. E.g. H. Riesenfeld ('The Messianic Character of Jesus' Temptations', p. 85); F. Filson (*The Gospel according to St Matthew* [New York: Harper & Brothers, 1960], p. 70); T.H. Robinson (*The Gospel of Matthew* [New York: Harper & Brothers, 1927], p. 19); M. Albertz, (*Die synoptischen Streitgespräche* [Berlin: Trowitzch & Sohn, 1921], pp. 42-43); L. Williamson ('Matthew 4:1-11', *Int* 38 [1984], p. 51); S.E. Johnson ('The Temptations of Christ', *BibSac* 123 [1966], pp. 346-47). For a full listing, see Bratcher, *Temptation of Jesus*, ad loc.

46. Again, the claim, typified by the remarks of Allen, *et al.*, noted above in n. 46 is relevant here.

47. Cf. Gerhardsson, *The Testing of God's Son*, p. 60.

48. U. Luz (*Matthew 1–7: A Commentary* [Minneapolis: Augsburg, 1989], p. 188 n. 27) maintains that despite the fact that there is no mention anywhere in the story of 'the public' (which, he notes, ordinarily would be expected, since, as he also notes, such a reference 'would belong to a demonstrative miracle'), the Devil's petition to Jesus to leap from the Temple should still be seen as a call for a *Schauwunder* on the grounds that 'in a temptation scene the public is not appropriate, for stylistic

And there is also the fact that while procuring bread from stones *might*, if witnessed, be a phenomenon that would be taken as a *Schauwunder* and a 'sign' certifying Jesus' Messianic credentials (i.e. as a 'manna' miracle),[49] it is difficult to see how a leap (even one interrupted at the last moment) from a height of the Temple would be recognized, let alone taken, in this way. To what contemporary Messianic expectation does it conform?[50] And it is even more difficult to construe

reasons'. One wonders, then, if this indeed is the case, why the 'public' (human witnesses) appear in such scenes in the Synoptic tradition (of Jesus under temptation) as Mk 8.11-13//Mt. 12.38-42//Lk 11.16, 29-32; Mk 10.1-12//Mt. 19.1-12; Mk 12.13-17//Mt. 23.15-22; Lk. 10:25-28; and especially Mk 15.22-32//Mt. 27.33-44.

49.   This supposition is heavily dependent upon three assumptions: (1) that there was within Judaism an actual expectation of an eschatological deliverer acting like Moses and recapitulating the wilderness 'manna miracles', (2) that the expectation is contemporary with Q and (3) that it stands as the context of interpretation of the petition about procuring bread. One should note, however (as Kloppenborg has shown, *The Formation of Q*, p. 255 n. 28), that the evidence that the Messiah—let alone ὁ υἱὸς τοῦ θεοῦ—was expected to perform a manna miracle is mostly circumstantial. Moreover, non-circumstantial evidence for this expectation (e.g. *Midr. Qoh.* 1.9 §1) is late. Furthermore, even if we take the circumstantial evidence as confirming a contemporary expectation, there is still reason to doubt that this expectation actually forms the background of the Devil's petition that Jesus should procure bread from stones. As Gerhardsson has noted (*The Testing of God's Son*, p. 44), according to the traditions, what the Messiah is supposed to do when he appears and seeks to authenticate himself is bring bread *from heaven*. We should be fully aware, then, in light of this consideration alone, of the great improbability that Q intended for the petition concerning the procuring of bread from stones to be taken as a 'sign' that certifies Jesus' Messianic credentials.

50.   Appeal is sometimes made either to Mal. 3.1, with its prediction of the Lord whom Israel seeks coming 'suddenly' (ἐξαίφνης, LXX) to his temple, or to *Pes. R.* §36 (126a) and its claim that 'When the King Messiah reveals himself' to proclaim salvation, 'he will come and stand upon the roof of the temple' and will point to a light shining above him (presumably to legitimize his claim), as evidence for a first-century Jewish expectation of a spectacular and sudden revelation of the Messiah in the Temple. But two things need to be noted here: (1) Mal. 3.1 of the appearance of *God* in the Temple, not the Messiah, and there is no evidence that it was ever understood otherwise, let alone as a text concerning where and how the Messiah would make himself known. (2) *Pesiqta Rabbati* is late. Moreover, it seems to me that *even if* the tradition *Pes. R.* §36 (126a) embodies concerning the locus of the appearance of the Messiah and what he will do once he has manifested himself, can be assigned a first-century date (a fact over which there is great doubt), to see this as the background of the Devil's petition in Mt. 4.5//Lk. 4.9 involves ignoring some fundamental differences between the tradition and the Q text. First, the 'wing' of the

'falling down and worshiping' God's rival in this manner. What miracle does this action represent? And how could it, once performed, and then issuing, as it is promised to do, in Jesus receiving the kingdoms of the world *from the Devil* (cf. Mt. 4.10//Lk. 4.6, 7b), ever be recognized, let alone serve as, an authentication to anyone of *divine* ordination?[51]

Moreover, we must recognize that acceptance of the 'proof to others' view creates an embarrassing, if not insurmountable, interpretative difficulty, at least in so far as the first petition is concerned. If, according to Q, the Devil's first petition is really a solicitation for Jesus to engage in a 'manna' miracle, and if Q is concerned to show that Jesus both saw this as contrary to the will of God and designated it as something that the υἱὸς τοῦ θεοῦ must refuse to engage in, what do we make of the fact that elsewhere within both the Synoptic and other Gospel traditions (i.e. in traditions behind Mark's stories of the miraculous feedings [Mk 6.30-44; 8.1-10] and in Jn 6) and, more importantly, within both of the two synoptic Gospels which use Q as a source (i.e. by Matthew and Luke at Mt. 14.13-21 and Lk. 9.10-17 [both from Mk 6.30-40] respectively; by Matthew at Mt 15.32-39 [from Mk 8.1-10]), Jesus is explicitly depicted as engaging in this very thing? Is the tradition inconsistent? Are

temple, whatever else it might be (for a discussion, see N. Hyldahl, 'Der Versuchung auf der Zinne des Tempels', *STL* 14/15 (1960–61), pp. 113-19), is not the 'roof'. Secondly, 'leaping' is not 'standing', nor can it—or anything else Jesus is here asked to do—be construed, except by a large 'leap' of the imagination, as a proclamation of salvation. And thirdly, how is rescue from dashing one's foot against stones the equivalent to manifesting light? One would think, if Q had indeed intended the expectation noted in the tradition to be seen as the background to the Devil's petition, that there would have been a more exact correspondence between what Jesus is asked to do and what, accepting the evidence of *Pesiqta Rabbati* as reliable and indicative, first-century Palestinian Judaism actually believed the Messiah would do.

51. It might be argued that in light of such texts as Rev. 13.2-4, 7-8, Jesus' possession of 'all the kingdoms of the world...and their glory' would be seen by his contemporaries as an indication of divine approval and a certification that he was 'of God'. But possession in and of itself is not the same as miraculous display, nor, as Rev. 13 itself shows, is possession most naturally or always viewed as a 'sign' of legitimization by God. Moreover, it seems to me that what would need to be seen for possession to be taken as a *Schauwunder* and legitimizing 'sign' is God himself, and not his enemy, acting to confer possession.

In any case, all of this is beside the point, since it is 'bowing down' before the Devil, engaging in προσκύνησις, and not what comes as a result of this activity, that is the center of attention here and what must constitute the *Schauwunder* if the 'proof to others' view is correct.

Matthew and Luke ignorant of, or in opposition to, the theology of one of their primary sources?[52] On the 'proof to others' view, the answer must be yes to all of these questions.[53]

52. It should be noted that similar questions could be asked about the Devil's second petition as well. If the petition involves a solicitation to Jesus to prove to his contemporaries through miraculous display and/or a 'sign' that he is indeed God's emissary, and if Jesus is presented here as delimiting such an enterprise as forbidden him, as advocates of the 'proof to others' view maintain, then the following question arises—what do we make of the presentation elsewhere in Mark and the Synoptic Gospels of Jesus not only as a miracle worker who sees, *and points others to*, his miracles as proof of his identity as 'the one who is to come' (cf. Mt. 11.2-6// Lk. 7.18-19, [20], 22-23; cp. Mt. 12.22-28//Lk 11.14-15, 17-20), but also as one who has no compunction against offering a 'sign' to confirm his identity as God's agent when the truth of that identity is questioned or in doubt (cf. Mk 2.1-12//1; Mt. 12.38-39//Lk. 11.16, 28-29)? (On the synoptic tradition's portrayal of Jesus as not resistant to giving 'signs', see below, Chapter 4, pp. 169-74, and Chapter 5, pp.198-99.)

Indeed, as Kloppenborg and others have noted, the 'proof to others' view, with its assumption that Jesus is viewed in Mt. 4.1-11//Lk. 4.1-13 as one who has the power to work miracles, renders the theology of the whole temptation story at odds not only with the Markan stream of the the synoptic traditions but also with that of the remainder of Q itself:

> The implication of the devil's invitations is that the Son of God is or should be a miracle worker. But in the rest of Q, miracles are treated not so much as *deeds of Jesus* as they are *events of the kingdom* whose presence or impending coming they portend...Their expected function is to produce repentance in those who witness them...Nothing in temptation story— either in the devil's invitations or in Jesus' responses—suggests this understanding of the miraculous (Kloppenborg, *Formation of Q*, p. 247-48; see also A.D. Jacobson, 'Wisdom Christology in Q' [PhD dissertation, Claremont, CA, 1978], p. 93).

Instead of questioning the validity of the assumption that the temptation story sees Jesus as a miracle worker, Kloppenborg attempts to solve the puzzle of the 'contradictions' between Mt. 4.1-11//Lk. 4.1-13 and the rest of Q on how the miraculous is to be regarded by declaring that the temptation story is a late addition to Q. This, however, ignores the difficulty of explaining why, if the theology of the Q story stands in contradiction with the remainder of Q, *it was ever added at all.* For an assessment of some of the explanations of this, as well as a thorough critique of the assumptions behind the view that Mt. 4.1-11//Lk. 4.1-13 is theologically or thematically disconsonant with the rest of Q, see C.M. Tuckett, 'The Temptation Narrative in Q', in F. Van Segbroeck, C.M. Tuckett, G. Van Belle and J. Verheyden (eds.), *The Four Gospels 1992: Festschrift Frans Neirynck* (3 vols.; Leuven: Leuven University Press, 1992), I, pp. 479-507.

53. Attempts have been made to explain or explain away this difficulty. But the

In light of these considerations it seems clear that, like the first view considered here, the 'proof to others' view also has little to commend it as an adequate or full interpretation of what the Devil is up to in Mt. 4.1-11//Lk.4.1-13.

c. *An attempt to get Jesus to choose a false way of being the Son of God.* What, then, of the third way of answering the question—that, according to Q, the Devil is trying to get Jesus to chose among what are, from Q's point of view, 'false' Messianic paths, thus pressing Jesus to work out for himself what being God's Son might mean? In its favour stands the consideration, highlighted by the advocates of this view,[54] that the answer is grounded more solidly than the others in the fact that the issue of *whether* Jesus *is* God's Son is not what Q intended to raise in the temptation story. But despite this, the answer still cannot be accepted as correct.

In the first place, it, too, seems to be heavily reliant upon the assumption that within the Q story Jesus is presented as a miracle worker.

Secondly, this view of what the Devil is 'up to' is predicated on the assumption that Q presents Jesus as having no concrete idea, both at the time of, and even during, his encounter with the Devil, *how* he is to work out being the Son of God. But this seems most unlikely. In Q the title υἱὸς τοῦ θεοῦ is not contentless. On the contrary, it connotes a

claims that such attempts are usually grounded in, e.g., that the miraculous feedings described in Mk 6.30-44 and pars. and Mk 8.1-10 and pars. were not demonic because the motive force behind them was compassion for the needs of others, or that, unlike the action envisaged in the petition, they were in conformity with the divine will and represent a submissive response to divine initiative, seem to me to be as questionable as they are question begging. On my view there is no need either to explain or view as negligible the contradictions between what is said in the Q temptation story and elsewhere in synoptic and other gospel traditions, or to engage in the kind of tendentious exegesis that is often used to do so. For if, as I claim, there is no solicitation in the Q story to Jesus to perform a 'manna miracle', and therefore no delineation by Jesus that such miracles are forbidden him, then the contradictions are more apparent than real.

54. E.g. Holst, 'The Temptation of Jesus', pp. 334-44; E. Lohmeyer, *Das Evangelium des Matthäus* (Göttingen: Vandenhoeck & Ruprecht, 1963), p. 57; T.W. Manson, *The Teaching of Jesus: Studies of its Form and Content* (Cambridge: Cambridge University Press, 1967), p. 196; A.B. Taylor, 'Decision in the Desert: The Temptation of Jesus in the Light of Deuteronomy', *Int* 14 (1960), p. 301; J.A. Kirk, 'The Messianic Role of Jesus and the Temptation Narrative: A Contemporary Perspective', *EvQ* 44 (1972), pp. 11-21, 91-102.

specific identity and destiny and a commission to a particular path of behaviour that is commensurate with it.[55] Furthermore, according to Q, Jesus accepts the fact that he has been granted the status of Son.[56] Accordingly, acceptance of this fact implies knowledge on Jesus' (and the Devil's) part of what this status requires of him.

Thirdly, there is no agreement among those who hold the 'false ways' view regarding just what the 'Messianic' paths supposedly embodied in the petitions actually are. Procuring bread from stones is, on one reading, tantamount to engaging in the economic crusade of the so-called 'social bandits' active in Palestine from the time of Herod to the outbreak of the Jewish war,[57] while on another reading it equates with taking up the mantle of the first deliverer Moses or his successor Joshua.[58] On yet other readings it amounts to assuming the role either of a glorious, triumphalistic θεῖος ἀνήρ,[59] or of the Messiah of the *Second Apocalypse of Baruch*, who, in manifesting himself, brings with him a period of abundance which includes the 'descent of the treasury of manna',[60] or even to adopting the political programme of the Sadducees.[61] Leaping from the Temple is claimed to represent an endorsement of the activities of such saviour figures as are to be found in *3 Enoch*, or *4 Ezra* 13.24-37, or Josephus, *War* 6.285-86, each of whom makes the Temple a nationalistic stronghold,[62] or of the triumphal-

55. On this, see below.

56. This is clear if only from the fact that he nowwhere challenges the Devil's ascription to him (Jesus) of the title.

57. Cf. G.A. Buttrick. 'The Gospel according to St Matthew: Exposition', in *IB*, VII, p. 271. Buttrick also sees the petition to procure bread from stones in terms of an attempt by the Devil to get Jesus to prove to himself the reality of his Sonship.

58. Lohmeyer, *Matthäus*, pp. 56-57; Schniewind, *Matthäus*, p. 28; Mahnke, *Die Versuchungsgeschichte*, pp. 72-103, among many others.

59. F. Hahn, *The Titles of Jesus in Christology* (London: Lutterworth, 1969), p. 303 n. 34.

60. P. Hoffmann, 'Die Versuchungsgeschichte in der Logienquelle: Zur Aueseinandersetzung der Judenchristen mit dem politischen Messianismus', *BZ* 13 (1969), pp. 214-15; B.H. Kelly, 'An Exposition of Matthew 4:1-11', *Int* 29 (1975), pp. 57-62, esp. 59.

61. On this, see S. Liberty, *The Political Relations of Christ's Ministry* (London: Humphrey Milford and Oxford University Press, 1916), pp. 59-60; J.A. Kirk, 'The Messianic Role of Jesus in the Temptation Narrative', p. 29.

62. On the saviour figure of *3 Enoch* as background for the second 'false way', see B.H. Kelly, 'Exposition', p. 60. On figures from *4 Ezra* 13.24-37 and Josephus, *War* 6.285-86, see Hoffmann, 'Die Versuchungsgeschichte', pp. 216-17; See also

istic King Messiah of *Pes. R.* 36 (126a),[63] or of the eschatological High Priest who will rid the Temple of all impurity,[64] or even that of the Pharisees.[65] Worshiping the Devil is equivalent, depending upon whom one reads, to advocating self-aggrandizement at the expense of others,[66] to following the example of the *imperium Romanum*,[67] or to accepting the ideals and tactics of the holy war ideology of the Zealots and other theocratically motivated terrorist/revolutionary groups,[68] or even to adopting the political programme and 'irreligion' of the Herodians.[69]

One might explain all of this as due more to scholarly inability to get behind Q's language and imagery than to the deficiency of the 'false ways' view. But in light of the sheer number and diversity of supposed 'false Messianic paths', surely we must question whether taking the Devil's challenges as 'false' ways of being God's Son is itself a 'false' way of viewing what he is up to. After all, what, specifically, is there, either in the form of the petitions themselves, or within the narrative line of the story, or in any of its particular details, which actually indicates that the petitions are intended to be seen as concretely embodying ways of being υἱὸς τοῦ θεοῦ? Is it not only a predisposition to see them as such which has led many to do so?[70]

And finally, if we accept the view that trying to get Jesus to choose a false way of being God's Son and pressing him to work out his own path is, according to Q, what the Devil is really up to in his petitions,

---

Kirk, 'The Messianic Role of Jesus in the Temptation Narrative', p. 95.

63. Lohmeyer, *Matthäus*, p. 58.

64. Mahnke, *Versuchungsgeschichte*, pp. 122-24; So also G. Friedrich. 'Beobachtungen zur messianischen Hohepriesterwartung in den Synoptikern', *ZTK* 53 (1956), pp. 265-311, esp. pp. 300-301.

65. Liberty, *Political Relations*, pp. 66-68. Liberty understands the Pharisees to be a party who not only advocated a rigid adherence to their understanding of the Law, but held the 'political dogma that God was pledged sooner or later to put the keepers of his Law in a position of supremacy' (p. 60).

66. B.H. Kelly, 'Exposition', pp. 61-62.

67. R. Morganthaler, 'Roma—Sedes Satanae', *TZ* 12 (1956), pp. 289-304.

68. P. Hoffmann, 'Die Versuchungsgeschichte in der Logienquelle', p. 214; Kirk, 'The Messianic Role of Jesus in the Temptation Narrative', pp. 97-98.

69. Liberty, *Political Relations*, pp. 68-71.

70. On this, see A. Schlatter, *Der Evangelist Matthaeus* (Stuttgart: Calwer Vereinsbuchhandlung, 1929), p. 111. Here Schlatter argues that when the exegete views the Devil's petitions as attempts to get Jesus to chose a ' false way' of being the Son, '[he] deals with the text on his own terms'.

then we are destined to run up hard against the fact that by the end of the story Jesus has not actually worked out in any concrete or positive fashion what, as Son, he is to do. All Jesus has done when the Devil leaves him has been to indicate what types of sonship and paths of behaviour are *not* to be his.[71] But is it likely that Q would want to leave the matter standing like this?[72]

In light of all these considerations, there seems little reason for accepting the 'false paths' view of what the Devil is up to.[73]

A New Understanding

We turn now to my contention that what the Devil is up to in the Q Wilderness temptation story is attempting to get Jesus to turn away from a particular and God-ordained pattern of sonship with which he is already familiar and to which he has already been called—a pattern essentially characterized by peaceableness and willingness to do good to the enemy (in full awareness of the cost to self that this entails).

In assessing the validity of this contention, let us begin—as we have with the other views—by examining its basic presuppositions, for if

71. Cf. T.W. Manson (*The Sayings of Jesus* [London: SCM Press, 1949], p. 46): 'And here we may note that Jesus does not set forth the positive features of His own conception of His ministry. He rejects a number of proposals quite decisively, *as much as to say: Whatever else God may have appointed me to do, it is not this or this*' (my italics).

72. The evidence of Mt. 5.39-46//Lk. 6.27-35, where Q has *Jesus* precisely delineate who sons of God are and what being υἱὸς τοῦ θεοῦ entails, speaks decisively against this. How can Jesus have such knowledge if after his temptation he was still unclear on what positively was involved in living out that office?

73. In addition to the objections noted above, there is perhaps one more consideration which might be taken into account when assessing the validity of the 'false ways' view: if the editor(s) of Q intended to present the Devil as attempting in his petitions to move Jesus into ways of being God's Son that were 'false', with each petition embodying a separate option, why are only *three* 'false' ways offered? Surely we should expect more. For it is difficult to suppose that in the cultural milieu in which the temptation story was formed and presented, there were only three ways of being υἱὸς τοῦ θεοῦ with which the editor(s) of Q would be familiar and which they would have labeled 'false'—especially if, as most of the supporters of the 'false ways' answer assume, the ascription υἱὸς τοῦ θεοῦ is here equivalent to Χριστός (on this, however, see Gerhardsson, *The Testing of God's Son*, p. 44). But in light of the fact that 'sets of three' seem to be traditional not only in ancient (and modern!) story telling, but also in 'temptation stories' as well (cf., e.g., *b. Sanh.* 89b), it is difficult to assess how much, if any, weight this consideration has.

these do not obtain, then the contention itself is groundless. The contention rests upon the assumptions, already hinted at, that Q presumes and expects those who read or heard the Wilderness temptation story to see:

1. That prior to his encounter with the Devil, Jesus has been given a commission to be υἱὸς τοῦ θεοῦ.
2. That Jesus and the Devil know that he [Jesus] has been called to the status and office of Son.
3. That being υἱὸς τοῦ θεοῦ is not a contentless undertaking, but entails a specific mission and involves accepting certain patterns of behaviour, to be employed in accomplishing that mission, as divinely mandated and normative.
4. That these patterns of behaviour, that is, the *means* of accomplishing the divine will, are those which mirror and proclaim the all-encompassing, indiscriminate, and limitless mercy and love of God, namely, forgiveness of all injury, non-retaliation, willing endurance of ridicule and suffering, uncomplaining submission to persecution, and, above all, love of one's enemies.

Now, evidence revealed above in my assessment of the traditional answers given to the question of what, according to Q, the Devil is trying to do with his petitions to Jesus, shows that there is no reason to doubt the truth of points (1) and (2). The reality of Jesus' divine appointment to the role of Son, as well as the acceptance on the part of both Jesus and the Devil of that appointment, are indeed fundamental presuppositions of the temptation story. Nor is there any reason to doubt the truth of point (3), in light of the fact that divine sonship is inextricably linked by Q, notably within the temptation story itself, with sovereignty over the world that is achieved through ardent and single-minded dedication to acting according to the will and ways of God. If there were doubt, it would be dispelled by the fact that at Mt. 5.39-46//Lk. 6.27-35 and then again at Mt. 11.25-27//Lk. 10.21-22, texts linked both thematically and terminologically to Mt. 4.1-11// Lk. 4.1-13, Q defines being υἱὸς τοῦ θεοῦ in terms of appointment to an office and a mission: to be the agent of God's kingdom and the one to whom 'all things are given' (cf. Mt. 11.27//Lk. 10.22), who is constrained to make known to Israel and to the world the true nature and character of God, the type of devotion he demands, and his ways of dealing with human beings *by acting as God acts*.[74] And truth of point (4) is confirmed from two considerations: (a) that according to Q (cf. Mt. 5.45-46//Lk. 6.35-36) the preeminent characteristic of God's way of acting in the world is universal mercy, even towards those who are hostile toward him; and (b) that to be worthy of the office and title of υἱὸς τοῦ θεοῦ, and to be called and appointed by God to them, one must exhibit the characteristics of an εἰρηνοποιός, which, according to Q, comprise non-violence, non-retaliation, and, preeminently, active love and concern for the enemy.[75]

But what evidence, if any, exists to indicate that for Q the Devil's objective is *winning a denial* from Jesus that this particular pattern of Sonship is truly a divine Son's destiny? There are, I think, five things.

First, there is the fact that Jesus' πειρασμός is presented in Q as *a struggle on Jesus' part to hold faithfully to a commission by accepting and remaining obedient to the constraints of behaviour deemed by God to be appropriate for bringing the commission to completion*. This is clear from the following:

    1.   From a literary-critical and history-of-religions point of view, the story of Jesus' temptation in the wilderness is, as we have already had occasion to observe, a prime example of the literary 'type' which Bultmann has labeled 'the temptation of the "Holy Men" who are put to the test (by evil) and emerge

---

74. '[These texts show that] sonship of God depends upon acting like God' (O. Piper, *Love your Enemies: Jesus' Love Command in the Synoptic Gospels and in the Early Christian Paraenesis* [Cambridge: Cambridge University Press, 1979], p. 62.

75. '[According to Q] God is kind to his enemies, therefore anyone who wants to be a Son of God must do the same' (Piper, *Love your Enemies*, p. 62).

On the characteristics of the εἰρηνοποιός according to Q (as well as in the New Testament in general), see R.A. Guelich, *The Sermon on the Mount: A Foundation for Understanding* (Waco, TX: Word, 1982), p. 92. Contrast this sense of εἰρηνοποιός with that which was current in the Hellenistic world, i.e. Greek and Roman rulers who establish peace, security and economic welfare for their people *through conquest of their enemies* (on this, see H. Windisch, 'Friedensbringer—Gottessöhn', *ZNW* 24 [1925], pp. 240-60, esp. pp. 240-41).

For a definitive discussion of the links between sonship, *imitatio dei*, indiscriminate mercy, non-violence/non-retaliation, and love of enemies in the teaching of Jesus as well as in Q, see M.J. Borg, *Conflict, Holiness and Politics in the Teaching of Jesus* (New York: Edwin Mellen Press, 1984), pp. 123-39.

victorious'.[76] Now it should be noted that the basic theme of
this 'type' is always whether or not the tempted pious one
would show himself faithful to a vocation or a commission
which had been given to him before, or at the immediate outset
of, his subjection to πειρασμός.[77] This is evident, for instance,
not only in the many biblical examples of this type (e.g. Gen.
22, the testing of Abraham by God; Job 1–3, the temptation of
Job by Satan, Wis. 2, the testing of the righteous 'Son of God'
by the 'ungodly'),[78] as well as in those found in the pseude-
pigraphic and rabbinic literature,[79] but also in such non-biblical
examples as stories where Gautama Buddha and Zarathustra
are the 'Holy Men' in question.[80] Here, just as in the biblical
and biblically dependent stories, the essence of the temptation
concerns whether or not these figures will abjure as foolish and
not worthy of obedience all that has been commanded of them
as necessary in the faithful service of 'true religion'.[81]

2.   The fact that the author of the Q account of Jesus' Wilderness
temptation presents Jesus' experience specifically in parallelism
with, indeed, as the *recapitulation of*, the temptation which
Israel, God's firstborn and υἱός was subjected to during *its*
wilderness wanderings, as this was recounted in Deuteronomy
6–8. Accordingly, in Q's eyes, the defining characteristic of
Israel's Wilderness temptation is also that of Jesus' experience:

76. *History*, p. 253.

77. On this, see Gerhardsson, *The Testing of God's Son*, pp. 25-27; Rengstorf,
Das Evangelium nach Lukas, p. 52. See also M. Kahler, 'Temptation', in *The New
Schaff–Herzog Religious Encyclopedia* (New York: Funk & Wagnalls, 1913), XI,
pp. 297-99; J. Korn, *ΠΕΙΡΑΣΜΟΣ: Die Versuchung des Gläubigen in der
griechischen Bible* (Stuttgart: Kohlhammer, 1937), p. 48-71.

78. See also the notation in Sir. 2.1 that 'testing' is the expected and inescapable
lot of anyone who feels, and acts upon by taking up, a calling to 'serve' God
(τέκνον, εἰ προσέρχῃ δουλεύειν κυρίῳ, ἐτοίμασον τὴν ψυχήν σου εἰς
πειρασμόν).

79. For a full listing and discussion of these pseudepigrapical and rabbinic stories
along with their biblical antecedents, see Korn, *ΠΕΙΡΑΣΜΟΣ*, pp. 48-76.

80. For the Buddha, see *Samyutta-Nikaya* 2.10 (text in J. Aufhauser, *Buddha und
Jesus in ihren Paralleltexten* [Bonn: A. Marcus & E. Weber, 1926], pp. 27-28). For
Zarathustra, see *Vendidad* 19.1.

81. U. Luz, *Matthew 1–7*, p. 185 n. 15.

the struggle to hold on to a vocation through remaining fully obedient to God's way of fulfilling it.

Now holding faithfully to a commission by accepting and remaining obedient to all that has been deemed appropriate for bringing it to completion is no struggle unless one has, or has been *given*, cause to doubt the propriety of such a stance. Accordingly, in presenting Jesus' temptation in the wilderness as a fight to remain faithful and obedient to the will and ways of God, Q indicates that the wisdom or propriety or prudence of that faithfulness and obedience has been brought into question. And this in turn implies that Jesus has been appealed to to see and to admit that what appear to be God's ways cannot possibly be so.

A second thing supporting my contention is implied in the occasion and ground of *all* of the Devil's challenges being, according to Q, Jesus having been brought by God into a state of 'hunger' (πεινάω).[82] The notice that Jesus, through God's directive, came into a state of 'hunger' recalls the notice in Deut. 8.1-13 (as well as in other Old Testament passages such as Exod. 16.2-7; Num. 11.4-5; 21.4-5) that before and during its wilderness πειρασμός Israel was specifically made 'to hunger' so that God might know whether Israel would 'keep his commandments' and 'remember his ways' by not doubting that the means he had given them to achieve their destiny would be sufficient unto that end. The notice, then, serves to place Jesus in exact parallelism with the wilderness generation. His situation is theirs. Accordingly, Q's statement that Jesus 'hungered' (ἐπείνασεν) is not, as is often assumed, a notice that Jesus suffered for food and craved physical sustenance. On the contrary, it is an indication that he was beset with doubts about the propriety of trusting in the ways God has deemed fit for a υἱὸς τοῦ θεοῦ to fulfil his mission and achieve his destiny. For as the Deuteronomic and related passages show, 'to be made to hunger' (ἐλιμαγχόνησέν σε) and 'to hunger' 'in the wilderness' as Jesus does is not to be reduced to

---

82. That Jesus' 'hunger' is the occasion and ground of *all* and not, as many commentators assume, solely *the first* of the Devil's challenges seems clear from the fact that formally the notice of it (καὶ οὐκ ἔφαγεν [καὶ] ὕστερον ἐπείνασεν) is part of the narrative introduction to the ensuing unified dialogue between Jesus and the Devil. We might note, too, that Matthew seems to see the 'hunger' in this manner, since at the end of his retelling of the Q story he gives a notice (the substance of which is borrowed from Mk 1.13) which presumably recounts Jesus being relieved from hunger. On Jesus' 'hunger' as a decree of God, see Gerhardsson, *The Testing of God's Son*, p. 51.

starvation but *to be made dissatisfied with what God appoints as the means appropriate for sustaining and attaining 'life'*.[83] So if, according to Q, this is the occasion and ground of the Devil's challenges, then their substance must suit what they rise out of.

Thirdly, there is implication of the fact that Jesus' Wilderness πειρασμός is explicitly noted in Q as something carried out by the Devil (ὑπὸ τοῦ διαβόλου). Now, as I have hinted at in the previous chapter,[84] in contemporary thought the Devil is a figure who puts the pious 'to the test', first by posing as one privy to the divine counsel, and then by attempting to get the pious to break their faithfulness and turn aside from obeying God, by bringing them to 'see' that what God has commanded them to do (or put their trust in) is not really 'of God'. This perception, found frequently in early Christian writings and in intertestamental and rabbinic literature,[85] finds perhaps its clearest expression in the midrash on the Genesis story of God's temptation of Abraham (Gen. 22) found in *b. Sanh.* 89b, a text that both structurally and thematically bears more than a passing resemblance to Mt. 4.1-11//Lk. 4.1-13.[86]

---

83. The OT texts make clear that during its wilderness wanderings Israel *always had food*. When they 'hungered' it was because they deemed the food they *had* (manna), the food which God gave them, as 'worthless' (διακένον, cf. Num. 21.5) and incapable either of sustaining them or bringing them into 'life', i.e., their destiny.

84. See above, Chapter 2, pp. 58-60.

85. It seems to stand behind both the Johannine claim at Jn 8.44 that the Devil 'has nothing to do with the truth…he speaks according to his own nature, for he is a liar and the father of lies' and the warning from Paul in 2 Cor. 11.14 that Satan disguises himself as an angel of light. It can be seen clearly in the Markan story of Peter's 'confession' at Caesarea Philippi (Mk 8.27-33) and its parallel in Matthew (where, by virtue of Matthew's addition of the macarism, the perception is perhaps emphasized even more strongly than in Mark), as well as in *Apoc. Abr.* 13 (cf. esp. vv. 9-13) and *The Testament of Job* (especially in chs 24–27, the dialogue between Sitis and Job), where it is a fundamental presupposition of the *Testament*'s portrayal of Azazel/Satan.

86. The text reads:

> *And it came to pass after these words, that God did tempt Abraham* (Gen. 22.1). What is meant by '*after*'?—R. Johanan said on the authority of R. Jose ben Zimra: *After* the words of Satan, as it is written, '*And the child grew and it was weaned. [And Abraham made a great feast the same day the child was weaned*' (Gen. 21.8)]

R. Simeon b. Abba said that the word *nā'* can only denote entreaty. This may be compared to a king of flesh and blood who was confronted by many wars which he

Here Abraham, on the way to Mount Moriah to sacrifice Isaac as God
has commanded him, is confronted by the Devil who has come to
Abraham to carry out the divinely ordained 'testing' of his (Abraham's)

> won by the aid of a great warrior. Subsequently he was faced with a severe battle.
> Thereupon he said to him, 'I pray thee, assist me in battle, that people may not say,
> there was no reality in the earlier ones'. So also did the Holy One, blessed be He, say
> unto Abraham, 'I have tested thee with may trials and thou didst withstand them all.
> Now be firm for my sake in this trial, that men may not say, there was no reality in the
> earlier ones.'
>
> > *Thy Son.*
> > [But] I have two sons!
> > *Thine only one.*
> > Each is the only one of his mother.
> > *Whom thou lovest.*
> > I love them both!
> > *Isaac!*
>
> And why all this [circumlocution]?—That his mind should not reel [under the
> sudden shock].

> > Thereupon Satan said to the Almighty: 'Sovereign of the Universe! To this
> > old man didst thou graciously vouchsafe the fruit of the womb at the age
> > of a hundred, yet of all that banquet which he prepared, he did not have one
> > turtle dove or pigeon to sacrifice before thee! Hath he done aught but in
> > honour of his son?' Replied He: 'Yet were I to say to him, "Sacrifice thy
> > son before Me", he would do so without hesitation'. Straightway *God did
> > tempt Abraham ... And he said, Take, I pray thee [nā'] thy son* (Gen.
> > 22.2) ... On the way Satan came towards him and said to him, *'If we assay
> > to commune with thee, wilt thou be grieved? ... Behold thou hast
> > instructed many; and thou hast strengthened the weak hands. Thy words
> > have upholden him that was falling and thou hast strengthened the feeble
> > knees. But now it has come to unto thee and thou faintest* (Job. 4.2-5 on
> > the basis of a verbal link between *nasâ* in Job and Genesis). He replied, *'I
> > will walk in my integrity'* (Ps. 26.2). *'But'*, said [Satan] to him, *'should not
> > thy fear be thy confidence?'* (Job. 4.6) *'Remember'*, he retorted, *'I pray
> > thee, who ever perished, being innocent?'* (Job 4.6) Seeing that he would
> > not listen to him, he said to him, *'Now a thing was secretly brought to me'*
> > (Job 4.12): thus have I heard from behind the curtain, *'the lamb for a
> > burnt offering* (Job 4.7) but not Isaac for a burnt offering'. He replied, 'It
> > is the penalty of a liar, that should he even tell the truth, he is not listened
> > to'.

As even a cursory glance at this text shows, the thematic and formal similarities
between *b. Sanh.* 89b and Mt.4.1-11//Lk. 4.1-13 are striking. The theme of both
stories is the demonstration of the faithfulness of the pious in and through

faithfulness. Notably, the Devil does so specifically by trying to show Abraham, through appeal to Scripture,[87] and the 'knowledge' of God's ways which he possesses by virtue of his privileged position as a member of the heavenly court,[88] that Abraham need not carry out God's command, for it is contrary to God's ways and not really what God demands of him.

So the fact that Q has the Devil carry out the temptation to which Jesus is subjected in the wilderness strongly indicates that at the center of that temptation lies an attempt to get Jesus to deny that the constraints of his office, the will and ways of God which he knows he must follow, are really 'of God'.

Fourthly, the form in which the Devil's petitions are cast has its own implications. Long ago Bultmann, following Bousset, noted that the way Q has the Devil argue and cite and use Scripture within the temptation story reflects the form, method and intent of rabbinic disputation.[89] Now disputations of this sort most typically involved a thesis being advanced by an interlocutor which not only countered a previous assumption on the question under debate, but at the same time showed the erroneousness of the entire position taken by the one to whom the Scriptural citation was addressed.[90] The hope was that the addressee would come to abandon his position, having been forced to deny its

---

πειρασμός. In both, the πειρασμός is divinely ordained. But also in both, it is not God but the Devil who carries out the 'testing'. Then like the Q story, the bulk of the structure of *b. Sanh.* 89b is shaped around a threefold and ultimately unsuccessful attempt by the Devil to sway the one he 'tests' from obedience to a divine command. Also, as in Q, each of these attempts is made by means of an appeal to a shared knowledge of how God works, what his wishes are for the pious, and what, in light of this, the pious have a right to expect from God. Likewise each appeal is solemnly rebuffed. And here, too, each appeal, as well as each of the pious one's responses to it, is grounded directly or allusively in Scripture.

Though there is hardly a case to be made for the literary dependence of one story on the other, there is little doubt that they are both derived from the same theological model of (1) the nature of πειρασμός, (2) the Devil's role within this experience, and (3) how the Devil goes about his task of determining the faithfulness of the pious.

87. Job 4.2-5; Job 4.6 and Job 4.12 combined with 4.7.

88. Cf. the Devil's remark, 'thus have I heard from behind the curtain'.

89. Bultmann, *History*, p. 254. On this, see also Dupont, 'L'arrière fond biblique', pp. 287-88; J. Jeremias, *New Testament Theology*, p. 69; Donaldson, *Jesus on the Mountain*, p. 90.

90. On this, see Bultmann, *History*, 39-46.

validity.[91] So even the *way* the Devil here speaks with Jesus and engages him in debate about what belongs to the υἰὸς τοῦ θεοῦ also indicates that winning a denial from Jesus on the validity of his position on Sonship is what the Devil's challenges are all about.

Finally, there is the import of Jesus' responses to the Devil's petitions. In the last of them, a quotation from Deut. 8.3, Q has Jesus strongly emphasize a sense of the necessity and seemliness of maintaining a wholehearted devotion to his understanding of the will of God; in the first, a quotation from Deut. 6.13, of trusting in the ways he knows God has chosen for his 'Sons', and in the second, a quotation of Deut. 6.16; the avoidance of doubting that following those ways puts in jeopardy God's worthwhile purposes. Why would Q have Jesus respond in this manner and with these words unless, according to Q, the Devil has called into question Jesus' understanding of the will and ways of God and the propriety of following them?

In light of these considerations, it seems we have good reason to conclude that, according to Q, what the Devil is trying to win from Jesus with his challenges to Jesus is a denial that the particular pattern of Sonship to which Jesus has committed himself is truly what God has in mind for his Son.[92]

91. I point again to *b. Sanh.* 89b for an excellent illustration of all of this.

92. This conclusion has to a large degree been anticipated by Donaldson in his *Jesus on the Mountain*. As Donaldson notes, 'The temptation is certainly not that Jesus should doubt the *fact* of his Sonship. Nor is its central thrust that Jesus should adopt another pattern of messiahship...It is a temptation *away from* sonship, rather than towards any specific pattern of messianism' (pp. 91-92, my italics). Donaldson, however, is not as specific as I am in outlining that pattern in terms of a commission to be an εἰρηνοποιός. He seems to assume that the pattern of Sonship that the Devil is trying to sway Jesus from is to be conceived solely in terms of the relationship between Israel and the divine Father as defined in Deuteronomy, and not in terms of how Sonship is defined by Q.

Bretcher (in the second half of his *The Temptation of Jesus in Matthew*, cf. pp. 122-248) has also examined the temptation story from the same general perspective as I have (i.e. that the temptation itself is a 'testing', not an enticement to evil, that there is no presupposition within the story of doubt on the part of Jesus and/or the Devil regarding the fact of Jesus' Sonship, that the idea of 'sonship' is not 'contentless', and that Jesus is not viewed there as one who possesses miraclulous power). Yet Bretcher arrived at a conclusion concerning what the Devil is 'up to' in his challenges that is somewhat at variance with what I have argued for here. In Bretcher's view the Devil is assuming the role of the 'ungodly' in Wis. 2.16-20 vis-à-vis the righteous Son of God, and in his petitions *taunts* Jesus and derides his

And so according to Q, the issue of Jesus' Wilderness temptation is whether or not Jesus, commissioned to be the divine agent responsible for bringing true knowledge of God into the world, will renounce the means God has given him for doing so. More specifically, it centers in determining if Jesus will stand against the idea that God's emissaries are to act in the world as God does, showing mercy and forgiveness towards all, refusing to retaliate injury for injury, accepting suffering and persecution as the price of living in conformity to God's will, and, most importantly, loving and not 'hating' (seeking or willing the destruction of) those ordinarily deemed the enemy.

The Outcome of the Temptation according to Q
According to Q Jesus' Wilderness temptation ends with Jesus affirming the necessity of wholehearted devotion to God (καὶ ἀποκριθεὶς εἶπεν αὐτῷ [λέγει] αὐτῷ ὁ Ἰησοῦς· γέγραπται· κύριον τὸν θεόν σου προσκυνήσεις καὶ αὐτῷ μόνῳ λατρεύσεις) and the Devil's departure (τότε ἀφίησιν αὐτὸν ὁ διάβολος). This should leave us in no doubt that for Q the outcome of Jesus' temptation was a successful one, with Jesus 'passing' the test by showing himself faithful and obedient to all that God has commanded of him. For the final declaration that Jesus makes to the Devil is obviously meant to be taken as much along the lines of what Jesus *has done* in the face of πειρασμός as it is a

(Jesus') apparent obsession with the word of God and with religious obedience, trying to get Jesus (1) to see that in the quest to obey God, absolute trust will ultimately be personally disastrous, and (2) to come to the conclusion that 'it is right, necessary, and inevitable, that a man exercise a measure of common sense, and by calculation of consequences, determine the degree of obedience that may be practicable in any given instance' (*Temptation of Jesus*, p. 207; cp. pp. 243-46). In other words, Bretcher sees the Devil's petitions primarily as a challenge to the wisdom of obedience and not, as I do, as an assault on the legitimacy of thinking that God intends his Son to mold himself according to the pattern of the εἰρηνοποιός. Now I do not wish to deny that challenging the wisdom of obedience is part of what the Devil does within the Q story, let alone within the petitions themselves. Nevertheless, I would argue that such a challenge is to be seen as a *tactic* used in the service of a larger purpose, and not, as Bretcher seems to think, as the purpose itself.

Notable in this regard is the fact that Bretcher does not spell out in any detail what it is that the tempted Jesus assumes he must be obedient to. This, I think, is because Bretcher nowhere examines the meaning which the title υἱὸς τοῦ θεοῦ has in Q (or Matthew), and, correspondingly, does not elucidate what, according to Q (or Matthew) *being* a faithful and obedient Son entails. Perhaps if he had done this, our conclusions regarding what the Devil is 'up to' would have been more in line with one another.

recommendation of what a 'faithful' υἱός is to do. Moreover, as we have seen previously, in Jewish thought the Devil's departure from one of God's sons is taken to be one of the primary indications of the fact that that son has shown himself steadfast in his covenant loyalty.

In light of this, we have, then, in the Q version of Jesus' Wilderness temptation a portrayal of Jesus designated as one not only 'called', and 'proved', but also 'obedient'.

3. *Q and Mark Compared*

As we have seen above, within the Synoptic tradition there are two 'primary' versions of the tradition of Jesus' temptation in the wilderness: that of Mark and that which stands as the principal source for the bulk of Mt. 4.1-11//Lk. 4.1-3, from Q. And as we have also seen, after having examined both accounts, each of these 'primary' versions is intent to say something specific about the nature and content of that temptation experience.

Remembering that the larger purpose in exploring these accounts is to lay the groundwork necessary for determining whether or not there was within the early Church a unified conception of the nature and content of Jesus' temptations, the question we must now ask is: Do the Markan and Q accounts of the Wilderness temptation agree with respect to what they individually present as the center and sum of the temptation? Is there between them a 'horizontal' unity of conception on these matters? The evidence adduced above indicates in no uncertain terms that the answer is yes. Both Q and Mark present the temptation as 'religious' in kind, designed to explore and determine Jesus' willingness to be faithful and obedient to divine decrees. Both Q and Mark indicate that the particular decrees against which Jesus' faithfulness and obedience is tested concern themselves with outlining the way in which Jesus is to manifest himself as God's son and accomplish the task that Jesus' appointment to that office lays upon him. And both Q and Mark see the divinely decreed way of the Son to be one that involves service, suffering and love, especially towards the 'enemy'. And so, at least in so far as the 'primary' traditions of Jesus' Wilderness temptation stand as evidence and testimony, we see no divergence in the early Church's portraits of Jesus under temptation.

Chapter 4

The Tradition of Jesus' Temptation in
the Demand for a 'Sign'

I turn now to an examination of the tradition that Jesus was tempted as the result of being asked to produce a 'sign'.[1] As I have stated in the introduction, the purpose of this examination is to determine exactly what the earliest stage of this tradition presents as the nature and content of Jesus' 'sign' demand temptation and thereby lay the foundation of evidence necessary for ascertaining whether the developed versions of the tradition convey an understanding of these matters which is different from that contained in the tradition's original form. To do this, we must be clear as to the shape, that is, the form and wording, of the tradition's earliest stage. And so we must begin our examination of the 'sign' demand tradition by investigating the history of its development within the Synoptic tradition in so far as the evidence provided by its various extant versions allows us to do so.

The Accounts and their Relationship

The tradition that Jesus was subjected to temptation when he was approached with a demand for a 'sign' is known to all three Synoptic Evangelists. Mark recounts one version of the tradition at Mk 8.11-13, Matthew another at Mt. 12.38-40 as well as at Mt. 16.1-2a, [2b-3] 4,[2]

---

1.   I have placed the English equivalent to the word σημεῖον in inverted commas here and elsewhere in the following pages because, as I will show in the next chapter (see pp. 161-64), throughout the versions of the tradition of Jesus' '"Sign" Demand temptation' the word σημεῖον is used with a particular technical sense related to, but distinct from, the more familiar and ordinary senses with which σημεῖον was normally employed.

2.   The originality of Mt. 16.2b-3 has long been doubted. The verses were probably added to Mt through the influence of Lk. 12.54-56. But see R. Gundry,

and Luke yet another at Lk. 11.16, 28-30. The similarities between the versions can best be seen by viewing them comparatively in a synopsis:

Mt. 12.38-40	Mt. 16.1-2a, 4	Mk 8.11-13	Lk. 11.16, 29-30
	καὶ	καὶ ἐξῆλθον	
τότε	προσελθόντες		
ἀπεκρίθησαν			
αὐτῷ τινες τῶν			ἕτεροι δὲ
γραμματέων καὶ			
Φαρισαίων	οἱ Φαρισαῖοι	οἱ Φαρισαῖοι	
	καὶ Σαδδουκαῖοι		
	πειράξοντες	καὶ ἤρξαντο	πειράζοντες
		συζητεῖν αὐτῷ,	
λέγοντες,			
διδάσκαλε,			
θέλομεν ἀπὸ	ἐπηρώτησαν	ζητοῦντες παρ'	
σοῦ	αὐτὸν	αὐτοῦ	
σημεῖον	σημεῖον	σημεῖον	σημεῖον
	ἐκ τοῦ	ἀπὸ τοῦ	ἐξ
	οὐρανοῦ	οὐρανοῦ,	οὐρανοῦ
		πειράζοντες	ἐζήτουν παρ'
		αὐτόν.	αὐτοῦ.
ἰδεῖν.	ἐπιδεῖξαι αὐτοῖς.		
		12 καὶ	
		ἀναστενάξας τῷ	
		πνεύματι αὐτοῦ	
			29 τῶν δὲ ὄχλων
			ἐπαθροιζομένων
39 ὁ δὲ	2 ὁ δὲ		
ἀποκριθεὶς	ἀποκριθεὶς		
εἶπεν αὐτοῖς,	εἶπεν αὐτοῖς,	λέγει,	ἤρξατο λέγειν,
		τὶ	
		ἡ γενεὰ αὕτη	ἡ γενεὰ αὕτη
γενεὰ πονηρὰ	4 γενεὰ πονηρὰ		γενεὰ πονηρά
καὶ	καὶ		ἐστιν·
μοιχαλὶς	μοιχαλὶς		
σημεῖον ἐπιζητεῖ,	σημεῖον ἐπιζητεῖ,	ζητεῖ σημεῖον;	σημεῖον ζητεῖ,
		ἀμὴν λέγω ὑμῖν,	
καὶ σημεῖον	καὶ σημεῖον		καὶ σημεῖον
οὐ δοθήσεται	οὐ δοθήσεται	εἰ δοθήσεται	οὐ δοθήσεται
		τῇ γενεᾷ ταύτῃ	
		σημεῖον.	

Matthew: A Commentary on His Literary and Theological Art (Grand Rapids: Eerdmans, 1981), pp. 323-24.

4. *The Demand for a 'Sign'* 121

αὐτῇ
εἰ μὴ τὸ σημεῖον
Ἰωνᾶ
τοῦ προφήτου.

αὐτῇ
εἰ μὴ τὸ σημεῖον
Ἰωνᾶ.

καὶ καταλιπὼν
αὐτοὺς

ἀπῆλθεν.

13 καὶ ἀφεὶς
αὐτοὺς
πάλιν ἐμβὰς
ἀπῆλθεν
εἰς τὸ πέραν.

αὐτῇ
εἰ μὴ τὸ σημεῖον
Ἰωνᾶ.

40 ὥσπερ γὰρ ἦν Ἰωνᾶς
ἐν τῇ κοιλίᾳ τοῦ κήτους
τρεῖς ἡμέρας καὶ τρεῖς νύκτας,

οὕτως ἔσται ὁ υἱὸς
τοῦ ἀνθρώπου

ἐν τῇ καρδίᾳ τῆς γῆς
τρεῖς ἡμέρας καὶ τρεῖς νύκτας.
(cf. Mt. 12.41-42)

30 καθὼς γὰρ ἐγένετο Ἰωνᾶς

τοῖς Νινευίταις σημεῖον,
οὕτως ἔσται καὶ ὁ υἱὸς
τοῦ ἀνθρώπου
τῇ γενεᾷ ταύτῃ.

(cp. Lk. 11.31-32)

Then some of the scribes and Pharisees	And the Pharisees and Sadducees came, and to test	The Pharisees came and began to argue with	while others, to test him,
said to him, 'Teacher, we wish to see	him they asked him to show them	him,	
a "sign" from you'.	a 'sign'	seeking from him a 'sign'	sought from him a 'sign'
	from heaven.	from heaven, to test him. 12 And he sighed deeply in his spirit, and	from heaven.
		said,	28 When the crowds were increasing, he began to say,

39 But he answered them,	2 He answered them,		
		'How [Why does] this generation	'This generation is
'An evil and adulterous generation	4 'An evil and adulterous generation		an evil generation; it
seeks for a "sign";	seeks for a "sign",	seek(s) a "sign"!(?) (Truly,) I say to you,	seeks a "sign",
but no "sign" shall be given to	but no "sign" shall be given to	no "sign" shall be given to this generation.'	but no "sign" shall be given to
it except the "sign" of the prophet Jonah.	it except the "sign" of Jonah'. So he left them and		it except the "sign" of Jonah'.
	departed.	13 And he left them, and getting into the boat again he departed to the other side.	
40 For as Jonah was		30 For as Jonah became a sign to the men of Nineveh,	
three days and three nights in the belly of the whale,			
so will the Son of man be		so will the Son of man be to this generation.	
three days and three nights in the heart of the earth.' (cf. Mt. 12.41-42)		(cf. Lk. 11.31-32)	

Critical scholarship has demonstrated that the second of the two Matthean versions (Mt. 16.1-2a, 4) is both secondary to Mk 8.11-13 and to a large extent literarily dependent on it.[3] However, the same cannot be said for the bulk of Mt. 12.38-42 or Lk. 11.16, 29-32. Literary- and source-critical studies show that from a traditions history point of view, these versions of the 'sign' demand tradition, while each at certain points drawing material from Mark's version,[4] should in the main be considered as essentially independent of Mark's account[5] and, given

3.   On this, see R.A. Edwards, *The Sign of Jonah in the Theology of the Evangelists and Q* (STB, 18, Second Series; London: SCM Press, 1971), p. 81; E. Schweizer, *The Good News according to Matthew* (Atlanta: John Knox Press, 1975), p. 333; D. Hill, *The Gospel of Matthew* (London: Oliphants, 1972) pp. 256-57; A.J. Hultgren, *Jesus and his Adversaries: The Form and Function of the Conflict Stories in the Synoptic Tradition* (Minneapolis: Ausburg, 1979), pp. 46-47. In asserting the dependence of Matthew's report in Mt. 16 on Mk 8.11-13, each of authors draws attention to the facts that Mt. 16.1-2a, 4 is not only close to Mark in vocabulary but also occurs in the same order of events as does the Markan version of the 'sign' demand' tradition, i.e., as the sequel to a miraculous feeding (cp. Mt. 15.32-39 with Mk 8.1-10) and before a castigation of the disciplines by Jesus, during a boat trip, over 'forgetting' bread (cp. Mt. 16.5-12 with Mk 8.14-21).

4.   As E. Schweizer notes (*The Good News according to Matthew* [Atlanta: John Knox, 1975], p. 291), Matthew seems to have taken over his notice at 12.38 of the Pharisees as the ones demanding a 'sign' from Mk 8.11 (contrast Luke's 'certain ones/others'). And, given that the Lukan notice at Lk. 11.16 that certain people sought a 'sign' from Jesus is agreed with Mk 8.11 and against Mt. 12.38, first in reporting the demand itself in indirect and not direct speech and, secondly, in using the simple form of the verb ζητέω within this report, much of the present wording of Lk. 11.16 also seems to be derived from Mk 8.11 (as R. Edwards, *The Sign of Jonah*, pp. 74, 90, 96, and J.A. Fitzmyer, *The Gospel according to Luke X–XXIV* [Garden City: Doubleday, 1985], p. 918, have argued). One might object, as C. Rowland has done in conversation with me, that it is unlikely that Luke has taken over the substance of Lk. 11.16 from Mk 8.11. given Luke's redactional tendency to avoid conflating Mark and Q. But notably we find Luke doing just this at Lk. 4.1-2, in the opening of his largely Q-dependent version of the tradition of Jesus' Wilderness temptation, when (coincidentally?) he takes up much of his notice of Jesus being led by the Spirit to be tempted by the devil from Mk 1.13.

5.   Among the considerations which lead to this conclusion are the following. First, both Lk. 11.16, 28-30; Mt. 12.38-40 agree against Mark in the matter of the context in which the demand is made. In the Matthean and Lukan accounts the story of the demand is interwoven, not as in Mk, with a story of a miraculous feeding (cf. Mk 8.1-9) and a story of a discussion between Jesus and his disciples about bread (Mk 8.14-21), but with the Beelzebub controversy (cf. Mt. 12.22-37; Lk. 11.14-28). Secondly, Luke and Matthew agree here against Mark on the matter of the occasion of the demand—a healing of a 'dumb' man (cf. Mt. 12.21//Lk. 11.14) as opposed to Jesus' feeding of a multitude (Mk 8.1-9). Thirdly, in their respective reproductions of

their formal and material similarity with one another, should also be taken as witnesses to the existence of another non-Markan version of the tradition which undoubtedly was part of the Synoptic source Q.[6] Accepting these conclusions, the investigation of the tradition of Jesus' 'sign' demand temptation must begin, then, with the question of the relationship between the Markan and Q accounts of that tradition. Are the two 'primary' accounts in any way literarily related? Or are they independent versions of an even more primitive story? To answer these questions, we must do three things: first, determine the original extent and wording of each text; second, determine whether and in what way, if any, each of the versions of the 'sign' demand tradition is a development of a more primitive account; and third, examine the nature and extent of the formal and verbal similarities that Mk 8.11-13, and the *Vorlage* behind it, if such there is, has with the account in Q.

The Extent and Wording of the Markan Account

The Extent of the Markan Account

In Mark's Gospel Jesus' temptation in the demand for a 'sign' takes place immediately after the story of the Feeding of the Four Thousand (Mk 8.1-9) and immediately before the story of Jesus' castigation of the disciples for their 'forgetting' bread (Mk 8.14-21).[7] There is good reason to believe that the present sequential connection between the 'sign' demand story and the story of the disciples' rebuke is not traditional but due, rather, to Mark's editorial and compositional activities.[8] But Mark's

---

the dominical saying against the demand, which is central to all versions of the 'sign' demand story (cp. Mk 8.12b; Mt. 16.4; Mt. 12.39; Lk. 11.29), Matthew and Luke agree against Mark, but with one another, on the matter of the form and wording of that saying.

6.   Edwards, *Sign of Jonah*, pp. 71-74; Schweizer, *Matthew*, p. 290; I.H. Marshall, *Commentary on Luke* (Grand Rapids: Eerdmans, 1978), pp. 482-83; T.W. Manson, *The Sayings of Jesus* (London: SPCK, 1937), pp. 89-91; and especially A. Vögtle, 'Der Spruch vom Jonaszeichen', in J.A. Schmid and A. Vögtle (eds.), *Synoptische Studien: Alfred Wikenhauser zum siebzigsten Geburtstag am 22 Februar 1953 dargebracht von Freunden, Kollegen und Schulern* (Munich: Zink, 1953), pp. 248-53.

7.   On the nature of this 'forgetting' and the reason for Jesus' rebuke in Mk 8.14-21, see my discussion, 'The Rebuke of the Disciples in Mark 8.14-21', *JSNT* 27 (1986), pp. 31-47.

8.   To be noted in this regard is the fact, to be shown below (see p. 138), that the

presentation of the story of the 'sign' demand as the sequel to the story of the miraculous feeding does not seem to be something he himself devised, despite the facts that from a form-critical perspective both Mk 8.11-13 and Mk 8.1-9 are complete in themselves and that the verse which now links these units (i.e. Mk 8.10) appears to be a secondary editorial seam[9] constructed by Mark himself.[10] For as E. Schweizer has noted,[11] the same sequence of miraculous feeding + demand for a 'sign' appears in Jn 6.1-3, 30.[12] So maximally the Markan version of the 'sign'

---

verse (i.e. Mk 8.13) which now provides not only the link between the two stories, but the occasion for, and the setting of, the events narrated in Mk 8.14-21, is wholly a Markan creation. This suggests that Mark, and not the tradition, is responsible for joining the two stories together. But more importantly, as E. Best (*The Temptation and the Passion: The Markan Soteriology* [Cambridge: Cambridge University Press, 1965], pp. 73, 78; idem, *Following Jesus: Discipleship in the Gospel of Mark* [Sheffield: JSOT Press, 1981], p. 134), R. Bultmann (*The History of the Synoptic Tradition* [Oxford: Basil Blackwell, 1963], p. 330), T.A. Burkill (*New Light on the Earliest Gospel* [Ithaca: Cornell University Press, 1972], p.50), R. Pesch (*Näherwartungen: Tradition und Redaction in Mk 13* [Düsseldorf: Patmos, 1968], p. 61), K.G. Reploh (*Markus—Lehrer de Gemeinde: Ein Redaktionsgeschichliche Studie zu den Jüngerperikopen des Markus-Evangeliums* [Stuttgart: Katholisches Bibelwerke, 1969], p. 78), E. Schweizer (*The Good News according to Mark* [Atlanta: John Knox, 1974], p. 160), V. Taylor (*The Gospel according to St Mark* [London: Macmillan, 1952], p. 363), E. Trocmé, *The Formation of the Gospel according to Mark* [London: SPCK, 1975], pp. 74-75 and n. 111, p. 142), and many others have shown or noted, the pericope delimited by Mk 8.14-24, that is, the story which follows Mark's version of the 'sign' demand temptation tradition, *is itself also a Markan creation*. The only traditional element within Mk 8.14-21—around which Mark has built up the story reported there—is the traditional dominical saying now preserved in Mk 8.15.

    9.   Cf. Taylor, *Mark*, p. 362.

    10.   See K. Kertlege, *Die Wunder Jesus im Markusevangelium* (Munich: Kösel-Verlag, 1970), p. 139; F. Neirynck, *Duality in Mark: Contributions to the Study of Markan Redaction* (Leuven: Louvain University Press, 1972), pp. 79, 117; Pesch, *Näherwartungen*, p. 61; J. Sundwall, 'Die Zusammensetzung des Markusevangeliums', in *Acta Academiae Aboensis*, IX (Åbo, 1934), pp. 1-86, esp. pp. 50-51; Taylor, *Mark*, p. 360; J. Gnilka, *Das Evangelium nach Markus (Mk 1–8.26)* (Zürich: Neukirchener Verlag, 1978), p. 300. Indications of Markan redaction in Mk 8.10 is the appearance there of such favorite words as ἐμβαίνω, μαθητής and πλοῖον. Cf. E.J. Pryke, *Redactional Style in the Markan Gospel* (Cambridge: Cambridge University Press, 1978), p. 143.

    11.   *Mark*, p. 158; idem, *Matthew*, p. 290.

    12.   I hold, with Schweizer and many other scholars, that Jn 6 and the tradition

demand tradition extends from Mk 8.1 to Mk 8.13 and consists of five elements:

a. a story of a miraculous feeding (Mk 8.1-9);
b. a notice of Jesus sending away the crowds he has fed and then departing with his disciples *via* boat from the scene of the feeding (Mk 8.10);
c. a description of opponents of Jesus coming to him, arguing with him, and making a request for a 'sign' (Mk 8.11);
d. a notice of Jesus responding to the demand which depicts Jesus first venting strong emotion over being subjected to it, then remarking on how typical it is for those who have made the demand to do so, and then refusing absolutely to produce what he is asked for (Mk 8.12); and
e. a notice of Jesus' departure with his disciples, again *via* a boat, from the scene of the demand and those who have made it (Mk 8.13).

The Wording of the Markan Account
The wording of Mark's version of the 'sign' demand tradition is in little doubt, for the textual tradition of Mk 8.1-13 is fairly uniform in the major manuscripts.[13] There is, however, one variant reading of Mk 8.12—Jesus' saying against 'this generation's' seeking a 'sign'— which, if original, would stand as evidence that Mark has had a greater hand in the redaction of the passage than he has generally been thought to have had.[14] Consequently it deserves our attention.[15]

The variant reading in question is that of $\mathfrak{P}^{45}$ and W which have ἀμὴν εἰ δοθήσεται, κτλ. instead of the ἀμὴν λέγω εἰ δοθήσεται, κτλ. of B and L or the ἀμὴν λέγω ὑμῖν εἰ δοθήσεται of ℵ A D and

embodied within it is independent of that which underlies the Synoptic Gospels.

13.   Within Mk 8.1-13 significant differences are limited to the variants between the major witnesses and D 1009 it[d,q] in 8.7 (where εὐχαριστήσας appears instead of εὐλογήσας αὐτά), D, θ *f*[1.13] 565 in 8.10 (where Μαγεδά[ν] or [τὰ ὅρια] Μάγδαλα appears over against τὰ μέρη Δαλμανουθά) and $\mathfrak{P}$45 and W in 8.12, to be discussed presently.

14.   See below, pp. 151-53.

15.   The other two major variants (see above, n. 13) can each be explained as assimilations (the first to the wording of Mk 8.6, the second to Mt. 15.39). Moreover, even if original, they need not be taken into considered here. They are not part of Mark's typical redactional vocabulary and therefore are of little consequence for determining the nature and extent of Mark's redaction within Mk 8.1-13.

the majority of manuscripts. In this I contend that 𝔓⁴⁵ and W preserve the original text. For, in the first place—and as the textual tradition itself seems to indicate—it is more likely that an absolute ἀμήν introducing a saying of Jesus would be expanded to a form of the ἀμήν formula frequently employed elsewhere in the Gospels,[16] than that the longer phrase would be shortened to an absolute form. Secondly, other than bringing the shorter phrase into conformity with the longer, more familiar, and more frequently employed expression, the phrases λέγω and λέγω ὑμῖν have no apparent function within the verse. Since the negation εἰ δοθήσεται is already solemnly and conclusively reinforced by the absolute ἀμήν, the phrases in question neither accentuate nor add anything substantial to the present ἀμήν's sense, and are, therefore, quite redundant in their present context. I am confident, then, in asserting that the reading of Mk 8.12 preserved in 𝔓⁴⁵ is the original Markan text of this verse.[17]

Accordingly, my view of the original text of Mk 8.11-13 differs little from that advocated by the majority of contemporary textual critics save that, for the reasons stated above, I see v. 12 as reading καὶ ἀναστενάξας τῷ πνεύματι αὐτοῦ λέγει· τὶ ἡ γενεὰ αὕτη ζητεῖ σημεῖον; ἀμήν, εἰ δοθήσεται τῇ γενεᾷ ταύτῃ σημεῖον.

3. *The Extent and Wording of the Q Version of the 'Sign' Demand Temptation*

The Extent of the Q Version
As a comparison in any synopsis shows, the Q version of the story of the demand for a 'sign' (1) occurs within the context of the so-called Beelzebub controversy (Mt. 12.25-30//Lk. 11.17-23) and in conjunction with the parable of the return of the evil spirit (Mt. 12.43-45//Lk. 11.24-26), (2) was most likely followed closely by a series of woes against the scribes and Pharisees (Lk. 11.37-51) which climaxed in a doom oracle

16. On the 'Amen formula' in the Gospels, see J. Jeremias, *New Testament Theology* (New York: Charles Scribner & Sons, 1971), pp. 35-36.
17. Cf. P.L. Couchoud, 'Notes sur le texte de St Marc dans le codex Chester Beatty', *JTS* 35 (os 1934), p. 13. The reading of 𝔓⁴⁵ and W of Mk 8.12 is also defended as original by G.W. Buchanan ('Some Vow and Oath Formulas in the New Testament', *HTR* 58 [1965], p. 235) because the omission of λέγω ὑμῖν brings the saying of Jesus against 'signs' into conformity with oath formulas in the Old Testament and Rabbinic literature (e.g. Num. 5.19; Deut. 27.15-16).

against 'this generation', and (3) was occasioned not, as in Mk, by Jesus feeding a multitude, but by Jesus' healing one of 'the dumb' (οἱ κωφοί, Mt. 12.22-23//Lk. 11.14-15). Such a comparison also shows, moreover, that in Q Jesus' response to the demand (Mt. 12.39//Lk. 11.29) is notably more complex and lengthier than its Markan counterpart, containing both a refusal to accede to what is asked of him that is less absolute than that found in Mk 8.12b,[18] as well as a unit of material in which Jesus first makes a comparison between Jonah and the Son of Man (Mt. 12.40//Lk. 11.30) and then a declaration (formally, a perfectly balanced double saying) about the witness of the Ninevites and the Queen of the South to 'this generation' (Mt. 12.41-42//Lk. 11.31-32).

Accordingly, the Q version of the 'sign' demand tradition was broader in scope than that found in Mk and consisted of at least nine elements:

a.   a report of Jesus healing (and/or exorcising) one of 'the dumb' before a crowd of witnesses (Mt. 12.22-23a//Lk. 11.14);

b.   a notice of the witnesses' response to the healing (Mt. 12.23// Lk. 11.14), which leads to

c.   a notice of one group from among the witnesses issuing a charge of demonic collusion against Jesus (Mt. 12.24//Lk. 11.15)

d.   a story of Jesus responding to the charge with the parables of the divided household and the binding of the strong man (Mt. 12.25-26, 29//Lk. 11.17-18, 21-22) and making the claim that his activities truly embody the Reign of God (Mt. 12.27-28//Lk. 11.19-20);

e.   a dominical judgment saying (Mt. 12.30//Lk. 11.23);

f.   a notice of a second group from among the witnesses to the healing making a demand for a 'sign' (Mt. 12.38//Lk. 11.16);

g.   a reply of Jesus to the demand which is prefaced by a remark about the identity and character of those who make it (Mt. 12.39//Lk 11.29);

h.   a comparison made by Jesus between Jonah and the Son of Man (Mt. 12.40//Lk. 11.30); and

---

18.   In contrast to Mark's account, where Jesus effectively says that he will not produce a 'sign' (or, in anticipation of what will be revealed below, that he will not produce *the particular 'sign' asked for*), Q has Jesus say that one 'sign', the ' "sign" of Jonah' (τὸ σημεῖον Ἰωνᾶ), *will* be given.

i.   a double saying of Jesus about the future witness of the
     Ninevites and the Queen of the South to those who have made
     the demand (Mt. 12.41-42//Lk. 11.31-32).

The Wording of the Q Version
Since our overarching concern is to examine the nature of the relationship, if any, between the Markan and Q versions of the 'sign' demand
tradition, and since the evidence that might allow us to say something in
this regard is most likely to be found at those points in the respective
Markan and Q versions of the tradition which bear the strongest formal
or thematic resemblance to one another, I shall not here attempt to
determine the wording of all nine of the elements basic to the Q version,
but only of those in the Q story where formally and materially the
overlap with the substance of Mk 8.1-13 is most conspicuous. These are
elements (f), (g) and (h), or Mt. 12.38//Lk. 11.16, Mt. 12.39//Lk 11.29,
and Mt. 12.40//Lk. 11.30.[19]

Mt. 12.38//Lk. 11.16: The Request for a 'Sign'. The original wording
of this element of the Q story is difficult to determine. This is not only
because, as the synopsis above shows, the only thing Matthew and Luke
here have in common is the word 'sign'. It is also due to the fact that
both the respective Matthean and Lukan versions of this section are
patently editorial. As I have noted above,[20] there is reason to believe that
Luke's wording here is not traditional but has been taken over from
Mk 8.11. And in Mt. 12.38 the words 'then' (τότε) and 'we wish'
(θέλομεν), the identification of the Scribes and Pharisees as Jesus'
opponents, the phrase 'they answered...saying' (ἀπεκρίθησαν...
λέγοντες), and the vocative 'teacher' reflect Matthean style and concerns.[21] So neither Mt. 12.38 nor Lk. 11.16 can be taken as representing

19.   While elements (a), (b), (c), (d), (e) of the Q version of the 'sign' demand
tradition have obvious parallels with Mk 3.22-30, they, along with element (i), have no
apparent counterpart with any of the elements basic to Mk 8.1-13. So there is no need
to attempt to reconstruct their original wording. Moreover, the wording of these
elements is in little doubt given the general extensiveness of the verbal agreement
between their respective Matthean and Lukan representations. For a recent
reconstruction, see J.S. Kloppenborg, 'Q 11:14-26: Work Sheets for
Reconstruction', *SBLSP 1983*, pp. 133-51.
20.   See above, n. 4. See also below, pp. 144-45.
21.   Gundry, *Matthew*, p. 243; Schweizer, *Matthew*, p. 290.

the original text of the request. And yet some sort of text involving a request for a 'sign' obviously stood here. My own guess is that it was one that read something on the order of θέλομεν ἀπὸ σοῦ σημεῖον ἰδεῖν[22] and was preceded by either λέγοντες,[23] ἔλεγεν, or εἶπαν.[24] Moreover, it also identified those who requested the 'sign' as 'others of them' (ἕτεροι [τινες] ἐξ αὐτῶν), that is, one group from among at least one other distinct party present with Jesus at the time of the demand.[25] Furthermore, if it is correct to view Lk. 11.16 as essentially taken over from Mk 8.11, we can be certain that original text behind Mt. 12.38//Lk. 11.16 did not contain the phrases ἀπὸ τοῦ οὐρανοῦ or ἐκ τῶν οὐρανῶν or any form of the word πειράζω.[26]

Mt. 12.39//Lk 11.29: The Reply of Jesus to the Demand. Since, as the synopsis shows, both Matthew and Luke report that the reply of Jesus to the demand for a 'sign' is a couplet, whose first element is, according to each evangelist, an accusation against 'this generation' (cp. Mt. 12.40a, b//Lk. 11.29a, b), and whose second element is a statement of refusal to produce a 'sign' (cp. Mt. 12.40c//Lk. 11.29c), we can be sure that this also was the *form* the reply had in Q. But what was its wording? The second element of the reply most certainly read 'and a "sign" shall not be given to it except the "'sign' of Jonah"', as there is an almost exact verbal correspondence between Matthew and Luke at this point.[27] And the first element, the accusation, most certainly contained the words 'generation', 'evil', 'sign', and some form of ζητέω. The question is, however, How were these words set out? Were they

22. As argues A. Harnack, *The Sayings of Jesus* (London: Williams & Norgate, 1909), p. 23.

23. So S. Shulz, *Q—Die Spruchquelle der Evangelisten* (Zürich: Theologischer Verlag, 1972), p. 251.

24. So A. Polag, *Fragmenta Q: Textheft zur Logienquelle* (Neukirchen–Vluyn: Neukirchener Verlag, 1979), p. 52.

25. Cf. Linton, 'The Demand for a Sign from Heaven', p. 117.

26. On this, see above, n. 4 and below, pp. 144-45. See also Edwards, *Sign of Jonah*, p. 81; Fitzmyer, *Luke 10–24*, p. 918; Linton, 'The Demand for a Sign from Heaven', p. 117; B. Lindars, *Jesus Son of Man* (London: SPCK, 1983), p. 199 n. 24.

27. Vögtle, 'Jonaszeichen', pp. 116-17; Kloppenborg, *The Formation of Q*, pp. 129-30. See also D. Zeller, 'Redaktionsprozesse und weckselnder "Sitz im Leben" beim Q-Material', in J. Delobel (ed.), *Logia: Les Paroles de Jésus—The Sayings of Jesus* (Leuven: Leuven University Press, 1982), pp. 395-409, esp. 397 n. 19.

arranged as Matthew has them (i.e. in a single clause, with the word 'generation' standing without a demonstrative pronoun but modified by the adjective 'adulterous' (μοιχαλίς) as well as by 'evil' (πονηρός), and the verb ζητέω intensified to ἐπιζητεῖ with an introduction of '...and he [Jesus], answering, said')? Or were they as Luke has them (i.e. in *two* clauses, the first describing what the 'generation' referred to *is*, the second what it *does*, with 'generation' standing with a demonstrative pronoun ['this'] and modified by the adjective 'evil' but *not* the adjective 'adulterous', and the verb ζητέω left unintensified, all of which is introduced by the notice 'And as the crowds were increasing, he [Jesus] began to say')? Several things seem clear. First, the terms here common to Matthew and Luke were set out, as in Lk. 11.29b, in a double clause, since the Matthean form of the accusation can be explained by Matthew's collapsing of two traditional clauses into one in order to bring the accusation into synthetic parallelism with the statement of refusal.[28] Secondly, Matthew's 'evil and adulterous generation' is more original than Luke's 'evil generation' since Luke is more likely to have excised the epithet 'adulterous' as a metaphor unintelligible to his readers than Matthew is to have added it.[29] Thirdly, Matthew's omission of Luke's 'this generation' is redactional, since it generalizes the accusation and makes it refer not only to Jesus' contemporaries but also to unbelievers in Matthew's own time.[30] Fourthly, the uncompounded form of ζητέω seems to be original to Q since Luke is fond of compounds and surely would have used it had it been in his source.[31] Fifthly, Matthew's introduction to the couplet (Mt. 12.39a) is secondary, since 'answering, he said' (ἀποκριθεὶς εἶπεν) is typical of Matthew's style.[32]

---

28. Gundry, *Matthew*, p. 243. For a contrary opinion, see M.D. Goulder, *Luke: A New Paradigm* (2 vols.; Sheffield: JSOT Press, 1988), II, p. 511. Goulder's view, it should be noted, seems largely conditioned by his 'new paradigm' that Luke is dependent here (and for all of the material which he and Matthew have in common) upon Matthew.

29. J.M. Creed, *The Gospel according to Luke* (London: Macmillan, 1930), p. 162; T.W. Manson, *The Sayings of Jesus* (London: SCM Press, 1937), p. 89; I.H. Marshall, *Commentary on Luke* (Grand Rapids: Eerdmans, 1978), p. 484.

30. Gundry, *Matthew*, pp. 242-43.

31. On this, see A. Plummer, *St Luke* (ICC; Edinburgh: T.& T. Clark, 1896), p. lii. While admitting Luke's tendency to create compounds, Harnack, on the contrary (*Sayings*, p. 23), maintains that Luke has here replaced ἐπιζητεῖ with ζήτει on the grounds that 'He [Luke] appreciates the special meaning of the compound'.

32. Gundry, *Matthew*, p. 243.

But on the other hand Luke's introduction can not be taken as original either, since ἐπαθροίζομαι, though a *hapax*, is most probably Lukan,[33] and the whole of Lk. 11.29a is Luke's replacement for what he used in 11.16.[34] Given, however, that here Matthew and Luke both have δέ and a form of λέγω, the probability is that the basis of the introduction to the couplet was ὁ δὲ εἶπεν[35] or ὁ δὲ ἤρξατο λέγειν.[36]

Mt. 12.40//Lk. 11.30: The Comparison between Jonah and the Son of Man. Careful attention to the synopsis of this section of the Q 'sign' demand story makes clear that the material here common to both Matthew and Luke is an 'eschatological' or 'prophetic correlative',[37] the wording of which was at the very least:

> For just (even) as Jonah became (was)...
> So shall the Son of Man be...[38]

But what else did the correlative say? Did it compare Jonah in the belly of the whale with the Son of Man being in the heart of the earth as Matthew has it? This is unlikely. With this wording the correlative not only has the most tenuous of links with its context;[39] it also presents Jesus as alluding to the death and resurrection of the Son of man, something which is not otherwise done in Q.[40]

Did it, then, as Luke has it, compare Jonah as a σημεῖον for the Ninevites with Jesus as a σημεῖον for 'this generation'? This seems most likely to be the case. For apart from the fact that Luke is generally reliable in reproducing the wording of Q,[41] Lk. 11.30 does not, as Mt. 12.40 does, jar with its context. Indeed, with this wording, the

---

33. Marshall, *Luke*, p. 483.

34. Fitzmyer, *Luke 10–24*, p. 934; Manson, *Sayings*, p. 89. See also E. Klostermann, *Das Lukasevangelium* (Tübingen: Mohr [Paul Siebeck], 1975), p. 128.

35. Harnack, *Sayings*, p. 137.

36. Cf. Polag, *Fragmenta Q*, p. 52.

37. On this, see Edwards, *The Sign of Jonah*, pp. 47-58, 86; D. Schmidt, 'LXX Gattung "Prophetic Correlative"', *JBL* 96 (1977), pp. 517-22.

38. Schweizer, *Matthew*, pp. 290-91.

39. Creed, *Luke*, p. 162; A.J.B. Higgins, *Jesus and the Son of Man* (Philadelphia: Fortress Press, 1964), p. 134.

40. Higgins, *Jesus and the Son of Man*, pp. 134-35; H.E. Tödt, *The Son of Man in the Synoptic Tradition* (London: SCM Press, 1965), p. 212.

41. On this, see Harnack, *Sayings*, p. 115.

correlative is the middle term for what precedes and follows it, and provides the thematic and linguistic links for what is otherwise disparate material.[42] It seems reasonable to conclude, then, that the original text of this section of the Q story of the demand for a 'sign' ran:

> For just as Jonah was a σημεῖον to the Ninevites,
> So shall the Son of man be to this generation.[43]

Therefore, when translated, our text seems originally to have run:

> And others (certain ones) [from that group who witnessed the healing of
>   one of οἱ κωφοί]
> were saying (said),
> 'We [in contrast to the others] wish to see a 'sign' from you'.
> But he said (began to say):
> 'This generation is a wicked and adulterous generation.
> It seeks a "sign".
> And no "sign" shall be given to it
>   except the sign of [belonging or given to][44] Jonah.'
> For just as Jonah was a σημεῖον to the Ninevites,
>   So shall the Son of man be to this generation.'

A Unified Tradition?

The question of whether the Q version of the 'sign' demand tradition is unitary or composite, reflecting both a traditional and redactional layer, especially within that section in which the Q/Mk overlap is most conspicuous, is, for our purposes, hardly an idle one. It has great potential for delimiting the kinds of evidence necessary for determining whether the Markan version of the tradition stands in a relationship of literary dependence with the Q account. One would be less inclined to posit Markan dependence upon Q here if the Q story is unitary, for one could

---

42. Higgins, *Jesus and the Son of Man*, p. 134.

43. Beare, *Earliest Records*, pp. 102-103; Edwards, *The Sign of Jonah*, pp. 818-22; Fitzmyer, *Luke 10–24*, p. 931; Manson, *Sayings*, p. 89; Marshall, *Luke*, pp. 482-83; Schweizer, *Matthew*, p. 290. I leave the term σημεῖον untranslated here because, as we will see below, there is some question as to whether in this instance it is used in the same sense with which the term is employed in Mt. 12.38-39//Lk. 11.16, 28-29.

44. As J. Jeremias has noted ("Ἰωνᾶς', *TDNT*, III, p. 408), the genitive here is ambiguous and may be either appositive, subjective or objective. So, from a grammatical standpoint, there are three possible renderings of the phrase τὸ σημεῖον Ἰωνῖ: 'the "sign" which was given *in* Jonah', 'the "sign" which Jonah gave', or 'the "sign" which was *given to* Jonah', that is, 'the "sign" which Jonah himself experienced'. Thus my parenthetical addition here.

then explain any similarities in form or wording between the Markan and Q accounts by appeal to reliance by Mark and Q on a common tradition. But if the Q tradition is composite and if the elements or features that Mark and Q share in common are those which in Q are to be attributed to Q's editorial activity, then we may reasonably suspect some dependence of Mark (or the tradition behind Mk 8.1-13) on Q, for we would then have concrete evidence that Mark (or his *Vorlage*) used not the tradition that stands behind Q, but Q itself. What, then, is indicated, at least with respect to the unit of material within the Q 'sign' demand story where Q and Mk 8.1-13 overlap?[45]

As we have seen, this unit of material consists of four elements: (1) a notice of certain bystanders making a demand for a 'sign' (Mt. 12.38// Lk. 11.16); (2) a reply of Jesus, conditionally refusing the demand, which is prefaced by a remark about the identity and character of those who seek a 'sign' from him (Mt. 12.39//Lk 11.29); (3) a comparison made by Jesus between Jonah and the Son of Man (Mt. 12.40//Lk. 11.30); and (4) a perfectly balanced double saying of Jesus about the future witness of the Ninevites and the Queen of the South to those who have made the demand (Mt. 12.41-42//Lk. 11.31-32). There is good reason to suspect that the double saying is secondary to its present context. In the first place, as B. Lindars has observed,[46] the very symmetry of the saying suggests it was originally a complete unit in itself. In the second place, thematically Mt. 12.41-42//Lk. 11.31-32 is inconsistent with the material which presently precedes it. In the double saying Jonah is presented as inferior to what Jesus proclaims is now being manifested to 'this generation', but in Mt. 12.40//Lk. 11.30, Jesus' comparison between Jonah and the Son of Man, Jonah is given a status equal to what Jesus proclaims 'this generation' shall have manifested to it through the Son of Man. Moreover, since the focus in the comparison and in the refusal saying is on the figure of Jonah (and his counterpart, the Son of Man), the reference to the Queen of the South and Solomon that appears in the double saying seems in its present context to be, as C.M. Tuckett has put it, 'rather otiose'.[47]

45. For a review and discussion of the question of the tradition history of Mt. 12.22-36//Lk. 11.14-28, see Kloppenborg, *The Formation of Q*, pp. 121-27.

46. B. Lindars, *Jesus Son of Man* (Grand Rapids: Eerdmans, 1983), p. 42.

47. C.M. Tuckett, 'Mark and Q', in C. Focant (ed.), *The Synoptic Gospels: Source Criticism and the New Literary Criticism* (BETL, 110; Leuven: Leuven University Press, 1993), pp. 149-75, esp. p. 159.

There is also strong evidence that the comparison, too, is secondary to the core tradition original to the Q 'sign' demand story. As we have noted, the comparison is cast in the form of an 'eschatological' or 'prophetic' correlative. Thus it is of a 'type' that could exist and be passed on in the tradition independent of its present context. When this is brought into conjunction with the facts that Mt. 12.38-39//Lk. 11.16, 28-29 is, from a form-critical perspective, also complete in and of itself,[48] and that the present juxtapositioning of the two originally independent units of tradition[49] is easily explained on the basis of their terminological similarity (Jonah, σημεῖον), then we are justified in concluding that Mt. 12.40//Lk. 11.30 is a comment secondarily appended to Mt. 12.39// Lk. 11.29.

But is there any evidence that the joining of these traditions is traceable to Q redactional activity? In answering this, it is important to take account of two facts: (1) that a polemic against 'this generation' is a dominant motif of the present form of Q, and (2) that this motif is worked out in terms of ideas drawn from Wisdom and the Deuteronomic theme of the rejection and violence that Israel's prophets suffer from their compatriots.[50] Accordingly, the juxtaposition in Q of elements associated with this motif, but which emphasize different aspects of it, is more than likely due to the work of the Q editor(s) and a strong indication of Q redaction.

Now, as even a cursory glance shows, a theme common to all three of the elements constituent to the section of the Q story here under consideration is a castigation or belittling of 'this generation'. But why 'this generation' is the object of castigation *varies from element to element*. In Mt. 12.39//Lk. 11.29 it is (as we will see below) because its members demand a particular proof of God's presence in Jesus. In Mt. 12.40// Lk. 11.30 it is because 'this generation' now is as the Ninevites were when Jonah first confronted them. And in Mt. 12.41-42//Lk. 11.31-32 it is castigated because of its refusal to respond to the great events of the

---

48. It is, to use V. Taylor's categorizations of the material in the Synoptic Tradition (cf. *The Formation of the Gospel Tradition* [London: Macmillan, 1949], a pronouncement story. And, ending as these stories should do, i.e. in a dominical saying towards which the saying's introductory material (here Mt. 12.38//Lk. 11.28) leads, it therefore needs no additional material following it.

49. I assume here that Mt. 12.40//Lk. 11.30 is traditional. This assumption, though widely accepted, has not met with universal assent.

50. Tuckett, *Mark and Q*, p. 157.

present. So we find, within Mt. 12.38-42//Lk. 11.16, 29-32, in the appearance in each of its constituent elements of an expression of a negative attitude toward 'this generation', just the kind of evidence that indicates the editorial hand of the Q editor(s) at work. In light of this, it seems clear that the joining of Mt. 12.39//Lk. 11.29, Mt. 12.40// Lk. 11.30, and Mt. 12.41-42//Lk. 11.31-32 has occurred, not in a pre-Q stage of the tradition, but under the auspices of the editor(s) of Q.[51]

The Tradition History of Mark 8.1-13

Preliminary Remarks

That Mark's version of the tradition of Jesus' 'sign' demand temptation, maximally construed, is based on a more primitive account of that tradition seems impossible to doubt.[52] The fact that the story appears not only in Q but also in John is testimony to the tradition's pre-Markan nature.[53] Moreover, if we assume that Mark has located the incidents narrated within his version of the tradition in the Decapolis, thereby associating them with the theme of the extension of God's mercies to the Gentiles,[54] there are elements within Mk 8.1-13, such as Mk 8.2, and the reference to the disciples, which, as Taylor has observed, are not necessary to Mark's purpose.[55] This, too, would seem to indicate that Mark is reproducing, and with some fidelity, existing tradition. But that Mark has reproduced the tradition exactly in the form and wording in which it appeared in his *Vorlage* seems equally dubious. Traces of his

51.   There is some disagreement among scholars who see Q redaction evident in Mt. 12.39-42//Lk. 11.16, 29-32 over the order in which the material comprising Mt. 12.40//Lk. 11.30 and Mt. 12.41-42//Lk. 11.31-32 was joined to Mt. 12.38-39// Lk. 11.16, 28-29. This issue, however, need not be discussed here, for our purpose has been simply to determine whether or not the passage has been edited by Q, a position that those who engage in the 'order' debate presuppose.

52.   *Contra* W. Schmithals, *Das Evangelium nach Markus: Kapitel 1–9,1* (Gütersloh: Mohn/Würzburg: Echter Verlag, 1979), pp. 366-68. Schmithals argues that all of Mk 8.1-10 is a Markan construction while Mk 8.11-13 is derived from Q.

53.   I am, of course, assuming not only that Jn and the traditions incorporated within it are independent of the Synoptics, but that Q is earlier than the Gospel of Mark. It is also worth noting that besides appearing in Q and apparently standing behind Jn 6, the tradition incorporated in Mk 8.1-13 may be alluded to in 1 Cor. 1.22.

54.   For a defense of this assumption, see Guelich, *Mark 1–8:26*, pp. 402-403.

55.   Taylor, *Mark*, p. 357.

hand are readily apparent not only, as we have noted,[56] at Mk 8.10, but, as many commentators have remarked, at Mk 8.1,[57] and, as we will see below, at Mk 8.13. To determine what this pre-Markan tradition looked like, and to secure the data necessary for establishing the nature of the relationship between Mk 8.1-13 and the Q version of the 'sign' demand tradition, we must attempt to outline the nature and extent of Mark's editorial contribution to the material now found between Mk 8.1 and 8.13. In other words, we must separate tradition from redaction within these verses. To do this I will follow the same methodology I used for distinguishing the traditional from the redactional in Mk 1.9-13, asking of each of the current passage's constituent verses whether its vocabulary is Markan, whether it is written in Markan style, and whether it contains or displays a Markan theme.[58] I will then check the results of my analysis, whatever they may be in each instance, by setting them against what form-critical investigation of these verses says with respect to their traditional nature.

I shall limit the scope of this investigation to Mk 8.11-13, for two reasons. In the first place, as virtually all others who have already subjected Mk 8.1-13 to the 'tests' outlined above have concluded, from Mk 8.2 to Mk 8.9 Markan intervention seems severely limited. Evidence of his redactional can be found only—and then not with a high degree of certainty—at Mk 8.7.[59] In the second place, it is at Mk 8.11-13, and not at all within Mk 8.1-10, where Mark's version of the tradition of Jesus 'sign' demand temptation is formally and materially closest to its counterpart in Q. Though both versions of the tradition have a miracle precede, and stand as the occasion for, the 'sign' demand, the miracles themselves—a feeding in Mk, an exorcism in Q—are quite different and bear no resemblance to one another. If we are to find clues for determining the nature and extent of the relationship between the tradition

56. See above, p. 125.

57. Among these are Taylor (*Mark*, p. 357), Guelich (*Mark 1–8:26*), p. 403, and J. Gnilka (*Das Evangelium nach Markus* [2 vols.; Zürich: Neukirchener Verlag, 1978], I, p. 315).

58. On this methodology as the proper 'tool' for ascertaining both whether a given verse in Mark's Gospel is Markan as well as the extent to which a verse in Mark possess Markan or pre-Markan material, I refer again to the article by R.H. Stein, 'The "Redactionsgeschichtlich" Investigation of a Marcan Seam (Mc 1:21f.)', *ZNW* 61 (1970), pp. 70-83.

59. Cf. D. Lührmann, *Das Markusevangelium* (HNT, 3; Tübingen: Mohr, 1987), p. 134; R.M. Fowler, Loaves and Fishes (Chico, CA: Scholars Press, 1981), pp. 53-54.

behind Mk 8.1-13 and the Q version of the 'sign' demand story, it is here, at Mk 8.11-13 and not within Mk 8.1-10, that we will find them.

I shall examine first Mk 8.13, Mark's conclusion to his version of the 'sign' demand story, then Mk 8.11-12a, the Markan counterpart to element (g) in the Q version of the story, and then I shall attend to the dominical saying in v. 12b-c, a saying which now stands at the heart of both Mark's and Q's version of the tradition.

Tradition and Redaction in Mark 8.13

καὶ ἀφεὶς αὐτοὺς πάλιν ἐμβὰς ἀπῆλθεν εἰς τὸ πέραν.

Among the three verses comprising Mk 8.11-13, this verse, Mk 8.13, has the lowest claim for being regarded as traditional: from beginning to end it gives every indication of being both secondary and Markan. It is loaded with characteristic Markan words or phrases (πάλιν, ἐμβὰς, εἰς τὸ πέραν).[60] In its employment of a double participle (ἀφεὶς...ἐμβάς) it is consistent with a noted Markan stylistic trait.[61] And its description of Jesus' abrupt departure to 'the other side' (i.e. to the eastern shore of the sea of Galilee)[62] is consistent with the Markan editorial interest in depicting Jesus in his pre-Jerusalem ministry as frequently departing to various places in, around, or near Galilee.[63] Furthermore, Mk 8.13 serves to frame the 'sign' demand incident by repeating the motif in which the verse beginning the incident is set—a device which Mark frequently employs in concluding pericopes.[64] Given all of this, I feel safe in concluding that Mk 8.13 is not only wholly redactional, but composed by Mark himself.[65]

---

60.   On the use of these words as part of Mark's redactional vocabulary, see J.C. Hawkins, *Horae Synopticae: Contributions to the Synoptic Problem* (Oxford: Oxford University Press, 1899), pp. 10-15; R. Morganthaler, *Statistik des neutestamentlichen Wortschatzes* (Zürich: Gotthelf-Verlag, 1958), pp. 181-85; L. Gaston, *Horae Synopticae Electronicae: Word Statistics of the Synoptic Gospels* (Missoula: Scholars Press, 1973), *passim*; Pryke, *Redactional Style*, pp. 136-38.

61.   On the use of two or more participles before or after the main verb of a sentence as a characteristic of Markan redactional style, see Pryke, *Redactional Style*, pp. 119-26; Neirynck, *Duality*, p. 82.

62.   Cf. Taylor, *Mark*, p. 361.

63.   See E. Trocmé, *The Formation of the Gospel of Mark* (Philadelphia: Westminster Press, 1975), p. 79 n. 2.

64.   On the frequency of Mark's employment of this 'framing' technique, see Neirynck, *Duality*, p. 97.

65.   On this, see also E. Mally, 'The Gospel according to Mark', in R.E. Brown,

Tradition and Redaction in Mark 8.11-12a

καὶ ἐξῆλθον οἱ Φαρισαῖοι καὶ ἤρξαντο συζητεῖν αὐτῷ, ζητοῦντες
παρ' αὐτοῦ σημεῖον ἀπὸ τοῦ οὐρανοῦ, πειράζοντες αὐτόν. καὶ
ἀναστενάξας τῷ πνεύματι αὐτοῦ...

Could what I have just said regarding the redactional nature of Mk 8.13
also be said of Mk 8.11-12a? Certain form-critical considerations constitute a *prima facie* case that the answer is no. It has been observed that
the saying which Mk 8.11-12a now introduces (i.e. Mk 8.12b, c) is formally analogous with the Greek *Chreiai*,[66] that is, pithy sayings that
always carried with them some introductory material which gave 'data
as to the situation' in which the sayings were spoken.[67] If so, and,
notably, if Mk 8.12b, c is in its present form authentic, that is, not composed by Mark but a faithful reproduction of a dominical saying,
Mk 8.12b, c is something which would never be handed on in the tradition without some attendant information attached to it indicating the
circumstances in which it was spoken. Accordingly, on form-critical
grounds, we should expect that Mk 8.12b, c would be preceded by and
transmitted with some material introducing and 'framing' it. Why not
the material which in Mk 8.1-13 presently performs these functions?
After all, Mk 8.11-12a not only does what it is supposed to do and
supplies the requisite 'data as to the situation' of Mk 8.12b, c, but seems
also to be *so* adequate to its task that it should be accepted as the
saying's original introductory material, material which Mark has simply
taken up from the tradition and reproduced more or less exactly as it
came to him.[68]

Now the truth of this form-critical argument for the traditional nature
of Mk 8.11-12a depends very heavily upon the accuracy of the observations concerning both the traditional nature of the saying which these
verses presently introduce as well as the saying's literary form. If the
form of the saying in Mk 8.12b, c is not that of a *Chreia*, then a major
link in the chain of argumentation necessary for establishing Mk 8.11-12

J.A. Fitzmyer and R.O. Murphy (eds.), *Jerome Biblical Commentary* (Englewood
Cliffs: Prentice–Hall, 1968), II, p. 39, in addition to the authors cited above in nn. 60,
61, 62, 63.

66. Cf. M. Dibelius, *From Tradition to Gospel* (New York: Charles Scribner &
Sons, 1933), p. 159.

67. On the form of the *Chreia*, see now J.R. Butts, 'The Chreia in the Synoptic
Gospels', *BTB* 16 (1986), pp. 132-38, esp. pp. 132-33.

68. So Dibelius, *From Tradition to Gospel*, p. 160.

as traditional is broken. And if the saying is not traditional but Markan, then whether or not the form of the saying is that of a *Chreia* matters little as far as the traditional nature of the saying's introductory verses goes, for all one could say then is that Mark has composed true to form. So how accurate are they? There is some reason to think, as I will attempt to demonstrate below, that the supposedly dominical saying at Mk 8.12b, c is actually a redactional product, or at least has been subjected to a certain amount of editorial activity.[69] And even if the saying as it appears now in Mark's Gospel is entirely traditional, it is by no means certain that formally it is of the sort which could not have been handed on in the tradition unless some 'framing', introductory material accompanied it.[70] So the observations may not be accurate, and the case built up from them may not be tenable.

But let us assume for the sake of argument that Mk 8.12b, c *is* traditional and possesses the form of a *Chreia*, that from the beginning of its transmission the saying possessed an introduction, and that it came to Mark in this extended form. Are we bound, then, to say that the particular narrative frame with which the saying is now introduced in Mark's Gospel is its original and traditional introduction? One need only ask the question to see that the answer is no. It is perfectly conceivable that only part of what appears now in Mk 8.12b, c comes from the tradition. Mark could have 'quarried' the traditional introduction, selecting from it only those of its constituent elements which he found useful for his purposes, and combined them with data of his own composition to create an introduction which was a mixture of traditional and redactional material.[71] It is also perfectly conceivable, even on the assumed reconstruction of the tradition history of the passage, that *nothing* of the saying's traditional introduction survives in the material which in Mark's Gospel currently stands before it. Mark could have entirely dispensed with the traditional introduction in favour of something which, in the light of the general context in which he placed the 'sign' demand episode, he felt was more appropriate. It seems necessary, then, if we are to determine whether or not Mk 8.11-12a is in any degree redactional, to subject these verses to the stylistic, linguistic and literary or thematic

69.   See below, 145-54.

70.   Dibelius's claim in this regard is by no means certain. He produces no evidence in support of it.

71.   R. Bultmann, *The History of the Synoptic Tradition* (Oxford: Basil Blackwell, 1963), p. 331.

tests which I applied to Mk 8.13. When this is done, the following three things stand out:

First, many of the words used in Mk 8.11-12a are typical of the Markan redactional vocabulary.[72] συζητέω is employed six times by Mark, notably always in redactional seams.[73] ζητέω appears ten times in Mark's Gospel[74] and its use is part of the evangelist's purpose.[75] ἔρχομαι is one of Mark's favourite words,[76] as is Φαρισαῖοι.[77] σημεῖον should probably be considered Markan at least in the sense that its appearance here is more than likely due to Mark having taken it up from the dominical saying in Mk 8.12b, c.[78] The possibility that πειράζαντες (αὐτόν) and ἀπὸ τοῦ οὐρανοῦ are also Markan will be considered below.

Secondly, Mk 8.11-12a is replete with characteristically Markan stylistic features. We find in these verses such typically Markan stylistic peculiarities as the use of cognate verbs within the span of two phrases (συζητεῖν...ζητοῦντες),[79] the use of ἔρχομαι,[80] and the use of ἄρχω as an auxiliary verb (καὶ ἤρξαντο συζητεῖν αὐτῷ), the blending of narrative and discourse into a formal and verbal correspondence,[81] and the stating of the realization (or in this case, the rejection) of a request in terms of the request's wording.[82] These traits, it should be noted, are not limited to only one portion of Mk 8.11-12a. They appear throughout its several parts.

---

72. Cf. Pryke, *Redactional Style*, p. 143.

73. Mk 1.27; 9.10, 14, 16; 12.28.

74. Mk 1.37; 3.32; (8.11, 12); 11.18; 12.12; 14.1, 11, 55; 16.6.

75. On this, see R.P. Martin, *Mark: Evangelist and Theologian* (Exeter: Paternoster, 1972), p. 168.

76. It occurs outside of Mk 8.11 some 83 times in Mark's Gospel. On ἔρχεσθαι as part of Mark's redactional vocabulary, see Pryke, *Redactional Style*, p. 143.

77. Pryke, *Redactional Style*, p. 138.

78. Cf. O. Linton, 'The Demand for a Sign from Heaven', p. 116.

79. On this aspect of 'duality' as a characteristic of Mark's style, see Neirynck, *Duality*, p. 77.

80. On the use of ἔρχομαι as a typical feature in Mark's compositional technique, see C.H. Turner, 'Marcan Usage: Notes Critical and Exegetical on the Second Gospel', *JTS* 28 (OS 1926), pp. 325ff.; Taylor, *Mark*, p. 48, Pryke, *Redactional Style*, pp. 79-87.

81. For this stylistic feature as typical of Mark, see Neirynck, *Duality*, pp. 115-19.

82. On this as a Markan editorial technique, see Neirynck, *Duality*, p. 121.

Third, the basic themes of Mk 8.11-12a—a journey of Jewish religious authorities to Jesus for the express purpose of disputing with him, a conflict between Jesus and the Pharisees, and Jesus as one who reacts to conflict with strong emotion—are all typically Markan.[83]

Accordingly, given all of this, and, of course, assuming the adequacy and appropriateness of these linguistic, stylistic and literary or thematic tests for determining when and where Mark has exercised his editorial hand, I feel safe in concluding not only that little if any of Mk 8.11-12a is traditional, but also that most, if not all, of Mk 8.11-12a is a Markan construction.

Several other things point towards this same conclusion. There is, first of all, the fact that there is a discrepancy between the information which Mk 8.11 gives concerning the identity of those who demand a 'sign' from Jesus and that which Mk 8.12b, c gives in this regard. Mk 8.12b, c—the dominical saying against the seeking of 'signs'—identifies not Pharisees, as does Mk 8.11, but 'this generation' as Jesus' addressees. This inconsistency is difficult to explain if we assume that the present Markan introduction to the dominical saying is traditional and an original part of the 'sign' demand temptation episode. A more comprehensive and less specific identification of those seeking the 'sign' would seem to be more appropriate.[84] However, the appearance in a Markan story of such an inconsistency becomes readily intelligible when we recall the fact, mentioned above, that it is one of Mark's tendencies to cast the Pharisees in the role of Jesus' opponents, especially during Jesus' pre-Jerusalem ministry,[85] and to do so not only where traditional material leaves opponents unidentified[86] but where there is no tradition that a saying of Jesus was occasioned by a confrontation with opponents. The fact that there is an inconsistency between what the various segments of Mk 8.11-13 have to say concerning the identity of those who demand a 'sign' from Jesus would seem, then, to support my contention that within the Markan 'sign' demand temptation episode, Mark's editorial hand is apparent.

---

83.   On the first of these three themes as typically Markan, see Bultmann, *History*, p. 52. On the second, see J.C. Weber, Jr, 'Jesus' Opponents in the Gospel of Mark', *JBR* 34 (1966), pp. 214-22. On the third, see Taylor, *Mark*, p. 222; Linton, 'The Demand for a Sign', p. 116.

84.   Bultmann, *History*, p. 51.

85.   See Weber, 'Jesus' Opponents', p. 214-22.

86.   Bultmann, *History*, p. 51.

Secondly, there is the fact that the description in Mk 8.11a of the Pharisees as 'coming out' to Jesus seems to be dictated more by an editorial need to relate the 'sign' demand temptation episode consistently with, and have it flow smoothly from, its general context rather than by anything which, given the 'principles' of form-criticism, is demanded by the dominical saying, even granting that formally it requires the provision of some 'data as to its situation'. In the verse immediately preceding the description of the Pharisees' action, Mark has located Jesus in a territory which is not the Pharisees' home ground (cf. Mk 8.10).[87] Accordingly, if the Pharisees are to engage Jesus in the demand for a 'sign', and if their appearance on the scene for this purpose in non-Jewish territory is not to create a difficulty in the mind of the reader, they must, by sheer editorial necessity, be brought out to Jesus.[88] And with this observation we find again that Mk 8.11-12a, or at least this portion of it, cannot be regarded as traditional. Now when this observation is combined with the fact, noted above,[89] that (ἐξ)έρχομαι is one of Mark's favourite words, then the Markan redactional character of the description of the Pharisees' action in moving towards Jesus is made certain.

Thirdly, there is the fact that on form-critical grounds the description in Mk 8.12a of Jesus 'sighing (or 'groaning') deeply' in his spirit (καὶ ἀναστενάξας τῷ πνεύματι αὐτοῦ) does not seem to be a necessary or integral part of the introduction to the dominical saying in Mk 8.12b, c. If it is removed from Mk 8.11-12, there still seem to be more than enough data remaining there so as properly to outline the situation in which the saying is spoken. Formally, the information which the description provides is gratuitous to its setting. *Thematically*, however, the description is wholly consistent with Mark's peculiar habit of drawing attention to, and emphasizing the emotions of Jesus.[90] We can be certain, then, that Mk 8.12a is Markan.

Given all of this, it seems clear that Mark was entirely responsible for constructing the verses which now at Mk 8.11-13 provide the 'data as

---

87. Cf. Edwards, *The Sign of Jonah*, p. 76. It is interesting to see the lengths to which H.B. Swete goes (*The Gospel according to St Mark* [London: MacMillan, 1905], p. 167) in order to maintain the essential historicity of the description in Mk 8.11.

88. Bultmann, *History*, p. 51; Edwards, *Sign of Jonah*, p. 76.

89. Cf. p. 141.

90. Linton, 'The Demand for a Sign', p. 116; cf. Mk 1.41, 43; 3.5; 7.34; 9.1.

to the situation' of the dominical saying preserved there. But before we can say this with absolute certainty, we must account for the appearance there of the phrases 'tempting him' (πειράζοντες αὐτόν) and 'from heaven' (ἀπὸ τοῦ οὐρανοῦ). Could these phrases be elements left over from an original, traditional introduction to the 'sign' refusal saying (again, assuming that before Mark there *was* such an introduction) which, when Mark discarded its other elements, were retained and preserved by him and used in his composition of the setting of the saying? Here our linguistic, stylistic and literary tests do not provide sufficient evidence to make a decision one way or the other. Yet evidence arising out of a comparison of Mk 8.11-13 with the other Synoptic versions of the tradition of Jesus' refusal to accede to the demand for a 'sign' tells against this, and indicates that the phrases 'tempting him' and 'from heaven' stem from Mark's hand. Let us see how this is so.

As we have seen, the tradition of the demand for a 'sign', minimally construed, occurs four times within the Synoptic tradition, at Mk 8.11-13; Mt. 12.38-42; Mt. 16.1-2a, 4; and Lk. 11.16, 28-32. And as we have noted, the bulk of the material in Lk. 11.28-32 and Mt. 12.38-42 is from a Synoptic source independent of Mk, undoubtedly Q,[91] while much of Mt. 16:1-2a, 4 as well as the Lukan notice at Lk. 11.16 derives from the Markan version of the tradition. So ultimately, with respect to their tradition history, the Synoptic versions of the tradition of the demand for a 'sign' fall into one or the other of two camps—those which are basically derived from Mark and those which are basically derived from Q.

Now it should be noted that within Mt. 12.38-42 and Lk. 11.28-32, whose material is not derived from the Markan version of the 'sign' demand tradition, but from Q, *no traces of the phrases 'tempting him' and 'from heaven' can be found*. They are absent both from the versions of the dominical saying against 'this generation's' penchant for seeking 'signs' to be found in these accounts (cf. Mt. 12.39, cf. 16.4; Lk. 11.30) as well as from the material which in each of these accounts gives the saying its setting (cf. Mt. 12.38; Lk. 11.29). Where they *do* appear, however, is within Mark's version of this tradition, more specifically in Mk 8.11, and in the material concerning Jesus and 'signs' which Matthew and Luke have taken over from Mark.

Since, then, the phrases 'tempting him' and 'from heaven' occur

---

91. Edwards, *Sign of Jonah*, pp. 71-74; Schweizer, *Matthew* (London: SCM Press, 1976), p. 290; Marshall, *Luke*, pp. 482-83; Manson, *Sayings*, pp. 89-91; and especially Vögtle, 'Jonaszeichen', pp. 248-53.

neither (a) within any of the Synoptic Tradition's versions of the dominical saying against 'this generation's' seeking a 'sign', nor (b) in any other part of the material comprising the versions of the tradition of Jesus' refusal to produce a 'sign' which are derived from a source other than Mark, nor (c) even in the redactional additions which Matthew and Luke have attached to this material,[92] but *only* in Mark's introduction to his version of the dominical saying and in the Matthean and Lukan material dependent upon and derived from it, surely *we must conclude that these phrases were brought into the tradition by Mark himself.*[93]

Thus with respect to what I have identified as elements (c) and (e) (i.e. Mk 8.11-12a and Mk 8.13) in the Markan version of the tradition of the demand for a 'sign', the extent of Mark's editorial contribution is quite large. Element (e), a notice of Jesus' departure with his disciples, again *via* a boat, from the scene of the demand and those who have made it, has been composed *de novo* by Mark; and element (c), Mark's descriptions of opponents of Jesus coming to him, beginning to argue with him, and making a request for a 'sign', though probably grounded in pre-Markan material, seem to have been so thoroughly worked over by him and recast according to his own concerns that little if anything of the material upon which it is based can be discerned.[94]

Tradition and Redaction in Mark 8.12b, c

The dominical saying which stands at the center of Mark's version of the story of Jesus' 'Sign' Demand temptation is not only generally regarded as traditional, but as unmodified by Mark.[95] But to determine the exact extent of Mark's editorial contribution to his 'sign' demand temptation account, we need to examine whether or not this is actually the case. Can Markan redactional activity be detected in Mk 8.12b, c? Using the same stylistic, literary and linguistic tests with which I distinguished tradition from redaction in the other elements of Mk 8.11-13, the answer would seem to be no. With the possible exception of the verb ζητέω this section of Mk 8.12 does not contain vocabulary which is

---

92. Mt. 12.40; Lk. 11.30.

93. See Linton, 'The Demand for a Sign', p. 116-18; Edwards, *Sign of Jonah*, p. 76.

94. Gnilka, *Markus*, pp. 305-306; Pesch, *Das Marcus Evangelium* I, pp. 405-10; Taylor, *Mark*, p. 361. See also Pryke, *Redactional Style*, pp. 143, 162.

95. Cf. Taylor, *Mark*, p. 361.

distinctly Markan,[96] nor does this section of text display a distinctly Markan theme. The rhetorical question (τί ἡ γενεὰ αὕτη ζητεῖ σημεῖον;) of v. 12b might be attributed to Mark's hand in that the use of rhetorical questions is a distinctive aspect of Mark's style and one of his favourite literary devices.[97] But rhetorical questions have also been taken over by Mark from the tradition (cf. Mk 2.7; 5.39; 9.19; 14.63).[98] And so it need not signal Markan redaction. Accordingly, Mk 8.12b, c would seem to be a piece of traditional material taken up by Mark and employed in the form in which it came to him.

It must be kept in mind, however, that the redactional techniques which Mark employs when editing and transmitting the sayings of Jesus are different from those which he uses when dealing with the narrative tradition or when he is composing freely.[99] There is still a question, then, as to whether, despite the absence in Mk 8.12b, c of the clues usually indicating Markan redaction, one can confidently assume that Mark had no hand in the manner in which the saying of Jesus presented there is now reproduced.[100] Let us consider what can be gleaned in this regard by the evidence that arises when the form and wording of the Markan version of Jesus' 'sign' refusal saying is compared with that of the other versions of that saying found at Mt. 12.39, 16.4 and Lk. 11.29.

When the respective versions of the saying are compared with one another, it is immediately apparent that Matthew reproduces the saying twice in virtually the same form,[101] that Luke has a form of the saying which is in essence identical with that found in Matthew,[102] and that

96. But see my remarks on 'amen (ἀμήν)' below, pp. 151-52.

97. See M. Zerwick, *Untersuchungen zum Markus-Stil: Ein Beitrag zur Durcharbeitung des Neuen Testaments* (Rome: Pontifical Biblical Institute, 1937), pp. 24-25.

98. Pryke, *Redactional Style*, p. 73.

99. See E. Best, 'Mark's Preservation of the Tradition', in M. Sabbe (ed.), *L'Evangile selon Marc: Tradition et Redaction* (Gembloux: Leuven University Press, 1974), pp. 21-34.

100. That Mark does not always reflect the pristine form of traditional dominical sayings is noted by, among others, N. Perrin, *Rediscovering the Teaching of Jesus* (New York: Charles Scribner & Sons, 1967), p. 187 and *passim*.

101. With the already noted exception that in Mt. 12.39 Matthew adds the phrase τοῦ προφήτου το τὸ σημεῖον Ἰωνᾶ.

102. On the differences in wording and word order between the Matthean and Lukan versions of the saying, see above, pp. 130-31. See also Hultgren, *Jesus and his Adversaries*, p. 61 n. 27; Perrin, *Rediscovering*, p. 172.

Mark records a version of the saying which is all his own.[103] Thus in the Synoptic tradition there are two principal versions of the dominical saying against producing 'signs', the first version being the one found in Matthew and Luke, and the second being the one found in Mark. The first version, which we have seen was derived from Q,[104] probably originally read ἡ γενεὰ αὕτη γενεὰ πονηρὰ καὶ μοιχαλίς ἐστιν· σημεῖον ζητεῖ, καὶ σημεῖον οὐ δοθήσεται αὐτῇ εἰ μὴ τὸ σημεῖον Ἰωνᾶ.[105] The second version read τί ἡ γενεὰ αὕτη ζητεῖ σημεῖον; ἀμήν, εἰ δοθήσεται τῇ γενεᾷ ταύτῃ σημεῖον.[106]

It seems clear that the two versions of the saying are variants of one basic, more original saying.[107] *But which of these two variants best represents the tradition basic and common to them both?* Many scholars have concluded that it is the Markan version.[108] The evidence upon which this conclusion invariably is based is that the Markan version displays a notable Semitism. The phrase εἰ δοθήσεται in Mk 8.12c is a literal rendering of a typical Hebrew oath formula of adjuration which was in use in Palestine in Jesus' day as a recognized way of saying 'no' forcefully.[109] Accordingly, on the grounds that sayings which display

103. Hultgren, *Jesus and his Adversaries*, p. 61 n. 27; Perrin, *Rediscovering*, p. 172.

104. Cf. above, pp. 123-24, and Linton, 'The Demand for a Sign', p. 119.

105. For a slightly different reconstruction of the original form of the Q 'sign' refusal saying, see Edwards, *Sign of Jonah*, p. 73.

106. See above, pp. 126-27, for the text critical problems of Mk 8.12b, c.

107. Perrin, *Rediscovering*, p. 172; Martin, *Mark: Evangelist and Theologian*, p. 165; Vögtle, 'Jonaszeichen', pp. 230-35. For the contrary opinion that the two versions are actually independent of one another and reflect words of Jesus spoken on two separate occasions, see J. Howton, 'The Sign of Jonah', *SJT* 15 (1962), pp. 288-89.

108. See, for instance, Edwards, *Sign of Jonah*, pp. 75-77: Taylor, *Mark*, p. 363; Martin, *Mark: Evangelist and Theologian*, pp. 165-66; F.W. Beare, *The Earliest Records of Jesus* (New York: Abingdon, 1962), p. 103; H. Anderson, *The Gospel of Mark* (London: Oliphants, 1975), p. 198; E. Lohmeyer, *Das Evangelium des Markus* (Gottingen: Vandenhoeck & Ruprecht, 1963), p. 156 n. 4; J. Wellhausen, *Das Evangelium Matthai* (Berlin: Druck & Verlag von George Reimer, 1914), p. 62.

109. Cf. Taylor, *Mark*, pp. 362-63; Edwards, *Sign of Jonah*, p. 75. On the import of the oath and the Semitic formula which underlies the text of Mk 8.12c, see *GKC*, pp. 471-72; P. Joüon, *Grammaire de l'Hebreu biblique* (Paris: Pontifical Biblical Institute, 1923), p. 505; and Buchanan, 'Some Vow and Oath Formulas', pp. 324-26. It has been argued by M. Black (*An Aramaic Approach to the Gospels and Acts* [Oxford: Oxford University Press, 3rd edn, 1967], p. 123) that a Semitism lies behind

Semitisms are older—or have a *prima facie* claim to be regarded as closer to the *ipsissima verba* of Jesus—than similar but less Semitized parallels, Mk 8.12c has been viewed as primitive and more traditionally original.[110]

There are, however, two considerations which suggest that this may be a hasty conclusion. The first consideration is the fact that the Q variant of the saying also contains a Semitism. Behind the conjunction of the variant's statement of refusal (καὶ σημεῖον οὐ δοθήσεται) with its 'exceptive clause' (εἰ μὴ τὸ σημεῖον 'Ιωνᾶ) stands a regular Aramaic idiom, the idiom of *relative negation*,[111] in which the exception is, in fact, an affirmation.[112] On the grounds of Semitisms, then, the assertion of the relative originality of the Markan version of the saying of Jesus against producing a 'sign' cannot be made with certainty.

The second consideration is that while εἰ δοθήσεται in Mk 8.12c is a literal translation of a Semitism, the phrase translated is not an Aramaism but a *biblicism*.[113] It represents a formula which anyone

Mk 8.12b (τί ἡ γενεὰ αὕτη ζητεῖ σημεῖον) with τί standing for *mah* exclamatory (How!). Thus instead of taking the expression as a (rhetorical?) question, it should be seen as an exclamatory declaration '*How* doth this generation seek a "sign"!' But since the use of τί as a question is also a standard Koine form, nothing certain can be said in this regard. On this, see J.H Moulton, *A Grammar of New Testament Greek* (Edinburgh: T. & T. Clark, 1963), III, p. 127; and E.J. Maloney, *Semitic Interference in Marcan Syntax* (Chico, CA: Scholars Press, 1981), pp. 142-44.

110. 'The form of the saying in Mk 8.12 appears to come closest to Jesus' original pronouncement...the Greek words "if a sign shall be given to this generation"...reflecting the idiomatic Hebrew manner of making a solemn asseveration "may I be accursed if God shall give a sign"...[points] to the authenticity of the form of the words in Mark' (Anderson, *Mark*, p. 198). With respect to this, it should be pointed out that the value of Semitisms as an indication of the relative antiquity and originality of sayings material is not beyond dispute. See the searching criticisms of this criterion of authenticity made by E.P. Sanders in his *The Tendencies of the Synoptic Tradition* (Cambridge: Cambridge University Press, 1969), pp. 190-255.

111. Cf. C. Colpe, 'Υἱὸς τοῦ 'Ανθρώπου', *TDNT*, VIII, pp. 400-87, esp. p. 449 n. 349; Marshall, *Luke*, p. 484.

112. On this, see A. Kuschke, 'Das Idiom der "relativen Negation" im NT', *ZNW* 43 (1950–51), p. 263.

113. As J.H. Moulton and W.F. Howard note (*Grammar of New Testament Greek* [Edinburgh: T. & T. Clark, 1929], II, p. 468-87), the formula underlying εἰ δοθήσεται did not exist in Aramaic. See also, Edwards, *Sign of Jonah*, p. 75; W. Lane, *The Gospel according to Mark* (Grand Rapids: Eerdmans, 1978), p. 278.

familiar with biblical idiom might have employed.[114] And in light of this, it cannot be viewed as providing decisive evidence as to the relative antiquity of the saying of which it is a part. For its appearance in Mk 8.12c could be traceable to editorial recasting of a traditional saying in conscious imitation of biblical speech rather than to faithful translation of an original word of Jesus.

There is good reason, then, to doubt the conventional view that Mk 8.12c best represents the tradition that stands behind it and its parallel in Q. But is there reason to opt for the converse of this view—to say, that is, that the Q version of Jesus' refusal to produce a 'sign' is more original in form and wording that Mk 8.12c? To my mind the answer is yes. This becomes clear when we take into consideration the data provided by the following observations and see how the major differences between the two variants of the 'sign' refusal saying arose and are to be accounted for.

There are two major differences in the manner in which Mark, on the one hand, and Q, on the other, reproduce the saying of Jesus against producing a 'sign'. The first difference consists of the fact, already noted, that the Q version of the saying contains an 'exceptive clause', in which it is said that one 'sign' *shall* be produced, whereas the Markan version of the saying contains no such clause. Thus the Q version of the saying presents Jesus' refusal as *conditional* while the Markan version of the saying represents Jesus' refusal to produce a 'sign' as *absolute*.

The second major difference between the two versions of the saying is that the version in Q lacks the authorizing 'amen formula' which appears in the saying's Markan version and functions there as a solemnizing preface to the refusal. The question with which we need to deal then is this: *If the Markan and the Q version of the saying of Jesus against producing a 'sign' arose from a tradition common to them both, how are these differences to be accounted for?* Let us examine each of the differences in turn.

The 'Exceptive Clause'. One way to explain the absence of the 'exceptive clause' in the Markan version of the 'sign' refusal saying and its presence in the version in Q is to assume that the clause was not originally a part of the tradition upon which the Q and Markan versions of the saying are ultimately based. Rather, it was only added subsequently to the tradition as the saying passed into, and was taken up in,

---

114. Cf. its use by the author of the Epistle to the Hebrews at Heb. 3.11; 4.3, 5.

the Q stream of the Synoptic tradition.[115] But the assumption that the tradition common to the Markan and Q version of the 'sign' refusal saying did not from the beginning contain the 'exceptive clause' seems highly unlikely. The clause was an enigma in the early Church.[116] Notable, too, is the fact that in its present setting, the clause has the effect of making the refusal saying cryptic. To suppose, therefore, that this clause was added subsequently to an already established, intelligible and self-contained saying of Jesus is to suppose that whoever was responsible for the addition acted in a manner contrary to the normal tendency, readily discernable in the history of the synoptic tradition, namely, for transmitters of tradition to join not the unintelligible to the intelligible, but the intelligible to the obscure—to clarify confusing, ambiguous or no longer comprehensible traditional material by adding to it other material, thereby interpreting it and making it lucid.[117] Moreover, it is difficult to explain, except on the basis of the originality of the 'exceptive clause', why the specific material (i.e. a correlation between Jonah and the Son of Man [Mt. 12.40//Lk. 11.30] and a double saying on the witness of the Ninevites and the Queen of the South to 'this generation' [Mt. 12.41-42//Lk. 11.30-31]) which in Q and in Matthew and Luke now follows the Q 'sign' refusal saying, should ever have done so. *For, as we have seen, this material was originally independent of the Q version of the saying*[118] and now depends for its connection with the saying on the catchwords σημεῖον, γενεὰ αὕτη and Ἰωνᾶ.[119] Accordingly, it seems far more plausible to think that the 'exceptive clause' was an element integral to the tradition basic and common to the Markan and Q versions of the dominical 'sign' refusal saying *which was later dropped*, than to think that it was not a part of the original 'sign' refusal tradition, but was added only subsequently.[120]

---

115. Cf. Martin, *Mark: Evangelist and Theologian*, p. 166; Edwards, *Sign of Jonah*, pp. 83-87.

116. Cf. Bultmann, *History*, p. 118.

117. 'The tradition is in the habit of recording and interpreting enigmatic sayings of Jesus, but not of inventing or gratuitously attributing them to him' (J. Jeremias, 'Die alteste Schicht der Menschensohn-Logion', *ZNW* 58 [1967], p. 169).

118. Cf. above, pp. 134-35. See also Higgins, *Jesus and the Son of Man*, p. 137; Kloppenborg, *The Formation of Q*, p. 128.

119. Cf. Vögtle, 'Jonaszeichen', pp. 248-49.

120. Bultmann, *History*, pp. 117-18 (cf. p. 118 n. 1); D. Hill, *The Gospel of Matthew* (London: Oliphants, 1972), p. 219; Schweizer, *Mark*, p. 158; *idem, Matthew*, p. 292; Vögtle, 'Jonaszeichen', p. 240; W.G. Kümmel, *Promise and Fulfilment*

Granting this, the Q version of the saying shows itself, in this aspect at least, to be the older and more original of the traditional saying's two Synoptic variants.

The 'Amen Formula'. We can account for the fact that the Markan version of the 'sign' refusal saying contains a prefatory, solemnizing 'amen formula', while the Q version does not, by assuming two things: *first*, that the original tradition underlying the saying's two principal variants originally possessed such a formula, but that as the tradition was transmitted into the Q stream of the synoptic tradition its 'amen formula' was dropped; and, secondly, that it was not dropped, however, when the tradition flowed into the stream of the synoptic tradition that came to Mark. But how likely is this assumption? Admittedly, Luke's handling of the Markan 'amen' sayings shows us that at a late stage in the synoptic tradition there was a tendency to drop the 'amen formula' from sayings which originally possessed it.[121] But it is questionable whether this would have happened in the tradition's earlier stages. For there seems to be no reason sufficient to account for how or why this might have happened. Luke deletes the 'amen formula' when he finds it because he generally rejects foreign words.[122] But to the editor(s) or compiler(s) of Q, the word 'amen' would hardly have been foreign.[123] In light of these doubts, it must be asked whether it is not more plausible to assume that the 'amen formula' was added to the saying of Jesus against producing a 'sign' than to assume that the formula was eliminated from it. We know from Matthew, John, and even Luke that the addition of the word 'amen' to solemnize originally unadorned sayings of Jesus was not an uncommon practice in the early Church.[124]

(London: SCM Press, 1957), p. 68; Schulz, *Q*, p. 252; Tödt, *The Son of Man in the Synoptic Tradition*, p. 211.

121. J.C. O'Neill, 'The Six Amen Sayings in Luke', *JTS* 10 NS (1959), pp. 1-9, esp. pp. 1-2.

122. Cf. H.J. Cadbury, *The Style and Literary Method of Luke* (Cambridge, MA: Harvard University Press, 1920), pp. 154-58; H. Schurmann, 'Die Sprache des Christus: Sprachliche Beobachtungen an den synoptischen Herrenworten', *BZ* 21 (1958), pp. 54-84, esp. p. 67.

123. Especially given the probable Palestinian provenance of Q.

124. Matthew twice adorns statements of Jesus with 'Amen, I say to you'. Cf. Mt. 19.23 (par. Mk 10.23; Lk. 18.24); Mt. 24.2 (par. Mk 13.2; Lk. 21.6). John, as is well known, always reduplicates the 'Amen formula' in the 25 times he employs it. Luke creates an 'Amen' saying out of Markan material. Cf. Lk. 4.24 par. Mk 6.4. On

Moreover, we also know that this was something in which Mark himself engaged.[125] It seems clear, then, that in not having the 'amen formula', the Q version of Jesus' 'sign' refusal saying reproduces more faithfully than its Markan counterpart the original tradition which is basic and common to them both.[126]

In light of these observations I conclude that the Markan version of the saying of Jesus against producing a 'sign' is secondary to the version now found in Lk. 11.29//Mt. 12.39.[127]

But my observations in this regard do not stop here. To my mind it is hardly likely that a saying initially embodying a conditional refusal to give a 'sign' would come to be a saying expressing an absolute refusal to do so (at least in the particular, peculiar, intensified form in which it now appears in Mark's Gospel), given what could be expected to happen to it in the course of the original tradition's transmission either from one environment to another or from its oral form to written literature. The variations in the form and wording of the Markan version of the saying from that in which the tradition underlying Mk 8.12b, c was originally cast *must be due to intentional redaction*. But who was responsible for this editorial activity? It is conceivable that the addition of the 'amen formula' to the saying, the elimination of the saying's 'exceptive' clause, and the change in the form of its statement of refusal from οὐ δοθήσεται to εἰ δοθήσεται could all have been made in the pre-Markan tradition by hands other than Mark's. But it is also conceivable that the redaction of the 'sign' refusal saying from its original to its present Markan form may have been carried out by Mark himself. A decision on this matter will depend on whether evidence can be produced which shows that Mark was familiar with a version of the saying similar in form and wording to the original saying as it is made known to us by the Q tradition.

Just such evidence seems to be found in the appearance of the phrase 'adulterous and sinful generation' (τῇ γενεᾷ ταύτῃ τῇ μοιχαλίδι καὶ ἁμαρτωλῷ) at Mk 8.38, a traditional dominical judgment saying which emphasizes the dangers of renouncing allegiance to Jesus.[128] The saying

this, see O'Neill, 'Six Amen Sayings', pp. 2-4.

125. Pryke (*Redactional Style*, p. 136) lists eleven of the thirteen times 'amen' appears in Mark as redactional. Cf. also F. Neirynck, 'The Redactional Text of Mark', *ETL* 57 (1981), pp. 144-62, esp. p. 151.

126. Perrin, *Rediscovering*, pp. 191-92.

127. As do the authors cited in n. 120 above, p. 150.

also appears at Lk. 9.36, where it is taken over from Mark,[129] and yet again at both Mt. 10.32-33 and Lk. 12.8-9, where it is taken over from Q.[130] Mk 8.38 is to be regarded as a secondary variant of the saying, best represented by Lk. 12.8-9, because the verb used in the Markan version of the saying (ἐπαισχύνομαι) has a more general meaning and is less Semitizing than those found in Lk. 12.8-9 (ὁμολογέω and ἀρνέομαι),[131] and because a call for a decision concerning Jesus and the proclamation (καὶ τοὺς ἐμοὺς λόγους), as is now found in Mark, would be a later demand than the one found in Luke concerning simply Jesus himself.[132] Significantly, unlike the Markan version of the saying, neither the Lukan reproduction of Mk 8.38 nor the Q version of the saying in either of its respective Matthean and Lukan forms contains the phrase 'adulterous and sinful' as a description of the γενεά before whom the denial of Jesus is likely to occur. In Q this is simply 'before men' (ἐνώπιον or ἔμπροσθεν τῶν ἀνθρώπων). This indicates that the phrase is a Markan addition to the saying.[133] But what is this addition's origin? Given not only that in Mark's Gospel the phrase is attributed to Jesus, but also that it is fully consonant with the authentic ἡ γενεά αὕτη sayings of Jesus,[134] there is a strong *prima facie* case for regarding the phrase as derived from words of Jesus embedded in the synoptic tradition. Yet the only place where the phrase 'adulterous and sinful (or 'wicked') generation' occurs is in the Q version of the saying of Jesus against producing a 'sign' (γενεὰ πονηρὰ καὶ μοιχαλὶς σημεῖον ζητεῖ, κτλ.).[135]

---

128. See E. Käsemann, 'Sentences of Holy Law in the New Testament', in his *New Testament Questions of Today* (London: SCM Press, 1969), pp. 68-81; Tödt, *Son of Man*, pp. 40-41.

129. Tödt, *Son of Man*, p. 41.

130. Tödt, *Son of Man*, p. 40; Manson, *Sayings*, pp. 108-109; Schweizer, *Matthew*, pp. 245-46; Marshall, *Luke*, pp. 510, 514-16; M.D. Hooker, *The Son of Man in Mark* (London: SPCK, 1967), p. 117.

131. Perrin, *Rediscovering*, p. 186; Tödt, *Son of Man*, p. 55 n. 2.

132. Käsemann, 'Sentences', p. 77; Perrin, *Rediscovering*, p. 186; F. Hahn, *The Titles of Jesus in Christology* (London: Lutterworth, 1969), pp. 28-29. On the secondary nature of Mk 8.38, see also E. Schweizer, 'Der Menschensohn', *ZNW* 50 (1959), p. 188 and M. Hooker, *Son of Man*, p. 119.

133. Hooker, *Son of Man*, p. 118.

134. On these, see Jeremias, *New Testament Theology*, p. 135. See also M. Meinertz, 'Dieses Geschlecht im NT', *BZ* 1 (1957), pp. 283-89.

135. Taylor, *Mark*, p. 383.

This observation leads to the conclusion that Mark must have been familiar with a version of the saying of Jesus against producing a 'sign' which was very similar in form and wording to the version of the saying now found in Q.[136] With this being so, then the modifications made to the form and wording of the dominical 'sign' refusal saying—the elimination of the saying's 'exceptive clause', the change from οὐ δοθήσεται to εἰ δοθήσεται, and the prefacing of the refusal saying with a solemn ἀμήν—should be viewed as stemming from Mark's hand.

Summary and Conclusions

I now draw together and review my findings concerning the nature and extent of Mark's redactional contribution to his version of the tradition of Jesus' 'sign' demand temptation. According to my analysis of Mk 8.11-13, Mark:

1. took up a traditional saying of Jesus against the seeking of 'signs' (reading very much like ἡ γενεὰ αὕτη γενεὰ πονηρὰ καὶ μοιχαλίς ἐστιν· σημεῖον ζητεῖ, καὶ σημεῖον οὐ δοθήσεται αὐτῇ εἰ μὴ τὸ σημεῖον Ἰωνᾶ) which he found prefaced by a story of Jesus miraculously feeding a multitude (Mk 8.2-9) and to which was probably attached a notice containing some 'data as to the situation' in which the saying was spoken. He eliminated the saying's 'exceptive clause', altered the form of the opening of the saying from a declaration to a rhetorical question/exclamation, changed the wording of the saying's statement of refusal to countenance the seeking of 'signs' from οὐ δοθήσεται to εἰ δοθήσεται, and prefaced the refusal section of the saying with a solemnizing ἀμήν formula. He then

2. appended to the new form of the saying a descriptive notice of Jesus undergoing and expressing fervent emotion (i.e. καὶ ἀναστενάξας τῷ πνεύματι αὐτοῦ); and then,

3. having dispensed with the dominical saying's traditional introduction, placed the saying and its attendant descriptive notice within the context of a redactionally created setting of a dispute between Jesus and the Pharisees, a dispute which, according to

136. Cf. B.W. Bacon, *The Beginning of the Gospel Story* (New Haven: Yale University Press, 1909), pp. 96-97; A.E.J. Rawlinson, *The Gospel according to St Mark* (London: Metheun, 1925), p. 105.

Mark, is not only initiated by the Pharisees, but also culminates in, and is characterized by, their seeking of a 'sign'. He also

4. specified the character of the disputation by designating it as something which subjected Jesus to temptation;[137] and finally he

5. made the demand more precise, changing what was asked for from an unspecified 'sign' to one ἀπὸ τοῦ οὐρανοῦ.

What, then, of Mark's *Vorlage*? Can it be recovered? If my observations concerning the nature and extent of Markan redaction of Mk 8.1-13 are correct, the answer is *yes*, but at one point in particular we must stop short. We need not have any doubts over what its form was like or what it contained: a feeding miracle followed by a demand from opponents of Jesus for a 'sign' which in turn was followed by a dominical saying in which Jesus both gives vent to his feelings about those who make the demand and conditionally refuses to accede to it. But the original wording of the demand is now irrecoverable.

Mark's contribution to both the appearance and shape of the tradition of Jesus' 'sign' demand temptation is, then, quite extensive. In fact, *on my analysis it would seem that he is actually responsible for the casting of the synoptic story of the demand for a 'sign' in terms of a 'temptation tradition'*. But is this the case? Was Mark here doing something entirely new, namely, creating a temptation tradition where previously one did not exist? Or was he in his own way only drawing out and making explicit something already implied in the traditional demand for a 'sign' material? To answer this question, we will, of course, have to do three things: first, determine what Mark portrays as the nature and content of Jesus' temptation in Mk 8.1-13; second, analyse the Q tradition of the demand for a 'sign' to establish whether it states or implies that Jesus was tempted in any way in being asked to produce a 'sign', and, if so, what understanding of the nature and content of the temptation lies

---

137. It should be noted, contrary to Taylor (*Mark*, p. 362) and Edwards (*Sign of Jonah*, p. 75), that Mark does not explicitly say that the Pharisees ask Jesus for a 'sign' *in order to* tempt him. He simply says that, *whether or not* the Pharisees intended their demand to do so, the demand put Jesus 'to the test'. Indeed, C.G. Montefiore (*The Synoptic Gospels* [London, Macmillan, 1927], I, p. 174) has shown that the participle πειράζοντες is used in Mk 8.11 without any reference to the purpose or intention of the Pharisees. Rather it is used *interpretatively* to indicate only that Jesus recognized the demand as a temptation/'testing'. On this, see also J.E. Carpenter, *The First Three Gospels: Their Origin and Relations* (London: Philip Green, 4th edn, 1906), p. 119.

there; and then, thirdly, we must compare the results of these examinations. But before all of this is undertaken we must first return to the question of the nature of the relationship between the Q account of the 'sign' demand tradition and the account found in, and lying behind, Mk 8.1-13, and determine whether Mark or his *Vorlage* is literarily dependent upon Q.

5. *Mark 8.1-13 and Q*

What, then, is the nature of the relationship between Mk 8.1-13 and the Q version of the tradition of the demand for a 'sign'? If we were to focus exclusively on the fact that the dominical 'sign' refusal saying taken up and used by Mark at Mk 8.12 seems originally to have been the same in form and wording as that underlying its Q parallel (Mt. 12.39//Lk. 11.29), then we might be forced to conclude that Mark 8.1-13 is directly dependent on and derived from Q. But if we take a wider view, and bring into consideration other features of Mk 8.1-13 vis-à-vis what is or is not found in Q, we must, I think, come to the opposite conclusion. In the first place, as Tuckett has observed, the story in Mark exhibits no parallel to the 'eschatological/prophetic' correlative found at Mt. 12.40//Lk. 11.30, nor does there seem to be an awareness there of Q's 'double saying' or of the editorial activity of the Q redactor in linking this unit of material with the traditional 'sign' refusal saying.[138] If Mk 8.1-13 is in any way literarily dependent on the Q version of the 'sign' demand tradition, should we not expect to find within the Markan account or its *Vorlage* some traces of this material or activity?[139] In the

---

138. Tuckett, 'Mark and Q', p. 161.

139. One may, of course, argue that the tradition behind Mk 8.1-13 *did* originally contain the correlative and the 'double saying', but that, as was done with the 'exceptive' clause in the dominical 'sign' refusal saying, these elements were also eliminated by Mark when he took up and modified the tradition. Retention of the correlative and the 'double' saying would, after all, so the argument might go, be hardly appropriate once the 'exceptive' clause was eliminated, since without the 'exceptive' clause and its reference to Jonah, the correlative and 'double saying', linked as they are to the dominical 'sign' refusal saying by the catchword Jonah, would no longer make sense within the context of Mk 8.1-13. Answer: In the absence of the 'exceptive' clause, the correlative would indeed not make sense, but the same cannot be said for the 'double saying'. So Mark had no reason to eliminate it had he known it, and had he known it, we should have expected him to have retained it. The fact that Mark shows no awareness of the 'double saying' indicates, then, that it (and

second place, neither the present text of the Markan version of the story nor its *Vorlage* shows any awareness of the literary arrangement by Q of the materials now constituent to the Q version of the 'sign' demand story maximally construed, which as we have seen above, involved the placing of the unit most particularly concerned with the demand for a 'sign' and Jesus' response to it (Mt. 12.38-42//Lk. 11.16, 28-32) within the context of the Beelzebub controversy (with its story of a healing, its neutrality saying [Mt. 12.30//Lk. 11.23] and its parable about the evil spirits [Mt. 12.43-45//Lk. 11.24-26]) and the series of woes against 'this generation'(Lk. 11.37-52). Would Mk 8.1-13 not show some indication of the literary structuring of the Q story and its wider context if its substance were drawn from that story?[140] Finally, and I think most tellingly, there is no indication in Mk 8.1-13 of an awareness of what Q presents as the occasion of the demand. This is all the more striking in light of the fact that Mk 8.1-13 resembles Q in noting that the demand follows, and is in response to, Jesus engaging in miraculous activity. But in Q the miracle is a healing/exorcism of one of the κωφοί, and in Mark a feeding of a multitude. One might argue that Mark has replaced the one miracle with the other, but this ignores the fact, noted above, that the connection in Mk 8.1-13 between the demand already appeared in Mark's *Vorlage* and is itself grounded in primitive tradition.

Mk 8.1-13 is, then, indeed based on tradition. And as in Q, that tradition's version of the dominical saying against producing 'signs' for 'this generation' originally included an 'exceptive' clause referring to the 'sign' of Jonah. But the tradition behind Mk 8.1-13 is not the Q version of the 'sign' demand story. It seems to be a source other than, and independent of, Q, one from which in all probability the Q version of the tradition was itself derived.[141]

---

by extension, the correlative with which it is most intimately linked) was not a part of his *Vorlage*.

140. Cf. Tuckett, 'Mark and Q', p. 161: 'Mark does have a version of the Beelzebub controversy (Mk 3:20-30), but it is not connected with the Sign pericope in Mark. Mark also has a parallel to the neutrality saying of Q [Mt. 12.30//Lk. 11.23], in Mk 9:40, but again in a totally different context. Mark has no parallel at all to the parable of the evil spirits. And Mark has no parallel to the series of woes in Q [Lk. 11.37-51]. (The one similar warning against the scribes in Mk 12.38-40 has no substantive parallel in the Q series of woes.) Thus Mark seems to have no awareness of all of the literary structuring of Q, insofar as this can be determined.'

141. Tucket, 'Q and Mark', p. 162.

Chapter 5

THE 'SIGN' DEMAND TEMPTATION ACCORDING TO MARK

The Nature of the 'Sign' Demand Temptation

In the foregoing analysis I noted that it was Mark who specifically designated the dispute between Jesus and the Pharisees in Mk 8.11-13 as something which subjects Jesus to temptation. My purpose now is to outline the particular way in which Mark intended the demand for a 'sign' to be seen as tempting Jesus. What, according to Mark was that temptation's nature or character? Did it, in his eyes, involve—as did the temptation in the wilderness—a proving of Jesus' faithfulness? Or was it something else that was put on trial? I shall attempt to settle the matter by focusing attention on, and drawing data from, the one place in Mk 8.11-13 which would seem to hold the most promise for providing the sort of information required for answering these questions. That place is Mk 8.12, Jesus' response to the demand that he should produce a 'sign'.

According to Mark, Jesus' response to the demand for a 'sign' is tripartite. Its first element is a deep and intensely expressive 'sigh' or 'groan' (καὶ ἀναστενάξας τῷ πνεύματι αὐτοῦ, Mk 8.12a), coming, as it were, 'from the very bottom of the heart'.[1] That Mark portrays Jesus responding in this manner goes a long way towards unveiling Mark's understanding of the nature of the temptation which he says Jesus experienced on account of the demand. For in Mark's time, the type of 'sighing/groaning' in which Jesus engages at Mk 8.12 was specifically thought to express the type of dismay or distress of spirit that comes only upon discovering that one has suddenly been placed by fate or circumstance into a situation where a prior commitment to a

---

1. H.B. Swete, *The Gospel According to St Mark* (London: Macmillan, 1905), p. 168.

given divine decree may be found foolish or wanting.[2] Accordingly, the fact that Mark has Jesus 'sigh (groan) deeply' when faced with the demand for a 'sign' is strong evidence for saying that Mark intended the temptation which Jesus experiences on account of the demand to be seen as of the 'religious' kind, that is, a 'testing' of Jesus' faithfulness and obedience to God.

The second element of Jesus' response to the demand for a 'sign' is a rhetorical question/remark (cf. Mk 8.12b) in which the enterprise of 'sign' seeking is identified as an activity which marks those who engage in it—in this case the Pharisees—as members of 'this generation' (ἡ γενεὰ αὕτη). This also seems to indicate that Mark intended the temptation embodied within the demand to be seen as 'religious' in nature. For in Mark's Gospel the phrase 'this generation' denotes human beings in their opposition to God.[3] Consequently, we should assume that, according to Mark, behind Jesus' characterization of the enterprise of 'sign' seeking as an activity undertaken by members of 'this generation', there lies a recognition on Jesus' part that should he accede to the demand for a 'sign', he, too, like the Pharisees, would then be setting himself against God and turning his back on God's ways. This is, of course, the essence of 'religious' 'testing'.

The final element of Jesus' response to the demand for a 'sign' is an oath—one in which Jesus invites curses upon himself should he accede to the Pharisees' desires (cf. Mk 8.12c).[4] Why, according to Mark, does Jesus do this? Since, as R.A. Edwards and others have noted,[5] an oath of this sort was employed as a way of saying 'no' forcefully to a suggested course of action, one answer is that the Markan Jesus uses the oath because he wants to let his interlocutors know in no uncertain terms that he refuses to accede to their demand. But it should be noted that saying 'no' is not the only or even the most important purpose for which this oath was used. For the oath is primarily an expression of

2. On this, see J.B. Gibson, 'Mk 8.12a. Why Does Jesus "Sigh Deeply"?', *BibT* 38 (1987), pp. 122- 25.

3. Cf. M. Meinertz, 'Dieses Geschlecht im Neuen Testament', *BZ* 1 (1957), pp. 283-89, esp. pp. 283-85.

4. Cf. above, Chapter 4, n. 7, p. 147. The oath is here abbreviated, as in Ps. 95.11, but on analogy with 2 Kgs 6.31 may be filled out as 'May I die' or 'may God curse me if I accede to your demand!'.

5. R.A. Edwards, *The Sign of Jonah in the Theology of the Evangelists and Q* (London: SCM Press, 1971), p. 75. See also W. Lane, *The Gospel according to Mark* (Grand Rapids: Eerdmans, 1974), p. 278.

extreme revulsion, specifically the revulsion one feels at being asked to engage in activity that cuts against the grain of one's integrity.[6] To utter it is to indicate abhorrence, *to demonstrate how absolutely imperative one feels is the necessity of avoiding the course of action which the oath disavows.*[7] And what, according to Mark, is more abhorrent to Jesus or more necessary for him to avoid, than consenting to do something that would run contrary to God's will?[8] The fact, then, that Mark portrays Jesus as uttering an oath of conditional self imprecation in response to the demand to produce a 'sign' indicates that the temptation to which Jesus is subjected on account of the demand is, in Mark's eyes, of the 'religious' kind.

In light of all of the above, we must conclude that Mark intended the temptation which he has Jesus face when confronted with the demand for a 'sign' to be seen as something which puts 'on trial' Jesus' faithfulness and obedience to God.[9]

The Content of the 'Sign' Demand Temptation

Having reached this conclusion, it is then necessary to ask: Why, according to Mark, does the demand for a 'sign' present Jesus with such a trial? How, in Mark's judgment, would Jesus be disobedient or unfaithful to God if he acceded to the Pharisees' demand and promised or produced what they asked for? In other words, what is Mark's understanding of the content of Jesus' 'sign' demand temptation. To determine this, it is important to resolve the following questions:

6.   Cf. G.W. Buchanan, 'Some Vow and Oath Formulas in the New Testament', *HTR* 58 (1965), pp. 319-26, esp. pp. 324-25.

7.   Cf. V. Taylor, *The Gospel according to St Mark* (London: Macmillan, 1955), p. 362; M.J. Lagrange, *L'Evangile selon Saint Marc* (Paris: Gabalda, 1929), p. 207; W.F. Howard, 'Appendix on Semitisms in the New Testament', in Vol. II of J.H. Moulton's and W.F. Howard's *A Grammar of New Testament Greek* (Edinburgh: T. & T. Clark, 1929), pp. 468-69.

8.   It is hardly insignificant that in Mark's Gospel the only other remark of Jesus that comes close in form, urgency and emotional tone to this oath is Jesus' rebuke of Peter at 8.33 when Peter suggests that Jesus should not 'think the things of God'.

9.   See R.P. Martin, *Mark: Evangelist and Theologian* (Exeter: Paternoster, 1972), p. 169; E. Best, *The Temptation and the Passion: The Markan Soteriology* (Cambridge: Cambridge University Press, 1965), pp. 31-32; *contra* H. Seesemann, 'πεῖρα, κτλ.', *TDNT*, VI, p. 28; H. Anderson, *The Gospel of Mark* (London: Oliphants, 1976), p. 199.

- What actually is it that is sought by the Pharisees from Jesus, and why, according to Mark, do they demand it of him?

- What is it about the Pharisees' perception of Jesus that brings them to make their particular demand?

- Why does Jesus not accede to the Pharisees' demand? What specifically would he become involved in should he do so?

As we shall see, it is only after these questions are dealt with that we will have at our disposal the data necessary for outlining Mark's understanding of the content of Jesus' 'sign' demand temptation. And so it is to answering these questions that I now turn.

The Meaning of the Term σημεῖον in Mark 8.11-13
The temptation to which Jesus is subjected in Mk 8.11-13 is related to whether or not he would 'give' a σημεῖον. But what is a σημεῖον? A survey of the instances of the use of the term in both Classical and Biblical Greek shows that a σημεῖον. was an object of (usually visual) sense perception which imparts in various ways insight or knowledge.[10] Thus a σημεῖον could be a 'signal' or 'hi-sign', that is, something which transmits specific information (such as a warning) from one party to another.[11] It is also, and most generally, could be an 'indicator', that is, a distinguishing, corroborating or authenticating 'mark' which contributes to the recognition of a person or a thing.[12] Sometimes, however, a σημεῖον was also more particularly thought of either (1) as an event worked by a deity or a thaumaturge which signifies and manifests the presence of the numinous and inspires awe,[13] or (2) as a 'portent', that is, something by which the future or the will of the gods is made known.[14] In the Greek Old Testament and the literature dependent on it a σημεῖον may also be any of the wondrous deeds performed by God in the time of Moses and Joshua to deliver the people of Israel from

10. On this, see K. Rengsdorf, 'σημεῖον', *TDNT*, VII, pp. 200-61, esp. pp. 200-208.

11. Cf. Herodotus, 7.128; Thucydidies, 1.49, 63; 3.91; 4.42; Polybius 5.69.

12. Herodotus 2.38; 8.92; Plato, *Rep.* 614c; Aeschylus, *Ag.* 1355; Diogenes Laertius 8.32 (of symptoms by which illness or health is detected); Sophocles, *Antig.* 257-58; Aristophanes, *Ra.* 933; Xenophon, *An.* 1.10, 12.

13. Sophocles, *Oed. Col.* 94; Plutarch, *Alex.* 75.1; *Sep. Sap. Conv.* 3 C II, 149c.

14. Plato, *Phaedrus* 244; *Apol.* 40b; Xenophon, *Cyr.* 1; *Rhes.* 529; Plutarch, *Alex.* 25 (1, 679b).

Egyptian bondage and secure their salvation.[15] And it is also thought of as a 'token of trustworthiness' or 'proof'.[16]

As these instances show, a 'proof' σημεῖον—a 'sign'—has several distinct characteristics:[17]

First, a 'sign' is always a public event. Its occurrence is meant to be seen or perceived, as well as publicly acknowledged as having happened.

Secondly, a 'sign' happens—or is anticipated as happening—not accidentally or fortuitously, but on command. It is something that can be sought, promised, worked or produced.

Thirdly, a 'sign' is sought, promised, worked or produced for one of two reasons: either to certify the truth of a distrusted prophecy, or to establish the validity of a disputed claim that a certain course of action and the person initiating it are 'of God'. The context of such activity is typically as follows:

- A claimant to divine authority or insight into the mind of God engages in an activity, or utters a prophecy or doctrinal statement, that in his or her eyes bears God's approval.

- Observers are struck by the fact that the action or the utterance is either (a) strange and surprising, or (b) contrary to common sense, conventional wisdom or practical considerations, or, worse, (c) a direct contravention of Mosaic Law. Given this, they conclude that the truth of the action or utterance and its divine origin is not immediately apparent.

- The claimant, wishing to secure acceptance of what has been said or done, responds to the skepticism with which the action or utterance is greeted by proposing (or agreeing to submit to)

15. Cf. Exod. 7.3; Deut. 4.34; 6.22; 7.19; 13.2-3; 26.28; 28.46; 29.2; 34.11; Isa. 8.18; 20.3; Jer. 32.20-21; Ps. 78.43; 105.27; 135.9; Neh. 9.10; Bar. 2.11; Sir. 36.5; Wis. 10.16.

16. This occurs at Gen. 4.15; Exod. 3.12; 4.8-9; Num. 14.11, 22; Deut. 13.1-12; Judg. 6.17; 1 Sam. 2.4; 10.1; 14.10; 1 Kgs 13.3; 2 Kgs 19.29; 20.8, 9; 2 Chron. 32.24; Neh. 9.10; Isa. 7.10, 14; 37.30; 38.7, 22; Pss. 78 [77].43; 105 [104].27; 135 [134].9; 2 Esdras 4.51; 6.11, 20; 7.25, 8.63; Josephus, *War* 2.258; 6.258, 288; *Ant.* 8.347; 10.28; 20.97-99, 168; Mk 13.4; 13.22; [16.17, 20]; Mt. 12.39; 16.4; 24.3,4; Lk. 2.12; 11.16, 29; 21.7; Jn 2.18; 6.30; Acts 4.16; 8.16; 14.3; 1 Cor. 1.22; 2 Thess. 2.9; Rev. 13.13-14.

17. For the substance of the following, I am indebted to the comprehensive discussion of 'signs' carried out by O. Linton, 'The Demand for a Sign from Heaven (Mk 8,11-12 and Parallels)', *StEv* 19 (1965), pp. 112-29.

a kind of test. The person selects (or accedes to a demand for) some phenomenon and promises to have it come to pass. This is done with the understanding that should the phenomenon occur both as and when the claimant says it will, the skepticism surrounding the disputed action or utterance will then vanish.

When, for instance, Ahaz doubts Isaiah's prophecy that 'within sixty five years Ephraim shall be broken', Isaiah offers to produce a 'sign' (cf. Isa. 7.8-15). When Isaiah wants to prove to Hezekiah that, contrary to all available evidence, he is not to die, Isaiah proposes to work a 'sign', letting Hezekiah himself choose between two such phenomena, one that is difficult or one that is 'easier' (LXX κούφων) to produce (2 Kgs 20.1-10; cf. Isa. 38.1-20). Theudas and other so-called 'Sign Prophets'[18] promise to work specific 'signs' expressly to substantiate their respective claims that they were anointed by God and divinely commissioned to the sacred purpose of delivering the Jewish nation from the yoke of Roman oppression (cf. Josephus, *War* 2.259, 261-263; *Ant.* 20.97-99, 167-168, 188).[19] A 'sign' is demanded of Jesus when he claims that divine authority stands behind his 'cleansing' of the Temple (Jn 2.18, cf. 2.13-18, esp. v. 16), and, later, when he teaches that he is sent from God (cf. Jn 6.29-30).

A 'proof' σημεῖον—a 'sign'—is, therefore, an event thought of as having the power to certify or confirm something that could otherwise be doubted and dismissed.

Fourthly, the function peculiar to a 'sign'—its ability to prove the truthfulness of a distrusted utterance or the legitimacy of a claim that a person's words and activities are 'of God'—is grounded in the public experience of a coincidence between a prior prophecy (what is designated as the 'sign') and a subsequent event (the 'sign's' actual manifestation). For instance, in the story of Jonathan and his armor bearer (1 Sam. 14.6-15) Jonathan is initially skeptical of the idea, placed in his mind by God, that if he but tries, he will be able to conquer a garrison of Philistines on his own. It is only when the requested authentication, the 'sign', actually occurs that he believes God and engages the Philistines in combat. Indeed, Jonathan himself admits that if the 'sign' had not come

18. On this as the proper or appropriate designation for Theudas and figures like him, see P.W. Barnett, 'The Jewish Sign Prophets—AD 40–70—Their Intentions and Origin', *NTS* 27 (1981), pp. 679-97. The activities and aims of these men will be discussed in more detail below.

19. That these men made these particular claims, see below, p. 187, and note 109.

to pass, he would not have risked the undertaking, being as it was, in purely practical terms, extremely foolhardy (cf. vv. 9-10). Accordingly, a 'sign' does its work when it is effectuated in exact conformity with its predicted or previously stipulated 'shape'.

Finally, as either promised or manifested, a 'sign' does not need to have a spectacular content in order to stand as a token of trustworthiness. In the instances cited above, 'signs' whose content is ordinary (e.g. the 'sign' promised to Ahaz by Isaiah in Isa. 7)[20] are offered or accepted as 'tokens of trustworthiness' as readily as those which are stupendous or extraordinarily miraculous (e.g. the 'signs' offered by Theudas and the other 'Sign Prophets' or the 'signs' of the 'False Prophets' of whom Moses speaks).[21] The important thing about a 'proof sign's' 'shape' is not whether it is in itself miraculous or ordinary, but whether, once manifested, it then appears in complete correspondence with its own terms, whatever they have been stated to be.

Is, then, the σημεῖον of Mk 8.11-13 of this type? Is it thought of by Mark as a 'token of trustworthiness', a 'sign'? The answer, of course, is yes, for, like the 'proof' σημεῖα above, the σημεῖον of Mk 8.11-13 is also something which is sought, something which Jesus is expected to produce when demanded. Moreover, the purpose of the Pharisees in seeking a σημεῖον from Jesus is, according to Mark, nothing less than to confirm the truth of things previously said or done by Jesus which were so offensive or scandalous to the Pharisees that they reqired special authentication. This is plain from the fact that according to Mark the setting of the Pharisees' demand is their action of coming out to Jesus expressly to voice anew objections they had thrown at him on previous occasions concerning the legitimacy of his activities and proclamations.[22]

But what were the actions or words of Jesus the import and truth of which were to the Pharisees in need of special proof? To answer this we must turn to Mark stories of the encounters between Jesus and the Pharisees which occur in the Gospel before the Pharisees confront Jesus

20. Isaiah's 'sign' for Ahaz was that a young woman whom Isaiah and Ahaz had no reason to know was pregnant would shortly be found to be so and would give birth to a boy by a particular time (on this, see J.L. McKenzie, 'Behold the Virgin', in his *The New Testament without Illusion* [New York: Crossroad, 1982], pp. 103-13, esp. pp. 105-106).

21. On the exact 'shape' of these 'signs', see below.

22. Cf. W.L. Lane, *The Gospel of Mark* (Grand Rapids: Eerdmans, 1974), p. 275 n. 17, p. 276. The phrase καὶ ἤρξαντο συζητεῖν αὐτῷ implies a previous discussion which is now being climaxed in the demand for a 'sign'.

with their demand for a 'sign', and determine what actions or words of Jesus cause contention on the occasion of these encounters.

Jesus and the Pharisees in Mark's Gospel

Before he brings them together at Mk 8.11-13, Mark has the Pharisees (or their representatives) come into contact with Jesus five times: when Jesus eats with a large company of tax collectors and 'sinners' (Mk 2.15-17), when it becomes known that his disciples do not engage in the practice of fasting (Mk 2.18-22),[23] when Jesus permits his disciples to pluck grain on the Sabbath (Mk 2.23-28), when he enters a synagogue on a Sabbath and cures a man whose hand has withered (Mk 3.1-6), and when, during a meal, Jesus' disciples are seen eating with 'unwashed' hands (Mk 7.1-15). Certain features of these encounters are noteworthy.

- They always occur on occasions in which Jesus is exercising his divinely endowed ἐξουσία.[24]

23. I am aware of the fact that nowhere in Mk 2.18-20 are the interlocutors of Jesus identified as Pharisees. Indeed, strictly speaking, on a purely literal reading of the passage, those who question Jesus about fasting seem to have no particular identity at all, for Mk 2.18 reads only καὶ ἔρχονται καὶ λέγουσιν αὐτῷ διὰ τί, κτλ. But that in Mark's eyes Jesus' opponents here are not Pharisees seems unlikely. These are the opponents that Jesus faces prior to and immediately following Mk 2.18-20 (cp. Mk 2.15-17; 23-28; 3.1-6). Moreover, both up to and for some time after this point in the Gospel, Pharisees are not only the only ones who question Jesus, but the *only ones who question him in the manner in which he is approached in Mk 2.18*. In light of this, the subject of ἔρχονται καὶ λέγουσιν can be regarded as unspecified (cf. C.H. Turner 'Markan Usage: Notes Critical and Exegetical on the Second Gospel', *JTS* 24 [OS 1924], p. 379) *only* when these similarities between the actions of this subject and those of the Pharisees are ignored and when Mk 2.18-20 is read in isolation from its larger context. It should also be noted in this regard that Mark employs this same phenomenon, namely, contextual identification as Pharisees (and Herodians) of initially unspecified opponents of Jesus at Mk 3.1-6 (cp. v. 1 with v. 6), and that Luke reads Mk 2.18 as though it were referring to Pharisees (cf. Lk. 5.33). Cp. also Mt. 9.14 where Matthew does this even more clearly.

24. Indeed, it is part of Mark's purpose in narrating these stories both to present Jesus as one who possesses ἐξουσία as well as to delineate the nature, extent, and divinely ordained ends for the use of that ἐξουσία. On this as the theme of Mk 2.15-17; 18-22; 23-28 and 3.1-6, see H.E. Tödt, *The Son of Man in the Synoptic Tradition* (London: SCM Press, 1965), pp. 113-25; N. Perrin, 'The Creative Use of the Son of Man Traditions by Mark', *USQR* 23 (1967/68), pp. 357-61; D.J. Doughty, 'The Authority of the Son of Man (Mk 2:1–3:6)', *ZNW* 74 (1983), pp. 161-81. On this as

- The Pharisees (or their representatives) always stand in opposition to Jesus and his ἐξουσία.

- Never, however, do the Pharisees express doubt in these encounters that Jesus possesses ἐξουσία or that the ἐξουσία which he wields is 'of God'.[25] Nor do the Pharisees ever express the opinion that Jesus is not entitled to the ἐξουσία which is evidently his.[26] On the contrary, in each of these encounters they approach Jesus always under the assumption that he has been invested with divine ἐξουσία.[27] What they oppose in each of these instances is *the manner in which, or the ends toward which,* Jesus exercises his ἐξουσία.

the theme of Mk 7.1-15, see R. Banks, *Jesus and the Law in the Synoptic Tradition* (Cambridge: Cambridge University Press, 1975), pp. 132-46).

25. It may be objected that Mk 3.22—the Scribal charges that Jesus is possessed by Beelzebul and that he expels demons by the prince of demons—stands as direct evidence against this. But setting aside the fact that the Scribes are not the Pharisees, and assuming, given Mk 2.16, that in Mark's view what is said by one of these two groups of Jewish religious authorities is meant to be taken as representative of the feelings of the other, this still can hardly be the case. For a close reading of the pericope in which Mk 3.22 appears shows that what is expressed in this verse *is not really what the opponents of Jesus believe about him.* On the contrary, given how it is characterized at Mk 3.28-30, not as an honest misperception, but as sheer, knowing, and calculated perversity, the view expressed by the Scribes in Mk 3.22 is *the very opposite of what they know is true.* On the charges as an attempt by Jesus' opponents to suppress what they themselves assume to be true, see J. Coutts, 'The Messianic Secret and the Enemies of Jesus', in E.A. Livingstone (ed.), *Studia Biblica,* II (JSNTSup, 2; Sheffield: JSOT Press, 1978), pp. 37-46, esp. p. 43.

26. Again, the strongest evidence against this seems to be the Scribal charges in Mk 3.22. But as I have argued in the previous note, the charges actually show that Jewish religious authorities, the Pharisees included, accept Jesus as entitled to his ἐξουσία.

27. Indeed, if the Pharisees did not assume this, it is difficult to explain why they approach Jesus in the first place, let alone argue with him. In support of this, it is important to note that in Mark's Gospel the encounters between Jesus and the Pharisees take place not only after, but specifically *as a result of,* Jesus' healing of a paralytic (Mk 2.1-12). Now, for Mark, this event is programmatic. The principles on which all the subsequent meetings of Jesus with religious authorities are to be interpreted are laid down there (cf. Coutts, 'Messianic Secret', p. 39). Notably, one of these principles is that Jesus is recognized by Jewish religious authorities as fully endowed with ἐξουσία. On this, see below.

- Jesus is portrayed (in the first of these encounters) as exercising ἐξουσία to bring to ἁμαρτωλοί, the 'sinners'—those who had, and, indeed, consciously wanted, no part in Israel[28]—what the Markan Pharisees thought belonged only to Israel.[29]

- Jesus exercises his ἐξουσία in the remainder of these instances to allow himself or others consciously to leave off following the practices of fasting (cf. Mk 2.18-22), Sabbath observance (cf. Mk 2.23-28), and avoidance of things thought to defile (Mk 7.1-15). Now it is important to note that in Mark's presentation of the Judaism in which Jesus carried out his ministry, observance of these practices was the very thing that the Pharisees and all the Jews regarded both as setting Israel apart from other nations and, even more importantly, *as necessary for maintaining one's membership in Israel and receiving the benefits that such membership secured.*[30] So here Jesus' ἐξουσία is directed toward making plain several things: first, that observance of these practices was useless as a criterion for 'holiness'; secondly, that insistence on the observance of these practices as the criterion for determining who is in the sphere of God's favour promotes an exclusivism that works against God's purposes and involves Israel in disobedience and covetousness;[31] and thirdly, that contrary to what the

28. On the identity of the ἁμαρτωλοί, see E.P. Sanders, *Jesus and Judaism* (Philadelphia: Fortress Press, 1985), p. 177.

29. When Jesus hosted the dinner described in Mk 2.15-17, he was, according to Mark, actually bringing to tax collectors and sinners not simply an experience of social generosity but a taste of the 'messianic banquet'—an end time redemptive event in which, in the mind of the Pharisees, Israel would have pride of place. On the concept of the 'messianic banquet', see J. Jeremias, *Jesus' Promise to the Nations* (London: SCM Press, 1958), pp. 59-62. On the meal in Mk 2.15-17 as an anticipatory celebration of the end time, see Jeremias, *New Testament Theology.* I. *The Proclamation of Jesus* (New York: Charles Scribner & Sons, 1971), pp. 115-16; E. Lohmeyer, *Das Evangelium des Markus* (Göttingen: Vandehoeck & Ruprecht, 1963), pp. 56-58; D.M. Mackinnon, 'Sacrament and Common Meal', in D.E. Nineham (ed.), *Studies in the Gospels* (Oxford: Oxford University Press, 1955), pp. 201-207.

30. This is most plainly stated in Mk 7.3-4, 6-13. But it is also implied by the fact that the Pharisees become upset with Jesus each time he ignores or runs roughshod over these practices.

31. Cf. Mk 7.6-13, 18-23. Cp. Mk 11.15-18.

Pharisees thought, those who did not observe these practices had as much, if not more, claim to be among the people of God as those who did.

- Jesus always justifies the particular manner in which he exercises ἐξουσία by claiming that he is constrained to do what he does *by* the very ἐξουσία with which he is endowed.[32] In this he seems to say that those with 'eyes' and 'ears' (to put it in Markan language) know that divine authority can be exercised in no other way, that it is always meant to be exercised in this way, and that opposition to this fact is not evidence of an honest disagreement about the ways and intentions of God, but a perverse and culpable 'blindness' and 'deafness' to them.[33]

From all of this it becomes apparent that the factor crucial to turning encounters between Jesus and the Pharisees into confrontations—and, therefore, what stands in Mark's Gospel as the background to the Pharisees' dispute with Jesus in Mk 8.11-12—is the Pharisees' perception of Jesus as one endowed with divine ἐξουσία who, nevertheless, in his use of ἐξουσία, not only contradicts their expectations concerning how one so endowed should act, but violates their sense of the ends toward which divine ἐξουσία is to be wielded. In Mark's presentation of things, *the bone of contention between Jesus and the Pharisees is that as God's envoy, Jesus proclaims, and in his actions manifests, that there is now to be an end to the institutions, rituals and ordinances by which Israel pretends to hold a position of power and privilege in God's purposes. Jesus announces that Israel's inheritance of salvation is to be shared with those traditionally thought to be 'not of Israel'.* Indeed, it is just such a proclamation and demonstration that Jesus engages in immediately before he is faced at Mk 8.11 with the Pharisees' demand.

---

32. As the 'Doctor' and 'the One who Came to Call Sinners' (cf. Mk 2.17) he can do nothing less than eat with them. As the Bridegroom (cf. Mk 2.19) he cannot let those with him fast. As one greater than David and the Lord of the Sabbath (cf. Mk 2.25-26, 28) he cannot help but be sovereign on that day. As one to whom God has given 'understanding' (συνείδησις) of the divine ways regarding clean and unclean and things that defile (cf. Mk 7.18) he has no choice but to allow his disciples to dispense with regulations that are not God's doctrines but the teachings of men. On the fact that there is a Christological constraint behind all of the actions of Jesus to which the Pharisees take exception, see R. Banks, *Jesus and the Law, ad loc.*

33. This seems to be the import of Mk 3.5a. It certainly is the assumption of Mk 4.11-12.

Acting as the Shepherd of the Flock of Israel, and, therefore, as one endowed with the authority of Moses and David, he duplicates an event performed originally on Israel's behalf for a large group of Gentiles (cf. Mk 8.1-10).[34]

Accordingly, when we ask why, according to Mark, the Pharisees demand a 'sign' from Jesus, we can see that it is *because they want 'proof' before they will accept an envoy of God who claims that the maintenance of national and religious exclusivism is both antithetical to the realization of God's purposes in history and unacceptable behaviour for a people which claims to be God's elect.*

Issues Surrounding Jesus' Refusal to Produce a 'Sign'

As I have noted above, in Mark's Gospel Jesus' response to the Pharisees' demand is entirely negative. Jesus balks at what they ask of him. But why, according to Mark, should Jesus refuse to countenance this demand?

The most common answer is that, in Mark's portrayal of things, Jesus feels his ministry to be by its very nature *self-authenticating*, needing no external or additional proof of its validity. To offer such proof would not only be a concession to unbelief, but would make unlikely, if not impossible, the response of radical faith which Jesus demands from all who are confronted by what he says and does.[35]

34. That the miraculous feeding depicted in Mk 8.1-10 is a duplication of the Exodus manna miracles is hardly disputable. On Gentiles as the recipients of this feeding, see A. Richardson, *The Miracle Stories of the Gospels* (London: SCM Press, 1941), pp. 97-98; G.H. Boobyer, 'The Miracles of the Loaves and the Gentiles in Mark's Gospel', *SJT* 6 (1953), pp. 77-78; B.E. Thiering, '"Breaking of Bread" and "Harvest" in Mark's Gospel', *NovT* 12 (1970), pp. 1-12. On Jesus here as the Shepherd of Israel, endowed with the authority of Moses and David (and, perhaps, Joshua as well), see S. Masuda, 'The Good News of the Miracle of the Bread: The Tradition and its Markan Redaction', *NTS* 28 (1982), pp. 191-219, esp. pp. 209, 213-14.

35. Among the many commentators who hold this view are E.P. Gould (*A Critical and Exegetical Commentary on the Gospel according to St Mark* [Edinburgh: T. & T. Clark, 1896], p. 145), A. Menzies (*The Earliest Gospel* [London: Macmillan, 1901], p. 163), H.B. Swete (*Mark*, p. 168), A.W.F. Blunt (*The Gospel according to Saint Mark* [Oxford: Clarendon Press, 1929], p. 193), A.E.J. Rawlinson (*The Gospel of Mark* [London: Methuen, 1925], p. 257), B.H. Branscomb (*The Gospel of Mark* [London: Houder & Stoughton, 1937], p. 138), C.E.B. Cranfield (*The Gospel according to St Mark* [Cambridge: Cambridge University Press, 1959], pp. 257-58),

This supposition seems, at least initially, to have something to be said for it. After all, according to Mark, it is those who are 'outside', those who have wilfully 'blinded' themselves to seeing and recognizing God's activity when it is in their midst, who make the demand.[36] And it is true that later on in his Gospel, within his story of the crucifixion, Mark portrays Jesus as tacitly refusing to use a 'sign' to engender belief in the truth of his mission and ministry even when he is capeable of doing so.[37]

It is my belief, however, that despite all of this, this supposition is untenable. Something other than a blanket opposition to offering proof of the validity of his ministry and message stands behind the Markan Jesus' refusal to comply with the Pharisees demand. My main reason for saying this is that in Mk 2.1-12, the story of the healing of the paralytic, Mark portrays Jesus as actually producing a 'sign' to prove that his proclamation is 'of God' when the truth of that proclamation and its divine origin are questioned. To show that this is so, let us turn to the story and review its details carefully.

The Markan version of the healing of the paralytic opens with Jesus

G. Delling ('Botschaft und Wunder im Wirken Jesus', in H. Rostow and K. Matthiae (eds.), *Der historische Jesus und der kerygmatische Christus* [Berlin, 1960], pp. 389-402), V. Taylor (*Mark*, p. 361), K. Rengstorf ('σημεῖον', p. 235), D.E. Nineham (*St Mark* [Baltimore: Pelican, 1963], pp. 210-12), C.F.D. Moule (*The Gospel according to Mark* [Cambridge: Cambridge University Press, 1965], pp. 60-61), K. Tagawa (*Miracles et Evangile: Le pensée personelle de l'évangeliste Marc* [Paris: Presses Universitaires de France, 1966], pp. 75-80), E.J. Mally ('The Gospel according to Mark', in R.E. Brown, J.A. Fitzmyer, R.E. Murphy (eds.), *The Jerome Biblical Commentary* [Englewoood Cliffs, NJ: Prentice–Hall, 1968], p. 39), E. Schweizer (*The Good News according to Mark* [Atlanta: John Knox, 1970], p. 159), R.P. Martin (*Mark: Evangelist and Theologian*, pp. 172-74), W.H. Kelber (*The Kingdom in Mark* [Philadelphia: Fortress, 1974], p. 61), W.L. Lane (*Mark*, pp. 277-78), W. Barclay (*The Gospel of Mark* [Philadelphia: Westminster Press, 1975], pp. 175-76), H. Anderson (*Mark*, p. 91); W. Harrington (*Mark* [Dublin: Veritas, 1979], p. 111), L. Williamson, Jr (*Mark* [Atlanta: John Knox, 1983], p. 143).

36. On the Pharisees as among 'those outside', see J. Coutts, '"Those Outside" (Mark 4,10-12)', *StEv* II (1964), pp. 155-57. On 'blindness', i.e., willful refusal to acknowledge the presence of God, as an identifying characteristic of 'those outside', see Mk 4.12 and E.E. Lemcio, 'External Evidence for the Structure and Function of Mark iv. 1-20, vii. 13-23, and viii. 14-21', *JTS* 29 (1978), p. 335. See also R. Pesch, *Das Markusevangelium*, II (Freiburg: Herder, 1977), p. 223, and M. Boucher, *The Mysterious Parable: A Literary Study* (Washington, DC: Catholic Biblical Association, 1977), pp. 60, 84.

37. Cf. Mk 15.27-32.

besieged in a house in Capernaum by a crowd which is eager to hear his word (Mk 2.1). It then goes on to narrate the attempt of four men to bring a paralytic to Jesus so that Jesus might heal him. When the men find that the press of bodies denies them normal access to Jesus, they go up to the roof of the house, break open the part of the ceiling directly above Jesus, and lower the paralytic down to him (Mk 2.3-4). Jesus, the story notes, is impressed with the obvious lengths to which they are willing to go to bring the paralytic into contact with his healing power. But he does not at this point act to fulfil their desires. Instead, he makes a formal statement that the paralytic's sins are forgiven (Mk 2.5). At this point particular members of the crowd, religious authorities whom Mark calls Scribes, having heard Jesus' declaration, realize that Jesus has in effect made a claim to be in possession of, and authorized to use, a power that they believe is reserved to God alone. The claim is all too much for them, and privately they refuse to accept it (Mk 2.6-7). But Jesus becomes aware of what is going on in their minds (Mk 2.8a), and in response to their musings he does two things. First, he openly expresses disappointment with the Scribes for doubting his word and the claim implicit within it (Mk 2.8b). Second, he proposes a test whereby the Scribes may see for themselves that their doubt is groundless (Mk 2.9), and then goes ahead and publicly submits himself to it (Mk 2.10-11). The story then ends with a notice that Jesus passes the test successfully (Mk 2.11), and that he is roundly acknowledged as having done so (Mk 2.12).

Several things should be noted here. First, the type of conflict that here prompts Jesus to cure the paralytic is the same as that which, according to the biblical phenomenology of 'signs', would prompt a 'sign' worker to produce a 'sign', namely, the rejection of a claim that at a given time, one is speaking or acting on God's behalf with divine approval. In this case, the claim rejected is both Jesus' possession of authority to forgive sins and whether or not his proclamation in v. 5 effectuates what it proclaims.

Secondly, the response that Jesus secures from the Scribes by healing the paralytic is identical with that typically won by 'sign' workers from their interlocutors when they effectuate the 'signs' they have added to their disputed words or deeds. The Scribes accept the truth of the utterance or the implications of the action for which the subsidiary prophecy stands as proof.[38]

---

38. See M.D. Hooker, *The Son of Man in Mark* (London: SPCK, 1967), p. 88. In

Thirdly, the activity that Jesus immediately resorts to after the Scribes' initial rejection of his words, and all they imply, is formally the same as that which Old Testament, Jewish and Christian 'sign' workers engage in when the truth of their words or deeds is challenged. Like those 'sign' workers, Jesus responds to the gauntlet thrown down against the validity and the import of his statement, not by initiating a discussion or an argument, *but by offering to make something happen.* Given its context, in function this response is nothing less that of offering a 'sign'.[39]

Finally, and perhaps most importantly, Jesus says that his reason for undertaking the cure of the paralytic is precisely to prove the claim that he has made in Mk 2.5. He makes clear at Mk 2.10 that he performs the healing so that those who have expressed doubt over the truth and the import of this claim may 'know that the Son of Man has authority on earth to forgive sins' (ἵνα δὲ εἰδῆτε ὅτι ἐξουσίαν ἔχει ὁ υἱὸς τοῦ ἀνθρώπου ἀφιέναι ἁμαρτίας ἐπὶ τῆς γῆς).[40] In other words, *Jesus*

support of this, it is important to note that Mark has cast Jesus' offer to make something happen in such a way as to call to mind the similiar offer on the part of Isaiah in the 'sign' story of the healing of Hezekiah in 2 Kgs 20.1-11. According to Mark, Jesus, like Isaiah, points out two courses of action that he is willing to take to meet the skepticism that he has encountered on account of his proclamation (cp. Mk 2.9 with 2 Kgs 20.9). Also, as does Isaiah, Jesus allows the decision about his course of action to be made for him. Finally, note the verbal resemblance between Jesus' question in Mk 2.9, 'Which is easier...?' (τί ἐστιν εὐκοπώτερον, κτλ.) and Hezekiah's remark in the LXX of 2 Kgs 20.10, 'It is easy...' (καὶ εἶπεν Ἐζέκιας, κοῦφων, κτλ.). On the correspondence between Mk 2.1-12 and 2 Kgs 20.1-11, see T.R. Hobbs, *2 Kings* (Waco: Word, 1985), p. 293. Curiously, I have found no other scholar besides Hobbs who has appreciated, let alone noticed, the correspondence between the two texts.

39. We must take seriously the fact that Mark does not exclude the Scribes from those who marvel at what Jesus does in his healing of the paralytic. It is, Mark notes at Mk 2.12, 'all' (πάντας) who were present on this occasion who 'were astounded and gave glory to God' (ὥστε ἐξίστασθαι πάντας καὶ δοξάζειν τὸν θεόν). To say, as does, for example, T.A. Burkill, that in Mk 2.1-12 'The impression produced [by the healing] on the hostile Scribes finds no mention, for they would hardly be included among those who glorify God in verse 12, and we are perhaps meant to take it for granted that they are temporarily put to silence' (*Mysterious Revelation* [Ithaca: Cornell University Press, 1963], p. 127) is to engage in special pleading.

40. J. Duplacy, following a suggestion first made by D.S. Sharp 'Mk. 2:10', *ExpTim* 38 (1927), pp. 428-29, contends that here ἵνα with the subjunctive εἰδῆτε expresses a command and therefore this verse should be translated 'Know that the Son of Man has authority on earth to forgive sins' ('Marc II, 10, note de syntax', in

himself here identifies his cure of the paralytic as a 'sign'.

If I am correct in these observations, then Mark's story of the healing of a paralytic presents Jesus as validating his actions or utterances by means of a 'sign'. Indeed, given what I have shown, *the story actually makes clear that in Mark's eyes, Jesus was quite ready ordinarily not only to produce 'signs' but to offer to do so when he or, notably, others, felt they were needed.* To argue that it says otherwise[41] is surely to refuse to allow both the story and Mark to speak on their own terms.[42]

This being the case, we may then dismiss as wholly untenable the conventional position on the reason why Mark has Jesus refuse to

Mélanges bibliques rédégos en l'honneur de A. Robert [Paris: Bloud & Gay, 1957], pp 421-27, esp. pp. 424-26; see also C.J Cadoux, 'The Imperitival Use of ἵνα in the New Testament', *JTS* 42 [1941], pp. 165-73; H.G Meecham, 'The Imperatival Use of ἵνα in the New Testament', *JTS* 43 [1942], pp. 179-80; and the summary of the evidence by C.F.D. Moule in his *An Idiom-Book of New Testament Greek* [Cambridge: Cambridge University Press, 2nd edn, 1959], pp. 144-45). If this is the case, then the deliberateness of Jesus' intention to prove his authority is all the more pronounced.

It has, however, frequently been suggested that Mk 2.10a was not meant by Mark to be seen as a statement of Jesus to the Scribes. Rather it is a parenthetical remark addressed by the evangelist to the Christian readers of the Gospel to explain the significance of the closing phase of the healing for them (cf. Dibelius, *From Tradition to Gospel* [New York: Charles Scribner & Sons, 1933], p. 67; Boobyer, 'Mark II, 10a', pp. 115-20; C.P. Ceroke, 'Is Mk. 2,10 a Saying of Jesus?', *CBQ* 22 [1960], pp. 369-90; Cranfield, *Mark*, p. 100; J. Murphy-O'Connor, 'Pêche et Communaute dans le Nouveau Testament', *RB* 74 [1967], pp. 181-85; L.S. Hay, 'The Son of Man in Mk. 2:10 and 2:28', *JBL* 89 [1970], pp. 71-73; N. Perrin, 'The Christology of Mark: A Study in Methodology' in *A Modern Pilgrimage in New Testament Christology* [Philadelphia: Fortress Press, 1974], pp. 112, 116 n. 24; Lane, *Mark*, p. 98; and R.M. Fowler, *Loaves and Fishes* [Chico: Scholars Press, 1981], pp. 161-62. I do not find this conjecture convincing in that it is based primarily on a questionable assumption, namely that the title 'Son of Man' is here a designation of transcendent dignity which Mark would not have Jesus publicly apply to himself so early in his ministry. For trenchant criticisms of this assumption, see Hooker, *The Son of Man in Mark*, pp. 84-85; C. Tuckett 'The Present Son of Man', *JSNT* 14 (1982), pp. 58-81; and J.D. Kingsbury, *The Christology of Mark's Gospel* (Philadelphia: Fortress Press, 1983), pp. 83-84.

41. As does, for instance, Anderson, *Mark*, p. 101.

42. 'The stated purpose of the healing was a demonstration that Jesus had the power to forgive sins. There is no escaping the language and intention of the text' (W. Wink, 'Mark 2:1-12', *Int* 38 [1984], p. 61).

produce a 'sign' at Mk 8.11-13. In light of the evidence of Mk 2.1-12, it does not seem possible to assert that Jesus, according to Mark, held principled reservations against involving himself in any of the activities associated with the phenomenon of 'signs'.[43]

But why, then, if the Markan Jesus is not in principle opposed to the enterprise of producing, or giving in to the demand for, 'signs', does he refuse to engage in this activity when, as Mark recounts, the Pharisees demand that he do so?

The 'Sign' Demanded of Jesus at Mark 8.11

The answer lies, I think, in focusing attention on the 'sign' that the Pharisees ask for, and assuming that it is of a peculiar type, a type which the Markan Jesus would find offensive. That this is indeed what must be assumed becomes clear when we consider the implications of the facts that in Mk 8.11-13 the 'sign' demanded of Jesus is (1) designated by a specific name, (2) associated with one expected by 'this generation', and (3) identified as one which is 'given'.

1. *The Name of the 'Sign' Demanded of Jesus.* At Mk 8.11 Mark calls the 'sign' by a specific name. It is, he says, one which is ἀπὸ τοῦ οὐρανοῦ. Now, it is often thought that this phrase means nothing more than 'from God', and therefore that what Mark is doing in using it here is making a statement concerning not the content but the 'author' of the 'sign' demanded of Jesus.[44] But this cannot be the case for the following

---

43.   It should be noted that both Mk 1.21-28 and Mk 3.1-6 also provide evidence for this conclusion. In Mk 1.21-28 Mark presents Jesus as healing a demoniac to demonstrate, in the face of mild skepticism to the contrary (cf. v. 22), that he is in rightful possession of the authority with which he speaks (cf. D. Hill, 'Jesus and Josephus' "Messianic" Prophets', in E. Best and R. McL. Wilson [eds.], *Text and Interpretation: Studies in the New Testament Presented to Matthew Black* [Cambridge: Cambridge University Press, 1979], p. 150). In Mk 3.1-6 Mark has Jesus propose, and then carry out, a healing of a man with a withered hand in order to show that, contrary to the opinions of Pharisees and Herodians (cf v. 6; cp. v. 2), his actions of 'doing good' and 'saving life' prior to this occasion (i.e. the actions described in Mk 1.16–2.27) are authorized by God even though they sometimes fly in the face of current fashions in interpreting the Mosaic Law.

44.   See, for instance, Rengstorf, 'σημεῖον', p. 235, Lane, *Mark*, p. 275 n. 18; F. Hahn, *The Titles of Jesus in Christology* (London: Lutterworth, 1969), p. 378; J. Gnilka, *Das Evangelium nach Markus (Mk. 1–8:26)* (Zürich: Neukirchener Verlag, 1978), p. 306; and J. Sweetnam 'No Sign of Jonah', *Bib* 66 (1985), p. 126.

reasons. In the first place, Mark had no need to specify who ultimately stood behind the 'sign'. It was of the very nature of 'signs' to be 'from God', otherwise they would never have been taken, as we have seen they were, as evidence of trustworthiness. A phrase meaning 'from God' would here be superfluous and redundant. If Mark had merely intended that the Pharisees should be seen as content to receive any 'sign' so long as it had God as its author, he would have written only...ζητοῦντες παρ' αὐτοῦ σημεῖον, κτλ. and not, as he does, ζητοῦντες παρ' αὐτοῦ σμηεῖον ἀπὸ τοῦ οὐρανοῦ, κτλ.[45] And in the second place, when Mark does want to designate something as having divine origin, and uses a circumlocution to do so, the phrase he employs is ἐκ τοῦ οὐρανοῦ (ἐξ οὐρανοῦ), not ἀπὸ τοῦ οὐρανοῦ.[46] Accordingly, Mark's calling the 'sign' demanded of Jesus ἀπὸ τοῦ οὐρανοῦ must have another purpose. And that must be to specify not the source of the 'sign', but its 'shape'. The phrase, then, is an appellative, and as such it indicates that the 'sign' demanded of Jesus is one of a peculiar type, in a class all of its own, distinct in its content from any or all other 'signs' that the Pharisees might have requested.[47] But in Mark's eyes then, what content did a 'sign' ἀπὸ τοῦ οὐρανοῦ have?

Could he have thought it to be, as some have suggested,[48] a celestial portent? This is possible, for οὐρανός does sometimes means 'sky' in Mark's Gospel, for example, at 1.10; 4.32; 13.25 and possibly 13.31.[49] But that, according to Mark, the 'sign' demanded of Jesus was a 'sign out of the sky'—as this understanding of οὐρανοῦ would render the phrase in question—seems unlikely. For in the first place, 'sky' as the meaning of οὐρανός is hardly normal for Mark. In the eleven other instances (excluding Mk 8.11) in which he employs οὐρανός it does not

---

45. Cf. Mt. 12.38 where a group of Pharisees (and Scribes) is portrayed in exactly this way and their demand is only διδάσκαλε, θέλομεν ἀπὸ σοῦ σημεῖον ἰδεῖν.

46. Cf. Mk 1.11; 11.30, 31.

47. See H. Traub, 'οὐρανός', *TDNT*, V, p. 509. On ἀπό with the genitive as an appellative, see BDF §209, p. 113.

48. Cf., e.g., Cranfield, *Mark*, p. 258.

49. At first glance, 'sky' might seem to be the meaning of οὐρανός at Mk 6.41 and 7.34 as well. But given that the contexts of the use of the word is Jesus carrying out part of the ritual involved (in the first instance) in prayer and meal blessing and (in the second) exorcism, it seems more likely that οὐρανός is understood in these instances as a periphrasis for God.

bear this sense,[50] and in three out of the four instances in which it *does* mean 'sky' the word is part of an Old Testament quotation.[51] Secondly, and more importantly, in Mark's time the phrase ἀπὸ τοῦ οὐρανοῦ, when used, as it is here in Mk 8.11, with an object seems to have had a specific, technical meaning. This is clear when we look at the usage of the phrase in the Greek versions of the Old Testament, in the Old Testament Pseudepigrapha, and elsewhere in the New Testament.

The phrase ἀπὸ τοῦ οὐρανοῦ appears twelve times in the extant Greek versions of the Old Testament. It is used appositively nine times, as an appellative for:

- the rain that God has used to rid the earth of sinful humanity (Gen. 8.2);

- the celestial phenomenon which the sun and moon worshipping heathen regard as portents of their gods (Jer. 10.2);

- a figure called a 'watcher' who pronounces and then brings doom on King Nebuchadnezzar of Babylon for not acknowledging Yahweh as the Supreme God (Dan. 4.13, 23 [4.10, 20, 28, Theodotion]);

- God's all-powerful word (ὁ παντοδύναμός σου λόγος) which, in the form of a 'stern warrior carrying a sharp sword' who 'stood and filled all things with death', was unleashed against the Egyptian first-born on the first Passover (Wis. 18.15);

- the particular but unspecified phenomenon which Judas Maccabeus and his men knew to have been the decisive factor in destroying a Galatian army that set itself against God and his power (2 Macc. 8.20);[52]

- the aid which, in the form of a spectacularly armored warrior angel, accompanies the Maccabean army and helps to bring defeat to Lysias, the commander of Greek forces besieging Jerusalem (2 Macc. 11.10); and

---

50. Cf. Mk 1.11; 6.41; 7.34; 10.21; 11.25, 26, 30, 31; 12.25; 13.27, 31; 14.62.

51. Dan. 4.12 in Mk 4.32, Isa. 34.4 in Mk 13.25 and Dan. 7.12 in Mk 13.31.

52. For the historical event referred to in this verse, see J. Goldstein, *II Maccabees* (Garden City: Doubleday, 1983), pp. 331-34.

- the divine intervention that had given victory to a hopelessly outnumbered Maccabean army (2 Macc. 15.8).

So, with one exception (i.e., Jer. 10.2), in the Greek versions of the Old Testament an object which is ἀπὸ τοῦ οὐρανοῦ is always something which is instrumental in bringing about divine wrath against God or Israel's enemies and/or salvation to the people of God.

In the Pseudepigrapha the phrase ἀπὸ τοῦ οὐρανοῦ occurs six times.[53] In five of these instances it is used appositively, as an appelative for:

- God's 'might' which appears in the 'day of tribulation' to destroy the ungodly and bring peace to the righteous and the elect (*1. En.* 1.5).

- the fire that destroys two companies of emissaries from the apostate king Azariah when they come to serve summons on Elisha for forestalling an attempt by Azariah to inquire of his fate from Baalzebub, the God of Ekron, and for issuing an oracle of doom against the king (*Liv. Proph.* 21.10; cf. 2 Kgs 1.2-16).

- the good order (εὐνομίη) and utopian peace that will come to the persecuted faithful once the 'avenger' (ἔκδικος) 'dispenses justice' and destroys Rome, the enemy of God's people (*Sib. Or.* 3.373)

- the eclipsed light of the sun, the occurence of which, along with the falling of 'dust' (κονιορτός) ἀπ' οὐρανόθεν, signals the onset of both the 'day of judgment' against the 'ignorant and empty minded' Greeks who besiege the Temple, and God's establishment of the escatological kingdom for the faithful (*Sib. Or.* 3.802).

- fiery light that convinces the Egyptians, as they pursue the Israelites through the cleft Red Sea, that God offers his elect 'succor' and their enemies 'destruction' and which portends the ravaging of Pharaoh's host (*Ezek. Traj. Exagoge* 9.29, 14.42 [line 234 in Charlesworth, *OTP*]).

---

53. *1 En.* 1.4; *Liv. Proph.* 21.10; *Sib. Or.* 3.373; 3.802; 4.134; *Ezek. Trag.* 9.29, 14.42 (preserved in Eusebius, *Praep. Ev.* 9.29.5, 1-14, 50).

178   *The Temptations of Jesus in Early Christianity*

So, here too, as in the Greek versions of the Old Testament, something which is ἀπὸ τοῦ οὐρανοῦ seems always to be a phenomenon which is instrumental in bringing about divine wrath against Israel's enemies and/or salvation to the people of God.

Apart from Mk 8.12, the phrase ἀπὸ τοῦ οὐρανοῦ appears eleven times in the New Testament.[54] Of these instances it is used appositively six times, as an appellative for:

- the fire that Jesus' disciples want God to rain down on certain Samaritan villages as punishment for their inhabitants' refusal to receive Jesus (Lk. 9.54, cf. Lk. 9.51-56);

- the fiery phenomena that the Lukan Jesus says will be manifested on the day that the Son of Man comes to judge human beings for their iniquities (Lk. 17.29, cf. Lk. 11.30);

- the terrors and great signs (σημεῖα!) that will herald the arrival of the 'day of retribution' (Lk. 21.11, cf. Lk. 21.22);

- an angel which appears to Jesus during his ordeal in Gethsemane (Lk. 22.23);

- the particular appearance of Jesus which, according to Paul, will signal the arrival of the Day of the Lord (2 Thess. 1.17);

- the wrath of God, the revelation of which betokens the decisive unveiling of the righteousness of God in judgment against the unrighteousness of human beings (Rom. 1.18).

So in the New Testament the objects with which the phrase ἀπὸ τοῦ οὐρανοῦ is associated are always apocalyptic phenomena which embody or signal the onset of aid and comfort for God's elect and/or the wrath that God was expected to let loose against his enemies and those who threaten his people.

There is, then, a striking consistency of usage in Greek biblical literature as far as the phrase ἀπὸ τοῦ οὐρανοῦ used appositively and as an appellative is concerned. It is almost always associated with objects which embody the twin aspects of divine judgment—deliverance for those who are faithful to God and/or destruction of those who stand against him or his people.

---

54. Mt. 24.29; Lk. 9.54; 17.29; 21.21; 22.43; Jn 6.38; Rom. 1.18; 1 Thess. 4.16; 2 Thess. 1.7; Heb. 12.25; 1 Pet. 1.12.

This being the case, then a 'sign' which was ἀπὸ τοῦ οὐρανοῦ is most likely a phenomenon which embodied 'Salvation'.[55]

2. *The Association of the 'Sign' with 'This Generation'*. In Mk 8.12b— a castigation by Jesus of the Pharisees' demand[56]—Mark has Jesus state that the 'sign' demanded of him is of a certain type. It is one of those 'signs' that 'this generation' expected it would be shown should one claiming to be 'of God' wish to ensure that it ('this generation') would put its trust in him. But in Mark's view of things, what type of 'sign' was this? For this information I turn to Mk 15.28-32.

> And with him they crucified two robbers, one on his right and one on his left. [29] And those who passed by derided him, wagging their heads, and saying, 'Aha! You who would destroy the Temple and build it in three

---

55. In support of this, it is important to note that in two of the three times in the LXX (the exception being Job 7.9), in the one time in the Pseudepigrapha, and in each of the five times in the New Testament (i.e. Wis. 16.20; Sir. 46.17; *Sib. Or.* 4.134; Mt. 24.29; Jn 6.38; 1 Thess. 4.16; Heb. 12.25; 1 Pet. 1.12) where ἀπὸ τοῦ οὐρανοῦ is used adverbially, to designate a place of origin, the phrase is also linked with events or phenomena embodying some aspect of salvation. In Wis. 16.20 it is recalled that Israel was saved from perishing in the wilderness by bread sent by God ἀπ' οὐρανοῦ (καὶ ἕτοιμον ἄρτον αὐτοῖς ἀπ' οὐρανοῦ ἐπέμψας). According to Sir. 46.17 the phenomenon that destroyed the Philistines and Tyrians besetting Samuel was God's thundering ἀπ' οὐρανοῦ (καὶ ἐβρόντησεν ἀπ' οὐρανοῦ ὁ κύριος). In *Sib. Or.* 4.134 divine wrath that is to be directed directed against those who 'destroy the blameless tribe of the pious' is presented as having the form of showers of volcanic ash falling ἀπ' οὐρανοῦ (ψεκάδες πίπτωσιν ἀπ' οὐρανοῦ). The author of Hebrews states that the Israelites who were punished for disobedience were those who were being warned ἀπ' οὐρανοῦ of the loss of their salvation (οἱ τὸν ἀπ' οὐρανῶν ἀποστρεφόμενοι, Heb. 12.25). It was, according to 1 Pet. 1.12, the phenomenon of the Holy Spirit being sent ἀπ' οὐρανοῦ (ἐν πνεύματι ἁγίῳ ἀπ' οὐρανοῦ) that stood behind the experience of salvation (σωτηρίας, cf. v. 10) enkindled in the readers of the epistle by the words of the early Christian evangelists. In 1 Thess. 4.16 it is the event of Jesus' coming ἀπ' οὐρανοῦ (ὁ κύριος... καταβήσεται ἀπ' οὐρανοῦ) that heralds the resurrection of the saints. In Jn 6.38 it is Jesus' 'coming down' ἀπὸ τοῦ οὐρανοῦ that 'does' the divine will (καταβέβηκα ἀπὸ τοῦ οὐρανοῦ οὐχ ἵνα ποιῶ τὸ ἐμὸν ἀλλὰ τὸ θέλημα τοῦ πέμψαντός με) and allows the impartation of 'eternal life' to those who see the Son and believe in him (cf. Jn 6.40). And in Mt. 24.29 the arrival of the Son of Man for judgment is accompanied by stars that fall ἀπὸ τοῦ οὐρανοῦ (καὶ οἱ ἀστέρες πεσοῦνται ἀπὸ τοῦ οὐρανοῦ).

56. On this, see M. Meinertz, 'Dieses Geschlecht im Neuen Testament', *BZ* 1 (1957), pp. 283-89.

days, [30] save yourself and come down from the cross!' [31] So also the Chief Priests mocked him to one another with the Scribes, saying, 'He saved others; he cannot save himself. [32] Let the Christ, the King of Israel, come down now from the cross, that we may see and believe'. Those who were crucified with him also reviled him.

As even a casual glance at these verses shows, this is a story in which Jesus is asked to prove certain claims he is believed to have made by making something happen. In other words, *it is a story in which Jesus is faced with a demand for a 'sign'*. Three things need to be noted here:

The first thing is that according to Mark those who demand a 'sign' from Jesus are members of 'this generation'. This is sufficiently clear from the fact that Mark has these particular people—passers-by, chief priests, and Scribes—mock Jesus and hurl insults at him. But Mark underscores this point in several other ways. (1) He portrays those here demanding a 'sign' specifically in terms of the wicked who in Psalms 22 and 109, Wisdom 2 and Lamentations 2 heap derision on God's elect.[57] (2) At Mk 15.32 Mark has the mockers contemptuously appeal to Jesus for help in 'seeing' when they obviously have no intention of doing so. In this, Mark recalls Jesus' declaration at Mk 4.11-12 that the behaviour especially characteristic of 'this generation' is a refusal to engage in the 'seeing' that would lead to belief.[58] And (3) at 15.29 Mark identifies the mockery engaged in by those who here demand a 'sign' as blasphemy,[59] that is, wilful and perverse rejection of the revelation of God. According to Mark, blaspheming is an identifying mark of 'this generation' (cf. Mk 3.28-30; 7.6-9).

Secondly, the claim that Jesus is here called upon to prove by means of a 'sign' is that he is, as he has said or is thought to have said, Lord of the Temple,[60] Saviour, and the King of Israel (cf. vv. 29b, 31b, 32a). In other words, the issue in dispute, especially in light of Jesus' present ignoble circumstances, is whether or not he himself is 'of God'.

---

57. On this, see Lane, *Mark*, p. 569; Taylor, *Mark*, pp. 591-92.

58. On the emphasis in Mk 15.32 on 'seeing' in order to believe as a reference to Mk 4.12, see F.J. Matera, *The Kingship of Jesus* (Chico: Scholars Press, 1982), p. 28.

59. καὶ οἱ παραπορευόμενοι ἐβλασφήμουν αὐτόν, κτλ.

60. This is the implication of mocking charge, 'You who would destroy the Temple and rebuild it in three days...' (Mk 15.29b). See D. Senior, *The Passion of Jesus in the Gospel of Mark* (Wilmington, DE: Michael Glazier, 1984), p. 119; F.J. Matera, *Passion Narratives and Gospel Theologies* (Mahwah: Paulist Press, 1986), p. 44.

Thirdly, here the members of 'this generation' not only demand that Jesus make something happen before they accept his claims. *They dictate to him what he must make happen before they will 'see and believe'* (cf. v. 32). They do not leave it up to him to decide the terms of the 'sign' they will accept from him. This fact is significant. It implies that the particular 'sign' here demanded of Jesus is the only type of 'sign' that would be taken by 'this generation' as proof for the truth of the claims that are now under dispute.

There is, then, according to Mark, a strong formal connection and correspondence between the 'sign' demanded of Jesus by the Chief Priests and others at Jesus' crucifixion and that demanded of Jesus by the Pharisees at Mk 8.11-13. In his mind the respective 'signs' are similar, if not identical, in 'shape'. Accordingly, once we determine the 'shape' of the 'sign' demanded of Jesus in Mk 15.28-32, we will also have determined the 'shape' of the 'sign' that Jesus is asked to produce in Mk 8.11-13.

What, then, is this 'sign'? Mark notes that it is Jesus 'saving' himself by 'coming down from his cross' (σῶσον σεαυτὸν καταβὰς ἀπὸ τοῦ σταυροῦ, v. 30; καταβάτω νῦν ἀπὸ τοῦ σταυροῦ, v. 32). In other words, the 'sign' demanded from Jesus is a phenomenon that embodies and effects 'deliverance'. But deliverance of whom, and from what? Certainly at the very least it is rescue of an individual from personal tragedy, since the challenge to 'save yourself' and 'come down from the cross' confronts a broken man who is embroiled in a life-extinguishing situation. But it is much more than this. For, in the first place, in Mark's Gospel to 'save oneself' by 'coming down from the cross' represents blatant self aggrandizement and not simply self preservation. This is clear from the fact that Mark has Jesus define 'saving oneself' through a wilful rejection of 'cross bearing' as tantamount both to asserting oneself over others at their expense[61] and to the attempt—on the part of individuals as well as nations—to gain and use worldly power to conquer and fiercely dominate their enemies.[62] In the second place, according to Mark, the appeal to Jesus to 'save himself' is addressed to him not just

---

61. Cf. Mk 8.34-38.
62. Cf. Mk 10.42-45. That Mark intended to have these verses seen as a continuation of Jesus' teaching at Mk 8.34-38 on the nature of 'cross bearing' seems abundantly clear if only from the fact that, as with Mk 8.34-38, Mark has prefaced Mk 10.42-45 with a 'passion prediction' of Jesus and a story of the disciples failing or refusing to understand this prediction (cf. Mk 8.31-33; cp. 10.32-41).

as an individual, but as the supreme Jewish national figure—'the King of Israel' (and therefore, the embodiment of the people of God)—who has been reduced to his present fate (the cross) in this identity by conquerors of Israel.[63] So, according to Mark, the deliverance attested to by the 'sign' of Jesus 'coming down from the cross' is the deliverance, through conquest and not suffering service, of Israel from national oppression.[64]

This being the case concerning the type of 'sign' that, according to Mark, 'this generation' typically seeks and desires, then the 'sign' demanded of Jesus at Mk 8.11-13—also a 'sign' that 'this generation' seeks (cf. Mk 8.12)—must have been, in Mark's eyes, a phenomenon of a particular kind, one that was associated with (and indeed, intimated) Israel's liberation from, and conquest of, its enemies.[65]

3. *The 'Sign' as One Which is to be 'Given'.* In Mk 8.12c Mark has Jesus define the 'sign' demanded of him as one which is to be 'given' (δοθήσεται). Significantly, this is a signal characteristic of the 'signs' which, according to Jesus in Mk 13.22, will be offered to the inhabitants of Jerusalem and Judea by certain 'sign' workers during a time of grave national crisis (cf. Mk 13.14ff.). These 'signs' are also ones that are to be 'given' (δώσουσιν σημεῖα, κτλ.).[66] It seems clear, then, because of

63. Cf. Mk 15.24-25.

64. Cf. Matera, *Passion Narratives*, p. 44; Senior, *Passion of Jesus*, pp. 119-21; J. Blackwell, *The Passion as Story: The Plot of Mark* (Philadelphia: Fortress Press, 1986), pp. 72-73.

65. It should be pointed out that in the New Testament this connection between 'this generation' and 'signs' of this type is not Mark's alone. Paul also knows it to be the case, as is apparent from 1 Cor. 1.22 where he attributes the rejection of a crucified Christ by Jews who are among 'the foolish' and 'those who are perishing' (Pauline equivalents for 'this generation') to a desire for 'signs' (σημεῖα). And the author of the Gospel of John makes reference to it when he has Jesus complain that belief does not arise in his contemporaries unless they 'see signs and wonders' (ἐὰν μὴ σημεῖα καὶ τέρατα ἴδητε, οὐ μὴ πιστεύσητε, Jn 4.48). On this, see R.E. Brown, *The Gospel according to John 1–12* (Garden City, NY: Doubleday, 1966), pp. 195-96. On the meaning of the term σημεῖα καὶ τέρατα, see below, pp. 189-90.

66. D *f*13 the Diatessaron a (Origen) Victor of Antioch and certain other witnesses describe these σημεῖα as those which will be 'shown' or 'performed' (ποιέω), rather than 'given' (δίδωμι). On δώσουσιν σημεῖα, κτλ. rather than ποιησοῦσιν σημεῖα, κτλ. as the preferred reading for Mk 13.22, see C.H. Turner, 'Western Readings in the Second Half of St Mark's Gospel', *JTS* (1928), pp. 9-10; Taylor, *Mark*, p. 516; and B.M. Metzger, *A Textual Commentary on the Greek New*

this, that in Mark's eyes the type of 'sign' that is demanded of Jesus at Mk 8.11 is cut from the same cloth as those which the 'sign' workers of Mk 13.22 are wont to produce. But what type of 'sign' are they? How does Mark envisage their content? He lets us know this in three ways: (a) by giving specific information concerning the identity of those who work these 'signs', (b) in calling these 'signs' σημεῖα καὶ τέρατα, and (c) in noting the effect that these 'signs' might have upon those who see them.

a. *The Identity of the 'Sign' Workers of Mark 13.22.* Mark, through Jesus, characterizes those who produce the 'signs' referred to in Mk 13.22 in three different ways. The first way is as 'false christs' (ψευδόχριστοι, cf. Mk 13.22). Now, for Mark, Jesus is the Christ (cf. Mk 1.1), and since Mark takes great pains to show that Jesus' identity *as* the Christ is grounded in suffering and service, and stands solidly against triumphalism, chauvinism and despotism (cf. esp. Mk 8.27-37; 9.31-37; 10.32-45), then Mark's designation through Jesus of the 'sign' workers of Mk 13.22 as 'false Christs' means one thing. They are Messianic pretenders who hold that their identity as Messiah is bound up in engaging in, and encouraging their followers towards, violence, conquest and war.[67]

The 'sign' workers of Mk 13.22 are also referred to as 'false prophets' (ψευδοπροφῆται, Mk 13.22). For Mark, a prophet is primarily one who calls Israel to become the people that God would have them be.[68] Accordingly, a 'False Prophet' is someone who leads the people of Israel towards national behaviour that is the antithesis of what God has ordained for them. Now, in Mark's Gospel Jesus is, among other things, a prophet.[69] And it is *as* a prophet that he warns Israel against taking its status as the chosen people as a pretext or justification for becoming involved in any form of exclusivistic nationalism.[70] He

Testament (New York: United Bible Societies, 1971), p. 112.

67. See Lane, *Mark*, p. 473; G.R. Beasley-Murray, *A Commentary on Mark Thirteen* (London: Macmillan, 1957), p. 83.

68. Cf. Mk 1.2-8, where John the Baptizer, who is, according to Mark, the embodiment of the prophet Elijah, does precisely this.

69. He is not only called this by others at Mk 6.15 and 8.28, but, according to Mark, he refers to himself as such at Mk 6.4. Moreover, Mark underscores the idea of Jesus as prophet by portraying Jesus as following in the footsteps of John the Baptizer. The idea of Jesus as prophet is also possibly intimated in Mark's designation of Jesus as ὁ ἐρχόμενος (on this, see Hahn, *Titles*, 380).

70. This is the import of such stories as the Calling of Levi (Mk 2.13-17) and the

calls Israel to see that its national identity as the people of God is bound up with being a servant to, and not a lord of, other nations.[71] By implication, then, for Mark, 'False Prophets' are people who advocate for Israel behaviour that is despotic in character and is set upon achieving worldly domination.

Finally, the 'sign' workers of Mk 13.22 are identified by Mark as identical with the 'many' (πολλοί) spoken of in Mk 13.5-6.[72] Now, according to Mark, the 'many' 'come in my name' (ἐλεύσονται ἐπὶ τῷ ὀνόματί μου) and they proclaim 'I am' (λέγοντες ὅτι ἐγώ εἰμι). What do these actions signify? With respect to 'coming in my name' a great number of scholars have taken up the view that this action signifies the laying of a claim on the part of people within the Christian community to be speaking to other Christians on Jesus' behalf[73] or even to *be* Jesus himself returned from on high.[74] In support of this view they point to two facts: (1) that the phrase 'to come in my name' generally means 'appealing to me as their authority', 'claiming to be sent by

---

Healing of the Syro-Phonecian Woman's Daughter (Mk 7.24-30), as well as of Jesus' teaching on the tradition of the elders (Mk 7.1-23).

71. This is most apparent in Jesus' teaching to the Twelve (i.e. the New Israel) in Mk 9.33-36 and Mk 10.42-45. But it is also the special import of Jesus' prophetic-symbolic act of 'cleansing' the Temple (Mk 11.15-19, cf. esp. vv. 17). On this, see D. Hill, 'Jesus and Josephus' "Messianic" Prophets', p. 150; G.W. Buchanan, 'Mark 11,15-19: Brigands in the Temple', *HUCA* 30 (1959), pp. 169-77; C. Roth, 'The Cleansing of the Temple and Zechariah 14:21', *Nov T* 4 (1960), pp. 174-81; W.W. Waty, 'Jesus and the Temple—Cleansing or Cursing?', *ExpTim* 93 (1981–82), pp. 235-39.

72. This is clear from the fact that Mark describes both groups in identical terms. They both 'lead astray' (cf. Mk 13.22; cp. Mk 13.5, 6).

73. Cf. J.V. Bartlet, *St Mark* (Edinburgh: T.C. & E.C. Jack, 1922), p. 352; C.H. Turner, *The Gospel according to St Mark* (London: Macmillan, 1928), p. 63; W. Grundmann, *Das Evangelium nach Markus* (Berlin: Evangelische Verlagsanstalt, 1965), p. 263; T.J. Weeden, *Mark—Traditions in Conflict* (Philadelphia: Fortress Press, 1971), pp. 88-89; W.H. Kelber, *The Kingdom in Mark: A New Time and a New Place* (Philadelphia: Fortress Press, 1974), p. 115.

74. This is, at least at first glance, a plausible position to take in this regard since the pronoun μου must refer to the speaker of the phrase ἐπὶ τῷ ὀνόματί μου, who is in this case Jesus (cf. Mk 13.5). But whether or not it is actually the case turns on knowing in what persona Mark has Jesus speaking here. Is it as the carpenter from Nazareth, the son of Mary, or is it more officially as God's anointed? On this, see below.

me',[75] and in this case probably 'usurping my identity',[76] and (2) that the personal pronoun in this phrase (μου) can only refer to the speaker, Jesus (cf. Mk 13.3).[77] But their view is untenable. In the first place, there is nothing in the text that would indicate that Mark intended the audience of the 'many' to be seen as the Christian community.[78] Certainly, Mark envisages here that Christians will *hear* the 'many' (cf. v. 5), but that seems to be only by accident. For in Mk 13.5-7, the people that the 'many' target and win over with their proclamations are specifically distinguished from the disciples and other followers of Jesus: they have never been privy, as the disciples and other followers of Jesus have (cf. v. 5), to Jesus' warnings about the ill effects of the proclamations of the 'many'.[79] Secondly, in Mk 13.5-7 Mark, through Jesus, designates the 'many' who 'come in my name' as originating *outside of* the circle of Jesus' followers. He does this by having Jesus speak of the 'many' in the third and not the second person. Had Mark wanted the 'many' to be seen as Christians, he would have had Jesus say something like 'many of *you* will come in my name...'[80] And thirdly, the referent of the phrase cannot be the name 'Jesus'. For a number of reasons, it must be a *title* that Jesus alone has the right to bear, namely the title 'Messiah':[81] (1) One cannot construe the phrase 'coming in my name' as a claim either to stand in for 'Jesus' (i.e. the man from Nazareth) or to *be* him without rendering the sentence in which it appears contradictory. As W. Weiffenbach long ago observed, 'He who legitimizes himself through

75. Cf. H. Bientenhard, 'ὄνομα', *TDNT*, V, p. 271; Cranfield, *Mark*, p. 359.

76. Cranfield, *Mark*, p. 359; W. Heitmuller, *'Im Namen Jesu'* (Göttingen: Vandenhoeck & Ruprecht, 1903); G.R. Beasley-Murray, *Mark Thirteen*, pp. 32-33; M. Hooker, 'Trial and Tribulation in Mark XIII', *BJRL* 65 (1982), p. 85.

77. Cf. E. Klostermann, *Das Markusevangelium* (Tübingen: Mohr/Siebeck, 1950), p. 133.

78. *Contra* J. Wellhausen, *Das Evangelium Marci* (Berlin: George Reimer, 1909), p. 101; W. Manson, 'ΕΓΩ EIMI of the Messianic Presence in the New Testament', *JTS* 48 (1947), p. 139, and all of the authors cited above in note 73.

79. Indeed, this is why they are seduced by the 'many'. See Hooker, 'Trial and Tribulation', p. 85.

80. Cf. E. Best, *Mark: The Gospel as Story* (Edinburgh: T. & T. Clark, 1983), p. 48; Beasley-Murray, *Mark Thirteen*, p. 31; Hooker, 'Trial and Tribulation', p. 85. In line with this, we should also note that there is no independent evidence (Acts 20.29-30 and 1 Jn 2.18 notwithstanding) of the existence of such Christians in the early Church.

81. Gould, *Mark*, p. 243; Swete, *Mark*, p. 298; Cranfield, *Mark*, p. 395.

the ὄνομα of Jesus cannot at the same time claim the same ὄνομα'.[82] (2) If Mark meant the 'many' to be seen as claiming to be standing in for Jesus or to be him, it is difficult to see why at v. 6 he did not write simply πολλοὶ ἐλεύσονται λέγοντες ὅτι ἐγώ εἰμι.[83] (3) Matthew understood the claim made by the 'many' in Mk 13.6 to be a claim to be the Messiah (cf. Mt. 24.5). (4) Most importantly, elsewhere in Mark's Gospel, when the phrase 'in (on) my name' appears on the lips of Jesus, the 'name' referred to is *not* the personal name 'Jesus' *but the title* χριστός.[84] The phrase 'coming in my name', then, in this context means claiming to be God's Anointed, his Deliverer,[85] and the activity it signifies is tantamount to attempting to rival Jesus for recognition as the figure empowered by God to bring salvation to Israel.[86]

And what of the second action, proclaiming ἐγώ εἰμι? D. Daube has shown[87] that the phrase ἐγώ εἰμι was associated in Mark's time primarily with Yahweh's presence, especially as that presence was made known during the time of the Exodus. Accordingly, to proclaim 'I am' is tantamount to announcing the dawning of the time in which Israel would be liberated from all enemies.

In light of all of this we may conclude that in identifying the 'sign' workers of Mk 13.22 with the 'many' of Mk 13.5-6 and in characterizing the many as those who both 'come in my name' and proclaim 'I am', Mark intended these 'sign' workers to be seen as those who claim to be divinely elected to be God's instrument in bringing about the deliverance of his people from their enemies and who also announce that

---

82. Weiffenbach, *Weiderkunftsgedanke Jesu nach den Synoptikern* (Leipzig: Druck & Verlag, 1873), p. 196. Cf. also Klostermann, *Das Markusevangelium*, p. 133.

83. Klostermann, *Das Markusevangelium*, p. 133; Beasley-Murray, *Mark Thirteen*, p. 32.

84. Cf. Mk 9.37, 39, 40.

85. Blunt, *Mark*, p. 239; Hooker, 'Trial and Tribulation', p. 85.

86. Gould, *Mark*, p. 243; Swete, *Mark*, p. 243; Branscomb, *Mark*, p. 235; Rawlinson, *St Mark*, p. 184; Blunt, *Mark*, p. 239; Klostermann, *Markusevangelium*, p. 133; Beasley-Murray, *Mark Thirteen*, p. 31; Cranfield, *Mark*, p. 395; Lane, *Mark*, pp. 456-57; M.-J Lagrange, *L'Evangile selon Saint Marc* (Paris: Gabalda, 1929), p. 336; H. Conzelmann, 'Geschichte und Eschaton nach Mc xiii', *ZNW* 50 (1959), p. 218; S.E. Johnson, *The Gospel according to St Mark* (London: A. & C. Black, 1960), p. 213; C.S. Mann, *Mark* (Garden City: Doubleday, 1986), p. 514.

87. Daube, 'The "I AM" of the Messianic Presence', in *The New Testament and Rabbinic Judaism* (London: Athlone, 1956), pp. 325-29.

the time of this deliverance is now at hand.[88]

Now it should be pointed out that these characteristics are exactly those of the so-called 'Sign-Prophets'—Theudas, the unnamed γοητής, the 'Egyptian'—who were active in Judaea in the years immediately preceding the outbreak of the Jewish Revolt against Rome[89] and who would have been known to both Mark and his readers. They, too, claimed that they were expressly sent by God to fulfil a divine plan of liberation and worldly exaltation of Israel which involved the violent overthrow of Israel's enemies,[90] and, announcing that the time of

88. Cf. Klostermann, *Markusevangelium*, p. 136. Notably, this is exactly how Luke understands this phrase. He renders it not as a statement of identity or a claim to dignity, but as the specific announcement ὁ καιρὸς ἤγγικεν (Lk. 21.8).

89. Theudas appeared during the procuratorship of Cuspius Fadus (44–48 CE); the 'Egyptian' and a group of γοητές appeared when Antonius Felix was procurator (52–60 CE); and an unnamed γοής appeared when Porcius Festus ruled (60–62 CE).

90. The claim of Theudas in this regard is inherent in his declaring himself to be προφήτης (προφήτης γὰρ ἔλεγεν εἶναι, *Ant.* 20.97), that is, one like Moses (on this, see R. Meyer, 'προφήτης', *TDNT*, VI, pp. 812-28, esp. p. 826; J. Jeremias, 'Μωϋσῆς', *TDNT*, IV, pp. 848-73, esp. 862) and Joshua *redivivus* (cf. *Ant.* 20.97), and that, as Gamaliel is recorded as noting in Acts 5.36, he 'gave himself out to be somebody' (λέγων εἶναί τινα ἑαυτόν), that is, God's instrument for salvation (on this, see O. Betz, 'Miracles in the Writings of Josephus', in L.H. Feldman and G. Hata (eds.), *Josephus, Judaism, and Christianity* [Detroit: Wayne State University Press, 1987], pp. 212-35, esp. p. 229). It also stands behind the fact that Cuspius Fadus felt constrained to send his troops against Theudas when Theudas's claims became known.

In the case of the 'Egyptian', the claim is clear from the fact that he, too, used the title ὁ προφήτης and presented himself as a new Joshua (*Ant.* 20.169-70) and that he proclaimed himself destined not only to overthrow the Roman garrison in Jerusalem but to 'set himself up as "leader (tyrant) of the people"' (τοῦ δήμου τυραννεῖν, *War* 2.262). It also is implied by the fact that the Roman governor of Judaea arrested him as a rebel against Rome (*War* 2.262).

The claim to this commission on the part of the γοήτες active during Felix's procuratorship is implied by the fact that they presented themselves as capable of bestowing the same blessings that Moses had from God for Israel (cf. *Ant.* 20.167-68; cp. 2.327) and in that, as Josephus reports things, they declared their activities to be 'in accord with God's plan of salvation' (κατὰ τὴν τοῦ θεοῦ πρόνοιαν γινόμενα). It is also implied by the fact that Felix regarded their posturings and promises as tantamount to a encouraging revolt (*War* 2.261). In the case of the unnamed γοής, this is clear from the fact that he declared that he was capable of bringing to Israel 'salvation' (σωτηρία) and 'rest from troubles' (παῦλαν κακῶν, *Ant.* 20.188). On all of this, see Hill, 'Jesus and Josephus' "Messianic Prophets"',

salvation had arrived, they gathered followers and encouraged them to rise up against their oppressors.[91] So not only is there a correspondence in Mark's Gospel between the 'sign' workers of Mk 13.22 and the historical 'Sign-Prophets' mentioned in Josephus and other sources,[92] there is a correspondence so exact that it cannot be anything but intentionally drawn. Accordingly, in describing and characterizing the 'sign' workers of Mk 13.22 in the particular ways he does, Mark was clearly identifying them with Theudas and his ilk.

Given this, it is extremely important to note that *the 'signs' offered by these 'Sign-Prophets' were phenomena copying the substance of one or another of the events of the time of the Exodus and Conquest which were instrumental in securing freedom from subjugation and dominance for the people of God.* The 'sign' that Theudas offered on his own behalf—and which, notably, was intended to grant safe passage for any who would march into Jerusalem against the Romans—was a re-enactment of Moses' division of the Reed Sea and/or Joshua's division of the Jordan.[93] The 'signs' offered by the unnamed γοητές active during the procuratorship of Antonius Felix were embodiments of the plagues which foreshadowed and brought about the liberation of God's people from their Egyptian bondage or re-runs of the events wrought by Moses when he confronted Pharaoh's court magicians that indicated the eventual subjugation of Pharaoh to God.[94] The 'signs' promised by the γόης who was active during Porcius Festus' procuratorship were to intimate the relief from slavery that the Israelites experienced when

pp. 147-48; Jeremias, 'Μωϋσῆς', p. 862; Betz, 'Miracles', pp. 226-31.

91. Cf. *Ant*. 20.97-99, 167-68, 169, 188; *War* 2.258-59, 261; 6.284-86.

92. Besides the passages from Josephus and Acts that I have already noted, references to the Judaean 'Sign-Prophets' can also be found in Acts 21.38; Eusebius, *History of the Church* 2.21; *b. Sanh.* 67a, and possibly Mt. 24.11-12, 24-26.

93. Cf. Meyer, 'προφήτης', p. 826; Jeremias, 'Μωϋσῆς', p. 862; Barnett, 'Jewish Sign Prophets', p. 681; Betz, 'Miracles', p. 228.

94. According to Josephus, the first of these 'signs' were 'signs of freedom' (σημεῖα ἐλευθερίας). Notably, this is a term which Josephus employs in his Exodus narrative for the plagues that foreshadowed the coming 'liberation' of God's people (cf. *Ant*. 2.327, τῶν...τὴν ἐλευθερίαν αὐτοῖς σημεῖον). The second of these were 'wonders and signs' (τέρατα καὶ σημεῖα) which were to 'accord with God's plan' (κατὰ τὴν τοῦ θεοῦ πρόνοιαν γινόμενα). This is a term which Josephus specifically applied to the σημεῖα wrought by Moses when he confronted Pharaoh's court magicians (cf. *Ant*. 2.286). On this, see Rengstorf, 'σημεῖον', p. 225.

Yahweh vanquished Pharaoh.[95] And the 'sign' that the 'Egyptian' sought to work—a 'sign' which, he thought, would in its manifestation specifically serve to overthrow the Roman garrison in Jerusalem—was the act of judgment performed by Joshua against Jericho.[96]

The ultimate effect, then, of Mark's characterization of the 'sign' workers referred to in Mk 13.22 as 'false christs', 'false prophets' and identical with the 'many' of Mk 13.6 is not only to identify these 'sign' workers with the historical 'Sign-Prophets' mentioned in Josephus and other sources. *It is to specify the type of 'sign' that, according to Mark, these 'sign' workers were wont to offer.* Since Mark intended the 'sign' workers of Mk 13.22 to be seen as identical with the likes of Theudas, the 'Egyptian', and Josephus' γοητής, then he also meant the 'signs' that the former group are said to offer to be taken as identical in type with those proffered by the latter. They, too, are 'signs of salvation', 'signs of freedom', phenomena betokening for Israel its impending deliverance from national oppression.

b. *The Name Given to the 'Signs' of Mark 13.22.* Through Jesus, Mark calls these 'signs' σημεῖα καὶ τέρατα (Mk 13.22). This phrase is sometimes found in ancient literature with the sense of 'miracle',[97] so Mark's calling the 'signs' offered by the 'sign' workers of Mk 13.22 by this name could be an indication more of character than of content. However, S.V. McCasland has demonstrated that in the LXX the phrase σημεῖα καὶ τέρατα was a *terminus technicus* for the 'mighty deeds', the acts of deliverance which God gave to Israel through Moses, Aaron and Joshua in connection with the Exodus and Conquest.[98] McCasland notes:

> Miraculous deeds are found in other places [in the Old Testament], such as Judges and Kings, especially in the careers of Elijah and Elisha, but these events are never referred to as signs and wonders in the characteristic passages in which the idiom occurs. It is evident that although the Hebrews believed in the continuous activity of God as the sovereign of history, who manifested his personal interest and power in all the great

95. On this, see Barnett, 'Jewish Sign Prophets', p. 685.

96. He promised that upon his command (ὡς κελεύσαντος αὐτοῦ) the walls of Jerusalem would collapse (*Ant.* 20.169). On the correspondence in the mind of the 'Egyptian' between Jerusalem and Jericho, see Barnett, 'Jewish Sign Prophets', p. 683; Betz, 'Miracles', p. 229.

97. Cf. Rengstorf, 'σημεῖον', pp. 206-207; M. Whittaker, '"Signs and Wonders": The Pagan Background', *SE* 5 (1965), pp. 155-58.

98. S.V. McCasland, 'Signs and Wonders', *JBL* 76 (1957), pp. 149-52.

experiences of the Hebrew people, it was his intention to deliver them from Egypt and lead them into Canaan which became the unique revelation of Yahweh's true character. The story was normative for the idea of God as far as signs and wonders were concerned.[99]

Now this is certainly the sense the phrase bears in Mk 13.22. For, in the first place, as McCasland also notes,[100] 'the mighty deeds by which God liberated Israel from Egypt' is the primary meaning which the phrase had not only in the Old Testament but in the New Testament as well, particularly in its writings or sections of writings that, like Mark 13, are apocalyptic in nature or tone. Secondly, Mark is careful always to use only the word δυναμεῖς when he wants to designate a deed or an event a 'miracle'.[101] And, thirdly, there is a specific allusion in Mk 13.22 to Deut. 13.2-3 ('If a prophet arises among you...and gives to you a sign or a wonder, and if the sign or the wonder comes to pass, and if he says, "Let us go after other gods", which you have not known, "and let us serve them", you shall not listen to the words of that prophet...for the Lord is testing you...'), where the expression 'sign or wonder' (σημεῖον ἢ τέρας) is a direct reference to the God's wonders in the days of Moses.[102]

So we may conclude that in calling the 'signs' of the 'sign' workers of Mk 13.22 σημεῖα καὶ τέρατα, Mark was identifying these 'signs' specifically with the liberating works carried out by God during the Exodus.

c. *The Effect of Seeing the 'Signs' of Mark 13.22.* According to Mark, the 'signs' referred to in Mk 13.22 are of a type that, once seen, threaten to 'lead astray' (πρὸς τὸ ἀποπλανᾶν, Mk 13.22) the people of Jerusalem and Judaea,[103] even though these people have witnessed the appearance of the 'abomination of desolation standing where he ought not' (cf. Mk 13.14). Now, for Mark, the abomination is an act of sacrilege so appalling that tribulation is certain to follow in its wake.[104]

99. McCasland, 'Signs and Wonders', p. 150.
100. McCasland, 'Signs and Wonders', p. 151; see also Rengstorf, 'σημεῖον', p. 241.
101. Cf. V.K. Robbins, 'Dynameis and Semeia in Mark', *BibRes* 18 (1973), pp. 5-20, esp. pp. 17-20.
102. Cf. Rengstorf, 'σημεῖον', p. 221. That Mark is alluding in Mk 13.22 to Deut. 13.1-3, see Swete, *Mark*, p. 310; Beasley-Murray, *Mark Thirteen*, pp. 83-84; Lane, *Mark*, p. 473.
103. Cf. Mk 13.14-21.
104. On this see, Lane, *Mark*, pp. 466-72.

Its appearance signals two things: first, that the destruction of the Temple and its environs is both inevitable and near,[105] and, second, that for the people of God flight from Jerusalem and Judaea is both imperative for survival and divinely mandated.[106] So in Mark's eyes, to be 'led astray' means to be made to think that all of this is not the case.

Accordingly, 'signs' that threaten to 'lead astray' are those which tempt one to believe, despite clear evidence and divine warnings to the contrary, that for the Temple and the people of Jerusalem and Judaea, deliverance, not destruction, is at hand.

But what kind of 'signs' would serve to convince a people whose survival and faithfulness depends upon fleeing, that flight is not only unnecessary, but actually a form of unbelief? What, if anything, was the 'shape' of these 'signs'?

To answer this I turn to Josephus, and his description in Book 6 of *The Jewish War* of an event in the last stages of the revolt of the Jews against Rome which in substance is an exact parallel (if not the actual historical referent) of that envisioned in Mk 13.22. The event occurred when Titus' soldiers breached the Temple Gates and began to mount the attack which ended in their setting fire to the Holy of Holies. Josephus tells us that just prior to this, the Jews of Jerusalem, ignoring clear and repeated warnings from God that the city was doomed and would be destroyed by the encroaching Roman forces (cf. 6.288-315), and oblivious to an abominating sacrilege committed in their midst by one of their number (cf. 6.201-219), had gathered in the inner sanctuary of Herod's Temple. There, they thought, they would be safe and could continue their rebellion undaunted, for they had convinced themselves that the Temple was still impregnable and the inner courts inviolable. So the breach of the gates sounded the death knell to Jewish hopes for the success of the revolt. It was the final and unmistakable signal that Jerusalem had met its end, and it made flight from the city imperative for those who wished to escape the Roman sword. Yet despite this, one man (whom, notably, Josephus labels a ψευδοπροφήτης, 6.288) was

---

105. Cf. Lane, *Mark*, p. 466; D. Daube, 'The Abomination of Desolation', in *The New Testament and Rabbinic Judaism* (London: Athlone Press, 1956), pp. 418-37; B. Rigaux, 'ΒΔΕΛΥΓΜΑ ΤΗΣ ΕΡΕΜΟΣΕΟΣ (Mc 13,14; Mt 24,15)', *Bib* 40 (1959), pp. 675-83.

106. Cf. Mk 13.14a-19. On this, see Daube, 'Abomination', pp. 422-23; Beasley-Murray, *Mark Thirteen*, pp. 57-58.

still able to induce 'thousands',[107] who were on the verge of fleeing the Sanctuary and saving themselves, not only to stay their ground, but to go out into the outer courts of the Temple to face the army that was waiting there to cut them down (6.288). He did this, Josephus says, by promising to effectuate specific 'signs', namely 'signs of salvation' (σημεῖα τῆς σωτηρίας, 6.288). Now, the expression 'signs of salvation' is one which Josephus uses for the actions of God during the Exodus which decimated the enemies of his people and led to the liberation of Israel from national subjugation.[108] It is clear, then, that the type of 'sign' that could serve to forestall and make light of necessary flight—the type of 'sign' which Mark, through Jesus, says the 'sign' workers of Mk 13.22 would offer—was that which, in content, embodied 'the mighty hand' and 'the outstretched arm' of Yahweh and recapitulated one of the 'great and terrible deeds' which God wrought on Israel's behalf at the time of the Exodus.

From all of this, it is abundantly clear that according to Mark 'signs' that are 'given' are 'signs' that embody and betoken the deliverance from bondage that Israel experienced at the Exodus. And since, as we have seen above, the 'sign' demanded of Jesus at Mk 8.11 is designated in the following verse as one such 'sign', then it, too, in Mark's view, is a phenomenon of this sort.

In summary, the fact that the 'sign' demanded of Jesus in Mk 8.11 is designated by Mark as ἀπὸ τοῦ οὐρανοῦ, together with the fact that it is associated with one expected by 'this generation' and is specified as one which is 'given', justifies my assumption that this 'sign' is of a peculiar type. From all that is implied by these facts, it is clear that according to Mark the 'sign' is a phenomenon whose content is apocalyptic in tone, triumphalistic in character, and the embodiment of one of the 'mighty deeds of deliverance' that God had worked on Israel's behalf in rescuing it from slavery.

The Issue at Stake for Jesus

In drawing this conclusion, it is important to note that in Mark's time these particular 'signs' seem to have been perceived in a particular way.

107. Josephus gives the total number as six thousand, including the women, children, and the elderly who had accompanied the last remnants of the Jewish army into the Temple.

108. Cf. Rengstorf, 'σημεῖον', pp. 223-25; Barnett, 'Jewish Sign Prophets', p. 686; Betz, 'Miracles', p. 227.

They were viewed as a 'means of confirmation' accrediting as 'of God' those in whose behalf they were to be worked. More importantly, *it appears that they were also thought of as something that, once manifested, would prompt a rerun of the saving action God undertook on Israel's behalf during the period of the Exodus and the Conquest.*[109]

It is also important to note that Mark shared this view. This is clear from the fact that, as we have seen, in his portrayal of the 'sign' workers of Mk 13.22, Mark notes that the offering of such 'signs' would give confidence to those both working and seeing them that, despite overwhelming evidence to the contrary, they would be saved from the imminent and certain destruction that was about to befall them.

Once we realize this—that for Mark 'signs' of the type which Jesus is asked by the Pharisees to produce were, given their content, 'levers' by which the hand of God could be activated, indeed, even forced, into bringing about the destruction of Israel's enemies[110]—then the reason why Jesus is portrayed at Mk 8.1-13 as refusing to accede to a demand

---

109. That this was indeed the case is the implication of the following:

First, that the 'Sign Prophet' Theudas was certain that after his 'sign' was effectuated he could walk, as he planned, into Jerusalem unmolested by the Roman forces stationed there despite his knowledge of the fact that these forces would certainly take his 'sign' as a challenge to their authority and act accordingly (Josephus, *Ant.* 20.97-99).

Secondly, that Theudas could gather followers who were willing to accompany him to the banks of the Jordan (where, as we have seen above, his 'sign' was to be manifested) despite the known risk that in response to doing so, Roman troops would be sent out against them (cf. Josephus, *War* 20.99).

Thirdly, that the 'Egyptian' could claim that immediately upon actuating his 'sign', the Roman garrison stationed in Jerusalem would be overcome and he would be set up as Ruler of Israel (on this, see *Ant.* 20.169; *War* 2.261; cp. Acts 21.38).

Fourthly, that the mere promise from the 'Egyptian' of his 'sign' roused 'thousands' to go on a march from the wilderness into Judaea in spite of the knowledge that the Roman authorities there would view such a march as a prelude to rebellion and take repressive action against it (cf. *Ant.* 20.169; *War* 2.261).

Fifthly, that anti-Roman sentiment stiffened among the Jews after the Roman procurator Felix prevented the Egyptian and his forces from getting near Jerusalem (cf. *Ant.* 20.169).

Finally, that, as already noted, a great multitude of Jews, who during the death throes of the Judaean revolt against Rome had been promised 'signs of salvation', were willing to rush into the outer courts of the Temple where these 'signs' were to be seen, even though they knew the soldiers of Titus, having breached the Temple's defenses, were waiting there to cut them down (cf. *War* 6.284-86).

110. Cf. Barnett, 'Jewish Sign Prophets', p. 688; Betz, 'Miracles', pp. 227-31.

for such a 'sign' becomes clear. *Mark has Jesus refuse this demand because for Jesus to do otherwise would be nothing less than to advocate, initiate and engage in triumphalism—a type of activity that, according to Mark, was forbidden to Jesus if he wished to remain faithful to the requirements of his divine commission.*[111]

It would seem, then, that the reason the Markan Jesus refuses to produce a 'sign' at Mk 8.11 when the Pharisees demand one of him is not because he is, according to Mark, opposed to the enterprise of producing 'signs'. Rather, given Mark's assumptions concerning the type of 'sign' demanded in this instance and what this 'sign' would activate once manifested, Jesus refuses because in producing such a 'sign' he would involve himself in the sort of triumphalstic, despotic and imperious activities that throughout Mark's Gospel he condemns and sets himself against.

Summary and Conclusions

My analysis of the Markan version of Jesus' 'sign' demand temptation leads to the following observations and conclusions:

First, given the various ways that Mark has Jesus respond at Mk 8.12 to what is asked of him, Mark presents the demand for a 'sign' as something which places Jesus in a situation of open choice between rebellion against the will of God or renewed submission to the ways that God has outlined for him. The temptation that Jesus experiences when faced with the demand is thus one which tests faithfulness.

Secondly, given his particular presentation of the intention and motivating force behind the Pharisees' demand, and the specific nature of the 'sign' which they seek from Jesus, Mark presents the demand for a 'sign' as something which places Jesus on the horns of a dilemma: to prove, as asked, the validity of his interpretation of the manner in which, and the purposes for which, divine ἐξουσία is to be wielded, and to succeed, as necessity urges, in winning the Pharisees over to his side, Jesus must in essence set himself against the exigencies and constraints of his divine commission. In substance as well as in form, the issue at stake for Jesus at Mk 8.11-13—and, therefore, the content of the temptation which he is there said to experience—is the same as that with

---

111. This is especially clear in Mk 8.27–9.1 (cf. eg. J.L. Mays, 'An Exposition of Mk. 8:27–9:1', *Int* 30 [1976], pp. 174-78), but it is a theme which permeates Mark's Gospel.

which Jesus must deal at Mk 15.2 when those mocking him at his crucifixion proclaim that they will 'see and believe' in the validity of the pattern of his ἐξουσία only if he comes down from his cross. To get the leaders of Israel to accept the fact that it is God's will for those endowed with ἐξουσία to 'call', 'serve' and 'ransom' those 'not of Israel', Jesus must show that he 'thinks the things of men', subscribing to 'mens'' standards concerning what God or those commissioned by him should or should not do in this regard.

On my analysis, then, not only is the temptation which the Markan Jesus experiences when confronted with the demand for a 'sign' 'religious', in that it has to do with the question of Jesus' obedience to a divine commission, but also, as with Jesus' experience of temptation in the wilderness, the temptation embodied in the demand centers in whether or not Jesus will engage in, or assent to, triumphalism.

Having determined Mark's understanding of the nature and content of Jesus' 'sign' demand temptation, I now return to the question, posed above, concerning whether or not in portraying Jesus as experiencing temptation when confronted with the demand for a 'sign', Mark has been innovative. Was he the one responsible for the appearance of the notion—a notion which also appears when the story of the demand for a 'sign' is taken up and reproduced in later stages of the synoptic tradition—that Jesus' experience of the demand for a 'sign' was an occasion of temptation for him? To put this another way, did Mark add this detail to a tradition which was previously devoid of it, thus radically transforming its basic theological thrust? Or was Mark only drawing out what he knew was already an essential element of the tradition?

My procedure for answering these questions will involve three steps. First I will analyze the Q version of the tradition of Jesus' being subjected to a demand for a 'sign', determining whether it implies that Jesus was tempted in any way by the demand. Second, if I find that the Q version of the tradition *does* contain this implication, I will then attempt to uncover just what this version presents as the nature and content of this temptation. Then, after this is done, I will compare the results of this analysis with what I have outlined above concerning what Mk 8.11-13 says in this regard.

Chapter 6

THE 'SIGN' DEMAND TEMPTATION ACCORDING TO Q

My purpose now is to determine whether or not the Q version of the tradition of the demand for a 'sign' implies that Jesus was in any way tempted by the demand. To do this it is, of course, necessary to examine not only the content of the demand as recorded in the story, but also the reason, according to Q, that it is made. In other words, attention must be paid to the question of Q's presentation of the occasion and cause of the demand.[1]

The Occasion and Cause of the Demand according to Q

In Q the occasion of the demand for a 'sign' is not, as in Mark, Jesus' feeding of a Gentile multitude (cf. Mk 8.1-10),[2] but Jesus' action of healing through exorcism, in the presence of a large Galilean crowd, a dumb man (κωφός) of his infirmity (Mt. 12.22-23//Lk. 11.14). It is, Q notes, only *after* this healing occurs, and *in direct response to it*, that Jesus is petitioned to provide a proof σημεῖον. So in Q the healing of one of 'the dumb' (οἱ κωφοί) is the demand's occasion. But why should the cure by Jesus of a speech-impaired man engender a demand for a 'sign'? Given the circumstances under which 'signs' were sought or offered,[3] the answer is, of course, that the undertaking was seen by

1. I assume here that what is demanded of Jesus in the Q story is, as in the story's Markan counterpart, a 'proof σημεῖον'. The arguments supporting this assumption are the same as those adduced above in Chapter 5 for seeing the σημεῖον refered to in Mk 8.1-13 as a token of trustworthiness, a 'sign'.

2. On the crowd Jesus feeds in Mk 8.1-10 as predominantly Gentile, see, e.g., G.H. Boobyer, 'The Miracles of the Loaves and the Gentiles in Mark's Gospel', *SJT* 6 (1953), pp. 77-87. See also R.A. Guelich, *Mark 1–8:26* (Dallas: Word, 1988), pp. 402-403, 409.

3. On this, see above, Chapter 5, pp. 162-63. See also K. Rengstorf, 'σημεῖον', *TDNT*, VII, p. 236.

those who make the demand as containing a claim whose content and import are so contrary to their expectations and beliefs that they cannot immediately accept the claim as true. But what, then, according to Q, is this claim?

One answer can be ruled out from the start. The claim is not that God, as opposed to some other force or authority, stands behind Jesus' action. This may have been an issue for some among those who witnessed the cure. But it is not the concern of those who demand a 'sign'. According to Q, those who make the demand accept the fact that Jesus acts with divine ἐξουσία, that he is one in whom God's sovereignty becomes active in the world, and the presupposition of their demand is their certainty that the cure was a manifestation of 'the finger of God'.

But if this is not the claim that engenders the demand, what is? It is, surely, that the one who is endowed with divine ἐξουσία, the one set apart to bring God's sovereignty into the world, is constrained by God to establish that sovereignty not, as expected, through vengeance and the destruction of the wicked but by extending the blessings of salvation, normally believed to be Israel's inheritance, to those regarded by Israel as not worthy or deserving of them. *For this is precisely the claim that is recognized as standing behind other of Jesus' healings of* οἱ κωφοί *when elsewhere in Q such healings are recounted.*[4] Moreover, *it is what Q has Jesus himself proclaim prior to the story of the healing, in the story of the Baptist's Question (Mt. 11.2-6//Lk. 7.18-23), as the import of these actions.*[5]

This being the case, then the cause of the demand for a 'sign' is according to Q, Jesus' insistence on, and demonstration of, the idea that God' does not will the destruction of the wicked and impure but their redemption, and that Israel's inheritance of salvation is to be shared with those traditionally thought to be 'not of Israel'.

Is the Demand a Temptation according to Q?

As I have noted above, unlike Mark, the Q version of the 'sign' demand tradition does not explicitly designate the demand as something which

---

4.	On this, see J. Jeremias, *Jesus' Promise to the Nations* (London: SCM Press, 1958), pp. 45-46; *idem, New Testament Theology. I. The Proclamation of Jesus* (New York: Charles Scribners & Sons, 1971), pp. 109, 246 n. 2.

5.	Cf. J.A. Fitzmyer, *Luke 1–9* (Garden City: Doubleday, 1981), pp. 665, 667-68.

subjects Jesus to any kind of experience of πειρασμός. The demand itself is nowhere labeled a temptation, nor is there any explicit reference in the account to an intention on the part of those who demand from Jesus a 'sign' to tempt him. Does this mean, then, that in the Q version of the 'sign' demand tradition, the demand for a 'sign' is not presented or meant to be understood as something in which Jesus encounters temptation? I think not. For even devoid of any explicit reference to 'testing', the challenge in the demand *is still portrayed as placing Jesus in a situation of having to choose between the alternatives of obedience or unfaithfulness to God.* This is clear from the fact that Jesus characterizes the particular enterprise in which he is petitioned to engage as an activity typical of, and only undertaken by, those who are an 'evil and adulterous' (πονηρὰ καὶ μοιχαλίς) generation. In this, Jesus is presented by Q not only as castigating his interlocutors for disobedience and unfaithfulness,[6] but as tacitly acknowledging that should he grant what is asked of him, he *too* would become involved in setting himself against God. Notably, this acknowledgement implies recognition on Jesus' part that in being confronted with the demand for a 'sign' his dedication to remain faithful and obedient to God is put on trial. For him, according to Q, the demand embodies a test. Given this, we can then say with some certainty not only that in the Q version of the tradition of the demand for a 'sign' the demand is something which subjects Jesus to temptation, but that the temptation which Jesus experiences on account of the demand is, according to Q, of the 'religious' kind.

The Content of the 'Sign' Demand Temptation according to Q

But how specifically does the demand for a 'sign' put Jesus to the test over his fidelity to God? Why, according to Q, would acceding to the demand enlist Jesus in the ranks of the unfaithful and the disobedient? One possible answer is that the Jesus of Q conducts himself under the assumption that his ministry and mission is self-authenticating; and, therefore, to give additional, confirmatory evidence on its behalf would be to make an impermissible concession to disbelief. But *does* the Jesus of Q feel that proving the validity of the manner in which he exercises his authority is something which faithfulness to the constraints of his mission will not allow him to do? This hardly can be the case. For in

---

6.   On this, cf., e.g., W.C. Allen, *The Gospel according to Matthew* (Edinburgh: T. & T. Clark, 1915), p. 138.

Mt. 11.2-6//Lk. 7.18-23 the Q tradition of the Baptizer's question and Jesus' answer, Jesus shows no hesitation to produce 'signs' when he is faced with an appeal for validation and authentication.[7] Moreover, it should be noted that within the Q version of the tradition of the demand for a 'sign' itself Jesus responds to the demand with a statement in which his refusal to accede to what is demanded of him is qualified by the affirmation that one 'sign' *shall* be given. Accordingly, in several ways it is made plain in Q that for Jesus, proving by means of 'signs' the legitimacy of the manner in which he conducts his ministry *is not in itself* synonymous with, or symptomatic of, covenantal disobedience. Indeed, the implication of Jesus' 'no "sign"/one "sign"' statement is that *Jesus objects to producing such proof only because of the particular 'sign' that is demanded of him.*[8]

To know, then, why according to Q acceding to the demand for a 'sign' would involve Jesus in 'evil and adulterous' behaviour, and show him to be unfaithful and disobedient to what God requires of him, we must first determine, if we can, what the 'sign' demanded of Jesus in the Q 'sign' demand story actually *is*, and what its 'shape' is there presumed to be.

In doing this it is instructive to recall the fact, noted above,[9] that Jesus' response to the demand for a 'sign' is cast in the idiom of relative negation. One of the upshots of this fact is that with respect to its nature and content the 'sign' which is demanded of Jesus is placed in contrast with the σημεῖον that Jesus *is* willing to produce.[10] It is marked out as something the 'shape' and import of which is the very opposite of the σημεῖον that at Mt. 12.39b//Lk. 11.29b Jesus says will be given. This is significant. For it means that *determining the 'shape' of the 'sign' Jesus is asked to produce here in the Q version will be a matter of outlining (1) just what the 'sign' Jesus does offer is here understood to be and then (2) inferring its opposite.*

---

7.   That this is the import of the story of the Baptist's question, see Fitzmyer, *Luke 1–9*, pp. 666-67.

8.   Cf. L. Goppelt, *Theology of the New Testament*, I (Grand Rapids: Eerdmans, 1981), pp. 148-49.

9.   See above, Chapter 4, p. 148.

10.   On this, see Colpe, 'Υἱὸς τοῦ Ἀνθρώπου', *TDNT*, IV (1972), p. 449 n. 349; Kuschke, 'Das Idiom des "relativen Negation"', *ZNW* 43 (1950–51), p. 263.

The 'Sign' That Will be Given
What, then, according to Q, is this 'sign'? In answering this, I will take into account the evidence provided by three things: (a) how Q has Jesus describe the 'sign' he offers, (b) what Q has Jesus say about those who are to receive this 'sign', and (c) the comparison Jesus makes in his response to the demand between Jonah and the Son of Man.

The Implications of Jesus' Description of the 'Sign' he Offers. In the Q 'sign' demand story Jesus not only announces that a 'sign' will indeed be given, he gives a description of what that 'sign' will be. It is, he says, 'Jonah's σημεῖον' (τὸ σημεῖον Ἰωνᾶ). Now, as many scholars have noted, this description is exceedingly brief, and in many ways puzzling.[11] Why? Could it be because Jesus wanted the nature of the 'sign' to remain obscure? This hardly seems likely. It would defeat the whole purpose of offering a 'sign', making it impossible for anyone to know whether or not any confirming evidence had actually ever been given. A far more plausible explanation is that Jesus was referring to a particular 'sign'—*one with which his listeners were already familiar*—and that, given this familiarity, *Jesus feels he need say no more than he does for his listeners to know what 'sign' he is talking about*, the terms of the description being sufficient in themselves to indicate or to call to mind just what the 'sign' in question is. So the issue is: just what 'sign' *would* be called to the minds of Jesus' listeners given the particulars of the manner in which the 'sign' promised to be given them is described? Three things need to be kept in mind here. First, his listeners are presumed in Q to be first-century Palestinian Jews. Secondly, the Jonah referred to in the description of the 'sign' that will be given is the Jonah of the book bearing that name, that is, the prophet sent by God to preach to the Ninevites.[12] Thirdly, the 'sign' referred to as Jonah's is a

---

11. Cf. e.g. Rengstorf, 'σημεῖον', p. 233; E. Schweizer, *The Good News according to Matthew* (Atlanta: John Knox Press, 1975), p. 291.

12. A number of scholars suppose there to have been a confusion in the tradition between the names *Jona(h)* and *Jona*, the latter being an abbreviation of *Jochanan*, and have argued that the Jonah referred to here is not the the prophet whose exploits are recounted in the book of Jonah, but *John the Baptist*. Cf. B.W. Bacon, *The Sermon on the Mount* (London: Macmillan, 1902), p. 232; W. Brandt, *Die jüdische Baptismen* (Geissen: Töpelmann, 1910), pp. 82-83; T.K. Cheyne and J.S. Black, *Encyclopedia Biblica: A Critical Dictionary of the Literary, Political, and Religious History, the Archeology, Geography, and Natural History of the Bible* (4 vols.; London: A. & C. Black, 1899–1903), II, p. 2502; J. Howton, 'The Sign of Jonah',

'proof σημεῖον', that is, something known to have been offered or demanded to dispel a voiced doubt about the validity of disputed actions or utterances.

In light of all this, the most reasonable deduction concerning the phenomenon Jesus referred to in speaking of τὸ σημεῖον 'Ιωνᾶ is that in effect if not in content it was the same as, or something very similar to, *whatever phenomenon is spoken of in the traditions about Jonah extant in the first century, and known to Palestinian Jews, as there having been offered or demanded to dispel a voiced doubt.*

Now, the traditions about Jonah extant in Jesus' time are recorded in Tob. 14.4, Sir. 49.10, *3 Macc.* 6.8, Josephus, *Ant.* 9.10.2, *PRE* 10; 43, *Midrash Jonah*, Mekilta de Rabbi Ishmael: *Pisha* 1.80, 82, 103-105, 112-113, *b. Sanh.* 89b; line 11 of the Jewish Synagogal prayer preserved in *Apostolic Constitutions* 7.37.1-5, *Martyrdom and Ascension of Isaiah* 4.22-22, *Sib. Or.* 2.245-50, *4 Ezra* 1.40, *Lam. R.* (Proem 31), *Liv. Proph.* 10, and, of course, the book of Jonah itself.[13] Significantly, when we examine these traditions we find that there is only one instance known or ever mentioned within them of a phenomenon given specifically to gain credibility for, and demonstrate the truth of, a doubted proclamation, namely, the phenomenon depicted in Jon. 4.6-9 which is given by God *to Jonah* when, despite evidence to the contrary, Jonah cannot bring himself to believe that it is right for God to demonstrate that his mercy is more than the exclusive possession of the Jews.[14]

SJT 15 (1962), pp. 288-304, E.H. Merrill, 'The Sign of Jonah', *JETS* 23 (1980), pp. 23-30; J.H. Michael, 'The Sign of John', *JTS* 21 (1919–1920), pp. 146-59; C. Moxon, 'Τὸ σημεῖον 'Ιωνᾶ', *ExpTim* 22 (1911), pp. 566-67; J.M. Creed, *The Gospel according to Luke* (London: Macmillan, 1930), p. 163; J.H. Kraeling, *John the Baptist* (New York: Scribners, 1951), pp. 136-37. For a skeptical assesment of this view, see Fitzmyer, *Luke 10–24*, p. 935; A. Vögtle, 'Das Spruch des Jonaszeichen', in J.A. Schmid and A. Vögtle (eds.), *Synoptische Studien: Alfred Wikenhauser zum siebzigsten Geburtstag am 22 Februar 1953 dargebracht von Freunden, Kollegen und Schulern* (Munich: Zink, 1953), pp. 230-77, esp. pp. 246-47.

13.   I assume here, desite the relatively late date of Mekilta de Rabbi Ishmael: *Pisha* 1.80, 82; 103-105, 112-13; *b. Sanh.* 89b, *Pirke de Rabbi Eliezer, Midrash Jonah*, and *Lamentations Rabbah* that the traditions contained therein date from the first half of the first century CE.

14.   At first glance *Pirke Rabbi Eilezer* might be taken as evidence that there was knowledge within first century Plaestinian Judaism of *another* 'sign' given to Jonah by God, namely, Jonah's preservation in, and deliverance from, the belly of a great fish. This text speaks of the sailors who were conveying Jonah to Tarshish turning from their idols to the God of Israel after seeing 'all the signs, the miracles, and the

None of the other human *dramatis personae* of these traditions, neither sailors nor Ninevites, or anyone else, are ever portrayed therein as doubting any proclamation that comes to them, let alone as calling out for, being granted, or being in special need of evidence to take a doubt away. It is only Jonah who is presented as recalcitrant. It is only Jonah who is shown to have a need for proof. *And, notably, it is only Jonah who is ever granted a 'sign'*.[15]

In light of this, the 'sign' that Jesus refers to in the expression the τὸ σημεῖον 'Ιωνᾶ would seem to be the 'sign' which the prophet is said to have received, the 'sign' *given to* Jonah in Jon. 4.[16] And the 'sign' that Jonah receives—the bush that grows to protect him from the sun—has the function of convincing Jonah that allegiance to God involves standing in solidarity with the free operation of God's grace even when that grace is extended to those who seem to have no right to it.[17]

It would seem, then, on the basis of these considerations, that in the Q

great wonders which the Holy One, blessed be he, did unto Jonah', which are here identified with Jonah's submarine adventures and his being 'vomited out' from the mouth of the fish intact. But given its linking with the terms translated as 'miracles' and 'great wonders', it is doubtful that the term translated 'signs' is being used in this text in the technical sense of 'proof'. Rather, 'signs' here means 'powerful works', and what the sailors witnessed was a token of the might of Israel's God.

15.   One might argue that this series of assertions is contradicted by *Lives of the Prophets* 10.10-11, which, if we follow C.C. Torrey's translation of these verses (*The Lives of the Prophets: Greek Text and Translation* [JBLMS, 1; Philadelphia: Society of Biblical Literature and Exegesis, 1946], p. 42) seems to speak of *Jonah* giving (presumably to Israelites) a 'sign'. According to Torrey, the text reads:

> And he [Jonah] gave a sign to Jerusalem, and to all the land: when they should see a stone crying aloud in distress, the end would be at hand; and when they should see all the Gentiles gathered in Jerusalem, the city would be razed to its foundations.

But, notably, in the Greek text the term which Torrey translates as 'sign' is τέρας, not σημεῖον. This, as well as the context in which the term appears, indicate that what Jonah is reported in *Lives* 10.10-11 as giving is not a 'sign', i.e., a 'token of trustworthiness', but a 'portent'.

16.   It is important to note that nothing in the grammar of the expression stands against this conclusion. In fact, if 'Ιωνᾶ is an objective genitive, as Jeremias ('Ιωνᾶς', *TDNT*, III, p. 408) admits is possible, it actually supports the conclusion that 'the "sign" of Jonah' is the 'sign' given to Jonah in that τὸ σημεῖον 'Ιωνᾶ would mean 'the "sign" that Jonah received'.

17.   Cf. L.C. Allen, *The Books of Joel, Obadiah, Jonah, and Micah* (Grand Rapids: Eerdmans, 1976), pp. 230-33.

'sign' demand story, the 'sign' that Jesus says will be given, the '"sign" of Jonah', was something that would confirm as 'of God' the message that, contrary to what was expected of him, God disowns religious nationalism, that his mercy does not belong solely to Israel, that he steadfastly refuses to endorse the point of view (and the life-style that springs from it) that wrath and not mercy will be shown towards Israel's enemies.

The Implication of Jesus' Description of those who are to Receive the 'Sign of Jonah'. In the Q story Jesus designates those who are to receive τὸ σημεῖον Ἰωνᾶ 'this generation', and about 'this generation' he has three things to say. The first thing is that it is 'wicked and adulterous' (πονηρὰ καὶ μοιχαλίς, cf. Mt. 12.39//Lk. 11.29), that is, perversely unfaithful and disobedient to what God has revealed as his will for his people.[18] In Q God's will for his people is that they should become gracious towards those who, by the standards of strict justice, deserve nothing but punishment.[19] It is in this way that the elect will truly reveal themselves to be 'Sons of God'.[20] So when Jesus here accuses 'this generation' of being 'wicked and adulterous', he is saying that it has refused to behave this way, accepting instead, as the proper and only standard for its dealings with its enemies, the idea of retributive justice.

The second thing Jesus says about 'this generation' is that it has stubbornly and wilfully not 'repented' (cf. Mt. 12.41//Lk. 11.32), that is, it has not taken up the covenantal obligations laid upon it by God when summoned to do so. In Q, these obligations involve accepting the fact of God's unrestricted extension of his mercy to the those not 'of Israel', including those by whose hands Israel has suffered, and acting accordingly.[21] So when Jesus says that 'this generation' has not 'repented', he is accusing it of two things: (1) thinking it has a claim on God's salvation that enables its members to set others outside of it, and (2) trying to exclude from God's mercies people whom God has determined are to be its recipients.

The third thing Jesus says about 'this generation' is that on the great

18. On this, see G. Harder, 'πονηρός', *TDNT*, VI, pp. 546-66, esp. pp. 554-55; and F. Hauck, 'μοιχεύω', *TDNT*, IV, pp. 729-35, esp. p. 734.
19. Cf. Mt. 5.43-44//Lk. 6.27-28; Mt. 5.48; 7.1-12//Lk. 6.36-38.
20. Cf. Mt. 5.45//Lk. 6.35.
21. Cf. Mt. 5.38-42; 45-47//Lk. 6.29-35.

day of judgment its members will find themselves in the heavenly court accused of faithlessness and disobedience by the Queen of the South and the people of Nineveh.[22] Now, the Queen of the South and the people of Nineveh are, notably, Gentiles who not only came to accept Yahweh as their God, *but did so specifically because of Israel's mediation*.[23] They are indisputable evidence of two facts: first, of God's universal salvific concern; second, that God's saving purposes cannot be fully realized apart from Israel's cooperation.[24] If, then, on the day of judgment, the Queen of the South and the people of Nineveh come to stand as plaintiffs against 'this generation', it must be because its members have adopted the view, against clear divine declarations to the contrary, not only that God desires to exclude those 'not of Israel' from his mercies, but also that Israel need have nothing to do with placing herself at the service of other peoples in extending to them the message of God's word.

Now, it is important to note that these three characteristics that, according to Jesus, typify 'this generation' are specifically *those of Jonah as he was before he received his 'sign'*. Indeed, in him they find their epitome. As the traditions about Jonah bear witness, he, too, grounded his life in the idea that evil should be punished, and he rejected as unjust any notion of God's not treating Israel's enemies strictly according to what they deserve.[25] He, too, thought God's mercies should be extended primarily to Israel, even in the face of a divine declaration to the contrary.[26] He, too, refused to cooperate with God when commanded to be the instrument by which the gift of salvation which Israel had known would be brought to other nations.[27] *Accordingly, that Jesus should speak of 'this generation' in terms of the characteristics typical of Jonah indicates that in the Q 'sign'*

22. Mt. 12.41-42//Lk. 11.31-32. For the legal imagery behind the phrases ἐγερθήσεται ἐν τῇ κρίσει...καὶ κατακρινεῖ, κτλ., see J. Jeremias, "Ἰωνᾶς", *TDNT*, III, pp. 406-10, esp. p. 408 n. 5.

23. That the men of Nineveh accepted Yahweh on account of Israel's mediation is clear in the book of Jonah. That the Queen of the South (Sheba) did so is recounted in Wis. 6.1-11.

24. On this, see T.E. Fretheim, *The Message of Jonah* (Minneapolis: Augsburg, 1977), p. 25.

25. Jon. 4.1-3.

26. Cf. Fretheim, *Message of Jonah*, p. 24.

27. Jon. 1.3; 4.2. See also *Mekilta de R. Ishmael: Pisha* 1.80-82 where R. Eleazar b. Zadok also explains Jonah's flight from Nineveh in these terms.

demand story Jesus is identifying 'this generation' with Jonah.
The implication of this designation is significant. It indicates that the
'sign' that Jesus says 'this generation' will receive is a phenomenon
confirming that God shows the enemy mercy and that those who wish
to be true children of God must do likewise. For inasmuch as 'this generation' is a latter-day Jonah, this, then, is the type of 'sign' it needs, the
type of 'sign' it deserves, the type of 'sign' that, given how God once
responded to 'this generation's' prototype, Jonah ben Amittai, it is
bound to receive.

Evidence from Jesus' Comparison between Jonah and the Son of Man.
But does not other information in the Q 'sign' demand story stand
against this conclusion? Does not the section of the story in which Jonah
and the Son of Man are compared (Mt. 12.40//Lk. 11.30), the eschatological or prophetic correlative, say explicitly that the '"sign" of Jonah'
was Jonah himself as he appeared to the Ninevites?[28] This is, certainly, a
widely held view.[29] But in the end it is untenable, for the assumptions
upon which it rests are incorrect.

The view's first assumption is that it was something of a commonplace in Judaism and Christianity, not to mention in the ancient world in
general, that a *person* could *be*, or *would be accepted as*, a 'sign'.[30]
Curiously, however, there is not one instance in all of the references in
biblical and other ancient literature to the phenomenon of 'signs' in
which a person serves in this capacity.[31] Nor do we ever find there any
support for the idea that a 'sign' was something a person could ever

28.   Or as Rengstorf ('σημεῖον', *TDNT*, VII, p. 233) puts it, Jonah in the
'particularity of his historical appearance'.
29.   Some of its advocates include, besides Rengstorf, G. Beasley-Murray (*Jesus
and the Kingdom of God* [Grand Rapids: Eerdmans, 1986], p. 255), R. Bultmann
(*History of the Synoptic Tradition* [Oxford: Basil Blackwell, 1963], p. 118), Creed
(*Luke*, p. 162), F.W. Danker (*Jesus and the New Age: A Commentary on St Luke's
Gospel* [Philadelphia: Fortress Press, 1988]. p. 236), H. Balforth (*The Gospel
according to Saint Luke* [Oxford: Clarendon Press, 1930], p. 214), A.B. Higgins
(*Jesus and the Son of Man* [Philadelphia: Fortress Press, 1964], p. 138), A.C. McNeil
(*The Gospel according to Matthew* [London: Macmillan, 1915], pp. 181-82),
J. Fitzmyer (*Luke 10–24*, p. 933), A. Vögtle ('Jonaszeichen', p. 120).
30.   On this, see Rengstorf, 'σημεῖον', *TDNT*, VII, p. 234.
31.   Rengstorf, of course, disputes this, claiming that Isa. 8.18; 20.3; and
Ezek. 12.6 are just such instances ('σημεῖον', p. 234). But these texts speak of
persons being *not* confirmatory phenomenon *but symbols of God's presence or
judgment*. Moreover, in Ezek. 12.6 the word used is τέρας not σημεῖον.

actually be, let alone *become*.[32] In light of this, then, the assumption
that within the correlative, Q equates Jonah with a 'sign' seems highly
unlikely.

The second assumption of the view that in the correlative Q says that
the 'sign' of Jonah was Jonah himself is that the word σημεῖον is used
within the correlative in its technical sense of 'sign', 'proof'. But against
this stands the fact that the noun is used here with reference to the
thing that Jonah 'came to be' (ἐγένετο) for the Ninevites (τοῖς
Νινευίταις).[33] In light of what I have noted above concerning the
apparent lack in the ancient world of any idea of a *person's* becoming a
'sign', this fact not only excludes any possibility that σημεῖον here
means 'sign'; it indicates that its meaning has to be 'ensign',

---

32. Isa. 7.14 and Lk. 2.12 notwithstanding. In both these instances, the 'sign' is
not a person, but the correspondence of the events surrounding that person's birth
with predictions made about them.

In conversation with me, D.R. Catchpole has questioned my assertion that a person
was never viewed in Judaism or Christianity as being, or as having the capacity to
become, a 'sign', arguing that Dan. 3.32 LXX (4.2 Theodotion) and Dan. 6.27 LXX
(6.28 Theodotion) present evidence to the contrary. In these texts, he claimed, we find
respectively the trio Shadrach, Meshach and Abednego and then Daniel himself
specifically catergorized as 'signs', i.e., 'tokens of trustworthiness'. But standing
against this is the fact that what the term σημεῖον is associated with in each of these
texts is *not* a person or persons, let alone the three young men or Daniel, but the
revelations of the power of Israel's God which the kings Nebucahdezzar and Darius
had received since Daniel came into their service. Moreover, since the term σημεῖον
is employed in each of these instances conjoined with the term τέρατα (τὰ σημεῖα
καὶ τὰ τέρατα, Dan. 3.32 LXX [4.2 Theodotion]; σημεῖα καὶ τέρατα ἐν οὐρανῷ
καὶ ἐπὶ τῆς γῆς, Dan. 6.27 LXX [6.28 Theodotion]), it seems clear that the meaning it
is meant to bear there is 'portent' or 'wondrous work' and not 'proof'. So even
should Catchpole be correct in seeing that in these texts the three young men and
Daniel are being categorized as σημεῖα, this would hardly be evidence that Judaism
and Christianity held to the view that persons could be or become confirmatory
phenomena or that they ever stood as such.

33.   According to P.D Meyer ('The Gentile Mission in Q', *JBL* 89 [1970],
pp. 405-17, esp. 407-409), the original text here specified that Jonah was a σημεῖον
not to the Ninevites but to *his generation*, that is, to his Jewish compatriots in Israel.
The appeal of this reconstruction is the symmetry it provides between the correlative's
two terms of comparison:

> Just as Jonah became (was) a σημεῖον to his generation
> so also will the Son of Man be to this generation.

There is not, however, any textual warrant for this reading.

'standard'.[34] Not only is there biblical precedent for using σημεῖον with this meaning to refer to a person,[35] but, among the many things which in the LXX and associated writings the word σημεῖον serves to designate,[36] 'ensign/symbol/standard' is both the only one that is linked with a person and *the only one that is ever spoken about as something that a person can 'become' or 'be'*.

The third assumption of the view that Q sees the σημεῖον referred to in the correlative as Jonah himself is that the function of the correlative within the Q 'sign' demand story is to *explain or interpret* what the 'sign of Jonah' is.[37] But this ignores something very basic about the way correlatives of this sort evidently function in the Gospels and their sources. When elsewhere in the synoptic tradition a prophetic or eschatological correlative appears as it does here, attached to a dominical saying, it does not explain the saying. Rather, *it justifies it*, that is, it gives the grounds for the content of the saying, answering any questions the saying provokes about *why* what is said has been said. At Mt. 24.27, for example, we find the following correlative uttered by Jesus:

> For as the lightning comes from the east and shines as far as the west, so will be the coming of the Son of Man.

The correlative follows on from a statement of Jesus about the foolishness and futility of attending to the announcement, given by messianic pretenders or their heralds to the people of Judaea shortly before the destruction of Jerusalem (cf. Mt. 24.23-24//Lk. 21.20-24, cf. Lk. 13.21-23),[38] that the Christ is about to appear in the desert or in the Temple[39] and deliver Israel from its enemies:

34. For this as a meaning of σημεῖον, see Rengstorf, 'σημεῖον', pp. 205-206.

35. Cf., in addition to the texts above, Isa. 11.10, 12; Mt. 24.30; Lk. 2.35.

36. Cf. above, pp. 205-206.

37. Typical in this regard is the remark of J.S. Kloppenberg that 'The correlative is constructed specifically as the explanation of [Mt. 12.39//Lk. 11.29]' (*The Formation of Q: Trajectories in Ancient Wisdom Collections* [Philadelphia: Fortress Press, 1987], p. 130). See also Beasley-Murray, *Jesus and the Kingdom*, p. 255; Edwards, *The Sign of Jonah*, p. 82; Higgins, *Jesus and the Son of Man*, p. 133 n. 2; B. Lindars, *Jesus Son of Man* (London: SCM Press, 1982), p. 39; Rengstorf, 'σημεῖον', p. 234, among others.

38. On this, see, Schweizer, *Matthew*, p. 453.

39. My assumption that ταμείοις is here a reference to the Temple, or, more precisely, the sanctuary of its inner court, seems natural in light of the fact that the confines of the sanctuary (a 'hidden place') was not only associated in Jewish expectation as one of several *loci* where Messianic salvation was to begin, but also, as

> So, if they say to you , 'Lo, he is in the wilderness', do not go out; if they
> say, 'Lo, he is in the inner rooms', do not believe it (Mt. 24.26//
> Lk. 17.23).

As even a cursory glance will show, in its present context the correlative serves not to interpret the saying to which it is attached, but to provide the saying's rationale. The correlative's purpose is to answer why expecting to see the Messiah in any particular locale, especially the desert or the sanctuary, and going out to those places in anticipation of experiencing there an act of divine liberation, is unwarranted and foolish and tantamount to being 'led astray'.[40]

If, then, the primary function of correlatives is to justify why something is said rather than to explain and interpret something, then the purpose of Jesus in comparing Jonah and the Son of Man is to outline *not* what the 'sign of Jonah' *is*, but *why it and no other is the one 'sign' that will be given.*

So the correlative is not evidence against the interpretation of the 'sign of Jonah' that I am arguing for here. On the contrary it actually provides evidence to support my view. As we have seen, the correlative contains Jesus' justification for giving no 'sign' except the 'sign of Jonah'. According to the correlative the justification is that as Son of Man Jesus must be to 'this generation' the same thing that Jonah was to the Ninevites. Now, as we have also seen, Jonah, according to the correlative, was an 'ensign' or 'standard'. But an 'ensign' or 'standard' of what? Given the thrust of the Jonah traditions, the answer, of course, is an 'ensign' or 'standard' of how boundless and all encompassing is God's love. So Jesus' justification for his giving no 'sign' but the 'sign of Jonah' is, then, that in his words and actions he must be nothing less than what Jonah ultimately was to the Ninevites, *an embodiment of the mercy and graciousness of God.* This means that any 'sign' that Jesus might give would have to be compatible with what he himself embodied. In light of this, the question to be asked, then, is: How else could the

---

Josephus notes, the only other place which, besides the desert, various 'false Christs' made the staging area for the manifestation and inauguration of their Messiahship. But for a different reading of what ταμείοις refers to here, see K. Stendahl, 'Matthew', in M. Black and H.H. Rowley (eds.), *Peake's Commentary on the Bible* (London: Nelson, 1962), p. 793.

40.   On this, see R. Gundry, *Matthew: A Commentary on his Literary and Theological Art* (Grand Rapids: Eerdmans, 1982), p. 485.

'sign of Jonah' do this unless its nature, content and import is as I have described it above?

Results of this Investigation on the Nature of the 'Sign' Jesus Offers. In light of the evidence provided by Jesus' description of the 'sign' that he offers to those who demand one of him, the implications of his description of those who are to receive it, and the implications of his comparison with Jonah and the Son of Man, we may conclude that the 'sign' that will be given to 'this generation', the 'sign of Jonah' is, according to Q, something that confirms the message that God intends his people to be lovers of those they consider their enemies.

The 'Sign' Demanded by 'This Generation'
We have seen above that it is assumed in Q that the 'shape' and import of the 'sign' demanded of Jesus in the Q 'sign' demand story is the exact opposite of the 'sign' that, according to Jesus, 'this generation' is bound to receive. In light of this, and having determined Q's view of the content and import of this latter 'sign', the 'sign of Jonah', we are now in a position to outline what Q views as the nature and content of the former, the 'sign' that 'this generation' demands from Jesus. Given that according to Q the 'sign' of Jonah is a 'sign' that demonstrates that God has love and concern for the 'enemy', the 'sign' which is demanded of Jesus—the 'sign' 'this generation' seeks and the 'sign' that Jesus refuses to give—must be *one that demonstrates that God seeks to punish and destroy the 'enemy'.*[41]

We are now in a position to answer the question posed above, namely, What, according to Q, would Jesus involve himself in should he produce the 'sign' that 'this generation' demanded of him? Given Q's view of the nature of that 'sign', *Jesus would in effect be advocating, if not himself actually engaging in, punishment rather than salvation of those 'this generation' regarded as 'the enemy'.* Now we have seen above that for the Jesus of Q such advocacy and engagement is inconceivable. It would represent a repudiation of what he knows to be God's will for him and for Israel, indeed, for 'this generation'. And yet 'this generation' will not be convinced of the truth of his claim about God's will for them unless he yields to their desires.

---

41. Goppelt, *Theology of the New Testament*, I, p. 148.

Conclusions on the Content of the 'Sign' Demand Temptation according to Q

In light of this, Q's view of the content of Jesus' 'sign' demand temptation becomes clear. Ironically, if Jesus is to get his compatriots to accept, on their own terms, the fact that God wishes his emissaries (including Israel) both to cease hoping for divine vengeance against Israel's enemies and to extend the gift of salvation to those who do not deserve it, then he will be forced to turn his back on the very message which he has been commissioned to bear and begin the process of judgment and punishment which, given his message, he repudiates.

Q and Mark Compared

In conducting this analysis of the Q 'sign' demand story I have been concerned with determining two things: (1) whether Q viewed the demand as subjecting Jesus to temptation, and, if so, (2) the view that Q presents regarding that temptation's nature and content. *But my main reason for doing this has been to lay bare the full nature and extent of Mark's editorial contribution to the version of the 'sign' demand story which he reproduces at Mk 8.11-13.* It will be recalled that when I initially dealt with this question, I argued among other things the following: (a) that Mark based his story on a primitive tradition about Jesus being petitioned to produce a 'sign', (b) that this tradition was also the basis of Q's 'sign' demand story, (c) that Q reproduced fairly closely—certainly more closely than did Mark—the basic shape and wording of this primitive tradition, (d) that the tradition which both Mark and Q took up and used as the basis for their respective accounts of the demand for a 'sign' was devoid of any explicit reference to Jesus being tempted by the demand, and (e) that the notice at Mk 8.11 that the demand confronted Jesus with temptation (πειράζοντες αὐτόν) is Markan. *The upshot of this was to raise the possibility that Mark was not only editorially but theologically innovative, that he had given to a tradition whose narrative theme was originally something other than that of temptation an entirely new thrust.* Deciding this, I argued, was a matter of determining whether or not the Q version of the tradition, and therefore also the more primitive account common to both Mark and Q, was *already* a temptation tradition, that is, whether or not, and in what if in any way, even devoid of explicit temptation terminology, it was concerned to present Jesus being 'put to the test'. If it could be shown that the Q (and, thus, the pre-Q) version of the story was indeed, like Mark's account of the demand for a 'sign', a temptation tradition, and, that, according to Q, the nature and content of that temptation was the same as that which Mark presents Jesus subjected to in Mk 8.11-13, then we would have good reason for saying that in his story of Jesus' 'sign' demand temptation Mark was not theologically innovative. On the contrary, we would be compelled to say that he was only in his own way drawing out and making explicit something implied in the 'sign' demand material which he took up and employed to write his version of the story.

This is precisely what we must say. For, as my analysis of the Q 'sign' demand story shows, (1) in Q the demand for a 'sign' is indeed an event which subjects Jesus to temptation; (2) this temptation is indeed, according to Q, 'religious' in nature, involving specifically a proving of Jesus' willingness to be obedient to commands God had given him; and (3) the content of this temptation is, as in Mk 8.11-13, Jesus being petitioned to reject the idea, which, again as in Mk 8.11-13, forms the basis of his mission, and which he has been commissioned to embody and promulgate, that God extends love to his enemies and that emissaries of God should do likewise.

The results of my analysis indicate, then, that while Mark has changed substantially the form and wording of the traditional 'sign' demand story, he has not made any essential changes to the story's narrative, thematic and theological thrust. Indeed, if anything, he has taken this up and passed it on, and, through his redactional changes to the form and wording in which it was originally couched, he has actually underscored and made even more explicit the story's point that for Jesus the demand for a 'sign' was a 'religious testing' involving a very specific issue: whether, contrary to what he believed God required of him, he would accept and countenance triumphalistic behaviour, and not non-violent suffering and service, even to the 'enemy', as the means by which Yahweh's sovereignty would be established in Israel and throughout the world.

Chapter 7

THE TRADITION OF JESUS' TEMPTATION AT CAESAREA PHILIPPI

The Accounts of the Tradition and their Relationship

Both Matthew and Mark record that Jesus was tempted at Caesarea Philippi, at Mt. 16.13-23 and Mk 8.27-33 respectively (cf. Lk. 9.18-22).[1] Neither the wording and word order nor the context of the Matthean (or for that matter, the truncated Lukan) version of this tradition differs sufficiently from that of its Markan counterpart to justify any suspicion that Matthew (or Luke) knew another 'primary' version of this temptation event. Indeed, they are so similar in this regard to what we find in Mk that we can hardly avoid the conclusion that the Matthean and the Lukan version of the tradition are each derived from that of Mark.[2]

1. The usual terminology that crops up in Synoptic 'temptation of Jesus' traditions, namely πειράζω, ἐκπειράζω, and πειρασμός, is absent from Mk 8.27-33//Mt. 16.13-23. That Jesus is, however, portrayed here as undergoing temptation need not be doubted since both Mark and Matthew make it clear that Jesus is (through Peter) attacked by Satan and that, as Jesus' response to this attack indicates (cf. Mk 8.33//Mt. 16.22, he views himself brought by this attack into a 'forced position' in which he must make a choice between obedience to constraints that God has laid upon him or rejection of them—a situation, which, as B.F. Van Iersel has shown (*The Bible on the Temptations of Man* [De Pere, WI: St Norbet Abbey Press, 1966], pp. 16, 23) is a constituent and characteristic element of πειρασμός.

2. The claim that Matthew's version of Jesus' temptation at Caesarea Philippi is even minimally, let alone wholly, dependent upon Mk 8.27-33 has been challenged not only by such scholars as C.S. Mann (*Mark* [Garden City: Doubleday, 1986], pp. 339-40) and W.R. Farmer (*The Synoptic Problem* [Macon: Mercer University Press, 1964], pp. 245-46), as we might expect, but also such a notable non-Griesbachian as R. Bultmann (*The History of the Synoptic Tradition* [Oxford: Basil Blackwell, 1963], pp. 257-59). In support of this view, they argue that what is unique in Matthew betrays a matrix which historically and theologically is more primitive than that assumed in the Markan account.

But against this position stand three considerations: (1) as A. Vögtle has noted

Accordingly, to lay the groundwork necessary for determining whether there was within the early Church a unified conception of the nature and content of Jesus' Caesarea Philippi temptation, we need to focus our attention on Mark's version of the tradition.

Jesus' Caesarea Philippi Temptation according to Mark

The Tradition History of the Markan Account

No consensus exists among scholars concerning the tradition history of Mk 8.27-33. Opinions run a full gamut from (a) the view that the entire pericope is a traditional, pre-Markan unit, cast early and transmitted from its inception in the synoptic tradition in the form and wording in which it now appears, with Mark making no or only minor changes,[3] to (b) the view that it is wholly a Markan composition,[4] with (c) the view, expressed in a variety of ways, that it is a mixture of tradition and

('Messiasbekenntnis und Petrusberheissung: Zur Komposition von Mt. 16,13-23 par.', *BZ* 1 [1957], pp. 252-72; *BZ* 2 [1958], pp. 85-103), what is peculiarly Matthean in Mt. 16.13-23 seems to be inserted into the Markan account and, more importantly, never contradicts what Mark says, but serves to clarify and amplify what is already there; (2) some small differences in wording between Mt. 16.14//Mk 8.28, where Matthew has ἕνα τῶν προφητῶν against Mark's εἰς τῶν προφητῶν, and οἱ δὲ εἶπαν· οἱ μὲν Ἰωάννην τὸν βαπτιστήν against Mark's οἱ δὲ εἶπαν αὐτῷ λέγοντες [ὅτι] Ἰωάννην τὸν βαπτιστήν, and Mt. 16.21//Mk 8.31, where Matthew has ἕνα τῶν προφητῶν against Mark's ἀποκτανθῆναι καὶ μετὰ τρεῖς ἡμέρας ἀναστῆναι, seem impossible to account for unless they are seen as Matthean attempts to deal with difficulties in the Markan text (on this, see Gundry, *Matthew: A Commentary on his Literary and Theological Art* [Grand Rapids: Eerdmans, 1982], pp. 329, 338); (3) the absence in Mk 8.33 of the phrase σκάνδαλον (cp. Mt. 16.23) and in Mk 8.32, if such there is (see below), of Peter's rebuke ἵλεώς σοι, κύριε· οὐ μὴ ἔσται σοι τοῦτο (cp. Mt. 16.22) is impossible to explain if Mk 8.27-33 is secondary to Mt. 16.3-23. Mark surely would have included these phrases in his own account, had he known, them since thematically they are consonant with the material that appears there.

3. Cf. C.E.B. Cranfield, *The Gospel according to St Mark* (Cambridge: Cambridge University Press, 1959), pp. 266-67; O. Cullmann, *Peter: Apostle, Disciple, Martyr* (London: SCM, 1953), pp. 176-86; V. Taylor, *The Gospel according to Mark* (London: Macmillan, 1955), pp. 374-75.

4. Cf. E. Haenchen, 'Die Komposition von Mk VIII 27-IX 1 und Par', *NovT* 6 (1963), pp. 81-109; D.R. Catchpole, 'The "Triumphal" Entry', in E. Bammel and C.F.D. Moule (eds.), *Jesus and the Politics of his Day* (Cambridge: Cambridge University Press, 1984), pp. 319-34, esp. pp. 326-28.

redaction standing in between.[5] Both extremes of the gamut are, I think, untenable. To say that Mk 8.27-33 is mostly (if not entirely) unretouched reproduction of traditional material seems to me to ignore the fact that there are clear indications of Mark's redactional hand in the pericope— vv. 30, 31a, 32b, for instance, being prime examples of this phenomenon.[6] To say that the pericope did not exist at all in any form before Mark, and that he created it *de novo*, is to ignore a basic feature of Mark's compositional technique, which is, with the exception of his 'seams' and other transitional material, never to produce even his most wholly Markan contributions to the tradition without using some traditional element as its base.[7] Moreover, the evidence of Jn 6.67-69 indicates that a story of Peter's 'confession' was a basic element in the

---

5.   Cf. E. Best, *Following Jesus: Discipleship in the Gospel of Mark* (Sheffield: JSOT Press, 1981), p. 25 (the pre-Markan tradition was Mk 8.31, 32b, 33); E. Dinkler, 'Peter's Confession and the "Satan" Saying: The Problem of Jesus' Messiahship', in J.M. Robinson (ed.), *The Future of our Religious Past* (New York: Harper & Row, 1971), pp. 176-89 ([8.27b], 29, 33); R.H. Fuller, *The Foundations of New Testament Christology* (New York: Scribners, 1965), p. 109 (the pre-Markan tradition is Mk 8.27-28, 33); F. Hahn, *The Titles of Jesus in Christology* (London: Lutterworth, 1969), pp. 223-25 (a 'biographical apophthegm' consisting of 8.27a...29b...33); U. Luz, 'The Secrecy Motif and the Markan Christology', in C. Tuckett (ed.), *The Messianic Secret* (London: SCM Press, 1983), p. 82 (the core of Mk 8.27-33 is Mk 8.27b-29, 31b, 33, which, originally three separate traditions, were joined together in the pre-Markan tradition); A. Merx, *Das Evangelien des Markus und Lukas* (*Die vier Evangelien nach ihrem ältesten bekannten Texte, II/2*) (Berlin: G. Reimer, 1905), pp. 88-91 (pre-Markan tradition is Mk 8.29b, 33); A. Meyer, 'Die Enstehung des Markusevangeliums', in *Festgabe fur Adolf Jülicher* (Tübingen: J.B.C. Mohr, 1927), p. 44 (original tradition was Mk 8.27-29, 33); R. Pesch, 'Das Messiahbekenntnis des Petrus (Mk 8,27-30)', *BZ* 17 (1973), pp. 178-95 (Mk 8.32b, 33b formed a unit by themselves and were united by Mark to Mk 8.27-30); J. Weiss, *Das älteste Evangelium* (Göttingen: Vandenhoeck & Ruprecht, 1903), pp. 235-38 (pre-Markan tradition consists of Mk 8.27b, 29, 33b), E. Wendling, *Die Enstehung des Mk-Evangeliums* (Tübingen: Mohr, 1908), pp. 113-19 (original text was Mk 8.29b, 30a, 33, 37, 37; 9.2).

6.   See below, pp. 216-18.

7.   As shown, for instance, above in the analysis of Mk 8.1-13. Cf. also Mk 8.14-21, which, though a narrative, is wholly a Markan composition, and still contains, and is built up around, a traditional dominical saying (Mk 8.15). For an extended defense of this view, see E. Best, 'Mark's Preservation of the Tradition', in *Disciples and Discipleship: Studies in the Gospel according to Mark* (Edinburgh: T. & T. Clark, 1986), pp. 31-48.

stock of early Christian traditions about Jesus.[8] The truth about the tradition history of Mk 8.27-33 must lie somewhere in between these views. We therfore turn to a traditio-critical analysis of the eleven elements constituent to Mk 8.27-33:

(a) the setting (v. 27a)
(b) the question, asked 'on the way', of who people say Jesus is (v. 27b)
(c) the disciples' response (v. 28)
(d) the question of who the disciples say Jesus is (v. 29a)
(e) Peter's response (v. 29b)
(f) the command to silence (v. 30)
(g) a passion prediction or 'death portent' (v. 31)
(h) the notice that Jesus spoke 'the word' 'openly' (v. 32a)
(i) Peter's rebuke of Jesus (v. 32b)
(j) a notice of Jesus turning to, and gazing at, the disciples (v. 33a)
(k) a notice of Jesus rebuking Peter and the 'Satan' saying (v. 33b, c)

Of these elements, the last, that is, element (k), Jesus' rebuke of Peter and the 'Satan' saying (ἐπετίμησεν Πέτρῳ καὶ λέγει· ὕπαγε ὀπίσω μου, σατανᾶ, ὅτι οὐ φορονεῖς τὰ τοῦ θεοῦ ἀλλὰ τὰ τῶν ἀνθρώπων), has a strong claim to being traditional. Linguistically and stylistically, there is little here that is typically Markan.[9] Indeed, as M. Black has shown,[10] it is doubtful whether one could even say that the

---

8. On this, see F. Hahn, *Titles of Jesus*, p. 227 n. 13; R.E. Brown, *The Gospel According to John, 1–12* (Garden City: Doubleday, 1966), pp. 301-303. See also R.E. Brown, K.P. Donfried and J. Reumann (eds.), *Peter in the New Testament* (Minneapolis: Augsburg, 1973), pp. 64-67. The assumption underlying this view—an assumption with which I agree—is that the Gospel of John is independent of the Synoptics.

9. M. Horstmann (*Studien zur markinischen Christologie* [Münster: Aschendorff, 1969], pp. 26-27) argues that ὀπίσω μου is redactional, having been drawn from 8.34. But he ignores the fact that the phrase, linked here with ὕπαγε, has an entirely different meaning. On this, see Best, *Following Jesus*, p. 26 n. 13.

The οὐκ (οὐ)...ἀλλά construction of 33c may be thought to represent Mark's style, since it appears with great frequency in his Gospel (some 34 times, if one counts allied constructions). But many of these instances are traditional. Cf., e.g., Mk 10.45.

10. M. Black, *An Aramaic Approach to the Gospels and Acts* (Oxford: Clarendon Press, 3rd edn, 1967), pp. 263-64. For a negative assessment of Black's

element originated in a Greek speaking milieu. Does it display a Markan theme? Bultmann,[11] T.J. Weeden and others[12] insist that it does. They rest their view on the assumption that disparagement of Peter is typical of Mark. But this not only begs the question.[13] It dismisses too readily the evidence from Jn 6.67-69 that a rebuke with Peter as its object and a word about Satan was traditional.[14] Moreover, it founders on the fact that Mark himself is here actually intent to mitigate the opprobrium that the rebuke places upon Peter by giving it a wider target.[15] So there is no reason to think that it is a secondary formation.[16] Indeed, there is a real possibility that it embodies a historical reminiscence.[17]

Now it should be noted that form-critically the rebuke/'Satan' saying is a 'pronouncement',[18] that is, a saying that caps and concludes a disputation or argument.[19] It presupposes (1) an action or a question to which it is the response[20] and (2) a setting, that is, some 'data as to the situation' for which it was uttered.[21] The question, then, that must be asked is: Could any of the other elements of Mk 8.27-33 have been these items?

A most definite 'no' must be placed against elements (f), (h) and (j). All three seem to be completely redactional. Element (f), the command to silence (καὶ ἐπετίμησεν αὐτοῖς ἵνα μηδενὶ λέγωσιν περὶ αὐτοῦ), is completely in line with Mark's theme of 'the messianic

argument, see Luz, 'The Secrecy Motif', p. 94 n. 60.

11. Bultmann, *History*, p. 256.

12. Weeden, *Mark: Traditions in Conflict, passim*; U.B. Müller, 'Die Christologische absicht des Markusevangeliums und die Verklärungsgeschichte', *ZNW* 64 (1973), pp. 159-93; E. Trocmé, *The Formation of the Gospel according to St Mark* (London: SPCK, 1975), pp. 125-30.

13. Cf. Dinkler, 'Peter's Confession', p. 174; E. Schweizer, *The Good News according to Mark* (Atlanta: John Knox, 1970), p. 165.

14. Brown, Donfried and Reumann, *Peter*, p. 67; Dinkler, 'Peter's Confession', p. 193; E. Best, 'Peter in the Gospel according to Mark', in *Disciples and Discipleship*, pp. 162-76, esp. p. 164.

15. Cf. Best, 'Peter', pp. 164-65.

16. Dinkler, 'Peter's Confession', p. 174.

17. Brown, Donfried and Reumann, *Peter*, p. 67.

18. Fuller, *Foundations*, p. 109.

19. On this, see R. Bultmann, *Form Criticism* (Chicago: Willitt, Clark & Co., 1934), p. 40; V. Taylor, *The Formation of the Gospel Tradition* (London: Macmillan, 1949), p. 63.

20. Bultmann, *Form Criticism*, p. 40; Hahn, *Titles of Jesus*, p. 223.

21. Fuller, *Foundations*, p. 134 n. 35.

Secret'.[22] Its style and wording—the use of καί and ἐπιτιμάω followed by ἵνα rather than by the infinitive—is Markan.[23] Element (h), the notice that Jesus spoke 'the word' 'openly' (καὶ παρρησίᾳ τὸν λόγον ἐλάλει), also betrays Mark's hand. The phrase λαλεῖν τὸν λόγον is an early church phrase meaning 'preach the Gospel'[24] and it is found in Mk 2.2 and 4.33, verses which are clearly secondary.[25] The form of the phrase, a verb with cognate accusative, is Markan style,[26] as is the use of the imperfect.[27] And the theme of the notice—that the one thing that Jesus speaks about 'openly' is the necessity of his passion and death—is the heart of Markan theology.[28] Element (j), Jesus' turning to, and seeing the disciples (ὁ δὲ ἐπιστραφεὶς καὶ ἰδὼν τοὺς μαθητὰς αὐτοῦ), not only fits very roughly with the rebuke/'Satan' saying (the rebuke/'Satan' saying is in the singular), and therefore seems only secondarily connected to its context,[29] it is consistent with Mark's interest in the disciples.[30] Moreover, the description of Jesus' action by means of a double participle (ἐπιστραφεὶς καὶ ἰδὼν) is part of Mark's style.[31]

A 'no' must also be placed against element (g). Whether or not the prediction of the suffering of the Son of Man is redactional[32] (δεῖ τὸν υἱὸν τοῦ ἀνθρώπου πολλὰ παθεῖν καὶ ἀποδοκιμασθῆναι ὑπὸ τῶν πρεσβυτέρων καὶ τῶν ἀρχιερέων καὶ τῶν γραμματέων καὶ ἀποκτανθῆναι καὶ μετὰ τρεῖς ἡμέρας ἀναστῆναι), its connection

22. Best, *Following Jesus*, 21; Brown, Donfried and Reumann, *Peter*, 66; Luz, 'The Secrecy Motif', 82; Hahn, *Titles of Jesus*, p. 223; R. Pesch, *Das Markusevangelium*, II (Freiberg: Herder, 1977), pp. 33-34.

23. Best, *Following Jesus*, pp. 21-22.

24. Best, *Following Jesus*, p. 24.

25. Schweizer, *Mark*, p. 174; E. Best, *The Temptation and the Passion: The Markan Soteriology* (Cambridge: Cambridge University Press, 1965), p. 70.

26. On this, see F. Neirynck, *Duality in Mark: Contributions to the Study of Markan Redaction* (Leuven: Leuven University Press, 1973), p. 76.

27. Best, *Following Jesus*, p. 24.

28. On this, see, among many others, Schweizer, *Mark*, pp. 380-86; R.P. Martin, *Mark: Evangelist and Theologian* (Exeter: Paternoster Press, 1972).

29. Best, *Following Jesus*, p. 24; Dinkler, 'Peter's Confession', p. 186.

30. Best, *Following Jesus*, p. 24; *idem*, 'The Role of the Disciples in Mark', in *Disciples and Discipleship*, pp. 98-130.

31. On this, see Neirynck, *Duality*, p. 82.

32. For a general survey of opinions on this matter, see G. Strecker, 'The Passion and Resurrection Predictions in Mark's Gospel (Mark 8.31, 9.31, 10.32-34)', *Int* 22 (1968), pp. 421-43.

with its present context is clearly secondary.[33] And if this is the case with this element, it must also be the case with element (i), Peter's rebuke of Jesus (καὶ προσλαβόμενος ὁ Πέτρος αὐτὸν ἤρξατο ἐπιτιμᾶν αὐτῷ), since one of the purposes of this element is to provide the transition between the passion prediction and the rebuke/'Satan' saying.[34] Moreover, as E. Dinkler has noted,[35] Peter's reaction picks up the ἐπιτιμᾶν from element (f), the command to silence (v. 30), but uses it with a different nuance. So the impression is that the reaction is not fully integrated with its context.

Doubtful, too, as originally part of the story leading to the rebuke/'Satan' saying is element (c), the declaration by the disciples regarding who people say Jesus is (οἱ δὲ εἶπαν αὐτῷ λέγοντες ὅτι Ἰωάννην τὸν βαπτιστήν, καὶ ἄλλοι Ἠλίαν, ἄλλοι δὲ ὅτι εἷς τῶν προφητῶν). The fact that there is in Mk 6.14-16 a doublet of what is here the disciples' declaration about Jesus suggests that this was a 'floating' tradition, no doubt ancient, but one having originally no connection with the 'pronouncement'.[36] And if this element is secondary, then so, too, is element (b), Jesus' question about who people say he is (καὶ ἐν τῇ ὁδῷ ἐπηρώτα τοὺς μαθητὰς αὐτοῦ λέγων αὐτοῖς...). This exists to introduce the report that people identify Jesus with John the Baptist, Elijah or one of the Prophets.

We are left, then, with elements (a), (d) and (e). Are these the original elements of the traditional pre-Markan 'frame' of the rebuke/'Satan' saying? Several considerations speak in their favour. First, each of these

---

33. This is clear from the fact that it begins with a formula (καὶ ἤρξατο διδάσκειν) that Mark uses to introduce a new piece of tradition. On this, see Luz, 'The Secrecy Motif', pp. 82, 94 n. 60.

34. Brown, Donfried and Reumann, *Peter*, p. 67; Hahn, *Titles of Jesus*, p. 223.

35. Dinkler, 'Peter's Confession', p. 185.

36. Brown, Donfried and Reumann, *Peter*, p. 65; Bultmann, *History*, p. 303; Schweizer, *Mark*, p. 132; J. Ernst, *Das Evangelium nach Markus* (Regensburg: Pustet, 1981), p. 178. Catchpole, however, has argued ('Triumphal Entry', p. 327) that no such 'floating' tradition ever existed. In his view both Mk 6.14-16 as well as Mk 8.28 have been composed by Mark himself, since 'the list of opinions [appearing in both texts] concerning the identity of Jesus [especially the suggestion that Jesus is John the Baptist] reflects no historical situation either before or after Easter but is an artificial construction serving [Mark's] christological ends'. But even if true, this conclusion matters little for our present purposes. For in the end it simply amounts to saying that v. 28 is, as I have already noted, secondary to its present context.

elements shows little evidence of stemming from Mark's hand.[37] They come, like the rebuke/'Satan' saying, from the tradition.[38] Secondly, from a form-critical perspective their combination results in a story which, given the shape of primitive, unitary 'pronouncement stories', not only is 'true to form' (with element [a] [καὶ ἐξῆλθεν ὁ 'Ιησοῦς καὶ οἱ μαθηταὶ αὐτοῦ εἰς τὰς κώμας Καισαρείας τῆς Φιλίππου] providing the setting, and elements [d] [καὶ αὐτὸς ἐπηρώτα αὐτούς· ὑμεῖς δὲ τίνα με λέγετε εἶναι;] and [e] [ἀποκριθεὶς ὁ Πέτρος λέγει αὐτῷ· οὐ εἶ ὁ χριστός] conveying the action to which the rebuke/'Satan' saying is the response[39]), but which bears no stamp of the secondary.[40] Thirdly, from a literary-critical point of view, the story they produce is not only coherent; it is fully appropriate given the nature and content of the 'pronouncement' toward which it builds. A confession of Jesus as ὁ Χριστός would produce the rebuke/'Satan' saying, and the rebuke/'Satan' saying is understandable as a response to such a confession.[41] Finally, these particular elements in this particular combination find their parallel in Jn 6.67-71, the Johannine counterpart of

37. This is more true of elements (d) and (e) than element (a). The use there of καί with a verb of motion (especially ἔρχεσθαι, or as here, one of its compounds) is Markan as is the use of a singular verb with a plural subject. But what about the reference to Caesarea Philippi? Is Mark responsible for this, too? The answer, I think, is no. *In the first place*, on a purely logical level, it is illegitimate to conclude that because the beginning of this element is Markan the remainder of it is as well. *Secondly*, the vocabulary of the reference is not distinctly Markan. (On this, see Luz, 'The Secrecy Motif', p. 93 n. 60). True, Mark uses οἱ δώδεκα ('the twelve') for the disciples, but μαθηταί is found in the tradition, too. *Thirdly*, the reference itself is imprecise ('in the villages of...') One would think that if Mark were introducing a geographical reference where one did not already exist, he would have been more specific. *Fourthly*, as Horstmann has pointed out (*Studien*, pp. 9-10), it is not Mark's habit to introduce new geographical data. *Fifthly*, it is a name that appears nowhere else in the Gospels. *Sixthly*, it is an unlikely site for Jesus and the disciples to be, even granting that Mark could be inferring—from references to Jesus' journey within the tradition—where Jesus and the disciples might have been when Jesus rebuked Peter. *Finally*, stylistically, the reference is disharmonious with its parallels in 7.31 and 8.22. To my mind then, what Mark has done here is to rework a traditional notice that read something like 'In the villages of Caesarea Philippi he asked his disciples...'

38. Cf. Dinkler, 'Peter's Confession', p. 178; Fuller, *Foundations*, p. 109.

39. Schweizer, *Mark*, pp. 171-74.

40. Fuller, *Foundations*, p. 109.

41. Dinkler, 'Peter's Confession', pp. 178-79; *contra* Bultmann, *History*, pp. 258-59.

Mk 8.27-33. There the story is also built on a structure of (1) a notice about Jesus' accompaniment by disciples (v. 66), (2) a question of Jesus to the Twelve (v. 67), (3) a 'confession' of Peter (v. 68-69), and (4) Jesus' reference to a devil among the Twelve (v. 70).[42]

So we find that the tradition history of Mk 8.27-33 begins with a pronouncement story looking somewhat like the following:

> And Jesus and his disciples came to the villages of Caesarea Philippi.
> And he asked them, 'Who do you say I am?'
> And Peter answered, 'You are the Christ'.
> And Jesus rebukes Peter and says, 'Get behind me, Satan.
> You do not think the things of God
> But the things of men'.[43]

Mark, then, in recounting his version of the episode, took this story up and added to it a notice of Jesus asking his disciples who people say he is (element [b]),[44] a tradition concerning how people have identified Jesus (element [c]),[45] casting it as the disciples' response to Jesus' question on who people say he is (element [b]), a passion prediction (element [g]),[46] the notice about the 'openness' of the prediction (element [h]), and the notice of Jesus turning to the disciples before he rebukes Peter (element [j]).

The Nature of Jesus' Temptation according to Mark

To be sure, neither the verb πειράζω nor the noun πειρασμός appear anywhere within Mk 8.27-33. But that Jesus is nonetheless presented here by Mark not only as tempted but tempted 'religiously', that is, put to the test over his faithfulness, is clear when we draw out the implications of the central feature of Mark's Caesarea Philippi account. That central feature is the presentation of Jesus and Peter as engaged in a heated dispute over the question of the means by which Jesus as

---

42. On this, see Brown, *John 1–12*, pp. 301-303.

43. On this as the original text, see n. 41.

44. This seems clear from the fact that this element is joined to its context by the phrase ἐν τῇ ὁδῷ, a phrase which is thoroughly Markan. On this, see below.

45. This seems clear from the fact that this element is joined to its context by a phrase (οἱ δὲ εἶπαν αὐτῷ λέγοντες [ὅτι]) which reflects Markan wording and style.

46. That Mark added this is clear from the fact that the prediction is prefaced by the phrase καὶ ἤρξατο διδάσκειν, a seam used by Mark to introduce new material. On this, see above, n. 35.

Messiah is to achieve the fulfilment of his messianic vocation.[47] In Mk 8.31 Jesus declares in the first of three passion predictions or, to use the phraseology of C. Myers, 'death portents'[48] that in accordance with his understanding of the will of God in this regard, the messianic task (which, as we have seen, is portrayed by Mark as the decisive victory of God's sovereignty over the world)[49] is to be accomplished only through suffering and a willingness to be subjected to death (πολλὰ παθεῖν καὶ ...ἀποκτανθῆναι) at the hands of enemies.[50] But at Mk 8.32 Peter disdains this declaration. In his demeanour towards Jesus and in his reaction to Jesus' announcement, he [Peter] vociferously asserts that, on the contrary, suffering and death are *not* God's plans for his Messiah, and he implicitly proposes that Jesus *as Messiah* should deny what he has just said and adopt some other means to execute his divine commission.[51] It should be noted that in Mark's portrayal of things this exchange of views is by no means merely academic. For at v. 33 he records that Peter's criticism is perceived by Jesus as nothing less than a suggestion coming from Satan himself, designed to induce disobedience to God.[52] Peter's response, therefore, is presented by Mark as something which

---

47. See J.L. Mays, 'An Exposition of Mark 8:27–9.1', *Int* 30 (1976), p. 174.

48. Cf. C. Myers, *Binding the Strong Man* (Maryknoll: Orbis Books, 1988), p. 238. The two other passion/death predictions appear at Mk 9.31 and Mk 10.33-34.

49. See above, Chapter 2, p. 77. See also Lane, *Mark*, p. 304; T.A. Burkill, *Mysterious Revelation* (Ithaca, NY: Cornell University Press, 1963), p. 154.

50. According to Mark, Jesus' perception of the path he is to follow in accomplishing the messianic task is rooted in his understanding of God's will. This is apparent from Mark's description (8.31a) of that path as something that Jesus knew he 'must' do (καὶ ἤρξατο διδάσκειν αὐτοὺς ὅτι δεῖ). For, as W.J. Bennett Jr has noted ('The Son of Man Must...', *NovT* 17 [1975], pp. 113-29, esp. p. 128), δεῖ here corresponds to, but in meaning is more pregnant than, γεγράπται ('it is written') and refers to a perception of particular compulsion or constraint, behind which stands the will of God. See, too, H. Anderson, *The Gospel of Mark* (London: Oliphants, 1976), p. 217.

51. Peter takes Jesus aside (προσλαβόμενος) and rebukes him (ἐπιτιμᾶν). The gesture described by προσλαβόμενος implies a presumptuous and patronizing sense of superiority on the part of Peter, and Peter's *rebuking* of Jesus, associated throughout the Gospel with the silencing of demons, expresses the heightened degree of his opposition to Jesus' declaration.

52. This is brought out clearly in the continuation of the 'Satan saying', οὐ φρονεῖς τὰ τοῦ θεοῦ ἀλλὰ τὰ τῶν ἀνθρώπων. On this, see Dinkler, 'Peter's Confession and the "Satan Saying"', p. 186; H. Seesemann, 'πεῖρα, κτλ.', *TDNT*, VI, p. 36.

places Jesus squarely in a situation of open choice between surrender to God's will or revolt against it.[53] In other words, it is, according to Mark, something which subjects Jesus to the experience of 'a testing of one's faithfulness and obedience', that is, to πειρασμός in its 'religious' sense.[54]

But what precisely in Mark's eyes is the sort of *alternative* messianic behaviour that Peter is advocating when he takes Jesus aside? What is the alluring activity that Peter, according to Mark, seeks to get Jesus to engage in, if he is to renounce suffering and still discharge his calling to be Messiah? In short, what does Mark hold the content of Jesus' temptation to be?

The Content of Jesus' Temptation according to Mark
Here we face a considerable problem, namely, a lack of information that would lead us to an answer to this question. For contrary to what is normally assumed, within the immediate confines of Mk 8.27-33 *Mark actually provides no data from which his conception of the content of Jesus' temptation may either be deduced or inferred.*[55] All that we are really told in this regard in these verses is what Peter thought Jesus ought *not to do.*

This being the case, must we then conclude that ultimately we cannot know Mark's idea of the real content of the temptation presented to Jesus by Satan through Peter at Caesarea Philippi? I think not. For while Mark nowhere within Mk 8.27-33 concretely specifies the content of the temptation that he there says Jesus faced, he nonetheless elsewhere makes plain what this content is. He does this in Mk 8.34–9.1 and in two other places in his Gospel, namely Mk 9.30-37 and 10.32-45. If certain information contained within these verses is taken into account, something quite definite can be said about Mark's conception of the particular messianic behaviour which Peter at Caesarea Philippi sought to move Jesus toward, and, therefore, some certainty can be gained concerning

53. On this, see Seesemann, 'πεῖρα, κτλ.', p. 36. See also K.W. Chase, 'The Synoptic Πειρασμόι of Jesus: Their Christological Significance' (ThD dissertation, New Orleans Baptist Theological Seminary, 1989), pp. 156-57.

54. On being placed in this type of situation as a basic element in the experience of temptation, especially that which 'tests' faithfulness, see Seesemann, 'πεῖρα, κτλ.', p. 36; B. Van Iersel, *The Bible on the Temptations of Man* (De Pere, WI: St Norbert Abbey Press, 1966), pp. 16.

55. P.J. Achtemeier, *Mark* (Philadelphia: Fortress Press, 1975), p. 43.

the actual content of the temptation which, according to Mark, Jesus faced. Let us see how this is so, first with Mk 8.34–9.1 and then with the other two units of material.

Mark 8.34–9.1 and the Content of the Caesarea Philippi Temptation. Mk 8.34–9.1 is a unit of material comprised of sayings of Jesus which are predominantly concerned with the subject of discipleship. The unit owes both much of its present form as well as its present place (as the sequel of Mk 8.27-33) to Mark's redactional activity.[56] In its present context the unit performs primarily two functions. First, it establishes Mk 8.27-30, Peter's 'confession',[57] as the introduction to, and the basis of, a formalized and carefully constructed pattern in which (a) a passion prediction made by Jesus (cf. Mk 8.31) is followed by (b) a dramatization of the failure of Jesus' disciples to understand or accept the prediction and the instruction about the destiny of the Messiah contained within it (cf. Mk 8.32b-33), and then by (c) teaching of Jesus on the subject of authentic discipleship (cf. Mk 8.34b-38). Secondly, the placement of the unit after Mk 8.27-30 highlights the Markan emphasis that discipleship is the correlative of messiahship.[58]

The discipleship which, by virtue of Mark's redaction, follows on from, and is deemed commensurate with, Jesus' declaration of the nature of his messiahship is typified in Mk 8.34–9.1 in the activity called

---

56. Bultmann, *History*, pp. 82-83; Taylor, *Mark*, p. 380. See also the detailed exposition of this position by E. Best, *Following Jesus*, pp. 28-54.

57. To call Mk 8.27-33 'Peter's Confession at Caesarea Philippi' is somewhat misleading and inaccurate. Peter's confession that Jesus is the Christ occupies only a few verses of the pericope. Moreover, it is only the initial stage of the drama of the piece that issues in an altercation between Jesus and Peter (cf. v. 32) and culminates in Jesus rebuking Peter (v. 33) and thereby in some sense discrediting his confession. The title 'The Confrontation between Jesus and Peter' is actually more accurate and appropriate (cf. W.H. Kelber, *Mark's Story of Jesus* [Philadelphia: Fortress Press, 1979], pp. 48-49). But since the former title is the more familiar, I will continue to use it here.

58. 'In the redactional sense the attachment of the logia about suffering and discipleship (vv. 34ff.) is materially appropriate; in these sayings the christological announcement is transcended and the following of the disciples becomes thematic; discipleship is interpreted as the acceptance of the fate of the suffering Messiah–Son of Man, and self-denial is made compulsory even for discipleship. So what is true for the way of the Messiah–Son of Man also applies to discipleship' (G. Strecker, 'The Passion and Resurrection Predictions', p. 673).

'cross bearing' (v. 35). It should be noted, however, that when within this unit of material the content of 'cross bearing' is spelled out (cf. esp. vv. 34-36), it is done so only paradoxically, that is, only through statements concerning what this activity does *not* involve—indeed, only through statements about the sort of behaviour which is the very opposite of 'cross bearing'. In other words, Mark has Jesus outline what the disciples of a suffering Messiah are expected to do by holding up and condemning examples of behaviour which are not only denials of 'cross bearing' but things which serve to frustrate the faithfulness to 'the things of God' (cf. Mk 8.33) that the willingness to 'take up the cross' displays. This behaviour, moreover, is programmatic in its concerns and scope, and, since it is the foil against which the pattern of behaviour deemed appropriate for the followers of Jesus is set, it is designated as a type of discipleship in its own right.

This being the case, certain conclusions are inescapable: first, within the context of the thematic emphasis provided by the Markan redaction for the teaching of Jesus on discipleship, the discipleship which Mark has Jesus oppose, like that which he has Jesus advocate, is meant to be seen as arising out of a particular conception of the nature of messiahship; and secondly, the Christology and Christological behaviour giving rise to the opposed discipleship is nothing other than that which in Mk 8.33 is delimited as Satanic. Consequently, what we need to do to determine the specific nature of the condemned messianic behaviour—and, therefore, the actual content of the 'testing' which it embodies—is, first of all, to examine the behaviour now redactionally designated as constituent to the discipleship which flows from the Satanic concept of messiahship, and then, secondly, move backwards from the results of this examination to whatever can be inferred from it about the nature of the condemned messiahship itself. It is to these tasks that I now turn.

The behaviour constituent to the discipleship which Jesus opposes is characterized in Mk 8.34 as involving the refusal to engage in 'self denial' (ἀπαρνέομαι), in Mk 8.35 as involving the wish to 'save' life or self (ὃς γὰρ ἐὰν θέλῃ τὴν ψυχὴν αὐτοῦ σῶσαι), and in Mk 8.36 as involving the desire for gain. Within the context that the Markan redaction has provided, these characteristics are linked together, reinforcing and mutually interpreting one another, making plain that the discipleship condemned holds as its own the right to preserve self or life from danger or death through a type of self-assertion which, in being exercised, seeks to gain 'the whole world' (κερδῆσαι τὸν κόσμον ὅλον).

The object of this self assertion is significant. In its abstract sense κερδαῖνω means simply to procure gain, advantage, profit. But with κόσμος as its object, κερδαῖνω means winning lordship over the world of human beings and gaining all the possibilities for self aggrandizement which such lordship allows.[59] In other words, *the constituent characteristic of the discipleship which Jesus condemns in Mk 8.34–9.1 is the seeking of worldly power and dominion.*

Now, a discipleship which considers power and dominion its right and self assertion its duty must be rooted in, and derived from, a conception of messiahship which possesses these same characteristics, since, as we have seen, discipleship and messiahship are in Mark's mind the two sides of a single coin. This is a significant conclusion, for it means that the messiahship which is labeled Satanic in Mk 8.33, being the ground and legitimization of the discipleship which Jesus condemns, is one which is involved with worldly power. And this in turn means that according to Mark the messianic activity which Peter at Mk 8.27-30 urges upon Jesus—the behaviour that, if adopted, would allow Jesus to refuse the suffering integral to his own messianic path while still pursuing the goal of his messianic appointment—is triumphalism.

But how in particular was this triumphalism to express itself? For this information I turn to Mk 9.30-37 and Mk 10.32-45, material which I believe was intended by Mark to be seen not only as formally and thematically related to the entire Caesarea Philippi episode, but also as explicating the content of the messianic behaviour which in that episode Peter sought to get Jesus to adopt.

The Relation of Mark 9.30-37; 10.32-45 to Mark 8.27–9.1. At Mk 9.30 and 10.32 there begin units of material which in a variety of ways are strikingly parallel to the redacted Caesarea Philippi episode (Mk 8.27–9.1). First, these units take up that episode's main theme and deal with the relationship between Christology and discipleship.[60] Secondly, they each begin with a precise geographical notice (9.30 '...from there and passed through Galilee'; 10.32 'going up on the road to Jerusalem')—something, notably, only infrequently found at the beginning of, or for that matter, within, Markan narrative pericopes, yet occurring conspicuously at Mk 8.27 ('to the villages of Caesarea Philippi'). Thirdly,

---

59. Cf. H. Schlier, 'κέρδος, κερδαῖνω', *TDNT*, III, p. 673.

60. Cf. N. Perrin, *Christology and a Modern Pilgrimage* (ed. H.D. Betz; Missoula: Scholars Press, 1974), p. 9.

structurally both Mk 9.30-37 and Mk 10.32-45 reproduce exactly
the passion prediction–misunderstanding–teaching pattern upon which
Mk 8.27–9.1 is built. And fourthly, as in the Caesarea Philippi episode,
Jesus' teaching on discipleship is set forth in both of these units in the
form of a paradox. All of this can be represented in tabular form:

Geographical reference	8.27	9.30	10.32
Passion Prediction	8.31	9.31	10.33-34
Misunderstanding	8.32-33	9.32	10.35-41
Teaching on Discipleship	8.34–9.1	9.33-37	10.42-45
Paradox	save life/lose life	first/last	great/least

But the similarities do not end here. The narrative setting of all three
units is, notably, 'on the road/way' (ἐν τῇ ὁδῷ, cf. Mk 8.27; 9.33;
10.32). Moreover, each of the 'teaching' sections of these units begins
with a notice of Jesus calling his disciples to him (Mk 8.34, καὶ
προσκαλεσάμενος τὸν ὄχλον σὺν τοῖς μαθηταῖς αὐτοῦ εἶπεν
αὐτοῖς, 9.35, καὶ καθίσας ἐφώνησεν τοὺς δώδεκα καὶ λέγει
αὐτοῖς, 10.42, καὶ προσκαλεσάμενος αὐτοὺς ὁ Ἰησοῦς λέγει
αὐτοῖς). Finally, the units beginning at Mk 9.30 and Mk 10.32 each
contain a notice that in following Jesus the disciples were afraid
(Mk 9.32, καὶ ἐφοβοῦντο, 10.32, οἱ δὲ ἀκολουθοῦντες ἐφοβοῦντο).

Now, both Mk 9.30-37 and Mk 10.32-45 are Markan constructions.[61]
Accordingly, the structural, formal and thematic similarities that exist
between these units of material and Mk 8.27–9.1 is hardly accidental. On
the contrary, these similarities indicate that Mark intended the Caesarea
Philippi episode, and especially its element involving Peter's 'confession', to be seen as presupposed in each of these units and, more

---

61. Arguing that Mk 9.31-37 was built by Mark out of originally separate units of
material, i.e., an isolated passion prediction, a story about the disciples boldness and
presumption, and logia on discipleship, see P.J. Achtemeier, 'An Exposition of Mark
9:30-37', *Int* 30 (1976), p. 178; F. Neirynck, 'The Tradition of the Sayings of Jesus',
Concilium 20 (1967), pp. 63-74; R. Schnackenburg, 'Mk. 9,33-50', in J.A. Schmid
and A. Vögtle (eds.), *Synoptische Studien: Alfred Wikenhauser zum siebzigsten
Geburstag am 22 Februar 1953 dargebracht von Freunden, Kollegen und Schülern*
(Munich: Zink, 1953), pp. 184-206, esp. p. 197; H. Fleddermann, 'The Discipleship
Discourse (Mark 9:33-50)', *CBQ* 43 (1981), pp. 57-75.

That the units of material clearly detectable in Mk 10.32-45 (i.e. vv. 32-34, 35-40,
42-45) were originally separate from one another, and not joined together before
Mark took them in hand, is maintained by Taylor, *Mark*, pp. 439, 442; Best,
Following Jesus, p. 123. See also R. McKinnis, 'An Analysis of Mark X 32-34',
NovT 18 (1976), pp. 81-100.

importantly, *as serving as the point of departure for the particular discussions on the nature of messiahship and discipleship that occur
within them.*[62] Indeed, given this, it is not too much to say that Mark
intended the information on the nature of messiahship and discipleship
contained within the material now incorporated in Mk 9.30-37 and
10.32-45 to be seen not only as co-ordinate with the material on
Christology and discipleship in the Caesarea Philippi episode but as an
explication of the view of the nature of messiahships advanced there by
Jesus and Peter. And so, in light of the question that I am here pursuing,
viz, the question of the actual content of Jesus' Caesarea Philippi
'testing', it is important that we turn now to examine just what these
units of material say in this regard.

Mark 9.30-37 and the Content of the Caesarea Philippi Temptation.
The unit of material comprising Mk 9.30-37 is most generally known as
'A Discussion concerning True Greatness'. It begins with Jesus making
his second passion prediction (Mk 9.30-31). In words substantially the
same as those contained within the passion prediction found at Mk 8.31,
Jesus' messiahship is here once again defined in terms of suffering and
death.[63] The prediction is then followed by an editorial statement that
the disciples 'did not understand the saying' (9.32). Mark then drama-
tizes, exemplifies and explains the nature of this 'misunderstanding' by
attaching a short scene of traditional and redactional material.[64] Certain
features of this section (vv. 33-37) bear notice. The first is that in vv. 33-
34, that is, the verses of the pericope's passion prediction–misunderstanding–teaching pattern which outline the disciples' inability to com-
prehend (or refusal to accept) Jesus' declaration on the nature of his
messiahship, Mark states that the disciples were occupied with a discussion concerning 'greatness' (...πρὸς ἀλλήλους γὰρ διελέχθησαν...
τίς μείζων). The term μέγας, from which μείζων is derived, has a
number of spatial, qualitative, and quantitative meanings. But when, as
here, it is applied to persons, it has to do with issues of rank and
dignity.[65] More closely defined, it serves in Mark's Gospel for those
who are set apart by power and might.[66] So here the disciples are

---

62. Cf. Perrin, *Chistology and a Modern Pilgrimage*, p. 9.
63. Cf. Lane, *Mark*, pp. 336-37.
64. Cf. above, n. 61.
65. W. Grundmann, 'μέγας', *TDNT*, IV, p. 529.
66. Cf. the parallelism in Mk 10.42 between the 'great ones' (οἱ μεγάλοι) and

portrayed as involving themselves with questions of social dominance. The second feature is that in v. 35, the verse of the pericope's passion–misunderstanding–teaching pattern which contains Jesus' teaching on discipleship, the 'greatness' which the disciples have been discussing is characterized as the desire to be 'first' (πρῶτος). The term 'first' can here only mean pre-eminence in worldly power, authority and might. For in the first place, when πρῶτος is not used adjectivally in Mark's Gospel (as it is in Mk 12.20, 28, 29; 14.12), it is consistently used as a designation for rulers and people of power (cf. Mk 10.44 and especially Mk 6.21 where the chief men of King Herod's administration are called οἱ πρῶτοι). In the second place, within the context of the verse, πρῶτος is set antonymically in contrast with ἔσχατος and διάκονος, terms which are there obviously meant as designations of worldly pow- erlessness.[67] And in the third place, within the context of the present passage, those who desire to be πρῶτος are set in contrast with a παιδίον, which there is not only a little child, but a servant, a helpless one.[68] So here the disciples are portrayed as concerned with questions of worldly social status.

The third feature of Mk 9.30-37 that bears notice is Mark's presenta- tion of the disciples' discussion as containing a personal reference. In v. 33 the disciples are said to be debating which of those within their circle (πρὸς ἀλλήλους) is 'great'. So power, prestige and privilege are things which the disciples view *as theirs by right*.

The fourth and last feature that concerns us is that, through the repe- tition of a key phrase, Mark carefully emphasizes not only that 'great- ness' was the disciples' favourite topic of conversation,[69] but, more importantly, that the disciples' passion for power and their confidence of their right to it *were based squarely on their assumptions concerning the nature of Jesus' messiahship*. Twice Mark notes that the discussion concerning 'greatness' takes place ἐν τῇ ὁδῷ (cf. vv. 33, 34), that is, on

the Gentile rulers who possess and exercise lordly authority.
    67. G. Kittel, 'ἔσχατος', *TDNT*, II, p. 698; H.W. Beyer, 'διακονέω', *TDNT*, II, p. 88.
    68. See the extended discussion of the Markan use of the term παιδίον by A. Ambrozic (*The Hidden Kingdom* [Washington, DC: Catholic Biblical Association, 1972], pp. 148-158), where Ambrozic concludes that in Mark a παιδίον is 'one who is last of all and expected to subject himself to others'.
    69. Kelber, *Mark's Story of Jesus*, p. 49.

the path of the Messiah.[70] This localization fixes the discussion within the context of the relationship which the disciples, as followers of Jesus, assume to have with him. They argue about their 'greatness' because the prominence and power which are its characteristics are the advantages which they assume their association with Jesus gives them.

When we turn to what can be inferred from all this with respect to the nature of the messiahship which the disciples here in Mk 9.30-37, like Peter in Mk 8.27–9.1, mistakenly assume that Jesus as Messiah embraces, one thing is clear. Jesus' messiahship as the disciples view it is bound up with being a king, a lordly sovereign, a 'great one' who will soon inaugurate his reign and reward those who have followed him faithfully with the positions and prerogatives of power. The disciples' assumption that their association with Jesus grants them a share in worldly 'greatness' presupposes that they think that Jesus as Messiah possesses such 'greatness' himself. The disciples here, like Peter at Caesarea Philippi, can turn a deaf ear to Jesus' profession of the real nature of his messiahship because they, like Peter, hold Jesus to be a Messiah full of this-worldly power.[71]

Mark 10.32-45 and the Content of the Caesarea Philippi Temptation. The second unit of material in Mark's Gospel which displays the passion prediction–misunderstanding–teaching pattern of the Caesarea Philippi episode is the Mk 10.32-45, the story of the request of James and John. It recounts that following an explicit and detailed passion prediction (Mk 10.32-33) the disciples James and John approach Jesus with a petition (διδάσκαλε, θέλομεν ἵνα ὃ ἐὰν αἰτήσωμέν σε ποιήσῃς ἡμῖν, 10.35) that he allow them to 'sit at [his] right and left hand' (10.37). Jesus responds to this request with an allusive and ironic remark that the disciples do not know what they are asking (10.38a). He then sets before them an enigmatic question concerning whether they will be able to partake of his 'cup' and his 'baptism' (10.38b). After James and John respond with an emphatic 'We can!' (10.39), Jesus summons all of the disciples together and addresses them with teaching on discipleship

---

70. On this, see Luz, 'The Secrecy Motif', p. 85; W. Michaelis, 'ὁδός', *TDNT*, V, pp. 42-43; W.H. Kelber, *The Kingdom in Mark* (Philadelphia: Fortress Press, 1974), pp. 67-69; W.M. Swartley, 'The Structural Function of the Term "Way" (*Hodos*) in Mark's Gospel', in W. Klassen (ed.), *The New Way of Jesus* (Grand Rapids: Eerdmans, 1980), pp. 73-86.

71. Kelber, *Mark's Story of Jesus*, p. 50.

(10.42-45) which culminates in the Son of Man 'ransom saying' (v. 45).
When this unit of material is examined in light of the information we
are seeking, it becomes clear that in almost every one of its features it is
implied that the view of the nature of Jesus' messiahship held by the
disciples is, again, one in which Jesus is seen to be a powerful king.
Consider, for instance, the initial address (διδάσκαλε) and the petition
of James and John (θέλομεν, κτλ.). The title διδάσκαλος as an appel-
lation for Jesus is found frequently in Mark's Gospel.[72] When it is used
by those outside the circle of Jesus' disciples as a form of address to
Jesus it means noting more than 'pedagogue', 'instructor', 'learned
man', albeit one of high standing.[73] But when it appears on the lips of
the disciples in direct speech to Jesus, it designates him not only as a
teacher in the ordinary sense, but as one in whom a powerful authority
resides.[74] The words of the initial petition not only implicitly express an
abundance of confidence in Jesus and assume that he has power at his
disposal, but in their particular form they recall the royal speech of King
Herod to the daughter of Herodias at Mk 6.22 (Αἴτησόν με ὃ ἐὰν
θέλῃς, καὶ δώσω σοι)[75] and give the petition the flavour of courtly
language. As Swete notes, 'Both the homage offered and the terms of
the petition suggests that [Jesus] is approached in the character of a king
who can gratify the desires of his subjects without limitation'.[76]

That the disciples here view Jesus as a powerful king is also the implication of the actual request of James and John in 10.37. This request is
to be allowed 'to sit on the right and on the left' of Jesus (δὸς ἡμῖν ἵνα
εἷς σου ἐκ δεξιῶν καὶ εἷς ἐξ ἀριστερῶν, κτλ.). Commentators
have long recognized that the form and imagery of this request is drawn
from contemporary courtly idiom. The disciples specifically ask Jesus to

72. Jesus so identifies himself, and is so identified by disciples, Jewish religious
leaders and others, 12 times in Mark's Gospel.

73. Cf. Mk 10.17; 12.14, 32.

74. On this, see P.J. Achtemeier, 'He Taught them Many Things: Reflections
on Markan Christology', *CBQ* 42 (1980), p. 480; *idem, Mark*, p. 62. See also
A. Ambrozic, 'New Teaching with Power (Mk 1:27)', in J. Plevnick (ed.), *Word and
Spirit: Essays in Honor of David Michael Stanley, SJ on his 60th Birthday*
(Willowdale, Ont.: Regis College Press, 1975), p. 113-49, esp. p. 114.

75. Taylor, *Mark*, p. 439. On the background and royal nature of this speech, see
K.H. Rengstorf, 'Old and New Testament Traces of a Formula of the Judean Royal
Ritual', *NovT* 5 (1963), pp. 229-244, esp. p. 236.

76. H.B. Swete, *The Gospel according to St Mark* (London: Macmillan, 1905),
p. 235.

'grant' something, indicating that the substance of the request is an official boon to be bestowed on them only through kingly *fiat*.[77] The seat 'on the right' (ἐκ δεξιῶν) and next to it the seat 'on the left' (ἐξ ἀριστερῶν or εὐωνύμων) are the places of honour next to a king.[78] Accordingly, the request of the disciples for these places, the form in which the request is couched, and the fact that the disciples approach Jesus as the one who is to speak in a royal manner and 'grant' them what they wish, imply that the disciples view Jesus not only as a king but one who can bestow upon those whom he chooses the privileges and prerogatives of kingly power: *for the request makes sense only if the disciples think that the prerogatives they desire belong to Jesus and are his to give.*

That worldly kingship and all that it entails is the essence of the disciples' assumptions concerning the nature of Jesus' messiahship is implied in the fact that the disciples' request is for positions of honour and power not only next to Jesus but within the sphere of Jesus' expected δόξα (ἐν τῇ δόξῃ σου). In the context of the courtly language and imagery of the request the word δόξα here carries the sense of 'royal splendour', 'imperial power', or, as Moffat translates it, 'triumph'.[79] As the Matthean parallel to Mk 10.37 shows, the term is here synonymous with both 'kingdom' and 'sovereignty'. Therefore, in conjunction with the preposition ἐν, the dative of δόξα here bears both a locative and a temporal meaning which gives the phrase ἐν τῇ δόξῃ the double sense of 'in your kingdom' and 'when you reign as king'.[80] Accordingly, by outlining where the disciples expect their petition to be granted, the phrase ἐν τῇ δόξῃ σου makes explicit that the disciples view Jesus as a king possessing the power to bestow upon them the lordly exaltation they desire.

77. Rengstorf, 'Old and New Testament Traces', pp. 233-36.
78. Cf. 1 Kgs 2.19; *1 Esd.* 4.29; Eccl. 12.12; Josephus, *Ant.* 6.11.9.
79. Cf. the similar use to which the word is put in Lk. 4.6.
80. The NEB combines admirably these two senses of the word by translating ἐν τῇ δόξῃ σου by 'grant us the right to sit in state with you'. On this, and for additional insights in to the nature of the request and what it implies about the disciples' view of the shape of Jesus' messiahship, see J. Muddiman, 'The Glory of Jesus, Mark 10.37', in L.D. Hurst and N.T. Wright (eds.), *The Glory of Christ in the New Testament: Studies in Christology in Memory of George Bradford Caird* (Oxford: Clarendon Press, 1987), pp. 51-58.

Jesus' expressive remark at Mk 10.38 that in their petition the disciples do not know what they are asking (οὐκ εἴδατε τί αἰτεῖσθε) likewise testifies that the disciples assume Jesus to be a worldly king, in that it acknowledges that the disciples approach him with this understanding of the nature of his messiahship. In denying that the disciples know what they are asking when they request the seats next to him, Jesus is not only making a statement of fact but an allusive comment implying two things. The first thing is that what sitting at his 'right and left hand' actually entails is totally opposite of what the disciples envisage this to be.[81] The second implication is that *if* the disciples knew this, they would not be so eager to have their request granted them, let alone to make it. For as Mk 15.27 shows, 'to sit on the right and on the left' of Jesus is to occupy not positions of power but a place in the shadow of the cross, for there it is recorded that those who are granted to be at the side of Jesus are those who are crucified along with him 'one on his right and one on his left' (ἕνα ἐκ δεξιῶν καὶ ἕνα ἐξ εὐωνύμων αὐτοῦ).[82] That the disciples are ignorant of this and, more importantly, think otherwise, is pointed out in the particular wording of Jesus' remark. The phrase οὐκ οἴδατε emphasizes that the request displays only ignorance and misunderstanding with respect to its object, and the use of the middle of αἰτέω calls attention the request's self-serving nature.[83] All of this makes plain that Jesus, in being aware of the expectations that the disciples mistakenly assume that they can and will have fulfilled through him, is also aware that the disciples approach him as king.

The view that Jesus is a worldly king, soon to exercise his power, also lies behind the emphatic, affirmative response of James and John in Mk 10.39 to Jesus' question concerning whether they will be able to drink his 'cup' and partake of his 'baptism' (cf. Mk 10.38). Jesus' 'cup' here stands for suffering, especially his divinely ordained messianic suffering,[84] and 'baptism' is a metaphor for the passion, which will plunge

---

81. 'Taking account of what immediately follows, the sense [of Jesus' remark] appears to be as follows: you do not know that in requesting to participate in my glory you ask at the same time to share in my painful destiny' (Lane, *Mark*, p. 379). See also D. Hill, 'The Request of Zebedee's Sons and the Johannine ΔΟΞΑ Theme', *NTS* 13 (1967), pp. 281-85, esp. 284-85.

82. Cf. Kelber, *Mark's Story of Jesus*, p. 51.

83. So Swete, *Mark*, p. 236.

84. On this, see A. Feuillet, 'La coupe et le baptême de la passion (Mc. x,35-40;

him into a sea of calamity and woe.[85] James and John are willing to drink Jesus' 'cup' and undergo his 'baptism' not because they misconstrue the meaning of Jesus' metaphorical speech and its significance as a description of the fate that lies in store for those who wish to be his disciples,[86] nor because they finally recognize and accept the fact, proclaimed by Jesus, that in the cross, and in the cross alone, is 'glory' to be manifested.[87] Rather, as C.H. Turner says, the two brothers are prepared to share Jesus' fate of suffering 'because they had now risen to the certainty that it would only be a transient preliminary to his triumph'.[88] This certainty, however, could only be entertained if the disciples see Jesus, whatever his immediate fate might be, as one who will in the end move beyond suffering to reign with worldly dominion and power. The words of Jesus in the teaching section of this unit's passion prediction–misunderstanding–teaching pattern also contain clear evidence that the disciples' assumptions concerning the nature of Jesus' messiahship are centered in the view that Jesus will soon reign as a worldly king. At Mk 10.42 Jesus not only openly states that the disciples seek worldly dominion,[89] but characterizes the type of dominion which the disciples assume that they, as his followers, will soon have as that which 'the great ones' (οἱ μεγάλοι) of the Gentiles, 'those who consider themselves to be the rulers of the nations' enjoy when they 'lord it over (κατακυριεύουσιν) their subjects and exercise authority (κατεξουσιάζουσιν) over them'. The term κατακυριεύω means 'to become master over' or 'to gain dominion over', and in its present context signifies the powerful and crippling rule of a mighty sovereign over a conquered people.[90] The term κατεξουσιάζω literally means, as

Mt. xx, 2-30; Lc. xii, 50)', *RB* 74 (1967), pp. 370-82.

85. Feuillet, 'La coupe', pp. 377-82; G. Delling, 'BAPTISMA, BAPTISTHENAI', *NovT* 2 (1957), pp. 92-115. See also W. Harrington, *Mark* (Wilmington, DE: Michael Glazier, 1979), p. 168.

86. So, many commentators. Cf., e.g., Harrington, *Mark*, p. 168.

87. Cf. Anderson, *Mark*, p. 256.

88. Turner, 'The Gospel according to St Mark', in part 3 of C. Gore and H.L. Gouge (eds.), *A New Commentary on Holy Scripture* (London: SPCK, 1928), p. 90. Cf. the acceptance of Jesus' lot of suffering on the part of Peter and the disciples at Mk 14.29-31 in contrast to their prior refusal at Caesarea Philippi to be party to this.

89. The οὐκ...ἀλλά form of Mk 10.42 carries the sense of 'but it is not *as you expect* to be with you; *on the contrary*...' Cf. below on Mk 10.45.

90. So W. Foerster, 'κατακυριεύω', *TDNT*, III, p. 1098. But see also K.W. Clark, 'The Meaning of (Kata)Kurieuein', in J.K. Elliot (ed.), *Studies in the*

noted in the translation above, 'to tyrannize', 'to exercise a power which tends toward compulsion and oppression'.[91] The prefix κατά, used twice within the parallelism of Mk 10.42, is not without significance, for it heightens the emphasis that the power which the rulers and 'the great ones' enjoy—and which the disciples are confident of receiving—is a type of dominion which is exercised more for the purpose of gaining and exploiting personal advantage over a foe than that of establishing order or peace. It follows from this, then, that the major presupposition lying behind, and giving rise to, the disciples' expectations of receiving such power from Jesus is a view of him and the nature of his messiahship which is commensurate with the content of the expectation. In the eyes of the disciples Jesus is one who will soon show himself to be a triumphalist, warrior king.

Finally, that the disciples view Jesus as a worldly, powerful king is also evident from Jesus' statement in Mk 10.45 concerning the nature of his role as Son of Man in the plan of redemption.[92] The statement serves to counter what Jesus, in the use of the words οὐ...ἀλλά, designates as a false set of expectations concerning his activity as the Son of Man, by contrasting what he recognizes is expected of him with the facts.[93] Since in its present context[94] the statement is addressed to the disciples, it is

---

New Testament Language and Text (NovTSup, 44; Leiden: Brill, 1976), pp. 100-105.

91. W. Foerster, 'κατεξουσιάζω', *TDNT*, II, p. 575.

92. Whether or not, or in what manner, the historical Jesus referred to himself as 'the Son of Man', and whether the phrase ὁ υἱὸς τοῦ ἀνθρώπου (Aramaic *bar-nash/bar nasha*') possessed, or was ever used in, a titular sense in the time of Jesus, it remains clear that Mark presents Jesus using the term as a self-designation with a specific apocalyptic, Christological sense. On this, see N. Perrin, 'The Creative Use of the Son of Man Traditions by Mark', in *A Modern Pilgrimage in Christology* (Philadelphia: Fortress Press, 1974), pp. 84-93; J.D. Kingsbury, *Jesus Christ in Matthew, Mark, and Luke* (Philadelphia: Fortress Press, 1981), pp. 38-40. On 'The Son of Man' in Judaism and early Christianity, see now the important work by M. Casey, *Son of Man: The Interpretation of Daniel 7* (London: SCM Press, 1979), and B. Lindars, *Jesus, Son of Man* (Grand Rapids: Eerdmans, 1982).

93. On this, see C.K. Barrett, 'The Background to Mark 10.45', in A.J.B. Higgins (ed.), *New Testament Essays* (London: SPCK, 1959), pp. 8-9; M. Hooker, *Jesus and the Servant* (London: SPCK, 1967), p. 141.

94. The break between Mk 10.44 and 10.45 caused by the introduction of the term 'the Son of Man' suggests that v. 45 was not originally one with the preceding logia, but was a secondary addition to that material. On this, see Best, *Following Jesus*, p. 125. Best, however, finds it unlikely that Mark was responsible for the redaction of v. 45 to the community rule of vv. 42b-44. On the question of the

they who hold the expectations about Jesus' role which Jesus insists are inappropriate. But what precisely are these expectations? They are not simply, as a cursory reading of what is negated by οὐ in Mk 10.45 might suggest, that Jesus is to be served and that he is not to give his life.[95] For in its context, what is negated is highly evocative and allusory, calling to mind in the first instance of negation the Son of Man of Dan. 7.14 who

> was given dominion, and glory, and kingdom
> that all the peoples, and nations, and languages
> should serve him,

and in the second instance the Son of Man of *1 En.* 46.4-5 and 69.27 who removes

> ...the kings and the mighty from their seats
> (and the strong from their thrones)...
> loosening the reigns of the strong
> breaking the teeth of the sinners
> because they do not extol and praise him
> nor humbly acknowledge whence the kingdom was
> bestowed upon them...

and sits

> on the throne of his glory...
> (causing) the sinners to pass away and be destroyed
> from off the face of the earth...

The Son of Man of these passages *takes* rather than ransoms the lives of his enemies.[96] Notably this Son of Man is also one who does not die, but instead is bestowed with 'the sum of judgment' (*1 En.* 69.27) but also with a 'dominion (ἐξουσία) which shall not pass away, and a kingdom

---

authenticity and the tradition history of the 'Ransom' saying, see the brief but succinct and informative summary by B. Lindars, 'Mark 10.45: A Ransom for Many', *ExpTim* 92 (1981–82), pp. 292-95.

95. Strictly speaking, the οὐ...ἀλλά contrast is not explicitly continued in the second part of Mk 10.45 where the idea of 'to give one's life' appears. But, nevertheless, especially as οὐ precedes the full statement of the purpose of the Son of Man's coming (καὶ γὰρ ὁ υἱὸς τοῦ ἀνθρώπου οὐκ ἦλθεν...δοῦναι τὴν ψυχὴν αὐτοῦ...), its sense is undoubtedly carried on. On this, see Barrett, 'The Background of Mark 10.45', p. 9.

96. Barrett, 'Background', p. 9.

(βασιλεία) 'that shall not be destroyed' (Dan. 7.15).[97] Accordingly, in the eyes of the disciples Jesus is seen as a king appointed to manifest his sovereignty by exercising a mighty and devastating authority against all who might be thought of as his foes.

Thus every major element of the story of the request of James and John and its sequel is constructed by Mark so as to show that as the disciples make ready to follow Jesus on his journey to Jerusalem (cf. Mk 10.33), they view him—just as they did at Caesarea Philippi and at Capernaum—as a worldly king who is soon to assert his sovereignty in a display of strength and glory.[98]

Conclusions: Mark's View of the Content of the Caesarea Philippi Temptation

The methodological assumptions with which the foregoing examination of the material contained within Mk 9.30-37 and Mk 10.32-45 has been undertaken are (a) that there is a redactional and thematic connection between Mk 9.30-37; 10.32-45, the stories about the disciples' discussion of 'greatness' and the ambition of James and John, and Mk 8.27-33, the story of Peter's 'confession' at Caesarea Philippi, and (b) that this connection was made by Mark to highlight and applicate the fact that the view of the nature of Jesus' messiahship held by the disciples in Mk 9.30-37 and by James and John in Mk 10.32-45 is founded upon, the same as, and growing out of that which was first put forth by Peter at Mk 8.27-33. Given this, my analysis of the information concerning the disciples' Christology contained within Mk 9.30-37 and Mk 10.32-45 leads to the following conclusion. As is the case with the disciples on the road to Capernaum and with James and John as they make their way with Jesus to Jerusalem, Peter's view of Jesus' messiahship expressed at Caesarea Philippi assumes as its constituent characteristic the ability, indeed the desire, to vanquish enemies and opponents through the use of domineering power.

This means, then, that the messianic behaviour which the Markan Peter, before he is rebuked at Caesarea Philippi, initially thinks Jesus embraces—and which, even after the rebuke, he still thinks would allow Jesus to claim the status of Messiah while avoiding the suffering that

97. Hooker, *Son of Man in Mark*, p. 141.
98. For a similar assessment, see J.B. Tyson, 'The Blindness of the Disciples in Mark', *JBL* 80 (1961), pp. 261-68.

Jesus' concept of messiahship entails—implies the exercise of a type of kingship which engages in conquest, exploits and dominates those over whom it reigns, and which uses its prerogatives for procuring personal advantage. And this in turn means that in Mark's eyes *the content of the temptation that Satan subjected Jesus to through Peter at Caesarea Philippi was for Jesus to fulfil his commission as Messiah by waging wars of deliverance.*

It should be noted, however, that this conclusion raises a serious question. Could Mark have really thought that such behaviour would have been the slightest bit attractive to Jesus, let alone sufficiently attractive that Jesus might have thought of it as a live option and given it serious consideration? The offer as I have outlined it, and as I think the evidence demands, is, after all, little short of an offer to act like Hitler. Could this in any way have been seriously alluring to Jesus, and therefore a real and not a sham 'test' of his faithfulness?

To be answered, this question must be set within the context of another. As I have noted above, in Mark's Gospel the task to which Jesus, as Messiah, is appointed and empowered is to establish and implement the sovereign authority of God over a rebellious world—a world dominated by Satan and his minions—by rescuing and permanently delivering those willing to submit to this authority from those forces hostile to God and his saving purposes. In light of this, the question then is: how successful, according to Mark, does Jesus feel that the path of suffering will be in the accomplishment of this messianic task?

The answer to this question lies not, I think, in Mk 8.27-33, nor in those passages which Mark has created in order to explicate the meaning of the 'confession' story, *but in Mk 14.32-42*, the story of Jesus' temptation in Gethsemane. And so it is to that story that I now turn.

Chapter 8

THE TRADITION OF JESUS' GETHSEMANE TEMPTATION

The Accounts and their Relationship

Each of the three Synoptic evangelists recounts that Jesus was tempted at Gethsemane: Matthew at Mt. 26.36-46, Mark at Mk 14.32-42 and Luke at Lk. 22.39-46.[1] With respect to the Matthean and Markan accounts, it is clear, given their high degree of structural and verbal similarity,[2] that a literary relationship exists between them. Moreover, it is also clear that the Matthean account is dependent on that of Mark.

1. At first glance, all three of the Synoptic versions of this tradition seem to be stories in which it is not Jesus but *only the disciples* who are (or are about to be) subjected to temptation as they enter Gethsemane. The terminology of temptation (specifically πειρασμός) is strictly speaking applied only to them (cf. Mt. 26.41// Mk 14.38//Lk. 22.46, cp. Lk. 22.40: 'pray that *you* might not enter into temptation'). But that we should regard each of these versions of this tradition as recounting an incident of temptation not only of the disciples, but of Jesus too, and, as R.S. Barbour argues, 'of him [Jesus] pre-eminently' ('Gethsemane in the Tradition of the Passion', *NTS* 16 [1970], p. 242), there can be little doubt. The tradition as it is presented to us in these versions not only assumes that the 'temptation' which the disciples are in danger of 'entering into' is something that Jesus himself is now faced with; it also presents Jesus as finding himself in a 'forced position', that is, a situation from which he cannot escape without showing how deep (or shallow!) is his commitment to obeying all that God requires of him (on this, see Barbour, 'Gethsemane in the Tradition of the Passion', pp. 231-51, esp. pp. 242-48). For a defense of an interesting suggestion, made originally by A. Loisy (*L'Evangile selon Marc* [Paris: E. Nourry, 1912], p. 415), that what Jesus actually said to his disciples was 'pray that *I* enter not into πειρασμός', see J. Héring, 'Zwei exegetische Probleme in der Perikope von Jesus in Gethsemane', in A.N. Wilder *et al.* (eds.), *Neotestamentica and Patristica: Eine Freundesgabe, Herrn Professor Dr Oscar Cullmann zu seinem 60. Geburtstag überreicht* (Leiden: Brill, 1962), pp. 64-69, esp. pp. 64-65.

2. On this, see F.W. Beare, *The Earliest Records of Jesus* (Nashville: Abingdon, 1962), p. 230.

Mt. 26.44, for instance, cannot be explained in any way except as an attempt by Matthew to make up the lack in Mk of any mention of Jesus' leaving his disciples for the third time.[3] And why would Mark, noting that Jesus prayed a second time, have stated, when recounting the substance of that prayer, only that Jesus said 'the same words' (i.e. those of Mk 14.36) and not, as in Matthew, 'My Father, if this cannot pass unless I drink it, thy will be done' (Mt. 26.42), had he had the Matthean text in front of him?[4]

It is, however, not so apparent that any relationship, let alone one of literary dependence, exists between Mk 14.32-42 and Lk. 20.39-46, for overall these texts have far more differences between them than similarities. For instance, the Lukan account is considerably shorter than that of Mark, and the incidence of common vocabulary is relatively low.[5] Moreover, the Lukan account contains many narrative details that either are not found in its Markan counterpart or give a significantly different emphasis to what appears there.[6]

1. At the beginning of Luke's account Jesus goes to the Mount of Olives (generically named) followed by unnamed disciples (cf. Lk. 22.39a, ἠκολούθησαν δὲ αὐτῷ καὶ οἱ μαθηταί). At the beginning of Mark's account Jesus goes to Gethsemane on the Mount of Olives (cf. Mk 14.32a) together with disciples (καὶ ἔρχονται...).

2. When, according to Luke, Jesus reaches this place, he instructs his disciples to pray (Lk. 22.40). Mark states that Jesus at this point tells his disciples to sit where they are while *he* goes to pray (Mk 14.32b). Furthermore, he then singles out Peter, James and John and tells them that he is beginning to experience distress and anxiety (Mk 14.33-34)—narrative details not recounted by Luke.

3. Next, according to Luke, Jesus withdraws some distance (καὶ αὐτὸς ἀπεσπάσθη ἀπ' αὐτῶν ὡσεὶ λίθου βολήν) from *all*

3. Beare, *Earliest Records*, pp. 229-30.

4. Notably, the priority of the Markan over the Matthean Gethsemane account is even admitted by such a prominent Griesbachian as C.S. Mann, *Mark* (Garden City: Doubleday, 1986), p. 588.

5. On this, see V. Taylor, *The Passion Narrative of St Luke: A Critical and Historical Investigation* (Cambridge: Cambridge University Press, 1972), p. 69.

6. For the substance of the following I am indebted to J.A. Fitzmyer, *The Gospel according to Luke, 10–24* (Garden City: Doubleday, 1985), p. 1437.

his disciples to pray (Lk. 22.41). According to Mark Jesus withdraws 'a little further' (καὶ προελθὼν μικρόν) from Peter, James and John (Mk 14.35a).

4. In both accounts Jesus then begins to pray (cp. Lk. 22.41b, Mk 14.35). But Mark gives Jesus' prayer first in indirect and then in direct discourse (Mk 14.35b-36). Luke, however, gives the content of Jesus' prayer entirely in direct discourse (Lk. 22.42).

5. In both accounts Jesus prays to the Father. But whereas in Mark the address is in Aramaic and then Greek (Αββα ὁ πατήρ), in Luke the address is only in Greek (cp. Mk 14.36a, Lk. 22.42a). Moreover, its form is the vocative, Πάτερ.

6. Luke reports that Jesus is granted angelic assistance and comfort after he prays (Lk. 22.43-44).[7] Mark knows of no such event.

7. Jesus in Luke prays once and then returns to all of the disciples (Lk. 22.45, cf. vv. 42-44). In Mark he prays three times and returns after each time only to Peter, James and John.

8. Jesus in Luke finds all the disciples asleep on account of grief (Lk. 22.45). In Mark Jesus finds only Peter, James and John asleep. There is no explanation given for their state (Mk 14.37, cp. vv. 40, 41).

9. According to both evangelists, Jesus then counsels the disciples to pray (Mk 14.37, cp. vv. 40, 41). But this for Luke is the second time this is done (cf. Lk. 22.40b), for Mark the first.

How are these differences to be accounted for? According to V. Taylor,[8] G.B. Caird,[9] and other scholars,[10] they can be explained only by

---

7. For a recent defense of the authenticity of Lk. 22.43-44, see J.H. Neyrey, *The Passion according to Luke* (New York: Paulist Press, 1985), pp. 55-58.

8. Taylor, *Passion Narrative of St Luke*, pp. 69-72.

9. Caird, *The Gospel of St Luke* (Baltimore: Penguin, 1963), pp. 25-26.

10. W. Grundmann, *Das Evangelium nach Lukas* (Berlin: Evangelische Verlagsanstalt, 2nd edn, 1961), p. 411; E. Haenchen, *Der Weg Jesu: Eine Erklärung des Markus-Evangeliums und der kanonischen Parallelen* (Berlin: Töpelmann, 1966), p. 495; K.G. Kuhn, 'Jesus in Gethsemane', *EvT* 12 (1952–53), pp. 260-85, esp. p. 271; M.-J. Lagrange, *L'Evangile selon Saint Luc* (Paris: Gabalda, 8th edn, 1948), p. 558; T. Lescow, 'Jesus in Gethsemane bei Lukas und im Hebräerbrief', *ZNW* 58 (1967), pp. 215-39; A. Loisy, *L'Evangile selon Luc* (Paris: E. Nourry, 1924), p. 525; F. Rehkopf, *Die lukanische Sonderquelle: Ihr Umfang und Sprachgebrauch* (Tübingen: Mohr [Siebeck], 1959), p. 84; A. Schlatter, *Das*

assuming that in recounting Jesus' Gethsemane experience, Luke and Mark have used separate, independent accounts of this tradition, with the one taken up by Luke being shorter and having details different from the one known and used by Mark. But, as J.A. Fitzmyer has recently shown, such a view is actually unnecessary, for each of the differences between Lk. 22.40-46 and Mk 14.32-42 can be accounted for on the assumption that Luke has simply redacted the Markan account.[11] Given Fitzmyer's evidence, it seems reasonable to conclude, then, that the Lukan account of Jesus' 'testing' in Gethsemane is, like that of Matthew, dependent upon, and secondary to, Mk 14.32-42.

Accordingly, the assumption guiding my investigation of the tradition of Jesus' Gethsemane temptation is that there is only one 'primary' Synoptic version of this tradition, namely, that now found in Mark's Gospel at Mk 14.32-42.

The Tradition History of Mark 14.32-42

Scholarly opinion on the tradition history of Mark's Gethsemane story divides itself into four main views: (1) that the story was traditional, coming to Mark and taken up and reproduced by him substantially as we find it now in his Gospel;[12] (2) that its present form represents successive redactions of a primitive narrative, with either vv. 32, 35, 37, 39, 40, 41a or vv. 32, 35, 37a, 39a, 40a,b, 41a, 40c, 41b or vv. 32 (part), 33b, 34, 35a, 36-37, 38b, 40b, 41 (part), 42 viewed as the earliest core tradition;[13] (3) that it is a Markan combination of two parallel sources:

Evangelium des Lukas: Aus seinen Quellen erklärt (Stuttgart: Calwer, 2nd edn, 1960), pp. 432-33.

11. Fitzmyer, *Luke 10–24*, pp. 1438-39. See also Neyrey, *The Passion according to Luke*, p. 49; J.M. Creed, *The Gospel according to St Luke* (London: Macmillan, 1930), p. 272; J. Finnegan, *Die Überlieferung der Leidens-und Auferstehungseschichte Jesu* (Geissen: Töpelmann, 1934), p. 18; E. Klostermann, *Das Lukasevangelium* (Tubingen: Mohr [Siebeck], 3rd edn, 1975), p. 215; E. Linnemann, *Studien zur Passionsgeschichte* (Göttingen: Vandenhoeck & Ruprecht, 1970), pp. 34-40; J. Schmid, *Das Evangelium nach Lukas* (Regensburg: Pustet, 4th edn, 1960), p. 335; G. Schneider, *Das Evangelium nach Lukas*, II (Gütersloh: G. Mohn, 1977), p. 457.

12. Cf. E. Lohmeyer, *Das Evangelium nach Markus* (Göttingen: Vandenhoeck & Ruprecht, 17th edn, 1967), pp. 313-21; R. Pesch, *Das Markusevangelium*, II (Freiburg: Herders, 1977), pp. 385-86.

13. The first position is that of R. Bultmann (*The History of the Synoptic Tradition* [Oxford: Basil Blackwell, 1963], pp. 267-68), the second that of

the first, source A, identical with vv. 32, 35, 40-41, and the second, source B, with vv. 33-34, 36-38;[14] (4) that the story is essentially a Markan creation built up from isolated fragments of tradition.[15]

Neither the first nor the second of these views is convincing. They suffer from being guided from the start by the question begging and increasingly questionable assumption that 'Mark is not sufficiently master of his material to be able to venture on a systematic construction himself'.[16] Further, they do not take seriously enough the fact that evidence of Mark's redactional and compositional hand can be found not just in small sections, but throughout the pericope.[17]

The third view is more solidly rooted in the text. For instance, many of the main features of the story—the introduction of the disciples, Jesus' prayer, a climactic dominical saying—are each reported twice. Moreover, the present text seems to be rife with logical and theological inconsistencies. Among the most notable are an eschatological use of the 'hour' motif (14.35, 41) versus a profane use (14.37), a reproach by Jesus of Peter that is abruptly deflected toward the other disciples (14.37-38), and a notice of the disciples' failure to 'answer' (14.40) which lacks an antecedent reprimand or questioning. But the view does not take into account the possibility, raised by F. Neirynck and others[18]

Bultmann's pupil, E. Linneman (*Studien zur Passionsgeschichte*, pp. 11-40), and the third that of H. Scheneke (*Studien zur Passionsgeschichte des Markus: Tradition und Redaction in Markus 14,1-42* [Würzburg: Echter Verlag, 1971], pp. 461-65).

14. Cf. Kuhn, 'Jesus in Gethsemane', pp. 260-85; H. Anderson, *The Gospel of Mark* (London: Oliphants, 1976), pp. 317-18; T. Lescow, 'Jesus in Gethsemane', *EvT* 26 (1966), pp. 141-59; Barbour, 'Gethsemane in the Tradition of the Passion', pp. 231-51; D.M. Stanley, *Jesus in Gethsemane* (New York: Paulist Press, 1980), pp. 107-108.

15. Cf. M. Dibelius, 'Gethsemane', *Crozier Quarterly* 12 (1953), pp. 254-65; E. Lohse, *History of the Suffering and Death of Jesus Christ* (Philadelphia: Fortress Press, 1964), pp. 55-68; W.H. Kelber, 'Mark 14:32-42: Gethsemane', *ZNW* 63 (1972), pp. 166-87, esp. 169-76.

16. Bultmann, *History*, p. 350. Cf. also Linneman, *Studien*, p. 32.

17. On this, see Kelber, 'Mark 14:32-42', pp. 169-76. See also R. Pryke, *Redactional Style in the Marcan Gospel* (Cambridge: Cambridge University Press, 1978), pp. 172-73.

18. F. Neirynck, *Duality in Mark: Contributions to the Study of Marcan Redaction* (Leuven: Leuven University Press, 1972); See also W.H. Kelber, 'The Hour of the Son of Man and the Sparing of the Hour', in W.H. Kelber (ed.), *The Passion in Mark* (Philadelphia: Fortress Press, 1976), p. 42. Kelber's view here is different from that which he espoused in 'Mark 14:32-42'.

in their work on 'duality' in Mark, that the contradictions and the doublets in the text may be as much evidence for Markan compositional activity as for the existence of two pre-Markan sources, each of which depicted an uncompounded, uniform Gethsemane story. More importantly, the view fails to explain why Mark should feel it necessary to combine two Gethsemane stories into one, as this view assumes he has done,[19] rather than simply using the one or the other.

What, then, of the fourth view? Of the four it is the only one which is consistent with the position, now gaining increasing acceptance among Markan scholars, that Mark is by no means simply a detached compiler and collector of traditions, but rather an author in the fullest sense of the word, actively participating in the final formation of his text.[20]

But is there any other evidence in its favour? Three things stand out. First, the story is replete throughout, and not just in certain sections, with Markan idiomatic features and theological themes. In v. 33 we find the characteristically Markan motif of the singling out of Peter, James, and John as Jesus' intimates,[21] as well as the separation of these three from the other disciples;[22] in vv. 37, 40 and 41 the motif of the disciples' failure to perform the duties of discipleship;[23] in vv. 34 and 37 the motif of watchfulness.[24] This distribution of Markan features throughout the story, not just at its beginning and end, is not what we would expect to find if, as the other views assume, Mark's contribution to his Gethsemane story was minimal and basically editorial.[25] It is, however,

19. Kelber, 'Mark 14:32-42', p. 168.

20. On the 'New View' of Mark, see W. Marxsen, *Mark the Evangelist* (Nashville: Abingdon, 1969); W. Telford, *The Interpretation of Mark* (Philadelphia: Fortress Press, 1985), pp. 14-15.

21. On this as Markan, see Lohse, *History*, p. 62; W. Wrede, *The Messianic Secret* (Cambridge: James Clarke, 1971), pp. 51-54.

22. On this as Markan, see Kelber, 'Mark 14:32-42', pp. 171-72.

23. This seems to have first been recognized as Markan by J.C. Hawkins (*Horae Synopticae: Contributions to the Study of the Synoptic Problem* [Oxford: Clarendon Press, 1909], p. 121). See also J.B. Tyson, 'The Blindness of the Disciples in Mark', *JBL* 80 (1961), pp. 261-68; T.J. Weeden, 'The Heresy that Necessitated Mark's Gospel', *ZNW* 59 (1968), pp. 145-58.

24. On this as Markan, see R. Pesch, *Näherwartungen: Tradition und Redaction in Mk 13* (Düsseldorf: Patmos, 1968), pp. 199-202. See also R.H. Lightfoot, *The Gospel Message of St Mark* (Oxford: Clarendon Press, 1950), pp. 48-59.

25. Mark's contribution to Mk 14.32-42 is limited to vv. 41c and 42 according to Bultmann (*History*, p. 268), to 37b, 41c, and 42 according to Linnemann (*Studien*,

wholly consonant with the view that the story is largely a Markan composition.

Secondly, the Gethsemane story is marked by a tripartite division, section one comprising vv. 32-38, section two vv. 39-40, and section three vv. 41-42.[26] Mark's predilection for threefold units is well-known.[27]

Third, as W. Kelber has shown,[28] every verse of the story except v. 36, which is constituted by Jesus' prayer Αββα ὁ πατήρ..., and v. 38, the sayings about praying to avoid entering πειρασμός and the conflict between the Spirit and flesh, displays characteristic Markan language and style.[29] Moreover, in addition to showing no characteristically Markan vocabulary or syntactical features, the exceptions are non-Markan thematically and have notable parallels in the liturgical and paranetic traditions of the early Church.[30]

In light of this, it seems clear that the fourth view on the tradition history of Mk 14.32-42 is the most convincing. The Gethsemane story is not traditional, nor is it a composition built up from two unified pre-Markan stories or successive pre-Markan redactions of a core tradition. Rather it is a Markan compositional product constructed from the ground up on the basis of two isolated traditional fragments of tradition, a prayer of Jesus and a dominical saying.

Mark's View of the Nature and Content of the Gethsemane Temptation

The Nature of the Temptation

In Mk 14.32-42, Jesus himself describes the time that he and his disciples spend at Gethsemane as a time in which they come face to face with

---

p. 32), or to v. 39, parts of vv. 40 and 41, and all of v. 42 according to Kuhn ('Jesus in Gethsemane').

26. Cf. Kelber, 'Mark 14:32-42', p. 171.

27. On this, see T.A. Burkill, *Mysterious Revelation: An Examination of the Philosophy of St Mark's Gospel* (Ithaca: Cornell University Press, 1963), pp. 123-24, 203; D.E. Nineham, *Saint Mark* (Baltimore: Penguin, 1967), p. 392.

28. Kelber, 'Mark 14:32-42', pp. 170-76.

29. On the non-Markan character of v. 36, see Kelber, 'Mark 14:32-42', p. 175. See also A. Suhl, *Die Function der alttestamentlische Zitate und Anspielungen im Markusevangelium* (Gütersloh: Gerd Mohn, 1965), pp. 49-50. On the non-Markan character of v. 38, see C.H. Turner, 'Marcan Usage: Notes, Critical and Exegetical, on the Second Gospel', *JTS* 29 (1928), pp. 356-59.

30. Compare v. 36 with Rom. 8.15; Gal. 4.6, and v. 38 with Mt. 6.13//Lk. 11.4.

πειρασμός (cf. 14.38). There is little doubt, then, that Mark intended Jesus to be seen here as subject to temptation.[31] But of what kind? The answer, surely, is that it is a 'testing' which probes the extent of Jesus' faithfulness to God, the kind which, as we have seen, is often labeled 'religious'.[32] This becomes clear when we take into consideration three things. First, there is the fact, indicated by the noun's usage by ancient writers, that in Mark's time, 'a test of faithfulness' is the meaning with which πειρασμός was most generally employed.[33]

31. *Contra* Kelber, 'Mark 14:32-42', pp. 177-78, 179. On this, see Barbour, 'Gethsemane in the Tradition of the Passion', pp. 236-38; and D. Senior, *The Passion of Jesus in the Gospel of Mark* (Wilmington, DE: Michael Glazier, 1984), p. 78.

32. By, for instance, H. Seesemann, 'πεῖρα, κτλ.', *TDNT*, VI, pp. 23-36, and K.W. Chase, *The Synoptic Πειρασμοί of Jesus: Their Christological Significance* (ThD dissertation, New Orleans Baptist Theological Seminary, 1989).

33. Aside from its use by the first century CE physician Pedanius Dioscorides (*Mat. Med. Praef.* 5.12) and the Alexandrian grammarian Aelius Herodianus (*Partitiones* 110.5) and by the author(s)/compiler(s) of a first-century CE 'Arabian Nights' known as the *Syntipas* (see p. 124 of the edition of the work edited by V. Jernstedt and P. Nikition and appearing in *Memories de l'Academie Imperiale des Sciences de St Petersbourg, 8me Serie, Classe des Sciences historico-philologique* [Tome XI, No. 1, 1912]), and that of the first-century CE work on magical curative powers of plants, stones and animals known as the Βίβλοι Κυπάνιδες (or Κοιράνιδες = *Cyranides*) (for the text, see F. de Mely and C.-E. Ruelle, *Les lapidaires de l'antiquite et du moyen age. II. Les lapidaires grecs* [Paris: Ernest Leroux, 1898], p. 40 line 24), the noun πειρασμός, 'a trial', is only known (before the end of the second century CE) *via* literature in the Greek biblical tradition. It occurs thirteen times in the Septuagint translation of the Hebrew Scriptures (Exod. 17.17; Deut. 4.34; 6.16; 7.19; 9.22; 29.3[2]; Ps. 94[95].8; Eccl. 3.10; 4.8; 5.2, 13; 8.16, accepting as authentic the reading of Alexandrinus in Eccl. 3.10; 4.8; 8.16, of Sinaiticus in 5.13, and of the three main textual witnesses in 5.2), seven times in the Apocrypha of the Septuagint (Sir. 2.1; 6.7; 27.5, 7; 36[33].1; 44.20; 1 Macc. 2.52), once in the Pseudepigrapha (*T. Jos.* 2.7), once in the extant fragments of non-Septuagintal Greek versions of the Hebrew Scriptures (Symmachus, Gen. 44.15), and 22 times in the New Testament (Mt. 6.13; 26.41; Lk. 4.13; 8.13; 11.4; 22.28, 40, 46; Acts 15.26 (D E), 20.19; 1 Cor. 10.13 (2×); Gal. 4.14; 1 Tim. 6.9; Heb. 3.18; Jas 1.2, 12; 1 Pet. 1.16; 2 Pet. 2.9; Rev. 3.10). πειρασμός is also used once in the *Didache* (*Did.* 8.2), once in Hermas (*Man.* 9.7), twice in the *Acts of John* (cf. 21.13 in the main text and 16.6 in the Recension), eight times in the writings of Clement of Alexandria (*Protrepticus* 9.84.3; *Stromata* 1.9.44; 1.17.86; 4.6.41; 4.7.47 (a quotation from 1 Peter); 4.20.129 (a quotation of 1 Peter); 7.12.76; *Excerpta ex Theodoto* 4.84.1), and nine times in the Clementines (*2 Cor.* 39.7; *Epistle of Clement to James* 2.3; 14.3; *Hom. 2* 39.1; *Hom. 16* 13.2; 13.5; 21.4; *Hom. 18* 20.2; 20.4. The noun also

Secondly, there is the import of the several ways Mark has Jesus characterize the πειρασμός that in Gethsemane he and his disciples face.

- According to Jesus, the πειρασμός is something which causes his 'soul' to become 'exceedingly sorrowful, even unto death' (cf. 14.34). As Pss. 42.6, 11; 43.5 and Jon. 4.9 show, to say that one's 'soul' (i.e. one's self) is 'exceedingly sorrowful' is to say that one is experiencing a crisis of faith over whether or not one should continue in a path of obedience to God.[34]

- The πειρασμός is also, according to Jesus, something for which 'watching' or 'vigilance' is the proper response.[35] In

appears once in the *Epitome Prior* [145.10] and once in the *Epitome Altera* [146.6]. But both of these instances are reduplications of *Epistle of Clement to James* 2.3).

In Biblical Greek, πειρασμός is almost never found *without* the meaning 'a test or trial of faithfulness' (the exceptions are, perhaps, Deut. 4.34; 7.19; 29.2 [but see S.R. Driver, *Deuteronomy* (Edinburgh: T. & T. Clark, 1895), p. 75] and Sir. 6.7; 27.5, 7 [πειρασμός = 'a test of integrity']). Moreover, even in Dioscorides, the *Cyranides*, Aelius Herodianus, and the *Syntipas* the noun seems always to be used with the sense of 'a trial which puts (someone or something) to the proof' in order to reveal or uncover something specific about the character of the person or thing 'tested'. In the case of objects (*Mat. Med. Praef.* 5.12), a thing's utility or value is proved, and in the case of human beings (*Syntipas*, the *Cyranides*), the nature and extent of a person's reliability, fortitude, or strength of character.

Seesemann ('πεῖρα, κτλ.', pp. 26-27), however, disputes the claim that the noun always stood for the idea of a 'trial' or 'test', let alone one of utility, integrity, or faithfulness. He argues on the basis of the instance in the *Cyranides*, where the noun is synonymous with κίνδυνοι (θαλασίων κινδύνων καὶ πειρασμῶν ἕν τε γῇ καὶ θαλασσῇ, καὶ ἀπὸ δαιμονόων καὶ πάσης νόσου), that πειρασμός was sometimes used in the ancient world, and indeed in the New Testament itself (e.g. in Lk. 22.28; Acts 15.26 [D E]; 20.19; 2 Pet. 2.9), to signify nothing more than 'dangers'. Given the term's usage in the *Cyranides*, there seems to be some truth to Seeseman's claim. But it is important to note that while literally true, it is substantially trivial, for the claim fails to ask what, according to the *Cyranides* (or Lk. 22.28; Acts 15.26 [D E]; 20.19; 2 Pet. 2.9, for that matter), these 'dangers' are thought *to do* to the person or persons experiencing them. A reading of the wider context shows that, at the very least, they have the function of determining a person's mettle. So the claim that in Mark's time πειρασμός bore the meaning 'test', and more specifically, 'a test of faithuness', seems sound.

34. Cf. Senior, *The Passion of Jesus in the Gospel of Mark*, pp. 70-73; A. Weiser, *The Psalms* (London: SCM Press, 1962), pp. 348-49.

35. Cf. Mk 14.34b, 37.

Mark's Gospel, things against which one must 'watch' (γρηγορέω) are things which sift a person's loyalty to God by falsely downplaying the necessity or desirability of devotion to him,[36] and the call 'to watch' (γρηγορεῖτε) comes at times when the possibility of being shown untrue to God is at its height.[37]

- Jesus further says that the πειρασμός is something that is to be resisted and overcome though prayer (cf. 14.38a), which in Mark's Gospel is the activity by which one offers one's commitment to God and receives strength from him to do his will.[38] What kind of temptation calls for prayer except one which is 'religious'?

- According to Jesus, the πειρασμός is something which, once 'entered into' (that is, not successfully resisted and overcome), allows σάρξ to triumph over God's Spirit and its purposes (14.38b).[39] Secular temptation has no such results.

Finally, that the nature of Jesus' Gethsemane πειρασμός is, according to Mark, one in which faithfulness and obedience are put to the test is clear from the fact that Mark portrays the temptation as plunging Jesus into a struggle over whether he should turn away from obedience to God's will (cf. 14.35-36). As we have seen many times in the preceding pages, such a struggle is the essence of 'religious' temptation.

Given, then, that Jesus' Gethsemane temptation *is* 'religious', what, in Mark's eyes, is its content? How, and over what issue, is the extent of Jesus' faithfulness to God 'put to the proof'?

The Content of Jesus' Gethsemane Temptation

To determine this, it seems best to turn to the point in the Gethsemane story where Jesus' struggle to maintain obedience and faithfulness is

---

36. On this, see W.L. Lane, *The Gospel according to Mark* (Grand Rapids: Eerdmans, 1974), pp. 515-16, 520.

37. Cf. Mk 13.33-37.

38. On this, see D.M. Sweetland, *Our Journey with Jesus: Discipleship according to Mark* (Wilmington, DE: Michael Glazier, 1987), p. 136; Lane, *Mark*, pp. 81-82.

39. For evidence that τὸ πνεῦμα here means God's Spirit, see Lane, *Mark*, p. 520; E. Schweizer, 'πνεῦμα', *TDNT*, VI, pp. 396-97; *idem*, 'σάρξ, κτλ.', *TDNT*, VII, pp. 123-24.

most clearly delineated—that is, in his direct address to God (Mk 14.36) —and to ask what, according to Mark, Jesus here seeks from God. In answering this question, it is important to keep the following in mind:

First, the address is a petition on the part of Jesus that his 'hour' might pass him by and that his 'cup' be removed. Now in Mark's eyes the 'hour' refers to Jesus' destiny to be handed over into the hands of sinners (cf. 14.41) and delivered up to the cross,[40] and the 'cup' is a cipher for the suffering and death ordained by God as the means that Jesus is to use in completing his messianic task (cf. 10.38).[41]

Secondly, the address is made by Jesus in the role not of a pious Jew, nor even of so notable a figure as the Suffering Righteous One, but that of the Son/Messiah. From start to finish it is as Son that Jesus speaks, and it is as Son that he expects to be heard.[42]

Thirdly, the occasion of the address is the awareness on the part of Jesus of two things: (1) that if he carries on in his dedication to obey God's will, his disciples will be scandalized by him and will desert and deny him (cf. 14.27-37; cp. 14.50), and (2) that he has arrived at the moment when he, as Messiah, armed only with his 'teaching' (cf. 14.49), must engage in the divinely willed, final, decisive confrontation with the representatives of the forces in the world opposed to God (cf. 14.41, 49).[43]

In light of these three considerations, it is clear that the aim of this petition is *nothing less than the elimination of the cross from the messiahship.*[44] *Jesus prays that as Messiah he will not have to suffer and die.*[45]

---

40. Cf. Kelber, 'The Hour of the Son of Man', in *the Passion in Mark*, p. 44.

41. On this, see Senior, *The Passion of Jesus in the Gospel of Mark*, pp. 75-76; M. Black, 'The Cup Metaphor in Mark xiv. 36', *ExpTim* 49 (1947–1948), p. 195; A. Feuillet, 'La coupe et le baptême de la passion (Mc. x,35-40; cf. Mt. xx,20-23; Lc. xii,50)', *RB* 74 (1967), pp. 363-88, esp. 363-64. On the 'cup' as an element of the imagery of 'religious' temptation, see J.H. Korn, *ΠΕΙΡΑΣΜΟΣ: Die Versuchung des Gläubigen in der griechischen Bibel* (Stuttgart: W. Kohlhammer, 1937), p. 67.

42. Cf. C.E.B. Cranfield, *The Gospel according to St Mark* (Cambridge: Cambridge University Press, 1972), p. 433.

43. On those who come to arrest Jesus as representatives of the forces in the world opposed to God, see below, n. 57.

44. Kelber, 'Mark 14:32-42', p. 177; Senior, *The Passion of Jesus in the Gospel of Mark*, p. 76; J. Blackwell, *The Passion as Story: The Plot of Mark* (Philadelphia: Fortress Press, 1986), p. 40.

45. It cannot be that when Jesus asks for the passing of the 'hour' and the

But why, according to Mark, should Jesus at this moment beg for the removal of the death warrant which in his own testimony he had accepted?[46] The words used in 14.34 to describe the motive force behind the petition indicate that Jesus' prayer stems from a sense of utter uncertainty and desperation.[47] But over what? Two frequently suggested possibilities are excluded from the start. First, it is not because, in Mark's eyes, Jesus is possessed by apprehension that the path of suffering to which he, as Messiah, had committed himself might not be after all the will of God for him.[48] For there is no hint in Mark's Gospel of doubt on the part of Jesus that God had mandated suffering to be the only means his Messiah could use to achieve the messianic task,[49] or that Jesus envisaged any other issue to his divinely directed life and mission than one involving his death on the cross.[50] Nor, secondly, is it because Jesus was beset with a loss of nerve as the reality of his impending arrest, torture and execution bore in upon him and, overcome with fear for his personal safety, suddenly realized that he might not be a match for what lay ahead.[51] Such a response stands in complete contradiction to what in Mark precedes and follows the Gethsemane account, especially Mark's portrayal of Jesus' resolute silence in the face of the

removal of the 'cup' he was attempting to drop completely out of his ministry and abandon his messianic role altogether. For, as I have noted above, it is as Son that Jesus prays *and expects to be heard*. Further, as C.K. Barrett notes, 'It may be taken as certain that Jesus' hope was not that a convenient way of escape might open up, so that he might slip away unobserved and so avoid the final peril. Not only is this in contradiction with the sense of the narrative; if Jesus had wished to escape he could in all probability have done so. He does not appear even to have tried' (*Jesus and the Gospel Tradition* [Philadelphia: Fortress Press, 1968], pp. 46-47).

46. Cf. not only the 'passion predictions' (Mk 8.31; 9.31; 10.33-34) but also Mk 9.12 and 14.21, 24.

47. Kelber, 'Mark 14:32-42', p. 177.

48. A position advocated by Barbour, 'Gethsemane', p. 250, and Barrett, *Jesus and the Gospel Tradition*, p. 120. A similar suggestion is made by Caird (*Luke*, p. 242) with regard to the motive behind Jesus' prayer in the Lukan Gethsemane account.

49. Cf. R.P. Martin, *Mark: Evangelist and Theologian* (Exeter: Paternoster, 1972), p. 204.

50. The latter half of Jesus' petition in Mk 14.36 (ἀλλ' οὐ τί ἐγὼ θέλω ἀλλὰ τί σύ) shows that even in Gethsemane this is the one thing of which Jesus is certain!

51. As O. Cullmann (*The Christology of the New Testament* [London, SCM Press], p. 96, *idem, The State in the New Testament* [New York: Charles Scribner & Sons, 1956], p. 40) and, to some extent, Cranfield (*Mark*, pp. 431-32) propose.

rigours of his trial and condemnation and of the covenant-making with his disciples at the Last Supper, where Jesus calmly contemplates his own death.[52] Moreover, the strength of the anguish and bewilderment that lies behind the prayer and petition betrays that there is more involved there than ordinary fear of death or horror and revulsion at the prospect of suffering.[53] The petition has its roots in questionings of another sort. But what are these questionings?

As I have noted above, Jesus, according to Mark, is aware as he prays at Gethsemane that carrying on with his commission to suffer in accordance with God's decree on the exigencies of messiahship entails the dissolution of the small band of followers whose response of loyalty and fellowship, however incomplete and varying, was in the end the only tangible result of his entire public ministry.[54] Accordingly, to submit to the passion is apparently to acquiesce in the complete failure of that ministry.[55] Jesus, according to Mark, is also aware[56] that in subordinating his will to that of God he consents to being 'delivered up ($\pi\alpha\rho\alpha\delta\acute{\iota}\delta\sigma\tau\alpha\iota$) into the hands of sinners', that is, he places himself, defenseless and powerless, at the mercy, whim and disposal of the seemingly absolute and arbitrary power of the forces which are committed to doing all they can to set him and his mission at nought.[57] So to

---

52. Cf. Mk 14.22-26. See also Barbour, 'Gethsemane', p. 248; Barrett, *Jesus in the Gospel Tradition*, pp. 48-49; Martin, *Mark: Evangelist and Theologian*, p. 204.

53. Cf. H.B. Swete, *The Gospel according to Mark* (London: Macmillan, 1905), p. 342; A.E.J. Rawlinson, *The Gospel according to St Mark* (London: Methuen, 1925), p. 211; G. Bertram, '$\theta\acute{\alpha}\mu\beta\sigma\varsigma$, $\kappa\tau\lambda$.', *TDNT*, II, pp. 4-7, esp. p. 7.

54. The Gethsemane story is preceded in the Markan narrative by the account of a double prophecy of Jesus (1) that his own suffering and death would cause his disciples to lose all faith in him and (2) that, in fulfilment of Zech. 13.7, his passion would both scandalize and cause the break up of the little community of believers who alone had remained loyal to him at the end of his ministry (Mk 14.27-31). The fact that this passage interrupts the flow of the narrative begun at 14.17, and that v. 32, the beginning of the Gethsemane story, follows on naturally from v. 26, the end of the Last Supper narrative, indicates that Mark has inserted vv. 27-31 at this point in order to emphasize that Jesus was thoroughly aware of the course of the events that would unfold in the hours ahead. As Lane notes, 'Within the Markan outline these verses serve to anticipate important sections of the subsequent narrative, but especially the flight of the disciples at the time of the arrest...and the denial of Peter...' (*Mark*, p. 510).

55. On this, see Stanley, *Jesus in Gethsemane*, pp. 138-39.

56. Cf. Mk 14.41. Compare Mk 9.31.

57. Cf. Mk 9.11. On the identification of the 'sinners' of Mk 14.41 with the

accept God's will also means risking the fate of John the Baptizer, who, like Jesus, was divinely commissioned to 'restore all things',[58] but who, trusting in God, was also 'delivered up' (cf. Mk 1.14, παραδοθῆναι) only to suffer an ignominious end[59] and have his mission defeated by those who opposed him.[60] To all appearances, then, obedience produces nothing but a literal dead end.[61] Accordingly, in Mark's view, the anguish and bewilderment, the hesitation and uncertainty to which Jesus is subject in Gethsemane arises out of a conflict between Jesus' desire to be faithful to his calling and to accomplish the messianic task and the apparent irrationality of submitting in obedience to a divinely decreed plan of action when it seemed that to obey was to jeopardize God's worthwhile purposes.

That this is the case is made certain by Jesus' use of the words περίλυπός ἐστιν ἡ ψυχή μου ἕως θανάτου in Mk 14.34 to describe to his disciples the type of distress which has seized him upon entering Gethsemane. In Jesus' lament are clearly recognizable allusions to the

forces of evil, see Holleran, *The Synoptic Gethsemane*, pp. 14, 66-67, 204; Lane, *Mark*, p. 522; M.D. Hooker, *The Son of Man in Mark* (London: SPCK, 1967), p. 162; H.E. Tödt, *The Son of Man in the Synoptic Tradition* (London: SCM Press, 1965), p. 200. As the parallelism between Mk 14.41 and 9.31 shows ('the hour is come; behold, the Son of Man is delivered up into the hands of sinners [ἁμαρτωλῶν]...'/'...the Son of man will be delivered up into the hands of men [ἀνθρώπων]...'), the term 'sinners' corresponds here with 'men', which in Mark's Gospel signifies not only the opponents of Jesus, and those who seek his death, but those forces aligned with Satan which seek to frustrate the work of God and his saving purposes (cf. Mk 8.31). On this, see B. van Iersel, 'Jesus' Way of Obedience according to Mark's Gospel', *Con* 30 (1981), pp. 25-33, esp. pp. 29-31. On the parallelism between Mk 14.41 and Mk 9.31, see F. Hahn, *The Titles of Jesus in Christology* (London: Lutterworth, 1969), p. 48 n. 4.

58. That John was viewed by Mark as commissioned for this task is clear from Mk 9.12, where Jesus, identifying John with Elijah (cp. v. 13), alludes to John's commission in terms of the function that Mal. 3.23 (LXX) ascribes to the forerunner, i.e., ἀποκαταστήσει, 'and he will restore' (see A. Oepke, 'ἀποκαθίστημι, ἀποκατάστασις', *TDNT*, I, pp. 387-89). This view also informs Mark's use in Mk 1.2 of the citation of from Isa. 40.3, Mal. 3.1 and Exod. 23.30 as an explanation of the advent of John and the purpose of his coming and Mark's allusions in Mk 1.6 to 2 Kgs 1.8 and Zech. 13.4. On this, see W. Wink, *John the Baptist in the Gospel Tradition* (Cambridge: Cambridge University Press, 1968), pp. 1-17.

59. Cf. Mk 6.27-29.

60. Cf. Mk 9.13.

61. Barbour, 'Gethsemane', p. 249-50.

refrain 'Why art thou cast down (περίλυπος εἶ), O my soul?' found in the twin Psalms of the Suffering Righteous one, Psalms 42–43 (MT); 41–42 (LXX)[62] and to Jonah's cry of anger and frustration in Jon. 4.3-9.[63] According to Mark, then, Jesus in Gethsemane finds himself in the same situation as Jonah and the Psalmist.[64] Notably, *that* situation is in both cases a condition of despair over the fact that faithfulness and obedience to the requirements of a divine commission had apparently no discernable effect of forwarding what the one commissioned thought were God's purposes in the world, but on the contrary seemingly brought those purposes to their ruin. Therefore, in Mark's Gospel Jesus prays to have pass by his 'hour' and to be relieved of his 'cup' because he doubts whether in the end the path of suffering will really be effective in achieving the task to which he has been commissioned. *Behind the petition in Mk 14.36 lies the question, 'How can I obey God, and trust in him, when he seems to be willing to jeopardize his own purposes?'*[65]

Now this observation is hardly without significance. Since Mark felt that Jesus, in desiring to succeed in his messianic commission, could

62. Cf. Holleran, *The Synoptic Gethsemane*, p. 14. See also R.H. Gundry, *The Use of the Old Testament in Matthew's Gospel* (Leiden: Brill, 1967), p. 59, who argues that in Matthew, and therefore *ipso facto* in Mark, the dependence on Pss. 41–42 (42–43) seems clear from the fact that περίλυπος is rare in the LXX and that the Hebrew means 'to be bowed (or cast) down'.

63. Cf. Bultmann, *TDNT*, IV, p. 323; Taylor, *The Gospel according to St Mark* (London: Macmillan, 1955), p. 553; E. Schweizer, *The Good News according to Mark* (Atlanta: John Knox, 1970), p. 312.

64. On this, see E. Lohmeyer, *Das Evangelium des Markus* (Göttingen: Vandenhoek & Ruprecht, 16th edn, 1963), p. 314.

65. Lohmeyer (*Markus*, p. 315) and Schweizer (*Mark*, p. 311) state that Jesus' command to his disciples in Mk 14.34 and his movement 'a little distance off' (cf. Mk 14.35) to pray is intended by Mark to be seen as an allusion to Gen. 22.5, thus casting Jesus at Gethsemane in the role of Abraham, who, on his mission to carry out the divine command to sacrifice his only Son, Isaac, was 'tested' (πειράξω) by God to see if he would obey even when obedience seemed certain to frustrate the achievement of God's stated purposes (cf. Gen. 22.1-8). If true, this would add further evidence in support of my view that Jesus' petition in Gethsemane is uttered because of Jesus' sense of the apparent hopelessness and irrationality of obedience. On the 'testing' of Abraham in Gen. 22, see B. van Iersel, *The Bible on the Temptations of Man* (De Pere, WI: St Norbert Abbey Press, 1966), pp. 5-17, esp. pp. 14-16; J.H. Yoder, *The Original Revolution* (Scotsdale: Herald Press, 1972), pp. 101-103. For an evaluation of the 'Jesus as Abraham' typology in Gethsemane, see Senior, *The Passion of Jesus in the Gospel of Mark*, p. 69 n. 31.

doubt, even momentarily, the instrumental propriety of suffering, then by implication he would not hesitate to portray Jesus as not only open to, but positively drawn toward, the use of means which in being antipathetic to suffering were apparently *ipso facto* more promising than suffering to bring about this end. Indeed, Mark does this very thing in his Gethsemane account.

It should be noted that, according to Mark, Jesus' Gethsemane prayer involves more than the petition to have the element of suffering removed from the Messiahship. Its particular conjunction of the affirmation that with God 'all things are possible' (πάντα δυνατά σοι, v. 36; cp. Mk 10.27) with the expression 'my will' not only implies that at Gethsemane Jesus contemplated the possibility that the wished-for future, the establishment of the sovereignty of God in Israel and throughout the world, could be brought about without suffering.[66] It also shows that the petition of Jesus entails the desire to be allowed to implement a plan of action to accomplish the Messianic task which is the very opposite of God's will in this regard,[67] one, namely, that uses violence and domination, instead of suffering and service, to achieve this end and envisages the punishment and destruction, not the inclusion within the mercies of God, of those 'not of Israel'. By placing this prayer on Jesus' lips in the particular wording in which it is now cast, Mark presents Jesus as seriously engaged with the idea of adopting messianic behaviour 'minded' to 'the ways of men'. To be sure, Mark has Jesus subsequently accept τὰ τοῦ θεοῦ as regards his sufferings, but only in such a manner that the strength of Jesus' attraction as Messiah to the 'ways of men' and the fervency with which he wishes to be allowed to side with them are emphasized.[68]

Gethsemane and Jesus' Temptation at Caesarea Philippi

I have undertaken this examination of the Markan account of Jesus Gethsemane temptation for two reasons: to outline Mark's presentation of the nature and content of Jesus' Gethsemane temptation, but also to answer a question posed above in my examination of the Markan

---

66. Barrett, *Jesus and the Gospel Tradition*, p. 49.

67. Swete, *Mark*, p. 344; Holleran, *The Synoptic Gethsemane*, p. 49.

68. Stanley, *Jesus in Gethsemane*, p. 137; van Iersel, *The Bible on the Temptations of Man*, pp. 46-47.

account of the temptation presented to Jesus by Peter at Caesarea Philippi. It will be recalled that after examining that account I reached the conclusion that, in light of the evidence given by Mark in this regard, it was Mark's intention to present that temptation as involving the invitation to Jesus to engage in the exercise of a type of kingship which engages in conquest, exploits and dominates those over whom it reigns, and which uses its prerogatives for procuring personal advantage, and to fulfil his commission as Messiah, not by suffering and service, especially to those 'not of Israel', but by waging wars of deliverance against them. I also noted, however, that the credibility of this conclusion depended upon whether it could be established that Mark could really have thought that such behaviour would have been the slightest bit attractive to Jesus, let alone sufficiently attractive that Jesus might have thought of it as a live option and given it serious consideration. If Mark did not think this, then the invitation would have been not a real but only a sham 'test' of his faithfulness, and therefore hardly a true 'religious' temptation.

I then argued that to be answered, this question must be set within the context of another. Since in Mark's Gospel the task to which Jesus, as Messiah, is appointed and empowered is to establish and implement the sovereign authority of God over a rebellious world by rescuing and permanently delivering those willing to submit to this authority from those forces hostile to God and his saving purposes, then the question is, how successful does Jesus, according to Mark, feel the path of suffering will be in the accomplishment of this messianic task? Does he have any doubts, given what he is ordained to do, about his mandated suffering's instrumental propriety and effectiveness? If Mark does not hesitate to portray Jesus as entertaining such doubts, then renouncing and abandoning suffering and adopting a different messianic path would be for Jesus a live and alluring option.

In light of what I have uncovered in this regard in Mark's Gethsemane story, we may indeed conclude that the invitation which Peter offered to Jesus at Caesarea Philippi was not, according to Mark, something Jesus could easily dismiss. It was in fact so alluring to him that it could be resisted only with supreme effort and the greatest of struggles. Accordingly, the invitation to take this alternative messianic path provided for Jesus a real and not a 'sham' temptation.

Has Mark Changed the Caesarea Philippi Tradition?

We have seen in the previous chapter that from a history-of-traditions point of view Mark's story of Jesus's Caesarea Philippi temptation is secondary. It is based upon, and developed out of, a more primitive traditional story of a confrontation between Jesus and Peter, the shape of which ran as follows:

> And Jesus and his disciples came to the villages of Caesarea Philippi.
> And he asked them, 'Who do you say I am?'
> And Peter answered, 'You are the Christ'.
> And Jesus rebuked Peter and says, 'Get behind me, Satan.
>   You do not think the things of God
>   But the things of men'.[69]

Given this, it must be asked if Mark's view of the nature and content of Jesus' Caesarea Philippi temptation is *also* secondary. Does Mark convey in Mk 8.27-33 something different from what is propounded in this regard in the material from which his story is derived? The answer must be no. For as E. Dinkler has decisively shown in his examination of the Casearea Philippi pericope,[70] the intent of the *Vorlage* of Mk 8.27-33 was to portray Peter's 'confession' specifically as a 'Satanic intention' or a 'temptation', that is, a 'testing of faithfulness', involving 'opposition to the Passion [and an] attempt to prevent the sacrifice of the cross', and to portray Peter himself as requesting that Jesus as Messiah eschew suffering and all that it implies as not God's way and construe his office along 'this-worldly', triumphalistic lines.[71] If Mark has done anything at all in his transmission, recounting and explication of the Caesarea Philippi episode, it is to ensure that the original tradition's understanding of the nature and content of Jesus' Caesarea Philippi temptation is passed on intact and made plain to his readers.

---

69. See above, Chapter 7, pp. 215-20.

70. E. Dinkler, 'Peter's Confession and the "Satan" Saying: The Problem of Jesus' Messiahship', in J.M. Robinson (ed.), *The Future of Our Religious Past* (New York: Harper & Row), pp. 176-89.

71. Dinkler, 'Peter's Confession', p. 186. See also, Schweizer, *Mark*, p. 165-66.

Chapter 9

THE TRADITION OF JESUS' DIVORCE QUESTION TEMPTATION

The Accounts of the Tradition and their Relationship

The tradition that Jesus was tempted when confronted with a question concerning divorce appears twice in the synoptic tradition, at Mt. 19.1-9 and at Mk 10.1-12. Some scholars, noting that there are certain notable differences between the two accounts, particularly in their respective descriptions both of the specific question that is asked of Jesus and of his response,[1] maintain that the two versions of the tradition are, from a literary point of view, independent of one another, and, therefore, represent separate incidents in the life of Jesus.[2] But this contention seems highly doubtful when the following information is taken into account:

- both accounts have (roughly) the same geographical setting (cf. Mt. 19.1; Mk 10.1).

- in both accounts the audience is the same—the Pharisees (cf. Mt. 19.3; Mk 10.2).[3]

- the wording of the question which in each of the two accounts occasions πειρασμός for Jesus is essentially the same.

- the Old Testament quotations found in each of the two versions of the tradition are the same (Deut. 24.1, cp. Mt. 19.7 and Mk 10.4; Gen. 1.27, cp. Mt. 19.4 and Mk 10.6; Gen. 2.24, cp. Mt. 19.5 and Mk 10.7-8).

---

1. On this, see R.H. Stein, 'Is it Lawful for a Man to Divorce his Wife?', *JETS* 22 (1979), pp. 115-21, esp. p. 116.

2. Stein, 'Is it Lawful', p. 116.

3. A variant reading of Mk 10.2, attested by a number of 'Western' witnesses, leaves the identity of the audience unidentified. But as I show below, this reading should not be considered original.

- in both accounts the Pharisees reply to Jesus' quotation of Gen. 2.24 by referring to Deut. 24.1 (cf. Mt. 19.7; Mk 10.4).

- in both accounts Jesus' explanation of the Mosaic prescriptions for divorce (Deut. 24.1) is the same: that Moses said what he said concerning divorce because of the hardness of men's hearts (cf. Mt. 19.8; Mk 10.25).

- in both Matthew and Mark's Gospel the tradition of Jesus' Divorce Question temptation is followed by the story of Jesus blessing the children (cf. Mt. 19.13-15; Mk 10.13-16).

Given both the nature and the extent of these similarities between the two versions of the tradition of Jesus' Divorce Question temptation. It is not only doubtful that in their respective accounts of this tradition Matthew and Mark are recounting and reproducing separate incidents; it is also more likely than not that one of the versions is the source of the other. But does Mk 10.1-12 stand as the source of Mt. 19.1-9, or was the Markan version of the tradition of Jesus' Divorce Question temptation derived from what Matthew recounts in this regard?

The answer typically given to this question is that the Matthean version of Jesus' Divorce Question temptation is derived from Mk 10.1-12. In the opinion of most scholars who have dealt with this issue, Mt. 19.1-9 is a revision by Matthew of material drawn by him from Mk 10.1-12.[4]

---

4.   Those who argue or assume this view include, but are by no means limited to, W.C. Allen (*A Critical and Exegetical Commentary on the Gospel according to St Matthew* [Edinburgh: T. & T. Clark, 1907], pp. 201-203), B.W. Bacon (*Studies in Matthew* [London: Constable & Co., 1930], p. 308), G. Bornkamm (*Jesus of Nazareth* [New York: Harper & Row, 1960], p. 99), B.H. Branscombe (*The Gospel of Mark* [London: Hodder & Stoughton, 1937], pp. 177-78), G.H. Box and C. Gore (*Divorce in the New Testament* [London: SPCK, 1921], pp. 15-17), R. Bultmann (*The History of the Synoptic Tradition* [Oxford: Basil Blackwell, 1963], pp. 26-27), D.R. Catchpole ('The Synoptic Divorce Material as a Traditio-Historical Problem', *BJRL* 57 [1974], pp. 92-127), F.H. Chase (*What did Christ Teach about Divorce?* [London: SPCK, 1921], pp. 54-61), C.E.B Cranfield (*The Gospel according to St Mark* [Cambridge: Cambridge University Press, 1963], p. 318), J.D.M. Derrett, 'The Teaching of Jesus on Marriage and Divorce', in *Law and the New Testament* [London: Darton, Longman & Todd, 1970], p. 367), J.A. Fitzmyer ('The Matthean Divorce Texts and some New Palestinian Evidence', *TS* 37 [1976], pp. 213-23, esp. p. 208), M. Grant (*Jesus: An Historian's Review of the Gospels* [New York: Charles Scribner & Sons, 1977], p. 85), E.P. Gould (*A Critical and Exegetical Commentary on the Gospel according to St Mark* [Edinburgh: T. & T. Clark, 1896], p. 184),

But in recent years several voices have been raised in opposition to the view that the Markan version of the story is more original than, and the source for, its Matthean counterpart. W.R. Farmer, for example, has declared that 'only with the greatest difficulty can one explain satisfactorily the history of the synoptic tradition on divorce by a redactional process in which Mark is placed first'.[5] Similarly, A. Isaksson has sharply criticized the idea of the priority of the Markan version of Jesus' Divorce Question temptation over that of Matthew because in his estimation such an idea is not so much based upon evidence derived from a careful examination and comparison of the two accounts as it is demonstrative of constraints imposed upon critical judgment by what he terms 'the Babylonian Captivity of the Two Document Hypothesis'.[6] These and other scholars[7] argue the case for the priority of Mt. 19.1-9 primarily on five grounds:

- The Markan version of Jesus' Divorce Question temptation shows signs of being composite. It has a double setting and a double audience, using Jesus' final retort to the Pharisees'

R.H. Gundry (*Matthew: A Commentary on his Literary and Theological Art* [Grand Rapids: Eerdmans, 1982], p. 375), P. Hoffmann ('Jesus' Sayings on Divorce in the New Testament', *Concilium* 55 [1970], pp. 51-66, esp. pp. 56-57), R. Hummel (*Die Auseinandersetzung zwischen Kirche und Judentum im Matthäusevangelium* [Munich: Kaiser, 1963], pp. 53-54), G.D. Kilpatrick (*The Origins of the Gospel according to St Matthew* [Oxford: Clarendon Press, 1946], p. 83), A.H. McNeil (*The Gospel according to Matthew* [London: Macmillan, 1915], p. 272), J.P. Meier (*Law and History in Matthew's Gospel* [Rome: Biblical Institute Press, 1976], pp. 140-41), *idem, The Vision of Matthew: Christ, Church, and Morality in the First Gospel* [New York: Paulist Press, 1978], p. 250), E. Schweizer (*The Good News according to Matthew* [Atlanta: John Knox, 1975], p. 380), R.H. Stein ('Is it Lawful', pp. 117-18), A. Stock ('Matthean Divorce Texts', *BTB* 8 [1978], pp. 24-33, esp. p. 25).

5.   Farmer, *The Synoptic Problem* (Macon, GA: Mercer University Press, 1964), pp. 255-57.

6.   Isaksson, *Marriage and Ministry in the New Temple* (Lund: Gleerup, 1965), pp. 70, 103.

7.   Cf. for instance, R.H. Charles, *The Teaching of the New Testament on Marriage and Divorce* (London: Williams & Norgate, 1921), pp. 85-90; D.L. Dungan, *The Sayings of Jesus in the Churches of Paul* (Philadelphia: Fortress Press, 1971), p. 122; K.G. Reploh, *Markus—Lehrer de Gemeinde: Ein Redaktionsgeschichtliche Studie zu den Jüngerperikopen des Markus-Evangeliums* (Stuttgart: Katholisches Bibelwerk, 1969), p. 182; C.S. Mann, *Mark* (Garden City: Doubleday, 1988), pp. 389-90.

divorce question as an address not to the Pharisees at the time of their inquiry, but to the disciples later on in a house (cf. Mk 10.10-12). On the other hand, however, the Matthean version appears to be much more of a unitary composition. It has its version of Jesus' retort the Pharisees' divorce question incorporated within, and not outside of, the confines of its story of the confrontation between Jesus and the Pharisees. The fact, then, that the Markan version of the tradition of Jesus' Divorce Question temptation possesses a formal arrangement of the material constituent to that tradition which is more ragged and less unified than that of the Matthean version indicates that the Markan version is secondary to that found in Matthew's Gospel.

- The Pharisees' question on divorce as posed in Mk 10.2 is inconceivable in a Palestinian Jewish setting where the legality of divorce was taken for granted.[8] The *Sitz im Leben* of the Markan version of the tradition of Jesus' Divorce Question temptation cannot, therefore, be a Palestinian milieu.

- Mk 10.11-12 speaks of a woman as well as a man pursuing divorce. Accordingly, the *Sitz im Leben* out of which the Markan version of the Divorce Question temptation tradition must have arisen is one in which Greco-Roman and not Jewish law prevailed, for it is only there that a woman also had the legal right to dissolve the marriage bond.[9]

- The earliest attestation of an attitude of Jesus towards divorce—Paul's discussion of marriage and divorce in 1 Corinthians 7, in which Paul quotes or alludes to sayings of the Lord to support his view on these issues—betrays an awareness on the part of Paul of the specifically Matthean form of the teaching of Jesus in this regard.

8. On this, see below, pp. 280-82. See also Dungan, *The Sayings of Jesus*, pp. 111-12.

9. Cf. *Cod. Iust.* 5.17.5-6; 8.38.2. See also H. Conzelmann, *The First Epistle to the Corinthians* (Philadelphia: Fortress Press, 1975), p. 145 n. 22; P.E. Corbett, *The Roman Law of Marriage* (Oxford: Clarendon Press, 1930), pp. 239-43. For the differences between Hellenic-Roman and Jewish marriage law, see B. Cohen, 'Divorce in Jewish and Roman Law', in *Jewish and Roman Law: A Comparative Study* (2 vols., New York: Jewish Theological Seminary, 1966), I, pp. 377-408.

- In the Matthean version of the tradition of Jesus' Divorce Question temptation, the question which is said to subject Jesus to temptation concerns the issue of the legitimate grounds for divorce and not, as in the Markan version of the tradition, the legitimacy of divorce itself. In this the Matthean version, then, reflects the debate on divorce being carried out in contemporary Judaism by the schools of Hillel and Shammai.[10] Given this, the Matthean version of the Divorce Question temptation tradition has its most plausible matrix in a Palestinian-Jewish setting.[11]

This is, at least at first glance, an impressive array of evidence. But does it really make the case for the relative primitiveness and priority of the Matthean version of the tradition of Jesus' Divorce Question temptation? I think not. For, as I will now show, upon examination the evidence enlisted to support the contention that Mk 10.1-12 is secondary to Mt. 19.1-9 *either turns out to be no evidence at all or does not do the job it is purported to do.* Let us review the evidence cited above item by item.

The Relative 'Ruggedness' of Mark 10.1-12

I agree that the Markan version of the tradition of Jesus' Divorce Question temptation is composite,[12] and that the Markan version possesses a less smooth arrangement of the material apparently ingredient to the tradition than that found in its Matthean counterpart. I fail to see, however, just how this can be counted as evidence for the view that Mk 10.1-12 is secondary to Mt. 19.1-9. Surely, if anything, the fact that Matthew's version of the tradition possesses a better formal arrangement of the tradition's constituent material than that of Mark indicates that *Matthew's* version is secondary. The tendency in the Synoptic tradition is for relatively rugged material to be smoothed out in the course

10. This debate centered around Deut. 24.1-4 and the question of how the words 'some indecency in her' should be interpreted. The school of Shammai took the words narrowly and said divorce was permitted only when there is some sexual indecency (i.e. adultery, unchastity). The school of Hillel took them in a wider sense to mean anything objectionable and so saw divorce as permissible for other, non-sexual offenses. For a report of the debate, see below.

11. Cf. Charles, *The Teaching of the New Testament on Marriage and Divorce*, pp. 29-31; Dungan, *The Sayings of Jesus*, p. 112.

12. For my analysis of the tradition history of Mk 10.1-12, see below, pp. 281-82.

of its transmission.[13] Moreover, it is, notably, a characteristic tendency of Matthew to restructure relatively jumbled material into formally more cohesive arrangements.[14] It should noted, too, that there is no purpose discernable for Mark to have broken up and re-arranged the Matthean order of the pericope in question, as those who assert the priority of Mt. 19.1-9 must assume he has done.[15] So this bit of evidence for the priority of Mt. 19.1-9 over Mk 10.1-12 turns out, upon examination, to be no evidence at all.

The Impossibility of a Palestinian-Jewish Setting for Mark 10.1-12

The assertion that the Pharisees' question as posed in Mark's Gospel is inconceivable in a Palestinian-Jewish setting is made because it is presumed that, given the fact of the legality of divorce in Judaism,[16] no one in Palestine would need to ask this question.[17] The thing to note here, however, is that this assertion is sound only insofar as it is certain that the question εἰ ἔξεστιν ἀνδρὶ γυναῖκα ἀπολῦσαι (Mk 10.2) is intended by Mark to be seen as one of *halakah*, with no motive behind its asking other than the desire to discover whether the Mosaic Law permitted divorce. As Dungan remarks,

> In view of the overwhelming evidence that nothing whatsoever in the law suggests that divorce is illegal, any commentator who proposes to defend the primitive historical character of Mark's version of the Pharisees' question, that it is more original than Matthew's, has no alternative... but to search for ulterior and sinister motives on the part of the Pharisees for putting such an obviously phony question to Jesus.[18]

But in the first place it is by no means certain that the Pharisees' question in Mk 10.2 is one of *halakah*. As I will show below, there are good reasons for thinking that ἔξεστιν, the key word in this verse, is not used in its strictest juridical sense of 'it is lawful'. If this is the case, then the question itself cannot be considered one which has its specific point of

---

13. Cf. Bultmann, *History*, p. 51.
14. Gundry, *Matthew*, p. 2.
15. Cf. Mann, *Mark*, pp. 393-94.
16. Again, see below, pp. 280-82.
17. Dungan, *Sayings of Jesus*, p. 112; See also D.E. Nineham, *Saint Mark* (Baltimore: Penguin, 1963), p. 260; J. Schmind, *Das Evangelium nach Markus* (Regensburg: Pustet, 1958), p. 186; E. Schweizer, *The Good News according to Mark* (Atlanta: John Knox, 1970), p. 202.
18. Dungan, *Sayings of Jesus*, p. 111.

reference in the Mosaic Law.[19] And, in the second place, that *no* sinister or ulterior motive lies behind the Pharisees' question is a highly questionable assumption, given the indications within the Markan version of Divorce Question temptation tradition—indications that will be noted below—that there is not only hostility shown by the Pharisees towards Jesus when they ask their question of him, but that there is also some awareness on their part that Jesus' position on divorce might be suspect. Consequently, even if ἔξεστιν in Mk 10.2 is to be taken as bearing the meaning 'it is lawful', the Pharisees' question cannot be labeled as one that would be inconceivable in a Palestinian-Jewish setting.[20]

The 'Dual Divorce' Terminology of Mark 10.2-12 and the Sitz im Leben of the Pericope

The assertion that Mk 10.1-12 is secondary to Mt. 19.1-9 is, as we have seen, made on the grounds that Mk 10.11-12 speaks of a *woman* as well as a man having the right to initiate divorce. This, it is argued, indicates that the Markan version of the Divorce Question temptation tradition was designed to mirror and address problems for Mark's readers which were created by the contingencies of living in a area where Greco-Roman and not Jewish law prevailed, since it is only there that a woman had the legal right to dissolve the marriage bond.[21] But, first of all, it is not all that certain that Mk 10.11-12 actually speaks of a woman as well as a man *divorcing* their respective spouses. The assertion that these

19. Cf. D.R. Catchpole, 'The Synoptic Divorce Material', p. 114. So also Fitzmyer, 'The Matthean Divorce Texts', pp. 22-23, but for different reasons. According to Fitzmyer, new evidence from Qumran (11QTemple 57.17-19) shows that, contrary to the received opinion, there were at least some Jews in first-century Palestine, i.e., the Essenes, who not only proscribed divorce but saw their proscription as demanded by the Law. In light of this, the question, 'Is it lawful for a man to divorce his wife?', is not as 'inconceivable' as has been thought, even should ἔξεστιν bear a juridical sense. Fitzmyer's contention rests, of course, on the adequacy of his interpretation of the Qumran texts. On this, see below, n. 86.

20. Catchpole, 'The Synoptic Divorce Material', pp. 114-15. See also H. Baltensweiler, *Die Ehe im Neuen Testament* (Zürich: Zwingli Verlag, 1967), pp. 46-47.

21. Charles, *The Teaching of the New Testament on Divorce*, p. 29; Dungan, *Sayings of Jesus*, p. 112; Farmer, *Synoptic Problem*, p. 256; R.P. Martin, *Mark: Evangelist and Theologian* (Exeter: Paternoster, 1972), p. 221. On women's rights in this matter in the Jewish and Gentile worlds, see B. Cohen, 'Divorce in Jewish and Roman Law', in *Jewish and Roman Law: A Comparative Study*, I, pp. 377-408.

verses *do* so speak is based upon the assumption that the correct text of Mk 10.11-12 is either that of the primarily Alexandrian (i.e. ℵ B L C etc.) or Byzantine (i.e. A W λ etc.) witnesses, both of which employ dual divorce terminology,[22] and not that found in the Western and Caesarean manuscript tradition which does not speak of a woman divorcing her husband.[23] But as I will show below, this assumption is highly questionable, and if it does not stand up to critical scrutiny, then the assertion that is grounded upon it cannot be maintained. But, secondly, even if Mk 10.11-12 does speak of a woman as well as a man having the right to divorce, it does not necessarily follow, as those advocating the priority of Mt. 19.1-9 assume, that Mk 10.1-12 is a pericope developed by Mark to address a problem arising from his readers' involvement in the vicissitudes of living in a Greco-Roman environment and that its *Sitz im Leben* is somewhere in the Hellenized world. For as D.R. Catchpole remarks,

> On the one hand, it would be quite possible for Jesus or the Palestinian Church or both to criticize the practice of fringe groups [see, e.g., the attitude toward divorce on the part of certain Elephantine Jews and Samaritans[24]]—a parallel which springs to mind is the anti-Qumran orientation of Matthew v. 43 f. = Luke vi. 27 f. On the other hand, it would be quite possible for Jesus or the Palestinian church or both to attack a principle which, while prohibited also by current custom, had been put into practice in certain notorious instances. Those instances were ready to hand in the actions of Salome against her husband Costabarus (*Ant.*, xv. 259) and of Herodias against Herod (*Ant.*, xviii. 136). Since Palestine was made sharply aware of the reality of Hellenistic procedure and influence by these cases, Mark x. 12 should not be dispatched too speedily to a place of origin beyond the frontiers.[25]

If, therefore, we cannot immediately proceed to categorize Mk 10.12 as stemming from a Hellenistic environment, then we cannot necessarily assume that the pericope in which these verses appear, namely

---

22. ὃς ἂν ἀπολύσῃ τὴν γυναῖκα αὐτοῦ.../καὶ ἐὰν αὐτὴ ἀπολύσασα τὸν ἄνδρα αὐτῆς...

23. Rather, it speaks of her 'abandoning' or 'separating from' (ἐξέλθῃ) her spouse. On the meaning of this phrase, see D. Daube, 'Terms for Divorce', in *The New Testament and Rabbinic Judaism* (London: Athlone Press, 1956), pp. 362-72, esp. p. 366.

24. On this, see E. Bammel, 'Markus 10:11f, und das jüdische Eherecht', *ZNW* 61 (1970), pp. 95-101, esp. pp. 100-101.

25. Catchpole, 'Synoptic Divorce Material', pp. 111-12.

Mk 10.1-12, is secondary to the Matthean version of the Divorce
Question temptation tradition.

Traces of Matthew 19.3-9 in 1 Corinthians 7

In 1 Corinthians 7 Paul is engaged in responding to questions from the
Corinthian congregation regarding the necessity and proprieties of marriage. One such question concerned just how seriously the married
among them should take their marriage vows. To this, Paul answers
with the following advice:

> To the married I give charge, not I but the Lord, that the wife should not
> separate from her husband (παραγγέλλω...γυναῖκα ἀπὸ ἀνδρὸς μὴ
> χωρισθῆναι)—but if she does, let her remain single or else be reconciled
> with her husband—and that the husband should not divorce his wife (καὶ
> ἄνδρα γυναῖκα μὴ ἀψιέναι) (1 Cor. 7.10-11).

According to those who support the originality of Mt. 19.3-9 over
Mk 10.1-12, the dominical saying appealed to here resembles Matthew's
version of Jesus' prohibition of divorce and remarriage (Mt. 19.9) more
than it does Mark's (Mk 10.11-12).[26] It should be noted, however, that
it is Mark and not Matthew who, as here with Paul, quotes Jesus as
addressing both men and women on the issue of divorce and remarriage. Jesus in Matthew gives a command only to men. Moreover, in
Mk 10.12 Jesus speaks of a woman not divorcing, but *leaving* her
husband.[27] This is also what is found in 1 Cor. 7.10.[28] So, if anything,
1 Corinthians 7 actually attests that Mark's version of the Divorce
Question temptation tradition is earlier and more original than
Matthew's.[29]

Matthew 19.1-9 and the Shammai–Hillel Debate on Divorce

Those who argue for the priority of the Matthean version of the Divorce
Question temptation tradition over that of Mark do so because they see
Mt. 19.1-9, but not Mk 10.1-12, as mirroring the debate about divorce
carried out in the Judaism of Jesus' day between the schools of Hillel

---

26. Dungan, *The Sayings of Jesus*, p. 131; Isaksson, *Marriage and Ministry*,
p. 71-72, 112.

27. See below, pp. 272-74.

28. γυναῖκα ἀπὸ ἀνδρὸς μὴ χωρισθῆναι. On this as meaning 'leaving',
'abandoning', see Daube. 'Terms for Divorce', p. 365.

29. Cf. C.K. Barrett, *A Commentary on the First Epistle to the Corinthians*
(London: A. &. C. Black, 1968), p. 162. See also Stein, 'Is it Lawful', p. 118.

and Shammai, and thus having a greater claim than its Markan counterpart to having arisen in a Palestinian-Jewish matrix, the matrix where primary synoptic traditions originated. But this observed coherence between Mt. 19.1-9 and the Hillel–Shammai controversy over divorce may be more apparent than real. As we have seen, the connection between the Matthean version of the Divorce Question temptation tradition and the Hillel–Shammai debate is made because the tempting question in Matthew (i.e. Mt. 19.2) is thought to center in the issue over which Hillel and Shammai found themselves in disagreement when considering the topic of divorce: not the legitimacy of divorce itself, but the legitimate grounds for divorce.[30] It should be noted, however, that the view that the tempting question in Mt. 19.1-9 is a query concerning what constitutes legitimate grounds for divorce may be based upon a *misreading* of the Matthean text.[31] And if this is the case, then neither the assertion that there is a coherence between the concern of Mt. 19.1-9 and that of the Hillel–Shammai debate on divorce, nor the conclusion that is drawn from it—namely, that the Matthean version of the Divorce Question temptation tradition has its most plausible matrix in a Palestinian-Jewish setting—can be maintained. But more importantly, what needs to be pointed out is that *even if* there is a coherence between Mt. 19.1-9 and the Hillel–Shammai controversy over the grounds for divorce, such a coherence no more proves the relative primitiveness of the Matthean version of the Divorce Question temptation tradition than does, say, the presence of Semitisms in general or Aramaisms in particular in sayings attributed to Jesus proves these saying's authenticity. For just as such features may mean only that the material in question stems

---

30. Catchpole, 'Synoptic Divorce Material', p. 93.

31. On this, see R.A. Banks, *Jesus and the Law in the Synoptic Tradition* (Cambridge: Cambridge University Press, 1975), pp. 146-47; Schweizer, *Matthew*, p. 381. If ἔξεστιν is taken here as 'Is it in your view right that...' rather than 'Is it lawful that...' (i.e. 'is it prescribed in the Mosaic Law'), then what Jesus is being asked is not whether he sides with Hillel or Shammai, but whether he thinks both authorities—as well as the Law!—are wrong. This view is strengthened by the fact that, as J. Bauer has shown ('De conigali foedere quid edixerit Matthaeus (Mt 5,31; 19, 3-9)', *VD* [1966], pp. 74-78), κατὰ πᾶσαν αἰτίαν most probably means 'for some cause' (with the corresponding answer, 'for no cause'), rather than 'for whatever cause one wishes'. On this, N. Turner, *Grammatical Insights into the New Testament* (Edinburgh: T. & T. Clark, 1965), p. 61; J.P. Meier, *Law and History in Matthew's Gospel: A Redactional Study of Mt. 5:17-48* (Rome: Biblical Institute Press, 1976), p. 146 n. 51.

from a writer familiar with Semitic or Aramaic idiom, so too, the coherence of the Matthean version of the Divorce Question temptation tradition with the Hillel–Shammai Divorce controversy may only indicate that the version was recast along the lines of the rabbinic/Pharisaic discussion by an author who, knowing the tradition in another form, wanted to give it a more 'Jewish' flavour than it already possessed.[32] So the use of the relationship (if such there is) between Mt. 19.1-9 and the Hillel–Shammai controversy on divorce to support the contention of the relative primitiveness of the Matthean version of the Divorce Question temptation tradition is, if not illegitimate, at least questionable and hardly convincing.

To my mind, then, the case for the priority of the Matthean version of the Divorce Question temptation tradition over the parallel version found in Mark's Gospel has not been made. More importantly, I do not think that it can be made. This is not only because, as we have seen, there is little or no evidence which actually stands in its favour, but because there are two considerations which stand forcefully against it. First, the assumption that the Matthean version of the tradition (or something very much like it) was used by Mark raises what can only be termed 'some thoroughly embarrassing questions'.[33] Why, for instance, does Mark roughen the transition between verses 5 and 6 (of his version), so that the subject of the verbs in v. 6 is not specified but is nevertheless different from the specified subject of the verb ἔγραψεν in v. 5—a roughness which is absent from Mt. 19.4-5, the Matthean parallel to these verses? Why does Mark shorten, as we must assume he does if he used Mt. 19.1-9 (or something similar to it) as his source, the quotation of Gen. 2.24 so as to omit κολληθήσεται τῇ γυναικὶ αὐτοῦ, and also omit οὐκ ἀνέγνωτε ὅτι... when both are thoroughly appropriate to his version, and when the latter introductory formula is paralleled at Mk 2.25 and 12.10, 26? Why, again, should Mark take the

32. Cf. Catchpoole, 'Synoptic Divorce Material', p. 99; P. Hoffmann, 'Jesus' Sayings about Divorce', pp. 59-60; H. Zimmermann, 'μὴ ἐπὶ πορνείᾳ (Matt. 19:9)—Ein literarisches Problem. Zur Komposition vom Mt. 19:3-12', *Cath.* 16 (1960), pp. 293-99, esp. p. 299. On Semitisms and Aramaisms as ambiguous criteria for judging the authenticity of material, see N. Perrin, *Rediscovering the Teachings of Jesus* (New York: Harper & Row, 1967), p. 37; R.S. Barbour, *Traditio-Historical Criticism of the Gospels* (London: SPCK, 1972), p. 4.

33. This phrase, as well as the list of questions themselves, come from Catchpole, 'Synoptic Divorce Material', pp. 101-102.

trouble to introduce αὐτοῦ in v. 7 of his version in qualification of τὸν πατέρα (and in agreement with the LXX), but fail to add it correspondingly τῷ τὴν μητέρα (as in the LXX), thus creating another stylistic awkwardness? Finally, why should Mark omit the words ἀπ᾽ ἀρχῆς δὲ οὐ γέγονεν οὕτως, which, given the assumption of Matthean priority, were presumably before him, when they fit so admirably with the tendency of his account to down-grade Moses? Answers to these questions are not readily forthcoming. And because they are not— indeed because, as D.R. Catchpole remarks, 'It is so difficult to envisage Mark's engaging in such inconsistent and less than thorough editorial activity'—I feel compelled to conclude along with Catchpole 'that the overwhelming suspicion left by a comparison of the two accounts [of the Divorce Question temptation tradition] is that the suggestion of the priority of Matthew...over Mark has stood the situation on its head'.[34]

The second consideration which stands against the contention of the priority of Mt. 19.1-9 over Mk 10.1-12 is the fact that the contention ignores a fundamental tenet in the logic of source criticism: a positive argument in favour of the priority of the Matthean version of the Divorce Question temptation tradition can be mounted, and a serious challenge against the view that the Markan version of the tradition is the source of that in Matthew can be made, only if the Matthean divergences from the Markan account as well as its other distinctive features can be shown to be untypical of the evangelist Matthew. But the fact is that the divergences and distinctive features of Mt. 19.1-12 are all typical of Matthew's approach to his source material. For instance, the form in which the material apparently ingredient to the temptation tradition is arranged in Matthew's Gospel, namely 'Question—Answer— Objection—Counter-Argument—Conclusion', is a typical rabbinic pattern belonging well within the overall character of Matthew's Gospel.[35] The extension of the Old Testament quotation (cp. Mt. 19.5 with Mk 10.7) is anything but surprising in an work so heavily weighted with such quotations.[36] The introductory formula οὐκ ἀνέγνωτε that appears at Mt. 19.4 is a typical Matthean expression, appearing also at

---

34. Catchpole, 'Synoptic Divorce Material', p. 102.

35. Catchpole, 'Synoptic Divorce Material', p. 102. On Matthew's assimilation to rabbinic patterns, see D. Daube, *The New Testament and Rabbinic Judaism* (London: Athlone Press, 1956), p. 61.

36. Catchpole, 'Synoptic Divorce Material', p. 102.

Mt. 12.3, 5; 21.16, 42; 22.31.[37] The mitigation of any collision between Jesus and Moses, a mitigation which occurs if we take Mt. 19.8 as a modification of Mk 10.25, is consistent with the intentions of an evangelist who is concerned with emphasizing the eternal validity of the Law (cf. Mt. 5.18-19).[38] Accordingly, since none of the divergences or characteristic features of the Matthean version of the Divorce Question temptation tradition are atypical of Matthew's editorial propensities and idiosyncracies, indeed, since they are the type of modifications we would expect if Matthew were to take up and employ the Markan version of the tradition, the contention of the priority of Mt. 19.1-9 over Mk 10.1-12 cannot be taken seriously.

Conclusions: The Relationship of the Accounts

With all of this before us, it seems impossible to regard Mt. 19.1-9 as the source for Mk 10.1-12. At most one might conclude that Mt. 19.1-9 appears to be the more primitive of the two synoptic versions of the Divorce Question temptation tradition. But as we have seen, appearances can be deceptive. On the contrary then, given what I have noted above, it would be irresponsible to say anything other than that Mt. 19.1-9 is a revision by Matthew of material drawn by him from Mk 10.1-12. Therefore, with respect to the tradition of Jesus' Divorce Question temptation, there is only one 'primary' version', namely, that now found in the Gospel of Mark.

Jesus' Divorce Question Temptation according to Mark

Now that I have established that the Markan version of Jesus' Divorce Question temptation is the earliest of the synoptic versions of that tradition, I must attempt to determine the nature and content of the temptation that in this version Jesus is said to have undergone. To do this it is important to be clear on two things: first, the exact wording of the Markan version of the Divorce Question temptation tradition, and, secondly, what, if any, particular features Mark may have added to it. Accordingly, before I attempt to outline just what Mark portrays as the nature and content of Jesus' Divorce Question temptation I will carry out an investigation of the textual tradition of Mk 10.1-12, and then a source-critical, tradition history analysis of the passage.

---

37. Cf. Gundry, *Matthew*, p. 378.

38. Catchpole, 'Synoptic Divorce Material', p. 102; Fitzmyer, 'Matthean Divorce Texts', p. 208.

The Original Text of Mark 10.1-12

The textual tradition of the Markan version of Jesus' Divorce Question temptation is not uniform. Significant variants appear in the most important manuscripts, particularly with respect to v. 1a, v. 2 and v. 12a. Given that (1) v. 1 establishes the location of Jesus' experience of temptation, (2) v. 2 recounts the identity of those whose question tempts Jesus, (3) v. 12a is Jesus' summation of the issue over which he is tempted, and that all three of these factors may be pertinent in determining the nature and content of Jesus' Divorce Question temptation, we must turn our attention to establishing which of variants of these texts is in each instance original.

Variants in Verse 1a. The text of v. 1a is found in three variant forms. Alexandrian manuscripts, including א B C* L Ψ and the Coptic versions, read that after Jesus 'rose up from there' (i.e. Capernaum, cf. Mk 9.33) 'he came into the territories of Judea and Transjordan' (ἔρχεται εἰς τὰ ὅρια τῆς 'Ιουδαίας καὶ πέραν τοῦ 'Ιορδάνου). A large number of Eastern ('Caesarean') and Western witnesses, including D W T fam. 1 fam. 13, 28, 565, the Latin and early Syriac, and the Armenian and Georgian versions, say that 'he came into the territory of Judea beyond Jordan' (ἔρχεται εἰς τὰ ὅρια τῆς 'Ιουδαίας πέραν τοῦ 'Ιορδάνου). A third group of witnesses, including A R 157 569 575 700 pl syr^h and *aeth*, tell us that 'he came into the territories of Judea via Perea' (ἔρχεται εἰς τὰ ὅρια τῆς 'Ιουδαίας διὰ τοῦ πέραν τοῦ 'Ιορδάνου).

Little can be said in favour of the originality of this last variant. Not only is its attestation relatively late and from generally inferior witnesses, but its implicit assumption that Perea was no more than a bridge between Galilee and Judaea is one which was geographically incorrect and unlikely to be held by anyone in the first century.

The originality of the second variant must also be doubted despite the antiquity and authority of its attestation. It presupposes that the province of Judaea extended east of the Jordan valley and included at least a portion of Perea. But the territory east of the Jordan was not considered a part of Judaea until the time of Ptolemy the astronomer, that is, the middle of the second century CE.[39]

39. Cf. Abel, *Géographie de la Palestine* (2 vols.; Paris: Gabalda, 1933–38), II, p. 164; W.L. Lane, *The Gospel according to Mark* (Grand Rapids: Eerdmans, 1975), p. 351 n. 1.

The first variant, that of Sinaiticus *et al.*, seems then to have the best claim to originality. And this is not only by default. Evidence of a positive nature also speaks in its favour. First of all, there is the fact that while all three variants record that the occasion of Jesus' Divorce Question 'testing' is a public appearance on his part after a journey (ἔρχεται εἰς τὰ ὅρια...), it is only the Alexandrian reading (our first variant) with its reference to *two* distinct scenes of Jesus' sojourning, that is consistent grammatically with the plural τὰ ὅρια. Secondly, and most importantly, there is the fact that *the textual tradition of Mk 10.1 could not be accounted for if the reading of our first variant was not original.* An omission of καί between τῆς 'Ιουδαίας and πέραν τοῦ 'Ιορδάνου is intelligible as due to assimilation to Mt. 19.1 (...καὶ ἦλθεν εἰς τὰ ὅρια τῆς 'Ιουδαίας πέραν τοῦ 'Ιορδάνου). The addition of the connective to a phrase which did not originally possess it is not. A change from ἔρχεται εἰς τὰ ὅρια τῆς 'Ιουδαίας καὶ πέραν τοῦ 'Ιορδάνου to ἔρχεται εἰς τὰ ὅρια τῆς 'Ιουδαίας διὰ τοῦ πέραν τοῦ 'Ιορδάνου is understandable. A scribe, assuming on the basis of Mk 10.2 that Jesus departed Capernaum with the express purpose of going to Jerusalem, and that the ἔρχεται of 10.1 implied non-stop movement towards that destination, made an attempt to explain Jesus' journey.[40] But what possibly could have motivated the substitution of καί for a more original διά? Accordingly, as T.W. Manson notes,[41] the reading with καί is intrinsically the best, and should be accepted as most original. Given this, the setting of the Divorce Question Story is, then, *not* a trip made by Jesus *from* Galilee to Jerusalem *but a ministry in Judaea and Perea.*

Variants in Verse 2. The text of Mk 10.2, the verse which relates the identity of those who ask the tempting question on divorce, appears in two forms in the manuscript tradition. The first form, attested by such witnesses as A B K L Δ Π Ψ fam 13 28 700 892, part of the Byzantine tradition, the Coptic and Gothic versions, and (with variations over the order and presence of the article) by א C X and many others, reads that 'And there came to him Pharisees asking him...' (καὶ προσελθόντες

---

40. Cf. H.B. Swete, *The Gospel according to St Mark* (London: Macmillan, 1898), p. 214; V. Taylor, *The Gospel according to St Mark* (London: Macmillan, 1952), p. 416.

41. Manson, 'The Cleansing of the Temple', *BJRL* 33 (1951), pp. 271-82, esp. p. 273.

φαρισαῖοι ἐπηρώτων αὐτόν). The second form, attested by Western manuscripts such as D it a,b,d,k,r1 syrˢ and Origen, omit the phrase καὶ προσελθόντες φαρισαῖοι, and tell us that 'they [i.e. unnamed persons, presumably from the crowd(s) which Jesus at this point was teaching, cf. Mk 10.1b] ask him...' (καὶ ἐπηρώτων αὐτόν), ἐπηρώτον here standing as an impersonal plural.[42] In favour of the originality of the second form of this verse stands the fact that the use of impersonal plurals is consistent with Mark's style.[43] But against accepting this reading as the original text of Mk 10.2 are a number of considerations. First of all, to accept this reading as original means that one must assume that the phrase προσελθόντες φαρισαῖοι came into the non-Western witnesses through the influence of the parallel to this verse in Mt. 19.3. But the correspondence between Mt. 19.3 and the reading of Mk 10.2 in the non-Western textual tradition is not exact, or at any rate as exact as it might be if this were the case; and this fact renders the assumption of the assimilation of Mk 10.2 to its Matthean parallel somewhat dubious if not wholly unlikely.[44] Secondly, while the Western reading 'they (or 'people') asked...' may be Markan stylistically, *it is hardly so thematically.* Rarely, if ever, are the common people, those of the ὄχλος, portrayed in Mark's Gospel as questioners of Jesus.[45] Never, certainly, are they presented as those who interrogate him, as is done here, about matters of the Law.[46] And nowhere in the Second Gospel are they ever reported as saying or doing anything which tempts Jesus.[47] It should be noted, too, given the fact that Jesus answers the questions put to him in v. 2 in a manner which in Mark's Gospel is reserved for his opponents,[48] that those who ask Jesus about divorce are presumed within the Markan version of the Divorce Question story to have approached Jesus in a spirit of antagonism.[49] But except for the

42. So Taylor, *Mark*, p. 417.

43. Cf. Taylor, *Mark*, pp. 47-48; C.H. Turner, 'Markan Usage: Notes Critical and Exegetical on the Second Gospel', *JTS* 29 (1927), p. 5.

44. K. Snodgrass, 'Western Non-Interpolations', *JBL* 91 (1972), pp. 369-79, esp. p. 378.

45. On this, see A. Ambrozic, *The Hidden Kingdom* (Washington, DC: Catholic Biblical Association, 1972), p. 57.

46. This is always done by members of the Jewish religious establishment.

47. Banks, *Jesus and the Law*, p. 145. Again, this is, according to Mark, only Satan (1.13), the Pharisees (8.11), and the Pharisees and Herodians (12.15, cp. v. 13).

48. Cf. Ambrozic, *Hidden Kingdom*, p. 57.

49. Ambrozic, *Hidden Kingdom*, p. 62.

people in the country of the Gerasenes (cf. Mk 5.15-16) and those in Nazareth (cf. Mk 6.1-2) the common people are always portrayed by Mark as *favourable* to Jesus. Even in the crucifixion accounts the crowds are portrayed as those who, if not for the agitation of the chief priests, would have remained loyal to Jesus.[50] Therefore, as K. Snodgrass has observed, 'If the Western text is correct in omitting the words in question (i.e. προσελθόντες φαρισαῖοι), the passage is certainly unique in Mark'.[51] On the other hand, the phrase προσ-ελθόντες φαρισαῖοι ἐπηρώτων αὐτόν is both stylistically and thematically Markan.[52] The Pharisees are frequently portrayed by Mark as 'coming out' to Jesus to be his interlocutors.[53] Their questions to him often concern a point of Law, and are generally asked in a spirit of antagonism. And, notably, in the two other places where, as is done in Mk 10.2, the verb πειράζω is used with reference to questioners, it is in both cases descriptive of the Pharisees.[54] Given all of this, it seems more than reasonable to conclude that the majority reading of Mk 10.2 is the original Markan text. And according to Mark, then, it is the Pharisees who ask Jesus a question about divorce, and in doing so tempt him.

Variants in Verse 12a. This verse, a saying of Jesus dealing with the circumstances under which a woman commits adultery (cf. v. 12b) appears in three forms in the manuscript tradition. Alexandrian wit-nesses, including א B C L Δ Ψ 517 579 892 1342, have Jesus declare that a woman commits adultery 'if she divorces her husband and marries another' (καὶ ἐὰν αὐτὴ ἀπολύσασα τὸν ἄνδρα αὐτῆς γαμήσῃ ἄλλον). Other (primarily Byzantine) witnesses, including A W λ 22 118 1071 *pl f g*[2] *r*[2] vg syr[p] syr[h] geo' and Augustine, have Jesus say that adultery occurs 'if a woman divorces her husband and marries another' (ἐὰν γυνὴ ἀπολύσῃ τὸν ἄνδρα αὐτῆς γαμήθῃ ἄλλῳ). A third set of witnesses, including such Western and Caesarean texts as D Θ Φ 28 543 363 700 a b ff (k) q syr[s] and arm, have Jesus state that adultery is committed 'if a woman separates (or 'departs') from her husband and marries another' (γυνὴ ἐὰν [ἐὰν γυνὴ D] ἔξελθη ἀπὸ

---

50. K. Snodgrass, 'Western Non-Interpolations', p. 378.
51. Snodgrass, 'Western Non-Interpolations', p. 378.
52. Cp., e.g., Mk 8.11.
53. Cf. Bultmann, *History*, p. 52. Cp. Mk 2.24; 7.1; 8.11; 12.14.
54. Banks, *Jesus and the Law*, p. 145; Snodgrass, 'Western Non-Interpolations', p. 378.

(τοῦ) ἄνδρης καὶ γαμήσῃ ἄλλον [γαμήθῃ ἄλλῳ]).

Most commentators and modern text critics favour either the reading of Sinaiticus *et al.* or that of the (primarily) Byzantine witnesses as the original Markan text of Mk 10.12a. But in my judgment the Western/ Caesarean reading of this verse has the strongest claim to priority. For, first of all, the priority of the non Western/Caesarean texts—which presuppose, contrary to the Western/Caesarean reading, a Greco-Roman and not a Jewish legal situation with respect to woman's right or ability to initiate divorce[55]—is asserted on the grounds that something like this would have had to have been written by Mark if he was to make the teaching of Jesus on divorce/adultery contained in both this and the previous verse applicable to his Roman readers.[56] *But that Mark should want to do this is an assumption that needs to be proven.* To hold it one must presume that Mark intended the saying of Jesus which appears at vv. 11-12 to be seen as something whose primary purpose was to give moral guidance to his readers on the issue of divorce/adultery. But given that in its present context the saying has the function of summarizing and clarifying the issue over which Jesus, in the story to which the sayings are appended, was confronted, this is highly questionable. Secondly, the Western/Caesarean variant is compatible with the ruling of Jewish Law regarding a woman's right to divorce, which is what we should expect, given that the issue Jesus is asked to comment upon in the story has its home in a Jewish and not a Hellenistic-Roman setting. Thirdly, the Western/Caesarean reading represents a textual tradition current at Antioch, Caesarea, Carthage, Italy and Gaul at least as early as 150 CE.[57] The Alexandrian and Byzantine readings are, by comparison, relatively late. Fourthly, the Western/Caesarean reading has an almost identical counterpart in 1 Cor. 7.10, a saying about divorce attributed to Jesus which also prohibits a woman from separating from (χωρίζομαι) her husband. Fifthly, and most importantly, the assumption of the priority of the Western/Caesarean reading best accounts for the textual

---

55. On this, see above, note 9.

56. Cf. Charles, *Teaching*, pp. 27-29; W. Grundmann, *Das Evangelium nach Markus* (Berlin: Evangelische Verlagsanstalt, 1965), p. 205; W. Harrington, *Mark* (Wilmington, DE: Michael Glazier, 1979), p. 156; E. Haenchen, *Der Weg Jesus* (Berlin: Töpelmann, 1966), p. 337; Martin, *Mark: Evangelist and Theologian*, p. 221; Nineham, *Mark*, p. 266; Schmid, *Markus*, p. 187; Schweizer, *Mark*, p. 201, and many others.

57. Cf. Lane, *Mark*, p. 352 n. 2.

tradition of Mk 10.12. A replacement of an original ἔξελθη by ἀπολύσασα (or another derivative) can be readily explained as due to an attempt either to bring v. 12 into symmetry with v. 11, where the action of a husband in 'dismissing' (ἀπολύω) his wife is also branded adultery, or, when Mk 10.12 fell into predominantly Hellenistic hands, to make the saying more relevant for those who would read it. But a substitution of ἔξελθη for an original ἀπολύσασα (or another derivative) is not so readily explainable. To account for it, one would have to assume that the Western/Caesarean versions of Mk 10.12a got their text from a source—or, more accurately, from sources—in which the saying in v. 12a had been Judaized. That at some point before 150 CE the verse *could* have been Judaized is by no means impossible. But as D. Daube has noted, 'the opposite evolution, the Hellenizing of an expression of a Rabbinic character, is more likely'.[58]

From all of this I conclude that the reading of Mk 10.12a preserved in the Western/Caesarean manuscript tradition best represents the original Markan text of that verse.[59] Accordingly, in v. 12a what Jesus designates as adultery on the part of a woman is not divorce but desertion and remarriage.

The Transmission History of Mark 10.1-12
Most commentators who accept the priority of the Markan version of the Divorce Question tradition usually trace the tradition history of Mk 10.1-12 along the following lines: To tell his story, Mark has (a) taken up and reproduced without substantial editorial modification a traditional pronouncement story, which now appears in vv. 2-9 of his Divorce Question story, (b) has given it an introduction (v. 1) of his own composition, and (c) has rounded off the traditional pronouncement story by appending to it traditional but originally independent dominical sayings on adultery (vv. 11-12) by means of a transitional seam (v. 10) which, like v. 1, he himself composed.[60]

58. 'Terms for Divorce', p. 367. See also N.B. Stonehouse, *Origins of the Synoptic Gospels* (Grand Rapids: Eerdmans, 1963), pp. 27-28.

59. Bultmann, *History*, p. 132; Lane, *Mark*, p. 354; Taylor, *Mark*, pp. 420-21. See also R.W. Herron, Jr, 'Mark's Jesus on Divorce: Mk 10:12 Reconsidered', *JETS* 25 (1982), pp. 273-81, esp. p. 278.

60. Cf. Bultmann, *History*, pp. 25-26; Taylor, *Mark*, p. 415; A. Albertz, *Die synoptische Streitgespräche* (Berlin: Trowitzch, 1921), pp. 39-41; E. Best, *Following Jesus* (Sheffield: JSOT Press, 1981), p. 100; G. Delling, 'Das Logion Mark 10:11 (und seine Abwandlungen) im Neuen Testament', *NovT* 1 (1956), p. 265; H.C. Kee,

That Mark composed the verses which introduce respectively what has been termed the 'kernel' of the Markan Divorce Question story (i.e. vv. 2-9)[61] and the sayings on adultery (vv. 11-12) I do not doubt. But that this is the extent of his contribution to his version of the Divorce Question tradition seems to me to be less than likely. In my opinion the pronouncement story in vv. 2-9, normally thought to be pre-Markan, also stems from Mark's hand. In support of this contention I offer the following considerations:

First of all, as R. Bultmann has asserted and A. Hultgren has demonstrated, the pronouncement with which the story now found in Mk 10.2-9 climaxes (i.e. v. 9) is a dominical saying that was originally in circulation independent of its present context and devoid of any introductory 'framing' material.[62] This means that the material which now introduces and 'frames' the saying (i.e. vv. 2-8), and thus provides a setting and a reason for the saying's utterance, is a secondary, redactional construction.

Secondly, within the 'frame' of the pronouncement of v. 9 Jesus is portrayed as quoting from the Greek and not the Hebrew version of the Old Testament.[63] This indicates that the provenance of the 'frame' of the pronouncement, and therefore, of the pronouncement story itself, is a Greek and not a Palestinian milieu. One could, of course, object that the presence of a quotation from the LXX on the lips of Jesus cannot *in and of itself* be used as evidence for determining the original provenance of the material in which the quotation appears. For, as B.M. Metzger has pointed out, it is historically demonstrable that scriptural quotations, within a given context that is transferred from one

---

Community of the New Age (London: SCM Press, 1977), p. 155; R. Pesch, *Das Markusevangelium* (2 vols.; Freiburg: Herder, 1977), II, p. 119. J. Gnilka (*Das Evangelium nach Markus* [2 vols.; Neukirchen–Vluyn: Neukirchener Verlag, 1978–79], II, p. 68) limits Mark's redactional contribution to v. 1.

61. So Taylor, *Mark*, p. 415.

62. Bultmann, *History*, p. 81; A. Hultgren, *Jesus and his Adversaries: The Form and Function of the Conflict Stories in the Synoptic Tradition* (Minneapolis: Augsburg, 1979), p. 120. See also E. Klostermann, *Das Evangelium nach Markus* (Tübingen: Mohr, 1950), p. 90; A. Suhl, *Die Function der alttestamenlichen Zitate und Anspielungen im Markusevagelium* (Gütersloh: Gerd Mohn, 1965), p. 78; K. Berger, *Die Gesetzsaulegung Jesu*, I (Neukirchen: Neukirchener Verlag, 1972), p. 536.

63. Cf. Hoffmann, 'Jesus' Sayings about Divorce', p. 55; Hultgren, *Jesus and his Adversaries*, p. 121.

language to another, often do not remain unchanged.[64] But it is to be noted that in this particular case both the comment which Jesus makes in Mk 10.8b vis à vis his quotation in Mk 10.7-9 of Gen. 2.24 (i.e. that a married couple are, because of their marriage, 'no longer two but one flesh', οὐκέτι εἰσὶν δύο ἀλλὰ μία σάρξ), and the argument for the indissolubility of marriage that is implicitly drawn from it, are not only based upon the Greek version of the verse quoted (where, in contrast to the standard Hebrew text, which reads 'and *they* shall become one flesh', the Greek text reads 'and *the two* (οἱ δύο) shall become one flesh'), they are entirely dependent upon that verse for their validity.[65]

From all of this, it must be concluded that the body of Mk 10.1-12 is a late redactional composition, originating in a Greek speaking milieu. Accordingly, in establishing this, there is satisfied a condition necessary for proving that Mk 10.2-9 is Markan, namely, that the pronouncement story contained in these verses would have to stem not, as would have to be the case if the assertion of the traditional nature of the pericope is to remain valid, from the earliest stages of the Synoptic Tradition, but from the tradition's later, secondary Hellenistic strata, where Mark's activities as redactor/author would have taken place.

But traditionists, redactors and authors other than Mark also worked to assemble or compose Synoptic pronouncement stories during this period and could, therefore, have been responsible for the construction of Mk 10.1-12. Is there anything which shows that the pericope originates with Mark? There are, I submit, four things.

First, there is the fact that the structure of the pronouncement story in Mk 10.2-9 is similar to that found in other Markan pronouncement stories which are demonstrably either redactional products built up of previously disparate material or wholly Markan compositions.[66]

Secondly, Mk 10.1-9 is replete with characteristically Markan stylistic traits such as multiplication of cognate verbs within the same immediate context (cf. vv. 1-2, ἔρχεται εἰς...συμπορεύονται...πρὸς...προσελθόντες),[67] the use of two participles within the span of a single

64. Argyle, 'Scriptural Quotations in Q Material', *ExpTim* 65 (1953–54), p. 125.

65. Hoffmann, 'Jesus' Sayings about Divorce', p. 55; Hultgren, *Jesus and his Adversaries*, p. 121.

66. Cp. Mk 12.13-17. On the redactional nature of this pericope, see my discussion of its tradition history in the following chapter, pp. 290-99.

67. On this as Markan, see F. Neirynck, *Duality in Mark: Contributions to the Study of Markan Redaction* (Leuven: Leuven University Press, 1972), p. 77.

sentence (cf. v. 2, προσελθόντες...πειράζοντες),[68] the repetition of a motif within the narrative and discourse material ingredient to a given context (cp. v. 2, καὶ προσελθόντες φαρισαῖοι ἐπηρώτων αὐτόν with v. 10, καὶ εἰς τὴν οἰκίαν πάλιν οἱ μαθηταὶ περὶ τούτου ἐπηρώτων αὐτόν, and cf. v. 8, καὶ ἔσονται οἱ δύο εἰς σάρκα μίαν· ὥστε οὐκέτι εἰσὶν δύο ἀλλὰ μία σάρξ),[69] correspondence in discourse, as between the vocabulary ingredient to a question and that of the question's answer (cp. v. 2, εἰ ἔξεστιν...ἀπολῦσαι with v. 4, ἐπέτρεψεν Μωϋσῆς βιβλίον ἀποστασίου γράψαι καὶ ἀπολῦσαι),[70] the use of the ἐπηρωτάω... ἀποκρίνομαι construction to bind a question and its answer together (cf. vv. 2-3, καὶ...ἐπηρώτων αὐτὸν...ὁ δὲ ἀποκριθεὶς εἶπεν αὐτοῖς),[71] correspondence between a biblical quotation and the interpretative comment that follows it (cp. vv. 6-8a, ἄρσεν καὶ θῆλυ ἐποίησεν αὐτούς· ἕνεκεν τούτου καταλείψει ἄνθρωπος...καὶ ἔσονται οἱ δύο εἰς σάρκα μίαν· with vv. 8b-9, ὥστε οὐκέτι εἰσὶν δύο ἀλλὰ μία σάρξ. ὃ οὖν ὁ θεὸς συνέζευξεν ἄνθρωπος μὴ χωριζέτω),[72] the use of double negatives (cf. v. 8, οὐκέτι εἰσὶν δύο ἀλλά..., and v. 9, συνέζευξεν...μὴ χωριζέτω),[73] and the casting of sayings of Jesus in antithetical parallelism (cf. v. 9).[74]

Thirdly, certain words—φαρισαῖοι, προσελθόντες, πειράζω, ἔξεστιν, ἐπερωτάω used in conjunction with ἀποκρίνομαι, ὥστε—which are key terms in the pericope, are typically Markan.[75]

Finally, two significant Markan themes—(1) the failure of the Pharisees to acknowledge that with Jesus a new situation arrives which clarifies the purpose for which the Mosaic regulations have been allowed, and, (2) the Pharisees as the embodiment of σκληροκαρδία—are given voice and developed within the pronouncement story.[76]

---

68. Cf. Neirynck, *Duality*, p. 82.
69. Cf. Neirynck, *Duality*, p. 97.
70. Cf. Neirynck, *Duality*, p. 126.
71. Cf. Neirynck, *Duality*, p. 130.
72. Cf. Neirynck, *Duality*, p. 124.
73. Cf. Neirynck, *Duality*, p. 92.
74. Cf. Neirynck, *Duality*, p. 133.
75. On this, see E.J. Pryke, *Redactional Style in the Markan Gospel* (Cambridge: Cambridge University Press, 1978), pp. 115-17.
76. On the first of these themes in Mark, see Banks, *Jesus and the Law*, p. 131. On the second, cf. Mk 3.4; 7.6-8. See also K. Berger, 'Hartherzidkeit und Gottes

Since, therefore, the pronouncement story in Mk 10.1-9 is not only a late, redactional composition originating in a Greek speaking milieu, but is also one which displays characteristically Markan style, vocabulary and thematic interests, I feel it more than reasonable to conclude that the story stems wholly from Mark's hand.

If my history-of-traditions analysis of Mk 10.1-12 is correct, we must then conclude that Mark himself is responsible not only for creating the story of the confrontation between Jesus and the Pharisees over a question on divorce, but also for the shaping of this story in terms of a temptation tradition. In other words, according to my analysis, *the tradition that Jesus was tempted when queried by the Pharisees on the issue of divorce originates with Mark and was not known to the early church before Mark constructed the story which now serves as its narrative 'vehicle'.* How this conclusion bears upon the larger question with which our overall examination of the individual New Testament temptation traditions is concerned (viz, whether or not there was within the early Church a uniform and widely known tradition concerning the content of Jesus' experience of πειρασμός) can only be ascertained after we have established what Mark presents as the nature and content of the temptation to which he says Jesus was subjected when he was confronted with the Pharisees' divorce question. And so it is to this issue that I now turn.

The Nature of the Divorce Question Temptation according to Mark
My purpose now is to establish the nature of Jesus' Divorce Question temptation as Mark portrays it. The question to be dealt with is whether Mark intended the temptation which he says Jesus experienced on account of his confrontation with the Pharisees' question on divorce to be seen as a 'secular' or a 'religious' 'testing', as involving a genuine search for truth or a 'putting to the proof' of Jesus' faithfulness to God. To determine this it is necessary to have answers to the following questions:

- What specifically is being asked by the Pharisees when they approach Jesus and say εἰ ἔξεστιν ἀνδρὶ γυναῖκα ἀπολῦσαι?

Gesetz: Die Vorgeschichte des antijüdischen Vorwurfs in Mc 10:5', *ZNW* 61 (1970), pp. 1-47.

- Is the question of Mk 10.2 sincere? That is, does it deal with an issue over which, according to Mark, the Pharisees themselves or the Judaism of which they are a part had no firm conclusion? And is it asked because Jesus' position on the matter at hand was unknown?

- Does Jesus, according to Mark, feel any sort of necessity or constraint to take the position with respect to divorce that Mark portrays him as taking.

To answer the first question we must examine the meaning with which the word ἔξεστιν, the key term in the question put to Jesus, is used in Mk 10.2. To answer the second question we must first outline what can be known from contemporary sources concerning the attitude or attitudes found in first-century Judaism on divorce, and then examine whether or not Mark presumes that Jesus' attitude towards divorce was something the Pharisees would have known before the events of the Divorce Question story. To answer the third question we must establish why, according to Mark, Jesus takes the stand on divorce that he does.

The Meaning of ἔξεστιν *in Mark 10.2.* Most commentators, noting that in Jewish writings ἔξεστιν (lit. 'it is lawful', 'it is free', 'it is permissible') often relates to the will of God and is used of legal definitions,[77] think that the term bears a juridical sense in Mk 10.2 and take it to mean 'commanded or forbidden by the Torah'.[78] If this is the case, then the question which the Pharisees put to Jesus in Mark's Divorce Question story is 'Does the Law of Moses allow a man to divorce his wife?'.[79] But that ἔξεστιν is used in a juridical sense in Mk 10.2 seems highly unlikely.

In the first place, 'it is prescribed in the Mosaic Law' *is not the only meaning that* ἔξεστιν *bears in Jewish writings*. A looser meaning of 'it is seemly' is attested, for example, in 2 Esd. 4.14; Est. 4.2; 1 Macc. 14.44. It appears with this meaning in Mt. 15.26; 20.25; Jn 18.31; Acts 8.37; 22.25 and 2 Cor. 12.4. And notably, *it is also used in this*

---

77. Cf. W. Foerster, 'ἔξεστιν, κτλ.', *TDNT*, II, p. 561.

78. Dungan, *Sayings of Jesus*, p. 111; Lane, *Mark*, p. 353; Nineham, *Mark*, p. 260; Schmid, *Markus*, p. 186; Schweizer, *Mark*, p. 202; Suhl, *Die Function*, p. 74; Taylor, *Mark*, p. 417.

79. Cf. Schweizer, *Mark*, p. 203; H. Anderson, *The Gospel of Mark* (London: Oliphants, 1976), p. 241.

non-juridical sense by Mark himself, at Mk 3.4 and 12.14.[80] Secondly, the assumption that ἔξεστιν is used juridically in Mk 10.2 makes the Pharisees' question moot at best, ridiculous at worst, *and certainly nothing which conceivably represents any kind of a 'test' for Jesus.* For, as is acknowledged by both Jesus and the Pharisees within the body of the Divorce Question story (cf. vv. 3-4), the Law at Deut. 24.1 *concedes divorce's legality*.[81] Thirdly, on the assumption that ἔξεστιν is used juridically in Mk 10.2, the Pharisees' response to Jesus' counter-question, τί ὑμῖν ἐνετείλατο Μωϋσῆς; (cf. v. 3), should not be their allusion to Deut. 24.1 (cf. v. 4) but something like 'That is, more or less, what we asked you'. *For on this showing, Jesus' counter-question simply repeats the Pharisees' original question to him.*[82] Fourthly, if we assume that ἔξεστιν is used juridically in Mk 10.2, then it is difficult to know why Mark has Jesus and the Pharisees exchange remarks beyond v. 4 of the Divorce Question story. For on the assumption that ἔξεστιν bears the juridical sense here, then the story should have ended with v. 4, since with the Pharisees' response of 'Moses allowed a man to write a bill of divorcement to put her away', the question which the Pharisees purportedly ask in v. 2 *is effectively answered and the matter at hand is settled.* Fifthly, the form of the whole Divorce Question story focuses not upon what is prescribed by the Law regarding divorce, but *upon what Jesus' view of the matter is*, and, as D.R. Catchpole notes, it is with this fact in mind that the meaning of ἔξεστιν in Mk 10.2 is to be determined.[83] In light of all of this, as well as given what I have noted above, I conclude then that ἔξεστιν in Mk 10.2 bears its looser, non-juridical sense. Accordingly, Mk 10.2 is to be rendered 'Is it in your [i.e. Jesus'] view right that a man should divorce his wife?' and *the question itself is to be seen as concerned with unveiling not Jesus' knowledge of the Law but his own opinion on the legitimacy of divorce.*

Divorce in Judaism. The evidence which allows us to outline the attitude (or attitudes) taken by Jesus' Jewish contemporaries towards divorce appears primarily in the following texts: Josephus, *Ant.* 4.8.23 (§253); 15.7.10 (§259); Philo, *Spec. Leg.* 3.5; the Mishnah, *Giṭ.* 9.10 (*b. Giṭ.* 90a).

80. Cf. Catchpole, 'Synoptic Divorce Material', p. 114.
81. On this, see below, p. 282.
82. Catchpole, 'Synoptic Divorce Material', p. 114.
83. Catchpole, 'Synoptic Divorce Material', pp. 114-15.

The first Josephan text, an exposition for non-Jewish readers of contemporary Jewish understanding of the Mosaic legislation contained in Deut. 24.1-4, reads:

> He who desires to be divorced from the wife who is living with him for whatever cause—and with mortals many such may arise—must certify in writing that he will have no further intercourse with her; for thus will the woman obtain permission to consort with another, which thing ere then must not be permitted. But if she be maltreated by the other also, or, if upon his death her former husband wishes to marry her, she shall not be permitted to return to him.[84]

The second Josephan text, the story of the divorce initiated by Salome, the sister of Herod the Great, against Costabarus, Herod's appointee to governorship of Idumea, reads:

> But sometime afterward, when Salome happened to quarrel with Costabarus, she sent him a bill of divorce, and dissolved her marriage with him, though this was not according to the Jewish Laws; for with us it is lawful for a husband to do so; but a wife, if she departs from her husband, cannot of herself be married to another, unless her former husband puts her away.

The Philonian text, an exposition of Deut. 24.2, reads:

> Another commandment is that if a woman after parting from her husband for any cause whatever marries another and then again becomes a widow, whether this second husband is alive or dead, she must not return to her first husband but ally herself with any other rather but him, because she has broken with the rules that bound her in the past and cast them into oblivion when she chose new love-ties in preference to the old.[85]

The Mishnaic text, a report of one of the debates between the Rabbis Hillel and Shammai, contemporaries of Jesus, with an addendum by Akiba, a Rabbi prominent in the early second century CE, reads:

> The School of Shammai say: A man may not divorce his wife unless he has found any unchastity in her, for it is written 'Because he has found in her indecency in anything' [Deut. 24.1a]. And the School of Hillel say: (He may divorce her) even if she spoiled a dish for him, for it is written 'Because he has found indecency in anything'. R. Akiba says, Even if he

---

84. Translation of this and the subsequent Josephan text is that of H. St John Thakeray, *Josephus*, V (New York: Putnam, 1926–65), p. 597.

85. Translation is that of F.H. Colson and G.H. Whitaker, *Philo* (Cambridge, MA: Harvard University Press, 1929–1962).

found another fairer than she, for it is written, 'And it shall be if she find
no favour in his eyes...'

Given all of this, and assuming that these texts are fully representative of
Jewish views on this matter, we may make the following observation:
Judaism in Jesus' time did not condemn divorce as such. On the contrary, it presupposed, on the basis of Deut. 24.1-4, the permissibility of
the dissolution of marriage, at least under certain circumstances.[86] *That
divorce was recognized as lawful within Judaism is also, notably, what
Mark presents to be the case.*[87] Indeed, as Mk 10.4 reveals, it is the very
presupposition under which Mark has the Pharisees approach Jesus in
the Divorce Question story.

The Pharisees' Knowledge of Jesus' Position on Divorce. Does Mark
presume that Jesus' position on the seemliness of divorce was something
which was unknown to the Pharisees when they ask εἰ ἔξεστιν ἀνδρὶ
γυναῖκα ἀπολῦσαι? To answer this we need to take into account all
that is implied by the fact that in Mark's Gospel Jesus is portrayed as
one who is readily recognized as 'John the Baptist all over again'.[88]

According to Mark, John is the Prophet of the end time, the eschatological messenger of Malachi,[89] a preacher of judgment,[90] one who

---

86. As noted above (n. 19), Fitzmyer contends that one group in first-century
Palestine, the Essenes, *did* prohibit divorce, seeing such action as mandated by the
Law. His evidence is 11QTemple 57.17-19. This, he claims, when read in light of CD
4.12b–5.14a, shows that the Essenes saw the Torah as proscribing divorce. But, as
G. Vermes has shown ('Sectarian Matrimonial Halakhah in the Damascus Rule', *JJS*
25 [1974], pp. 197-202; cf. also B. Vawter, 'Divorce and the New Testament', *CBQ*
39 [1977], pp. 528-42), the issue at the center of these texts is not divorce but
polygamy. In light of this, the conclusion that divorce as such was accepted as
legitimate by all parties in first-century Judaism still stands.

87. In Mark the Pharisaic position on a given matter is meant to be seen as
normative for Judaism in general. Cf. Mk 7.3.

88. Cf. Mk 6.14, 16; 8.28. On this as the meaning of Herod's statement, Ὅν ἐγὼ
ἀπεκεφάλισα Ἰωάννην, οὗτος ἠγέρθη (Mk. 6.16), see Branscomb, *Mark*, p. 109;
T.W. Manson, *The Servant Messiah* (Cambridge: Cambridge University Press,
1953), p. 69; A.E.J. Rawlinson, *The Gospel according to St Mark* (London: Metheun,
1931). p. 79; Taylor, *Mark*, p. 309; J. Wellhausen, *Das Evangelium Marci* (Berlin:
Reimer, 1909), p. 46.

89. Cf. W. Wink, *John the Baptist in the Gospel Tradition* (Cambridge:
Cambridge University Press, 1968), p. 3.

90. Cf. Mk 1.7-8.

summons Israel to repentance,[91] and, of course, a Baptizer.[92] But in the Gospel he is also and, perhaps, best known as one who stood adamantly opposed to the dissolution of marriage, particularly when this dissolution was undertaken so that the parties initiating such action could take to themselves other spouses.[93] Accordingly, then, for Jesus to be recognized and publicly proclaimed, as he is according to Mark, as John's alter ego,[94] then *he, too, had to be known as one who stood opposed to divorce and remarriage*.[95] That Mark indeed presumes this to be the case and, more importantly, that he intended it to be seen as *a fact that was both widely known and generally apparent long before Jesus' post-Galilean, pre-Judaean, Perean public ministry*, is confirmed by the fact that well in advance of the 'date' of the Divorce Question story he presents Herod Antipas himself—then the tetrarch of Galilee and Perea who, on account of putting away his first wife in order to marry his brother's spouse, was the prime target for John's anti-divorce/remarriage polemic—as overcome with worry that given Jesus' ascendancy to the role of noted and outspoken public figure, John's charges against him (Herod) were going to be made all over again.[96]

From this we may conclude, then, that according to Mark, when the Pharisees approach Jesus on the occasion of his appearance in Perea, they are satisfied that if pushed to state openly his opinion on the seemliness of divorce, Jesus would pronounce against it.

The 'Necessity' of Jesus' Teaching on Divorce. According to Mark, Jesus stands adamantly against divorce, especially divorce undertaken

91. Cf. Mk 1.4-5.

92. Cf. Mk 1.4-5, 8, 9.

93. Cf. Mk 6.18. On John's stance, see H.W. Hoerner, *Herod Antipas: A Contemporary of Jesus Christ* (Cambridge: Cambridge University Press, 1972), pp. 137-40.

94. On this as the implication of the view that Jesus was John *redivivus*, see Hoerner, *Herod Antipas*, p. 190. That Jesus was not only widely known but also publicly proclaimed as John's *alter ego* is the clear implication of Mk 6.16 and 8.28. In both instances people (i.e. the general public), not just a few individuals, say (λέγειν—probably not to be understood as 'think to themselves'), and say repeatedly, that Jesus was John.

95. Cf. F.C. Burkitt, 'Jesus and Divorce', *JTS* 5 (1904), pp. 628-29.

96. According to Mark, Herod's hearing about Jesus and his [Herod's] voicing of his fears take place while Jesus was still in the early stages of his 'Galilean' ministry.

for the purpose of rendering one free to take another marriage partner.[97] But why, in Mark's eyes, does he take this position? It is not because Jesus had come under the influence of the teaching of any of his contemporaries on this subject. For Jesus' absolute prohibition of the dissolution of marriage is something quite new in relation to the teaching on the permissibility of divorce which, as we have seen above, both historically, as well as in Mark's presentation of things, prevailed in first-century Judaism. What, then, according to Mark, is the origin of Jesus' anti-divorce/remarriage teaching? Given that Mark has Jesus use Gen. 1.27 and 2.24 as scriptural proof that marriage is indissoluble (cf. Mk 10.7-9), it might be thought that according to Mark Jesus arrived at his position against divorce as a result of an ethical revaluation of contemporary thought on the matter which in turn was reached through a study of the first two chapters of Genesis. But this is very unlikely since in Mark's Gospel, when Jesus quotes scriptural passages in response to questions or accusations of his opponents, *he does so only to support a standpoint which he has already arrived at for reasons other than those contained in the scriptural proofs adduced on these occasions.*[98]

A more plausible explanation for the reason the Markan Jesus takes his particular stance on the indissolubility of marriage is that Jesus feels that adopting such a position is one of the exigencies of the ἐξουσία with which he is endowed. That this is indeed the case is clear for two reasons. First, Jesus' teaching on the indissolubility of marriage possesses a form and a tone of authority which is remarkably similar to that of the dominical teaching which elsewhere in the Gospel Jesus utters when he is speaking under the aegis and constraint of his divinely imputed ἐξουσία.[99] Secondly, Jesus' teaching is presented by Mark as a prophetic pronouncement[100] the validity of which stems solely from the fact that it is Jesus, the Messiah, who propounds it.[101] In Mark's view, then, Jesus takes the stance he does with respect to divorce and

---

97. Cf. Mk 10.11-12.

98. Cf., e.g., Mk 2.23-28. See also Isaksson, *Marriage and Ministry*, p. 145.

99. Cf. Mk 2.8-11; 25-28; 7.6-8, 9-13.

100. Catchpole, 'Synoptic Divorce Material', p. 126; J. Jeremias, *New Testament Theology. I. The Proclamation of Jesus* (New York: Charles Scribner & Sons, 1971), p. 225.

101. On this, see Banks, *Jesus and the Law*, pp. 150-51. See also, H.J. Schoeps, 'Restitutio Principii as the Basis for the Nova Lex Jesu', *JBL* 66 (1947), pp. 456-64, esp. pp. 453-55.

remarriage because, given the authority he possesses, and the manner in which this authority informs his vision concerning both the will of God and what is to be proclaimed in light of it, he stands impelled to do so. His showing himself, if pressed on the matter, as standing against divorce/remarriage is in the end wholly a matter of remaining faithful to the divine commission he has been called to fulfil.

Conclusions. With all of this before us, what then can be inferred concerning Mark's view of the nature of the temptation which Jesus experiences on account of the Pharisees' question on divorce? It is undoubtedly that the temptation is intended to be seen as of the 'religious' and not of the 'secular' kind. For the question which puts Jesus 'to the test' is not presented as something which arises out of a genuine search for truth. It was not asked to make something clear which was unknown, or to help settle a dispute raging within the various sectors of Judaism, or to resolve a doubt which plagued the Pharisees. Rather, it is presented as a challenge to Jesus to state openly a position which the Pharisees already know Jesus is bound to take if he is what his words and his works proclaim him to be, a position which Jesus himself feels constrained to uphold if he is to remain faithful to the divine commission he has received.

The Content of Jesus' Divorce Question Temptation

But why, according to Mark, should being forced to state openly his opinion on the seemliness of divorce bring Jesus to the brink of unfaithfulness? How, in Mark's presentation of things, does the Pharisees' question on divorce plunge Jesus into a situation where disobedience to God's will is a possible, if not a desirable option? What, in short, is the content of Jesus' Divorce Question temptation?

To answer these questions let us focus on just what, according to Mark, Jesus would become involved in should he give an open and unambiguously negative answer to the Pharisees' question. There are, I think, two main things. The first thing Jesus would become involved in is a direct contravention of the Mosaic Law and a denial of its validity.[102]

The second thing is a confrontation with Herod Antipas, the tetrarch of the territory in which Jesus was teaching when faced with the

---

102. Taylor, *Mark*, p. 417.

Pharisees' temptation question on divorce.[103] For, as Mark well knew, Herod had divorced his first wife, the daughter of Aretas, king of the Herodian's traditional enemies, the Nabataeans,[104] to marry his brother's wife, Herodias[105] (who in turn deserted her husband to marry Antipas).[106] In this he had shown himself more interested in placing the satisfaction of his own desires ahead of both obedience to the Torah and the welfare of his people. His actions not only violated Mosaic restrictions on divorce and remarriage,[107] they also jeopardized the safety of those he governed, since they nullified a peace treaty that had been established with Nabatea through Antipas' marriage of Aretas' daughter[108] and, as N. Glueck expressed it, 'sounded the tocsin of war'.[109] So, given where Jesus was, and, consequently, whose jurisdiction he was under, *an open statement on his part on the illegitimacy of divorce and remarriage would have been tantamount to a condemnation of Herod's personal morality and public policies,*[110] a condemnation Herod could not easily ignore.

Now it is important to note that the two things that Jesus would become involved in are not matters of little consequence. On the contrary, *they are specifically things which would render him liable to death.* To contravene the law and declare it invalid was considered

---

103. J.W. Bowman, *The Gospel of Mark* (Leiden: Brill, 1965), p. 208; Cranfield, *Mark*, p. 319; Herron, 'Mark's Jesus on Divorce', pp. 278-79; Lane, *Mark*, p. 354; Nineham, *Mark*, p. 264; Stein, 'Is it Lawful', p. 118 n. 9; Taylor, *Mark*, p. 417. On Jesus being in Herod (and Herodias's domain), see above on the text-critical discussion of Mk 10.1. See also Hoehner, *Herod Antipas*, p. 55. Herod Antipas was appointed tetrarch of Perea (as well as of Galilee and Trachonitis) by Augustus in 4 BCE and ruled there until 39 CE. Cf. Josephus *Ant.* 17.188.317-18; *War* 1.664.

104. Cf. Josephus, *Ant.* 18.100-25, esp. 110. On the Nabataeans and Nabatean–Herodian hostility, see N. Glueck, *Deities and Dolphins: The Story of the Nabateans* (London: Farrer, Straus & Giroux, 1966), pp. 40, 375; Hoehner, *Herod Antipas*, pp. 142-43; C.H. Kraeling, *John the Baptist* (New York: Charles Scribner & Sons, 1951), pp. 88-91.

105. Cf. Mk 6.17-18; Josephus, *Ant.* 18.100-25.

106. Cf. Josephus, *Ant.* 18.136.

107. Cf. Lev. 20.21; 18.16. See also the extended discussion of this issue by Hoehner, *Herod Antipas*, pp. 137-39 (n. 4).

108. Hoerner, *Herod Antipas*, p. 143; Kraeling, *John the Baptist*, pp. 89-91.

109. Glueck, *Dieties and Dolphins*, p. 40.

110. Hoerner, *Herod Antipas*, p. 146; Kraeling, *John the Baptist*, p. 90-91; Taylor, *Mark*, p. 311.

'leading Israel astray',[111] an activity the penalty for which was stoning.[112] To criticize Herod in the matter of his marriage to Herodias was, in Herod's eyes, an act of disloyalty, indeed, sedition,[113] punishable by arrest, imprisonment and, eventually beheading.[114]

Further, a willingness to confront Herod over the matter of his divorce could be taken as a declaration in support of the idea that those who, like Herod, flouted God's Law, and consequently pushed themselves 'beyond the pale' into the realm of 'sinners' or 'the wicked', were not deserving of God's forgiveness, but only his judgment.

In light of this, it becomes clear why, according to Mark, the Pharisees' forcing Jesus to state openly his opinion on the seemliness of divorce brings Jesus to the brink of unfaithfulness. To do so is for him to run the risk of losing his life. In the face of this risk, the path of not speaking forthrightly, of denying what God has revealed to be the truth in this matter, is most assuredly the more desirable option. But to take this path would be to hold that 'saving one's life' was more important than proclaiming the Gospel.

So the content of Jesus' Divorce question temptation is whether he is willing to obey God both when such obedience entails bringing about his own destruction and when in not doing so, in not remaining obedient, he could 'save himself'.

---

111. Catchpole, 'Synoptic Divorce Material', p. 127.

112. *M. Sanh.* 7.4.

113. Cf. Josephus, *Ant.* 118-19. As Kraeling (*John the Baptist*, pp. 90-91) notes, to criticize Herod's divorce and remarriage 'meant aligning the pious Jewish inhabitants of Perea with those of Arabic stock against their sovereign and thus fermenting sedition and encouraging insurrection'.

114. Mk 6.17-18, 27.

Chapter 10

THE TRADITION OF JESUS' TAX QUESTION TEMPTATION

The Accounts of the Tradition and their Relationship

I turn now to an analysis of the tradition that Jesus was tempted when confronted with a question concerning the legitimacy of paying taxes to Caesar. The tradition appears three times in the Synoptic Gospels, at Mt. 22.17-18, at Mk 12.14-15 and at Lk. 20.23,[1] each time within the context of a story which outlines an attempt of members of the Jewish religious establishment to entrap Jesus in his speech (cf. Mt. 22.15-22; cp. Mk 12.13-17; Lk. 20.20-26).[2]

Given the amount of material common to, and the extent of the verbal agreement both between and among, the three Synoptic versions of the tradition *and* their respective contextualizing stories, the versions cannot be regarded as independent of one another.[3] One is the basis for the other two. So, unlike the Synoptic accounts of Jesus' Wilderness temptation and the demand for a 'sign', behind the canonical Gospel accounts of Jesus' Tax Question temptation there seems to be only one 'primary' tradition. But which of these three versions of Tax Question story best represents that 'primary' tradition'? This surely is that of

---

1.   Accepting the reading of A C D W Θ Ψ, among other manuscripts. It also appears at *Egerton Papyrus 2* frag. 2 recto. See below for a discussion of this text.

2.   So, too, the story surrounding the tradition to be found in *Egerton Papyrus 2* Frag. 2 recto (as is apparent from context). The tradition of Jesus being confronted with a question about paying Caesar's tax is reproduced by Justin in *Apol.* 1.17.2 (for the text, see below, n. 16) but those who present the question are identified only as 'some people'.

3.   On both the exact amount of material common to, and the extent of the verbal agreement between, the Matthean, Markan and Lukan versions of the Tax Question temptation Tradition and their respective contextualizing stories, see C.H. Giblin, 'The Things of God in the Question concerning Tribute to Caesar (Lk. 20:25; Mk 12:17; Mt. 22:21)', *CBQ* 33 (1971), pp. 515-16.

Mark. For both the Matthean and the Lukan versions of the tradition can be shown to be secondary to and derived from Mk 12.13-17.[4]

4. Cf. F.W. Beare, *The Earliest Records of Jesus* (New York: Abingdon, 1962), p. 212. For a contrary opinion, see W.R. Farmer, *The Synoptic Problem: A Critical Analysis* (Macon, GA: Mercer University Press, 1964), pp. 262-64; C.S. Mann, *Mark* (Garden City: Doubleday, 1988), pp. 471-72.

That the Matthean version of the tradition is both secondary to, and derived from, that found in Mark seems clear from the following considerations: (1) The wording of Mt. 22.17-18, as well as that of Mt. 22.15-16; 19-22, is primarily that of Mk 12.13 and Mk 12.16-17 respectively (on this see J.C. Fenton, *St Matthew* [Baltimore: Pelican, 1963], p. 352); (2) As R.H. Gundry (*Matthew: A Commentary on his Literary and Theological Art* [Grand Rapids: Eerdmans, 1983], pp. 441-45) has shown, in those instances where the Matthean version of the temptation tradition and its contextualizing story differ in wording from that of the Markan version of these elements, the differences are usually stylistic and grammatical improvements upon what is found in Mark. Moreover, these differences are often replete with Mattheanisms; (3) As is evident in Mt. 22.17—where the Matthean phrase τί σοι δοκεῖ (cp. Mt. 17.25) appears between the Markan phrases οὐ γὰρ βλέπεις εἰς πρόσωπον ἀνθρώπων and ἔξεστιν δοῦναι κῆνσον Καίσαρι ἢ οὔ, found at Mk 12.14—what is peculiarly Matthean in both Mt. 22.17-18 and Mt. 22.15-16, 19-22 rarely replaces elements integral to the respective Markan parallels of the verses in Matthew, but is inserted into the framework of these parallels.

That Mark's version of the Tax Question tradition is the source for that of Luke seems clear for several reasons. First, Luke follows Mark's lead in placing the tradition and its contextualizing story after the parable of the Wicked Husbandmen (Lk. 20.9-19; cp. 12.1-12) and before the story of the Sadducees' Question about the Resurrection of the Dead (Lk. 20.27-40; cp. Mk 12.18-27); secondly, the wording of Lk. 20.23, as well as that of Lk. 20.20-22 and 20.24-26, while differing at specific points (for these, see J.A. Fitzmyer, *Luke X–XXIV* [Garden City: Doubleday, 1985], pp. 1289-90), is, as T. Scramm has demonstrated (*Der Markus-Stoff bei Lukas* [Cambridge: Cambridge University Press, 1971], pp. 168-70), still basically that of Mk 12.13 and Mk 12.16-17 respectively. More importantly, in those instances where the Lukan version of the temptation tradition and its contextualizing story differ in wording from that of the Markan version of these elements (e.g. v. 21 [cp. Mk 12.14], where Luke does have not have Mark's difficult καὶ οὐ μέλει σοι περὶ οὐδενός, and has the Septuagintism λαμβάνεις πρόσωπον instead of Mark's curious βλέπεις εἰς πρόσωπον ἀνθρώπων, and v. 20 where Luke has an explicit statement about Roman political jurisdiction and the prefect's authority that cannot be found in Mk), the differences are not only stylistic improvements upon, or explications of, what is found in Mark. As Fitzmyer (*Luke X–XXIV*, p. 1289) has noted, they also serve Luke's interest in showing how the Roman social order was to be evaluated in light of the standard of the social patterns that he proclaimed as God's will. (For an extended discussion of these patterns, see R.J. Cassidy, *Jesus, Politics, and Society: A Study of*

Accordingly, to lay the groundwork necessary for determining whether there was within the early church a unified conception of the nature and content of Jesus' Tax Question temptation, we need to focus our attention on Mark's version of the tradition.

The Markan Version of Jesus' Tax Question Temptation

The Tradition History of the Markan Tax Question Story

Most commentators who have dealt with the issue of the tradition history of the Markan story concerning the Question of the Payment of Taxes to Caesar (Mk 12.13-17) regard the story not only as pre-Markan in origin, but also as owing little of its present, particular Markan form to Mark's editorial activities. With the exception of vv. 13 and 17b, what we now find in Mk 12.13-17 is generally thought to be a faithful and substantially unaltered reproduction of a traditional unit of material which was already fixed in its present form and wording long before it was taken up by Mark.[5] To its proponents, this view of the tradition-

---

Luke's Gospel [Maryknoll: Orbis, 1978].) Finally, assuming Lukan priority here is not without its difficulties. Why would Mark have eliminated Lk. 20.26 (the explicit statement that Jesus' opponents were not able to catch him [ἐπιλαβέσθαι] in anything he said), as the view of Lukan priority assumes he has done, had Mark had Lk before him? The statement is, after all, consistent not only with Mark's notice in Mk 12.13 that this (i.e. entrapment) is what Jesus' opponents had explicitly set out to do, but also with Mark's remark in Mk 12.17 (and with his interest in showing, cf. Mk 12.34) that they are roundly frustrated in their objective. And why would Mark have substituted the Latinism κῆνσος for φόρος when the latter was the proper Greek term for the tax discussed within the story, and why would he replace πανγουρίαν with ὑπόκρισιν when 'trickery' serves—just as admirably as does 'play acting'—Mark's ostensible purpose of emphasizing that Jesus is not taken in by his questioners? (With respect to the alleged substitution of κῆνσος for φόρος, it is no argument to state that Mark did this as a service to his [Roman] readers to help them understand which tax Jesus was questioned about. For even assuming a Roman provenance for Mark's Gospel, φόρος as a term referring to the particular tax that is the subject matter of the debate in Mk 12.13-17 was hardly unknown to them, as Rom. 13.6 shows.) Of course, other opinions have been voiced. Farmer (*The Synoptic Problem*, pp. 262-64) and Mann (*Mark*, pp. 471-72) see Mk 12.13-17 as a conflation of Mt. 22.15-20 and Lk. 20.20-26 with the Lukan text as the preferred model. And B. Weiss (*Die Quellen des Lukasevangeliums* [Stuttgart: J.G. Cotta, 1907], pp. 212-14) argues that here Luke employs his own special source. On the validity of these opinions, see T. Scramm, *Der Markus-Stoff*, p. 170.

5.   Cf. V. Taylor, *The Gospel according to St Mark* (London: Macmillan, 1955),

history of the Markan story is substantiated by conclusions drawn from three interrelated considerations. First, form-critical analysis shows that Mk 12.13-17 is to be considered a 'pronouncement story' (to use Vincent Taylor's terminology) in that, in conformity with the particular characteristics of this 'form', the story of the Question of the Payment of Taxes to Caesar culminates in a saying of Jesus (v. 17a, b) which expresses some ethical or religious precept, and the narrative element of the story (vv. 13-16) which leads up to the saying serves only to 'frame' the saying by noting both the situation in which the word was spoken and its occasion.[6] Secondly, the apodictic saying of Jesus in v. 17 with which the story climaxes is not only undoubtedly traditional,[7] but it is also of the sort which could never have circulated independently, devoid of some 'data as to the situation' in which and for which it was spoken.[8] Thirdly, the verses which lead up to the saying, which give it its setting

---

p. 478; R. Bultmann, *The History of the Synoptic Tradition* (Oxford: Basil Blackwell, 1963), p. 26; D.E. Nineham, *St Mark* (London: Penguin, 1964), p. 314; M. Albertz, *Die Synoptischen Streitgespräche* (Berlin: Trocwitz, 1921), pp. 26-27; A. Hultgren, *Jesus and his Adversaries: The Form and Function of the Synoptic Conflict Stories in the Synoptic Tradition* (Minneapolis: Augsburg, 1979), pp. 75-76; R. Pesch, *Das Evangelium nach Markus* (Freiburg: Herders, 1977), II, pp. 224-29. According to J. Gnilka (*Das Evangelium nach Markus: Mk. 8:27–16:8* [Zürich: Neukirchener Verlag, 1979], pp. 150-55), v. 14b is also redactional.

6.   On the form of the 'pronouncement story' see V. Taylor, *The Formation of the Gospel Tradition* (London: Macmillan, 1935), pp. 63-87; R. Bultmann, *Form Criticism: A New Method of New Testament Research* (New York: Harper, 1962), pp. 39-40; M. Dibelius, *From Tradition to Gospel* (New York: Charles Scribner & Sons, 1931), pp. 37-69, esp. 48-58; Hultgren, *Jesus and his Adversaries*, pp. 39-64. For the most up to date discussion of the 'pronouncement story', see *Semeia* 20 (1981). The whole volume is dedicated to a discussion of the the form and its types, not only in the New Testament but in Gnostic and Christian Apocryphal literature as well.

7.   Bultmann, *History*, p. 26; H. Anderson, *The Gospel of Mark* (London: Oliphants, 1976), p. 274.

8.   Bultmann, *History*, p. 26. That the saying never circulated independently seems to be confirmed by the fact that in each of the three occasions in which it is extant in non-canonical contexts (i.e. Logion 100 of the *Gospel of Thomas*, Justin Martyr, *Apol.* 1.17.2, and *Egerton Papyrus* 2, Fragment 2 recto, ll. 43-59) it appears not as an uncontextualized utterance of Jesus, but as a pronouncement in response to a question. On *the Gospel of Thomas*' version of the Tax Question Story and its bearing upon the question of the tradition-history of the Markan version of the story, see below, pp. 294-97. On the bearing of *Apol.* 1.17.2 and *Eger.* 2 on this matter, see below, n. 16 and n. 29 respectively.

and provide the occasion and *raison d'être* for its utterance, appear, at least at first glance, to be so excellently constructed in forming a complete unity with the saying in v. 17, so 'formally' correct in reducing the narrative element of the story to almost the barest essentials (and thus allowing, as the compositional 'laws' of the story's form demand, all emphasis to fall on what Jesus says), so appropriate for moving the story dramatically to its climax, and so effective in providing just the right foil for drawing out the ethical and religious import of the dominical saying, that they cannot be regarded as secondary to the saying. Rather, they represent the saying's original, traditional narrative 'frame'.[9] That the saying of Jesus which 'caps' the story of the Question of the Payment of Taxes to Caesar is traditional, and that it never circulated independently of some accompanying introductory and 'framing' material, is, I think, indisputable. But that the material which in Mark presently introduces and 'frames' the saying is also traditional and original to the saying seems to me to be less than likely. I have three reasons for holding this position:

First, in form and structure the Markan Tax Question story resembles not so much a primitive pronouncement story (as it should do if it is relatively early in origin) *as a late one*. The form and structure of the Markan story is built up around three exchanges between Jesus and interlocutors, the first exchange marked off by the phrases 'And they came and said to him' (vv. 13-16a) with 'But he...said to them' (v. 15b), the second by 'And they brought' (v. 16a) with 'And he said to them' (v. 16b), and the third by 'They said to him' (v. 16c) with 'Jesus said to them' (v. 17). Notably, this triadic construction is atypical of the form and structure of those pronouncement stories which have been transmitted in the synoptic tradition relatively free of editorial modification.[10] What they display is either a monadic or a diadic structure, with either only a question/accusation alone or a question/accusation followed by a counter-question respectively setting up and leading into the given story's apodictic saying.[11] Such a construction is, however, characteristic of the form and structure of several Synoptic pronouncement stories which are, from a tradition-history point of view, late, in that they are each, in their present form, demonstrably

---

9. Bultmann, *History*, p. 26; Taylor, *Mark*, p. 378; Hultgren, *Jesus and his Adversaries*, p. 76.

10. Cf. J.D. Crossan, 'Mark 12:13-17', *Int* 37 (1983), p. 397.

11. Crossan, 'Mk 12:13-17', p. 397; Bultmann, *Form Criticism*, p. 40.

redactional adaptations of received material.[12] The resemblance, then, between the form and structure of the Markan Tax Question Story and that of these late, non-unitary pronouncement stories suggests that rather than being a primitive, traditional unit of material, the Markan Tax Question Story is late in origin, and a product of redactional activity.

Secondly—and this is crucial in order for the narrative of the Markan Tax Question story to establish the conflict which is at the story's center—it is obvious that the compliment paid to Jesus in Mk 12.13 is false, and, therefore, that there is a huge discrepancy between the stated and the actual intentions of Jesus' interlocutors in their asking Jesus the tax question. This is made plain and emphasized through the use of a device which is found more frequently in literary works than in concretized oral tradition which Mk 12.13-17 is reputed to be. That the compliment is false is apparent due to its explicitness, verbosity and redundance.[13] The redundance and verbosity of the compliment makes the compliment sound overdone and hollow, especially when contrasted with the terseness both of the description which precedes it (v. 13) and the discourse that follows (v. 15). It has the effect of producing a sense that those who engage in such badinage are not only insincere, but involved in deceitful trickery.[14] It is important to note, then, that the use of a phrase of unusual explicitness and redundance to bring out a contrast between pretense and the reality of a situation is a narrative device found typically not in *Kleinliteratur* nor in material taken over from oral tradition, but in works composed by authors skilled in rhetorical technique.[15] That such a device is employed within, and as so integral a part of, the Markan Tax Question Story indicates that the story is, from a history-of-traditions point of view, late, originating at the literary and not the preliterary stage of the synoptic tradition.

My third reason for asserting the secondary nature of the bulk of the Markan Tax Question story is the fact that an investigation of the

---

12. I have in mind such stories as the Healing of the Paralytic (Mk 2.1-12), The Plucking of Grain on the Sabbath (Mk 2.23-28), The Tradition of the Elders (Mk 7.1-13), and the Matthean version of the Beelzebub Controversy (Mt. 12.22-37).

13. Cf. R.C. Tannehill, *The Sword of his Mouth* (Philadelphia: Fortress Press, 1975), p. 172.

14. Tannehill, *Sword*, p. 172.

15. Cf. R. Breymayer, 'Zur Pragmatik des Bildes. Semiotische Beobachtungen zum Streitgespräch Mk 12,13-17 ("Der Zinsgroschen") unter Berücksichtigung der Spieltheorie', *LB* 13-14 (1972), pp. 19-51, esp. pp. 41-42.

tradition history of Logion 100 of the *Gospel of Thomas* reveals that the Tax Question story originally circulated in a form devoid of most of the material which now appears in Mk 12.13-17.[16] Logion 100, a *Chreia*, reads as follows:

> They showed Jesus a gold (coin) and said to him: Caesar's men ask taxes from us. He said to them: Give the things of Caesar to Caesar; the things of God to God and give me what is mine.[17]

Now, there are obviously significant differences between this version of the Tax Question Story and its parallel in the Gospel of Mark.[18] Nevertheless, it is still evident that in Mk 12.13-17 and in Logion 100

---

16. In Justin Martyr, *Apol.* 1.17.2 the Tax Question story is also devoid of most of the material in which it is couched in Mark, reading,

> For once in his time some came to him and asked whether it were right to pay taxes to Caesar? And he answered, 'Tell me, whose image is on the coin'. They said, 'Caesar's'. And he answered them again, 'Then give what is Caesar's to Caesar and what is God's to God' (translation by E.R. Hardy, *The First Apology of Justin Martyr*, in *The Library of Christian Classics*. I. *Early Christian Fathers* [London: SCM Press, 1953], p. 253).

But since it is unclear whether or not Justin is here passing on intact, and as it came to him, a primitive (oral?) tradition or is summarizing one of the gospel accounts of the story (Matthew's?), the value of this text for ascertaining the tradition history of Mk 12.13-17 is uncertain.

17. On the text and the translation of *Thomas* Logion 100, see K. Aland, *Synopsis Quattour Evangeliorum* (Stuttgart: Württembergische Bibelanstalt, 7th edn, 1971), p. 528.

18. The pronouncement of Jesus concerning the payment of taxes is extended in *Thomas* beyond what is found in Mk in this regard by the addition of a phrase which imbues the pronouncement with a decidedly Gnostic tinge and gives it a Christological import missing in the Markan version of the saying. While, as in Mk, there is also in *Thomas* a conflict situation described, it is not expressed there in story form as it is in the Markan account. Further, in *Thomas* it is the followers of Jesus (or at least non-opponents) who come onto the scene, show the coin and report the issue of conflict to which Jesus' pronouncement is the response. Moreover, the conflict situation in *Thomas* arises as a result of contact of Jesus' questioners with members of Caesar's party. In Mark's Gospel, by contrast, there is an open confrontation in story form and in direct dialogue between Jesus and interlocutors who are not followers of Jesus: they arrive on the scene, they ask a question to entrap Jesus, the question is followed by an exchange of dialogue and the presentation of a specific coin at Jesus' request, and Jesus' final reply is said to amaze and silence his opponents.

we have the same incident related in two different forms.[19] But what is the relationship between the two versions of the Story?

Some scholars[20] have suggested that Logion 100 represents a late condensation of Mk 12.13-17, supporting their view with inferences drawn, on the one hand, from the fact that much of *Thomas* is clearly derived from the canonical Gospels, and, on the other, from the results of experiments conducted by Vincent Taylor to illustrate that the direction of the development and transmission of a given folk tradition, such as that underlying the written Gospels, is towards abbreviation.[21] But not all of *Thomas* is derived from the canonical Gospels, not even many of the logia which, in form and language, are strikingly similar to material in Matthew, Mark, Luke and John;[22] and the results of Taylor's experiments are of doubtful value in determining whether Logion 100 in *Thomas* is dependent upon Mk 12.13-17 because, as Taylor himself clearly states, they were meant to uncover tendencies in the transmission of oral and not written material.[23] Moreover, as R. Mcl. Wilson and Q. Quispel have shown, the tendency evident in *Thomas* is actually to expand and not to summarize or abbreviate the material that it does take

---

19. Hultgren, *Jesus and his Adversaries*, p. 43.

20. Cf. R.M Grant, *The Secret Sayings of Jesus: The Gnostic Gospel of Thomas* (Garden City: Doubleday, 1960), p. 116, 178; R. McL. Wilson, *Studies in the Gospel of Thomas* (London: SCM Press, 1960), pp. 59-60; W. Schrage, *Das Verhältnis des Thomas-Evangeliums zur synoptischen Tradition* (Berlin: Alfred Töpelmann, 1964), pp. 189-92; P. Perkins, 'Prouncouncement Stories in the Gospel of Thomas', *Semeia* 20 (1981), pp. 121-32, esp. p. 126.

21. Cf. Taylor, *Formation*, pp. 202-209.

22. Cf. O. Cullmann, 'The Gospel of Thomas and the Problem of the Age of the Tradition Contained Therein', *Int* 16 (1962), pp. 418-38; R. McL. Wilson, 'Thomas and the Synoptic Gospels', *ExpTim* 72 (1960–61), pp. 36-39; *idem*, '"Thomas" and the Growth of the Gospels', *HTR* 53 (1969), pp. 231-50. For the latest comprehensive discussion of the issue of the relation of *Thomas* with the canonical gospels, see H. Koester, *Ancient Christian Gospels* (Philadelphia: Trinity International Press, 1990), and S.J. Patterson, *The Gospel of Thomas and Jesus* (Sonoma, CA: Polebridge Press, 1991). Patterson concludes, after examining all of the reputed parallels of *Thomas* with canonical Gospel material, that despite the fact of the existence of parallels between *Thomas* and the Synoptics (which he labels 'Synoptic twins', 'Synoptic siblings' and 'Synoptic cousins', depending on the degree of verbal, thematic and formal correspondence with their Synoptic counterparts), there is no evidence of literary dependence of *Thomas* on the Synoptics. To use his words, *all* of the material in *Thomas* is 'autonomous'.

23. Taylor, *Formation*, p. 202.

over from written Gospel sources.[24] It should also be noted that it would be difficult, if not impossible, to explain why the author(s)/compiler(s) of *Thomas* would have made the changes to Mk 12.13-17, which it must be supposed were made, if the Markan version of the Tax Question story was used as a source for Logion 100. Why, given what is known of Gnostic theology in general and the theological emphases of *Thomas* in particular, would the *Thomas* traditionist(s) have omitted the reference in Mk 12.14 to Jesus as 'Teacher' who is himself 'true' (ἀληθής) and who 'truly' teaches 'the way of God' (ἐπ' ἀληθείας τὴν ὁδὸν τοῦ θεοῦ διδάσκεις)? The term 'way' and the ascription to Jesus of the titles 'teacher' and 'true' do, after all, feature prominently in Gnostic literature. They are, more importantly, found in *Thomas*.[25]

These considerations suggest that the *Gospel of Thomas* preserves a version of the Tax Question story which is parallel to, but independent of, the Markan version of this story. Accordingly, the question is, how old is the version of the tradition that it preserves? Given (a) that its structure is 'monadic' and therefore resembles that of primitive pronouncement stories,[26] and (b) that the narrative element of the story is reduced to the barest of essentials and sets up the saying of Jesus in such a way that all attention falls on what Jesus says (a formal characteristic of 'pure' pronouncement stories),[27] it seems clear that Logion 100 of the *Gospel of Thomas*, sans the (Gnostic?) command of Jesus to 'give me what is mine', dates from an early stage of the logia tradition, earlier certainly than that of the Markan version of the Tax Question story.[28] Indeed, it is not unreasonable to conclude, given the appearance in Mk 12.13-17 (and also in Mt. 22.15-20 and in Lk. 20.20-26) of the *Chreia*'s notice of a showing of a 'coin' and its specific 'dominical saying', that this *Chreia* is the *fons et origo* of the Synoptic Tax Question tradition. And if this is the case, then much of the substance of the Markan version of the Tax Question story must be regarded as

24. Wilson, 'Thomas', p. ; Q. Quispel, 'The Gospel of Thomas and the New Testament', *VC* 11 (1957), pp. 189-207.

25. Cf., e.g., Logion 13. It should also be noted that the term εἰκών, which figures prominently in Mark's version of the Tax Question story but which does not appear in *Thomas*, Logion 100, is part of *Thomas*'s terminology (cf. Logia 22, 50, 83, 84).

26. On the structure of primitive pronouncement stories, see above, p. 291.

27. On the formal characteristics of pronouncement stories, see the literature cited above in n. 6.

28. So Patterson, *Gospel of Thomas*, pp. 68-69.

secondary to, and a late adaption of, a received tradition, a tradition preserved in Logion 100.

I contend, therefore, that the three considerations outlined above lead to two conclusions: first, that the Markan version of the Tax Question story does not represent a faithful and substantially unaltered reproduction of primitive, traditional material, and, secondly, that much of Mk 12.13-17, though grounded in a primitive *Chreia*, is an editorial construction, created at the literary stage of the Synoptic Tradition.[29]

29. It has been suggested by J.D. Crossan (*Four other Gospels: Shadows on the Contours of Canon* [Minneapolis: Winston Press, 1985], pp. 77-87) that there is another consideration, besides those I have already listed, which also lends support to these two conclusions, namely, that the tradition of the Tax Question temptation appears in a form similar to, but in wording and substance different from, and in length shorter than, the Markan version of the tradition in *Egerton Papyrus* 2, frag. 2 recto, ll. 43-59. As J. Jeremias ('An Unknown Gospel with Johannine Elements', in E. Hennecke [ed.], *New Testament Apocrypha*, I [Philadelphia: Westminster Press, 1963], p. 97) translates the somewhat corrupt and presumably incomplete text (on this, see H.I. Bell and T.C. Skeat, *Fragments of an Unknown Gospel and other Early Christian Papyri* [London: Trustees of the British Museum and Oxford University Press, 1935], p. 28; *idem*, *The New Gospel Fragments* [London: Trustees of the British Museum and Oxford University Press, 1935], p. 13]), this version of the tradition reads:

> <ca>me to him to put him to the pro<of> (ἐξ[εράσ]τικος) and to tempt him (ἐπείραζον αὐτόν), whilst <they said>: [45] 'Master (διδάσκαλε) Jesus, we know that thou art come <from God>, for what thou doest bears a test<imony> (to thee) (which) (goes) beyond (that) of al(l) the prophets. <Wherefore tell> us: is it admissable <to p>ay the kings the (charges) appertaining to their rule? <Should we> pay or not?' But Jesus say through their <in>tention, became angry, and said to them: 'Why call ye me with yo<ur mou>th Master and yet <do> not what I say. Well has Is<aiah> prophesied <concerning y>[55]ou saying: This <people honours> me with the<ir li>ps but their heart is far from me; <their worship is> vain. <They teach> precepts <of men>

The truth of Crossan's thesis is, however, entirely dependent upon the truth of certain assumptions that Crossan, largely following C.H. Dodd ('A New Gospel', in *New Testament Studies* [Manchester: Manchester University Press, 1953], pp. 12-52, esp. pp. 36-40), makes about the text, namely, that the *Egerton Papyrus* fragment's version of the Tax Question temptation tradition is not only independent of any of the versions of that tradition found in the Synoptic Gospels, but represents the tradition's earliest form. (Notably, according to Crossan, *Thomas* Logion 100 is the latest of the tradition's forms.) But these assumptions are not without their difficulties (on these, see Jeremias, 'An Unknown Gospel', pp. 94-96; M. Rist, 'Caesar or God [Mark

This being the case, who is responsible for the creation of the Markan version of the tradition? A number of factors indicate that it was Mark himself. First, as I have already noted, the story possesses a triadic structure, involving three interchanges between Jesus and his interlocutors. Mark's fondness for triadic structure is well known.[30] Secondly, the story is replete with stylistic and thematic 'duality'. There is (a) a double dialectic of question and answer as well as of entrapment and escape;[31] (b) a doubling of all the main items in vv. 14-15a;[32] (c) a dualism in having both the Pharisees and Herodians as Jesus' questioners; (d) a reversed or chiastic dualism in 12.14a;[33] and (e) a correspondence between command and fulfilment in vv. 15b-16.[34] As F. Neirynck has demonstrated, such 'dualism' is the preeminent characteristic of Markan style.[35] Third, other stylistic features of the story, notably, τί used as an exclamation (cf. v. 15), the οὐ...ἀλλά construction in v. 14, the use in v. 16b of καὶ λέγει αὐτοῖς to introduce a saying of Jesus, are all Markan.[36] Finally, certain items of the story's vocabulary—items such

12:13-17]? A Study in *Formgeschichte*', *JR* 16 [1936], pp. 317-31, esp. p. 330); further, as Koester has noted (*Ancient Christian Gospels,* pp. 214-15), 'it is unlikely that the pericope of *Papyrus Egerton 2* is an independent older tradition [of the Tax Question story]'. However, he also notes that, for a variety of literary considerations (among them the fact that the pericope is cast in 'a language that is pre-johannine and pre-synoptic' and that none of individual building blocks of sayings from which the structure of the pericope is constructed 'has been formed by the literary activity of a previous gospel writer'), one cannot claim dependence either; it is at least *possible* that the *Egerton* version of the Tax Question story rests upon memory of the oral tradition which formed the basis of Mk 12.13-17 (p. 215). If this is the case, then there is some evidence that, contrary to what I argue below, the tradition of Jesus' Tax Question was originally transmitted as a 'temptation' tradition, and that Mark himself was not responsible for making it (or explicating it as) one.

30. On the triadic structures in Mark, see F. Neirynck, *Duality in Mark* (Leuven: Leuven University Press, 1972), pp. 110-12.

31. Cf. Crossan, 'Mark 12:13-17', pp. 397-98.

32. Teacher/teach; true/truly; no/not; pay or not/pay or not.

33. (a) teacher; (b) true; (c) not; (b′) truly; (a′) teach. Cf. Crossan, 'Mark 12.13-17', p. 398.

34. Jesus says 'bring me (φέρετε) a denarius that I might see it' and his questioners 'brought (ἤνεγκαν)' it.

35. Neirynck, *Duality,* pp. 75-137.

36. On τί exclamatory in Mark, see M. Black, *An Aramaic Approach to the Gospels and Acts* (Oxford: Clarendon Press, 1967), p. 123. On the οὐ...ἀλλά construction as Markan, see Neirynck, *Duality,* pp. 90-94. On καὶ λέγει αὐτοῖς as Markan, see J. Jeremias, *The Parables of Jesus* (New York: Charles Scribner &

as διδάσκαλος, διδάσκειν, ἀληθής/ἀληθείας, οἶδα, πειράζω, φέρω, βλέπω—are Markan.[37] In light of this, it seems reasonable to conclude that Mark is responsible for the particular form and, save for that of the dominical saying at Mk 12.17, also much of the wording of his version of the story concerning the Question of the Payment of Taxes to Caesar.

It will be noted that this conclusion, and especially that aspect of it which sees Mk 12.15 as a Markan addition to a more primitive and much briefer Tax Question story, raises a question which, given the larger objective I am pursuing in investigating this and other Synoptic versions of the traditions of Jesus under temptation, is of no little significance. If it was Mark who has labeled Jesus' confrontation with the question on the legitimacy of paying taxes to Caesar as something which 'tempts' Jesus, then there is the possibility that Mark has *created* a 'temptation tradition' and is responsible for its appearance in the synoptic tradition. Has Mark, in his particular handling of the Tax Question tradition, been thematically and theologically innovative?

To answer this we must know whether the version of the story upon which Mk 12.13-17 is ultimately based was itself a temptation tradition, affirming that Jesus was subjected to πειρασμός when the issue of paying taxes to Caesar was laid before him. But before we turn to this question, let us first attempt to discover and outline Mark's understanding of the nature and the content of Jesus' Tax Question temptation.

Mark's View of the Nature of Jesus' Tax Question Temptation
In his study of the πειρασμοί of Jesus, H. Seesemann contends that the temptation which, according to Mark, Jesus experiences when confronted with the question concerning the legitimacy of paying taxes to Caesar should be considered a 'testing' only in what he calls the 'secular' sense of the idea.[38] Jesus' remark τί με πειράζατε at Mk 12.15 is, Seesemann asserts, intended by Mark to be seen primarily

---

Sons, 1963), p. 14; Taylor, *Mark*, p. 218; W. Marxsen, 'Redactiongeschictliche Erklärung der songennanten Parabel-Theorie des Markus', *ZTW* 52 (1955), p. 262.

37. On these words as Markan vocabulary, see F. Neirynck, 'The Redactional Text of Mark', *ETL* 57 (1981), pp. 144-62.

38. H. Seesemann, 'πεῖρα, κτλ.', *TDNT*, VI, p. 35. In Seesemann's mind this is in contrast to 'to test faithfulness and obedience', i.e., what he terms the 'religious' sense of πειράζω.

as indicating a recognition on Jesus' part that he is being 'examined' academically, not 'put to the proof'—that is, that his opinion on a matter of some consequence is being solicited for inspection.[39] Now Seesemann acknowledges that Jesus' remark is also meant to be seen as expressing a sense of exasperation. This in turn, he notes, is to be taken as an indication that, according to Mark, Jesus knows that his 'examination' is being conducted with hostile intent, that is, under the hope that it will reveal something which can be used 'to bring about his downfall'.[40] And therefore Seesemann is willing to admit that in the Markan Tax Question story πειράζω is used with a meaning which bears a tinge of what he calls the special 'religious' sense of tempting/ temptation.[41] But despite this, he still goes on to say that here one 'should not overstress...the element of tempting in the true sense'.[42] The tempting question of Mk 12.14 can hardly be regarded, he maintains, as a temptation in the sense of Mt. 4.1-11 and Lk. 4.1-13.[43]

But is Seesemann's contention convincing? I think not. In the first place, it is highly dubious linguistically. There is not a single example in all of the pre-second-century CE instances of the use of πειράζω in either biblical or non-biblical Greek literature which indicates that 'examine academically', 'to test knowledge' was ever thought to be part of the semantic range of the verb.[44] In the second place, the contention

---

39. See also K.W. Chase, *The Synoptic Πειρασμοί of Jesus: Their Christological Significance* (ThD dissertation, New Orleans Baptist Theological Seminary, 1989), p. 161, who in agreement with Seesemann claims that πειράζω is used in Mk 12.15 only 'in a strictly secular sense without any hint of the distinctly religious connotations' [which for him involves either enticement to commit some particular sin or placing someone in a situation to 'prove' his real character]. To Chase the word here means '"to attempt, to strive, to make an effort" to cause Jesus to say something [the Pharisees and Herodians] could use against him'. And rather than being a 'test of faithfulness and obedience to God', the nature of the temptation in Mk 12.13-17 is, in Chase's eyes, 'a test of defective doctrine'. It should be noted, however, that Chase's view is rooted in the idea that Jesus' opponents appear in the Tax Question story as *not knowing where Jesus stands on the matter of the* κῆνσος. As I will show below, this idea is highly questionable.

40. Seesemann, 'πεῖρα', p. 28. So, too, Chase, *The Synoptic Πειρασμοί*, p. 161.

41. As we have seen (n. 39 above), Chase does not, however, draw this conclusion.

42. Seesemann, 'πεῖρα', p. 28.

43. Seesemann, 'πεῖρα', p. 35.

44. The same thing may also be said with respect to Chase's claim that part of the semantic range of πειράζω was the meaning 'to test for defective doctrine'. For a

is grounded in the questionable assumption that in the New Testament period any tempting of the 'religious' kind was thought to be instigated only by Satan or by one of his agents.[45] Now it is a fact that there is no explicit indication in the Markan Tax Question story that the words or actions of Jesus' questioners are regarded or portrayed as an attack upon Jesus by Satanic forces.[46] But in the biblical witness—and more significantly, in the view of Mark—an attack by Satan or his minions is neither a necessary nor even an essential concomitant of being tempted in the 'religious' sense of the idea. Thirdly, Seesemann's contention assumes that Jesus' remark τί με πειράζατε is intended by Mark to be seen as an analysis on Jesus' part of the intention of Jesus' questioners. But it is more likely that it serves in Mark's eyes to indicate a recognition on the part of Jesus that the question on paying taxes to Caesar represents something that puts him on trial.[47] Finally, and most importantly, Seesemann's contention founders because it does not take into account the implications of Jesus' immediate retort. His questioners have expressed ignorance of his position regarding the legitimacy of the tax[48] as well as the desire to be instructed and guided in this matter by his opinion,[49] but this is specifically designated by the Markan Jesus as an instance of ὑπόκρισις (cf. v. 15a), that is, of a quite deliberate pretense.[50] Accordingly, inasmuch as this designation implies that Jesus' questioners are *neither interested in being instructed by Jesus* in how to respond to the issue raised by the demand for Caesar's tax, *nor ignorant of Jesus' position on this matter*,[51] the experience to which Jesus is subjected as a result of their question must embody a 'test' of a quite different order from an 'examination'.[52]

---

listing of the instances of the usage of πειράζω prior to 2 CE, see, pp. 325-26.

45. Seesemann, 'πεῖρα', p. 36.

46. The question remains, however, whether in Mark's eyes a Satanic attack is here implicit. For a defense of the position that it is, indeed that in Mk all of the confrontations between Jesus and his opponents are extentions of Jesus' confrontations with Satan, see J.M. Robinson, *The Problem of History in Mark* (London: SCM Press, 1957), pp. 44-46, esp. p. 45.

47. Cf. C. Myers, *Binding the Strong Man: A Political Reading of Mark's Story of Jesus* (Maryknoll, NY: Orbis, 1988), p. 311.

48. This is implicit in the double question δῶμεν ἢ μὴ δῶμεν.

49. This is implicit in their approach and address to Jesus as 'Teacher'.

50. Cf. U. Wilkens, 'ὑποκρίνομαι, κτλ.', *TDNT*, VIII, pp. 559-70, esp. p. 568.

51. Wilkens, 'ὑποκρίνομαι', p. 568.

52. On this, see E. Best, *The Temptation and the Passion: The Markan*

Is, then, the temptation/'testing' which, according to Mark, Jesus here experiences 'religious' in nature? Certain considerations strongly suggest that it is. There is, first of all, the consideration arising from the fact, demonstrated above in preceding chapters, that in every instance of the Markan usage of πειράζω outside of Mk 12.15 the verb bears the specifically 'religious' sense of 'to be put to test over one's faithfulness to God'. Such a consistency of usage throughout the Gospel of Mark constitutes a *prima facie* case that πειράζω is employed also in Mk 12.15 with the same meaning.

Secondly, there is the consideration arising from the fact, established in my analysis of Mk 8.11-13 and 10.1-12, that on those occasions in his Gospel where, as in Mk 12.13-17, questions or challenges from Jesus' opponents are specifically said to tempt Jesus (cf. Mk 8.11; 10.2; cp. Mk 12.15), Mark consistently portrays the temptation/'testing' which Jesus therein experiences as a 'testing of faithfulness and obedience to God'. Would not the sense πειράζω has in these passages also obtain in Mk 12.15, where, as in Mk 8.11-13 and 10.1-12, it is again employed not only *in conjunction with the same thematic and stylistic elements ingredient to these passages* (i.e. the Pharisees as opponents of Jesus, a description of the Pharisees 'coming out' to Jesus which employs ἔρχομαι,[53] a verb of speaking prefacing the tempting question[54]), but *in accordance with the formal and thematic pattern into which these elements have been constructed*?[55]

More importantly, there is the fact that the question which tempts Jesus is indirectly designated by Mark as a challenge to Jesus to demonstrate how truly he is devoted to the 'way of God' (τὴν ὁδὸν τοῦ θεοῦ).[56]

It seems safe to conclude, then, given the cumulative weight of these considerations, that in Mark's eyes the temptation to which Jesus was subjected when confronted with the question concerning the legitimacy of paying taxes to Caesar is, to use Seesemann's terminology, 'religious'

Soteriology (Cambridge: Cambridge University Press, 1965), pp. 32-33.

53. ἐξῆλθον Mk 8.11; προσελθόντες Mk 10.2, cp. ἐλθόντες Mk 12.14.

54. συζητεῖν Mk 8.11; ἐπηρώτων Mk 10:2; cp. λέγουσιν Mk 12.14.

55. The pattern is (a) the approach of the opponents to Jesus; (b) a request/question; (c) a notice that the request/question subjects Jesus to temptation.

56. On this, see W.L. Lane, *The Gospel according to Mark* (Grand Rapids: Eerdmans, 1974), pp. 422-23.

in nature. It involves a proving of Jesus' loyalty and devotion to God. This being the case, what, then, is this temptation's content?

Mark's View of the Content of Jesus' Tax Question Temptation
To discover and outline Mark's understanding of the content of Jesus' Tax Question temptation we must find answers to the following questions:

• What precisely is the tax over which the question of the legitimacy of its payment is raised?

• What did this tax and its payment represent to the Jewish people in both Jesus' and Mark's time?

• What, in light of the answer to the previous question, would a pious Jew be likely to feel was the proper response to the demand to pay the tax?

• What would an open remark on the illegitimacy of the tax countenance and make one liable to? and

• What does Mark portray as Jesus' attitude toward the payment of this tax?

The Tax of Mark 12.15
The tax over which the Pharisees and Herodians question Jesus in Mk 12.15 is designated by Mark as the κῆνσος ('census'). This is the poll or head tax which was imposed upon the people of Judaea by Caesar Augustus in 6 CE when Archelaus, then Ethnarch of Judaea, was deposed from his office and the territory which he had governed became an Imperial province, subject to direct Roman rule.[57] The tax flowed into the *fiscus*, the imperial treasury,[58] through the hands of the prefect (later, procurator) of Judaea who, by virtue of his office and

---

57. Cf. Josephus, *Ant.* 5.1.21. D.M. Rhoads (*Israel in Revolution 6–74 CE* [Philadelphia: Fortress, 1976], pp. 30, 49), citing S. Safrai and M. Stern (*Compendia Rerum Iudaicarum ad Novum Testamentum*, I [Philadelphia: Fortress Press, 1974], p. 334), states that the poll tax was imposed in the time of Pompey. But for a decisive argument against this, see E. Schürer, *The History of the Jewish People in the Age of Jesus Christ*, I (ed. G. Vermes and F. Millar; Edinburgh: T. & T. Clark, 1973), pp. 416-20.

58. Taylor, *Mark*, p. 479; G. Bornkamm, *Jesus of Nazareth* (New York: Charles Scribner & Sons, 1960), p. 121.

appointment, was responsible for the tax's collection.[59] The κῆνσος subsidized the maintenance of three things: the Roman civil and military administration in Judaea, the splendour of the Imperial Court in Rome, and the cult of the Roman state.[60] It was calculated, and its payment conducted in, two types of *denarii*: first, from the inception of the tax until 15 CE, in the *denarius* of Augustus, and then, from 15 CE onwards, in that of Tiberius. The *denarius* of Augustus was a coin which bore on its obverse a laureated head or bust of the emperor along with the inscription CAESAR AVGVSTVS DIVI F PATER PATRIAE (= *Caesar Augustus, Divi Filius, Pater Patriae*, 'Caesar Augustus, Son of God, Father of his Country'), and on the reverse a depiction of the imperial princes, Gaius and Lucius, each with a spear in his hand, which was set on a background of crossed spears, with a star representing heavenly sanction, an image of the *stipulum*, the ladle employed by Roman priests in their libations, and the *litius* of the augurate together with the inscription PRINCIPES IUVENTUTIS ('Leaders of Youth') also adorning the depiction. The *denarius* of Tiberius was a coin which on its obverse bore both the legend TI CAESAR DIVI AVG F AVGVSTVS (= *Tiberius Caesar Divi Augusti Filius Augustus*, 'Tiberius Caesar, Son of the Divine Augustus, Augustus!') as well as an image of Tiberius *laureate*, and on its reverse side a depiction of a seated lady (perhaps Livia) as Pax with a palm(?) branch in her left hand and an inverted spear in her right, and the inscription PONTIF MAXIM (= *Pontifex Maximus*, 'High Priest', i.e., of the Roman State), referring to Tiberius.[61] The tax's collection was accomplished through methods that were never less than militantly forceful, and often savage, and inability to pay was, as Kennard notes, 'punished by confiscation, slavery, and death'.[62]

---

59. On the office and duties of the praefectus/procurator in Judaea, see Schürer, *History*, I, pp. 357-58.

60. Cf. F.C. Grant, *The Economic Background to the Gospels* (Oxford: Clarendon Press, 1926), p. 103; J.S. Kennard, *Render to Caesar* (New York: Charles Scribner & Sons, 1950), p. 31. See also F.F. Bruce, 'Render to Caesar', in E. Bammel and C.F.D. Moule (eds.), *Jesus and the Politics of his Day* (Cambridge: Cambridge University Press, 1984), p. 254.

61. Cf. H. St.J. Hart, 'The Coin of "Render unto Caesar…"' (A Note on some Aspects of Mark 12:13-17; Matt. 22:15-22; Luke 20:20-26)', in Bammel and Moule (eds.), *Jesus and the Politics of his Day*, pp. 241-48, esp. pp. 243-44; E. Stauffer, *Christ and the Caesars* (London: SCM Press, 1955), pp. 124-28; Kennard, *Render*, pp. 73-87. The κῆνσος was paid only in the *denarius*: see Bruce, 'Render', p. 258.

62. Kennard, *Render*, p. 28. See also, M. Rostovtzeff, *Social and Economic*

What the Tax Represented to the Jews

An Economic Burden. The κῆνσος was by no means the only tax the people of Judaea had to bear. On the one hand, the Romans demanded certain taxes besides the κῆνσος, some more indirect than others.[63] And on the other, the Jews of the province were also obliged by their own law to pay the following: a tithe for the maintenance of the Jerusalem Temple and its large staff of priests, Levites and other Temple servants, a Deuteronomic 'second tithe', which was originally an alternative to the first tithe, but which by the time of Jesus had to be paid in addition to it every third year, and at least nine other religiously prescribed dues.[64] These 'religious' taxes were in themselves an exceptionally heavy burden for those subject to them, taking at least ten percent of a provincial Judaean's income.[65] But when added to the amounts due to meet civil obligations, the burden they represented became even more grinding.[66] And when the weight of the imperial κῆνσος was superimposed upon that represented by the other civil and religious taxes and duties demanded of the Jews, the economic burden was nothing short of intolerable. F.C. Grant estimates that during the years 6 to 66 CE the total taxation of the Jewish people under the civil, religious and political levies imposed upon them must have approached the level of at least 30 to 40 percent of the provincial income, and may have been higher still.[67] But notably, even apart from the tax burden experienced on account of other civil and religious duties, the financial demand of the κῆνσος in itself was thought to be insufferable.[68]

History of the Roman Empire (Oxford: Clarendon Press, 1926), pp. 300-302.

63. On the number and nature of the direct civil taxes levied upon the Jews by the Romans, see Schürer, *History*, I, pp. 401-43; G.H. Stevenson, *The Cambridge Ancient History*, X (Cambridge: Cambridge University Press, 1934), pp. 191-93. On the number and nature of the indirect taxes for which the Jews of Judaea might be liable, see Schürer, *History*, I, pp. 373-74; Safrai and Stern, *Compendia*, I, pp. 332-34.

64. On the number and nature of these 'religious' taxes, see Grant, *Economic Background*, pp. 92-100.

65. Grant. *Economic Background*, p. 103.

66. D.L. Mealand (*Poverty and Expectation in the Gospels* [London: SPCK, 1980], p. 7) estimates that the Roman *tributum soli* (the tax on agricultural produce) alone amounted to a tax of twelve and a half percent of the harvest of Judaea.

67. Grant, *Economic Background*, p. 105.

68. This is the implication of Tacitus' report (*Annals* 2.42.6) that in 17 CE provincials from Syria and Judea petitioned for a reduction in the scale of the payment of the κῆνσος. Cf. Schürer, *History*, I, p. 373; Bruce, 'Render', p. 254.

Payment for the Maintenance of Hated Institutions. The monies derived from the κῆνσος were used to defray the expenses of occupying and maintaining a Roman presence in Judaea, as well as to subsidize the maintenance of the splendour of the Imperial Court in Rome and the cult of the Roman State.[69] The Roman occupation of Judaea denied the Jews the national sovereignty that was theirs by virtue of their religious heritage, and which also was necessary for sustaining the purity of their religion and worship.[70] The occupation's authority was that of a heathen, 'idol worshipping' empire.[71] Its history was characterized by a persistent inability, if not a consciously adopted unwillingness, to take into account fundamental Jewish sensibilities, and its implementation was often carried out through brute force.[72] The splendour of the

69. See above, note 60.

70. ' ...what was it that most threatened the due loyalty to Torah and Temple through which the covenant people could enjoy life in the promised land? It was the threat of an "alien" occupying power to both Torah and Temple. So long as the Seleucids or the Romans—or indeed, any other power—ruled the land which belonged to Yahweh, so long would observance of the Torah and reverence for the Temple be precarious...History had taught the Jews...that a foreign ruler could disrupt the conditions under which the covenant people could live in the promised land...[so that] they could only dwell securely in the promised land when it was not occupied territory' (W.D. Davies, *The Gospel and the Land* [Berkeley: University of California Press, 1974], p. 95). Cf. also *Ps. of Sol.* 17.23-31. On this issue, see also W.R. Farmer, *Maccabees, Zealots, and Josephus* (New York: Charles Scribner & Sons, 1956).

71. Grant, *Economic Background*, p. 100.

72. 'The Romans...had practically no comprehension of the Jewish character. As they knew nothing of the religious views of the Jews or of the many laws governing daily life, so they had no idea that for the sake of superficial and apparently unimportant things and entire people would be capable of offering the most extreme resistance, even to the point of death and self-annihilation. The Jews saw in the simplest administrative rulings, such as the initial census, an encroachment on their most sacred rights and came increasingly to believe that direct Roman rule, which they had desired at Herod's death, was incompatible with theocracy. Even with the best of intentions on both sides, tension and hostility were therefore inevitable. But such goodwill as existed was only partial. Except during the reign of Caligula, those at the head of government were ready to make concessions and exercise forbearance, sometimes in very large measure. But their good intentions were always foiled by the ineptitude of the governors, and not infrequently by gross miscarriages of justice on their part. These officials of lower rank were, like all petty rulers, above all conscious of their own arbitrary power, and through their infringements they in the end so

Imperial Court was manifested in ceremonies and displays of pomp which to the Jews involved the height of wantonness.[73] The cult of the State propagated ideas that the Roman people and Republic (personified in the goddess Roma) were a repository of deity, and that the Emperor was both an emissary, as well as one of, the Roman gods, worthy of προσκύνησις.[74] Consequently, payment of the κῆνσος implicated those who gave way to the tax in supporting, and making a tacit acknowledgement of the legitimacy of, institutions which few pious Jews could countenance.

A Symbol of Slavery. The κῆνσος was a tax imposed only upon conquered, subject peoples. 'Sons' and certain allies of Rome never felt the weight of its demands.[75] Accordingly, to the Jews in Judaea, whose heritage was the Exodus from Egypt, the Davidic Kingdom, and the divinely inspired exploits of the earlier Hasmoneans, the κῆνσος represented a yoke of bondage,[76] incompatible with their identity as the covenanted people of a liberating God.[77]

---

aggravated the people that in wild despair they plunged into a war of self annihilation' (Schürer, *History*, I, pp. 356-57).

73. Kennard, *Render*, p. 31.

74. Kennard, *Render*, p. 73-78.

75. Roman citizens were freed from the burden of the tribute in 167 BCE. That such freedom was viewed as the inherent right of a Roman citizen is indicated in the fact that when Augustus was in financial straits at the end of the civil wars, he could still impose only minor dues, such as manumission and sales taxes, on the people of Rome.

76. In the words of Judas of Gamala and Zaddok the Pharisee, who together led the revolt in 6 CE against imposition of the κῆνσος in Judaea, the tax was 'an introduction to slavery' (τὴν τῇ ἀποτίμησεν οὐδὲν ἀλλὸ ἢ ἄντικρυς δουλεῖαν ἐπιφέρειν..., Josephus, *Ant.* 1.1.4). A capitation tax, similar to the κῆνσος, imposed upon the Jews of Judaea in the last decade of Ptolemaic rule, is described by the author of *3 Maccabees* as an 'enrollment for slaughter' (cf. *3 Macc.* 2.28).

77. Cf. Deut. 23.17 (LXX), 'None of the daughters of Israel shall be subject to tribute (τελισφόρος) nor the sons of Israel to toll (τελισκομένος)'. The incompatibility of the κῆνσος with the Jews' identity as 'Sons' of God's Kingdom is also reflected in *Gen. R.* 20.1, 'In the world to come God will say to the Gentiles, "Why did you impose a fine (i.e. κῆνσος) on my people?"'. On the identity of 'fine' with κῆνσος, see H. Lowe, *'Render to Caesar' Religious and Political Loyalty in Palestine* (Cambridge: Cambridge University Press, 1940), pp. 43-44. Noteworthy, too, in this regard is the fact that in Jewish belief even Israel's own kings were not legally entitled to tribute from their Jewish subjects.

A Desecration of the Holy Land. Since, as I have noted, the κῆνσος was payable in the *denarius* first of Augustus and then of Tiberius, the imposition of this tax upon the Jews involved the importation of 'graven images' into Judaea,[78] a land which, because of its holiness, was to be kept free of such profane and desecrating objects.[79]

Assent to Blasphemy. The κῆνσος was demanded as tribute by, and collected on behalf of, one who claimed to be not only in possession of divine dignity and honour, but, as the devices and legends on the κῆνσος coin show, the Image and Manifestation of the King of Heaven on Earth.[80] To the Jews, who held that no human being had the right to claim the dignity and titles belonging properly only to Yahweh,[81] payment of the κῆνσος represented involvement in blasphemy.

A Denial of God's Ownership of the Land of Israel. Fundamental to first-century Judaism was the belief that the soil of Judaea belonged only to Yahweh.[82] The whole legislative system of Sabbatical and Jubilee years was grounded upon the idea of God's ownership of the land,[83] as were the Jewish laws stipulating that no Gentile could own property in Palestine.[84] The seriousness with which this belief was taken is indicated by the fact that even until the close of the rebellion of 132–135 CE non-Jews were still regarded as tenants in *eretz Israel*, subject to tithes, the

78. That the *denarius*, with its particular images and inscriptions, was regarded as a 'graven image', is indicated by two facts: (a) certain of the pious in Israel would not look upon the coin for fear of violating Lev. 19.4 (cf. *j. 'Abod. Zar.* 3.1; cp. *b. Pes.* 104a; Hippolytus, *Refutatio Omnium Haeresium* 9.26; see J.D.M. Derrett, 'Render to Caesar', in his *Law in the New Testament* [London: Atheneum, 1970], pp. 329-33); and (b) Jews regarded the *phalare*, the medallions on the standards of the Roman occupying forces which bore inscriptions and images identical with those found on the *denarius*, as idols, and were willing to risk death to prevent their introduction into Judaea (cf. M. Rist, 'Caesar or God: A Study in *Formgeschichte*', *JR* 16 [1936], pp. 317-31, esp. pp. 319-21; J.S. Kennard, 'Judaism and Images', *Crozier Quarterly* 23 [1946], pp. 259-65.

79. On this, see Ps. 81.9.

80. This is the meaning of the title 'Augustus'. Cf. Stauffer, *Christ and the Caesars*, p. 126. On the claims implicit in the imagery and inscriptions of the imperial *denarius*, see Kennard, *Render*, pp. 78-87.

81. Cf. Jn 10.33.

82. Cf. Lev. 25.23 where Yahweh explicitly declares '...the land is mine'.

83. On this, see Philo, *De Humanitate* 11.

84. On this, see the statements of Rabbi Meir in *m. 'Abod. Zar.* 1.8.

Sabbatical fallow year, and to other Jewish land laws.[85] Yet the κῆνσος was imposed and collected specifically on the basis of the Roman imperial philosophy, taken over from the Ptolemies of Egypt and popularized by Sulla and Julius Caesar, that provincial territory was the personal property of the Emperor, to be exploited as he chose.[86] The κῆνσος was, then, viewed by Jew and Roman alike as a sort of rent,[87] and as such its payment constituted an implicit recognition that Judaea was owned by Caesar and not by God.[88]

A Violation of the First Commandment. All Jews were bound by virtue of their religious heritage to the duty to 'have' and 'acknowledge' no other god 'beside' the Lord whom they worshipped.[89] The κῆνσος was, therefore, a violation of this fundamental obligation. As tribute to one who claimed to be not only a god, but also—given what Caesar thought was implied by his conquest of Judaea—one greater in power, might and authority than the God of the Jews,[90] the κῆνσος represented a demand for idolatry, and its payment represented a tacit 'having' and 'acknowledging' of a god and lord other than Yahweh.[91]

The Response of the Pious Jew to the Demand to Pay the Tax
In light of all of this, what, in Mark's eyes, would pious Jews be likely to feel was the proper response to the tax and the demand to pay it? The answer is clear. They would feel obliged to disavow the κῆνσος's

85. Kennard, *Render*, p. 105.

86. Cf. G.H. Stevenson, 'The Provinces and their Government', in *The Cambridge Ancient History*, IX (Cambridge: Cambridge University Press, 1932), pp. 437-74, esp. pp. 468-70.

87. Cf. Kennard, *Render*, p. 105.

88. Cf. Josephus, *War* 7.8.1; *Ant.* 18.1.1. For further discussion of the Jewish view that payment of the κῆνσος represented an acknowledgement that Judaea was owned by Caesar and not God, see M. Hengel, *The Zealots* (Edinburgh: T. & T. Clark, 1989), pp. 131-34.

89. Cf. Exod. 20.2-3; Deut. 5.6-7; 6.13-17, and how this duty is accepted and acknowledged in the *Shema* and the *Shemoneh Esreh*, the chief prayers of Judaism in the first century CE. On this, see E. Schürer, *The History of the Jewish People in the Age of Jesus Christ*, II (ed. G. Vermes, F. Millar and M. Black; Edinburgh: T. & T. Clark, 1979), pp. 454-63.

90. On this, see L. Gage, 'La théologie de la Victoire imperiale', *Rev. Hist.* 171 (1933), pp. 1-44.

91. Cf. Josephus, *Ant.* 18.1.6.

legitimacy and deem it necessary to refuse to pay it, seeing that one's dedication to do so was a vital measure of how loyal and devoted one was to God and his Law.[92]

The Import of Open Anti-Statements

What effect would open, voiced advocacy of refusing to pay the κῆνσος have? The answer to this question becomes clear when set it against the fact that in the eyes of Rome to refuse to pay the tax was an act of sedition, an offense meriting execution, and that to call for and publicly support non-payment was to foment and incite, if not to engage in, rebellion,[93] a capital crime punishable by crucifixion. Accordingly, one effect of open advocacy of refusing to pay the κῆνσος was *to render the one engaging in such activity liable to death*. But there is another. We read in Josephus' works accounts of the career of Judas of Galilee (cf. *War* 2.8.1; 7.6.1-4; *Ant.* 18.1.1, 1.6), a quasi-messianic claimant[94] and founder of the so-called 'fourth philosophy' of the Jews (i.e. the Zealots[95]), who refused to the point of death to make any confession of Caesar as Lord (*Ant.* 18.25) and who 'reproached his fellow country-men for patiently paying tribute to Rome' and 'for being submissive to the Romans next to God' (*War* 2.118). Inasmuch as this advocacy of refusing to pay the κῆνσος was specifically grounded in either the profession that Yahweh alone was Lord or the belief that acceptance of the κῆνσος reduced the people of Judaea to a type of slavery which theologically, politically and economically was an intolerable condition for a nation whose Lord was Yahweh, it follows that to call for and

92. Cf. Bruce, 'Render to Caesar', p. 257.

93. Cf. Josephus, *Ant.* 18.1.1; 18.1.6; cp. *War* 2.8.1.

94. On this, see Stauffer, *Christ and the Caesars*, p. 117; Hengel, *The Zealots*, 291-93; F. Loftus, 'The Anti-Roman Revolts of the Jews and the Galileans', *JQR* 68 (1978), pp. 78-98, esp. pp. 87-88; V.A. Tcherikover, *Corpus Papyrorum Judaicarum*, I (Cambridge, MA: Harvard University Press), p. 90 n. 2.

95. Recently scholars, following the lead set out by K. Lake (*The Beginnings of Christianity*. I. *The Acts*, I, *Prolegomena* [London: Macmillan, 1920], pp. 421, 423) have been wont to question not only whether 'the Zealots' was the actual name of the 'fourth philosophy' founded by Judas in 6 CE, but whether there was ever any party known by that name, let alone any real, organized, radical liberation *movement* whose aim was an open people's war with Israel's Roman oppressors, before the outbreak of the Jewish revolt in 66 CE. For the definitive defense of these contested positions, see Hengel, *The Zealots*, pp. 61-78, and esp. pp. 380-404. See also S.G.F. Brandon, *Jesus and the Zealots* (New York: Charles Scribner & Sons, 1967), pp. 26-64.

publicly support refusal to pay the κῆνσος was tantamount to a summons to Jews to 'vindicate their liberty' (τῆς ἐλευθερίας ἐπ' ἀντιλήψει, *Ant.* 18.1) *through armed struggle* and to help establish, through the destruction of the Roman occupation forces and all who supported or cooperated with them, Yahweh's sovereignty in Israel and throughout the world (*War* 7.6.1-4; *Ant.* 17.1.1). So a second effect of open advocacy of refusing to pay the κῆνσος was *to render the one making it an advocate both of a war of liberation with Rome and of the demise of those who had no loyalty to the Law of God.*

Mark's Portrayal of Jesus' Attitude toward the Tax
What, according to Mark, was Jesus' position regarding the legitimacy of the payment of Caesar's κῆνσος? The majority of scholars who have commented on this question have declared that *Mark presents Jesus as advocating payment of the tax* or at least acknowledging its legitimacy.[96] This, however, seems to be a seriously deficient appraisal of Mark's opinion on the matter. In the first place, it ignores the fact that in Mark's Gospel Jesus is presented as one who stands adamantly against the type of economic exploitation which the imposition of the κῆνσος caused. Stinging criticisms are leveled by Jesus against people who deprive inheritors of property from their right of benefit (cf. Mk 7.9-13),[97] or who, believing they are divinely favoured, make use of their privileged status to wring forth exactions from those who can least afford them (cf. Mk 12.38-40, esp. v. 40).[98] Spleen is vented upon rulers who regard their appointment to positions of power as a license to take advantage of their subjects (cf. Mk 10.42).[99] In light of this, it is highly doubtful that Mark presents Jesus as one who endorses Caesar's κῆνσος.

In the second place, the view that Jesus, according to Mark, advocated paying the κῆνσος or accepting its legitimacy ignores the implications of the fact that in Mark's Gospel—and, significantly, nowhere more preeminently than in the Tax Question story itself—Jesus

96. See the list of scholars cited by Giblin as holding the view: 'The Things of God', pp. 510-14.

97. Cf. Lane, *Mark*, p. 251.

98. On the denunciation of the Scribes for economic exploitation, see J.D.M. Derrett, '"Eating Up the Houses of Widows": Jesus' Comment on Lawyers?' *NovT* 14 (1972), pp. 1-9; H. Fleddermann, 'A Warning about the Scribes (Mark 12:37b-40)', *CBQ* 44 (1982), pp. 52-67, esp. pp. 61-63.

99. Cf. Lane, *Mark*, p. 382. Taylor, *Mark*, p. 443. H.B. Swete, *The Gospel according to St Mark* (London: Macmillan, 1905), p. 239.

is presented as one who holds that absolute and undivided loyalty to God is the prime duty for those who believe in him.[100] Given, then, both this and the patent idolatry involved in paying the κῆνσος, it is difficult to think that the Markan Jesus could assent to the legitimacy of the demand. In doing so he would implicate himself in a violation of his own explicit profession that one must always be 'minded' to τὰ τοῦ θεοῦ, loving God with all of one's soul, mind, and strength.[101]

In the third place, to say that the Markan Jesus advocated the payment of the κῆνσος is to ignore the significance of the fact that Jesus, according to Mark, does not carry on his person the particular coin with which the κῆνσος was paid and studiously avoids touching it when it is brought to him (cf. v. 15).[102] As we know from Josephus,[103] the second-century Christian writer Hippolytus,[104] and certain rabbinic sources,[105] such actions are those of one who stood in opposition to, not advocacy of, the κῆνσος and all that it implied.[106]

Finally and most importantly, the view that Jesus, according to Mark, advocated paying the κῆνσος ignores the implications of the fact that in Mark's Gospel the κῆνσος question is presented as the answer given by those who seek to destroy Jesus to their own question concerning how they might bring about his death.[107] According to Mark, the opponents

---

100. On Jesus' call for absolute loyalty to God in the Tax Question story, see Giblin, 'The Things of God', pp. 524-25; M. Hengel, *Was Jesus a Revolutionist?* (Philadelphia: Fortress Press, 1971), p. 33; *idem*, *Christ and Power* (London: SCM Press, 1977), pp. 19-20.

101. Cf. Mk 12.28-32.

102. On this as Mark's presentation of Jesus in Mk 12.15, see L. Hurtado, *Mark* (San Francisco: Harper & Row, 1983), pp. 180, 186.

103. *War* 2.118.

104. *Refutatio Omnium Haeresium* 9. 26.

105. On these, see Hengel, *The Zealots*, pp. 195-96.

106. On Jesus' actions as an expression of a 'theology of opposition' to the κῆνσος, see T. Mommsen, *Römisches Geschichte* (5 vols.; Berlin: Weidmann, 1933), V, p. 514.

107. Pesch, *Das Markusevangelium*, II, p. 225; W. Harrington, *Mark* (Wilmington, DE: Michael Glazier, 1979), p. 186. According to Mark, those who send the Pharisees and Herodians to question Jesus about the legitimacy of the κῆνσος (cf. Mk 12.13) are those who, because of Jesus' Temple 'cleansing' and parable of the Wicked Husbandmen, 'sought a way to destroy (ἀπολέσωσιν)' Jesus (cf. Mk 11.18) and to have him 'arrested' (κρατῆσαι) (cf. Mk 12.12). On this, see Taylor, *Mark*, p. 478; Swete, *Mark*, p. 273; M.-J. Lagrange, *L'Evangile selon Saint*

of Jesus are confident in the hope that the κῆνσος question will be a key instrument in bringing Jesus to destruction. This, then, implies a certainty on their part that once faced with the challenge to adhere to the way of God with regard to the question, Jesus could reply only in a manner which would make him appear to be taking sides with those who, with respect to the κῆνσος question, urged non-cooperation with, and resistance to, Rome—for no other answer would suffice to accomplish this end. But how could the opponents of Jesus be certain that the κῆνσος question would have this outcome unless they knew beforehand that Jesus did not endorse the tax?[108]

It must be concluded then, that in Mark's Gospel Jesus is assumed to be, indeed, is portrayed as, one who opposes the payment of tribute to Caesar.

Given these four observations—(a) that the tax that Jesus is questioned about is the κῆνσος, the poll tax paid in tribute to the Roman Emperor, (b) that to those like Jesus, for whom God alone was King, the tax was offensive and blasphemous and would involve any one who paid it in idolatry and apostasy, (c) that voicing anti-κῆνσος sentiments made the one voicing them both liable to death and an advocate of a violent revolution whose end was to see Israel supreme over its enemies, and (d) that in Mark's eyes Jesus was, and was known by his enemies to be, opposed to the tax—we can now see just *how*, according to Mark, the κῆνσος question puts Jesus' faithfulness to God to the 'test'.

That he would suffer death should he state openly his own position on the tax makes saying that the tax *should* be paid an attractive option. But in doing so Jesus would be capitulating for the sake of self-preservation, which he himself has condemned at Mk 8.34-35 as inappropriate for anyone who, like him, lives to 'follow the way' and 'take up the cross'. This would amount to refusing to 'deny himself' and attempting

Marc (Paris: Gabalda, 1929), p. 312; E. Klostermann, *Das Markus Evangelium* (Tübingen: Mohr, 1926), p. 138.

108. 'It is hard to see how the denarius question could have been thought by those who put it [to Jesus] to be a serious trap, unless Jesus' repudiation of the Roman occupation were taken for granted, so that he could be expected to give an answer which would enable them to denounce him' (J.H. Yoder, *The Politics of Jesus* [Grand Rapids: Eerdmans, 1972], p. 53). See also on this, Derrett, 'Render', p. 321 n. 4; Hengel, *The Zealots*, p. 194; Pesch, *Das Markusevangelium*, II, p. 225; Stauffer, *Christ and the Caesars*, p. 120; and especially R.A. Horsley, *Jesus and the Spiral of Violence* (San Francisco: Harper, 1987), pp. 307-308.

to 'save his life'. But should he actually 'deny himself' and give voice to what he actually thinks about the legitimacy of the κῆνσος, he would not only sanction in the name of teaching 'the way of God' an activity which Jesus, according to Mark, had previously declared characteristic of being 'minded' to τὰ τοῦ ἀνθρώπου,[109] but he would also deny the truth of the Gospel that it is though suffering and service, not conquest and domination, that God wishes his elect to establish his sovereignty over the world.

Has Mark Changed the Tradition?

I have shown above in my examination of the tradition history of Mk 12.13-17 that Mark's version of the tradition of Jesus' Tax Question is a secondary, and largely Markan, expansion of a pre-Markan narrative which is to be found preserved in, and best represented by, Logion 100 of the *Gospel of Thomas*.[110] I have also shown that in recounting the story of Jesus Tax Question Mark has altered the narrative upon which his version is based in at least two ways. First, he *transformed the form* of the original version of the tradition from that of a *Chreia* to that of a full fledged, non unitary, 'conflict story' or 'controversy dialogue'. Secondly, he both *modified the substance* of the contextualizing intro-duction of the original tradition by making those who come to Jesus and raise the issue of the tax Jesus' opponents and not his compatriots,[111]

109. On this, see above, Chapter 7.

110. Without, of course, what is evidently a secondary (Gnosticising?) addition, i.e., Jesus' pronouncement 'But give me what is mine'. In other words, the original version of the Tax Question tradition read:

They showed Jesus a gold (coin) and said to him: Caesar's men ask taxes (φορος) from us. He said to them: Give the things of Caesar to Caesar; the things of God to God.

111. In the *Chreia* the identity of those who come to Jesus and report that Caesar's men are demanding taxes is left unspecified (*'They* come to Jesus...and say...'). That they are compatriots, indeed, co-religionists, and not opponents of Jesus is indicated by three considerations. (1) As we will seem below (see note), in their report that 'Caesar's men demand taxes from us', they seem to regard Jesus as a member, if not the leader, of their group. (2) Their motivation in seeking out Jesus and reporting to him what Caesar's men are demanding seems to be an actual desire to have Jesus advise them on how to respond to the demand. Moreover, they seem to be willing to be bound by his advice. (3) They seem to be genuinely bothered by the demand and are thus presented as devotees of God.

and he *added much to it* by giving the story a concrete setting (in Jerusalem in the last week of Jesus' life), by linking what goes on within the story with a plot line begun early in the Gospel (the move by Jewish religious authorities to destroy Jesus, cf. Mk 11.18, cp. Mk 3.16), and by explicitly noting that the question on the legitimacy of the tax subjects Jesus to an experience of πειρασμός in which his resolve to avoid the 'things of men', especially as regards the acceptance of violence, is put to the test. In light of this, the question arises as to whether Mark altered the basic narrative theme of the original tradition as well. In designating the story of the tax question as a 'temptation' tradition, and in explicating the content of the temptation recounted therein as he does, has Mark been theologically innovative? Or was he only drawing out and emphasizing a theme which was, or which he took to be, already present within the *Chreia* upon which his own telling of the Tax Question story is based?

This depends of course on two things: first, whether or not the primitive *Chreia* was, or was likely to have been taken as, a 'temptation' tradition; secondly, *if* the *Chreia* was indeed a 'temptation' tradition, or was readily perceived as such, whether the nature and content of temptation presented there was the same as that presented in Mk 12.13-15. It is to these questions that I now turn.

Was the Chreia a 'Temptation' Story?

At first glance it would seem that this was not the case. There is no appearance or usage within the *Chreia*'s contextualizing introduction (i.e. the narrative 'framework' leading to the dominical saying) of the terminology or *dramatis personae* typical of 'temptation' stories (e.g. πειράζω or one of its cognates or synonyms, the figure of Satan). Nor is there anything within the response of Jesus to the issue posed to him on the order of his τί με πειράζετε found at Mk 12.15.

But, despite this, there are, I think, two considerations which, when taken together, indicate that the *Chreia* that was the ultimate source for Mk 12.13-17 was, or could easily be taken as, a 'temptation' tradition. First, it is presupposed within the *Chreia* that the demand to pay the tax is made of Jesus as much as it is of his compatriots.[112] Secondly, in his

---

112. As we have seen, those who come to Jesus with the report of the imposition of the tax announce that 'Caesar's men demand taxes of *us*'. Admittedly, the 'us' here could be a referent to a special group of which Jesus is not a member, which nevertheless recognized Jesus as a wise man from whom they might gain counsel on

pronouncement, 'Give the things of Caesar to Caesar and the things of God to God', Jesus characterizes the demand as one which places those subjected to it in a 'forced position' of having to chose between remaining obedient to God or abandoning what he commands.[113] Now, as we have had many occasions to observe, being brought into this sort of position is the essence of a πειρασμός, especially a πειρασμός involving faithfulness. So in characterizing the demand in this fashion, Jesus is in effect noting that he has experienced a 'religious' testing. And this notation would not be lost on a first-century audience.

The Presentation of Content of the Temptation

We have seen that the most primitive version of the tradition of Jesus' Tax Question presents Jesus as being subjected to temptation of the 'religious' kind. But what according to this version is the content of this temptation? How does being confronted with the issue of paying taxes to Caesar put Jesus' faithfulness 'to the test'? Surely it is that it might force him into having to admit that faithfulness to God cannot be maintained without countenancing some form of 'holy war'. This becomes clear when we take into account four facts. First, when his compatriots approach him and report that Caesar's men are demanding that Jews pay a certain tax, Jesus is in effect being asked whether he thinks a Jew loyal to God should capitulate to the demand or refuse to do so. Though there is nothing in the *Chreia* on the order of Mk 12.14c-15 ('...Is it lawful to pay taxes to Caesar, or not? Should we pay them, or should we not?' RSV), this question or one very much like it seems presupposed there. Secondly, the tax that Jesus is asked about in the *Chreia* is the same one he is asked about in Mk 12.13-14, the κῆνσος. Thirdly, the background of the story told in the *Chreia* is the assumption that for a Jew to say 'yes' to the payment of the κῆνσος was to abandon faithfulness to God, while to say 'no' openly was in effect to issue a clarion call to arms against Rome. And fourthly, Jesus is portrayed as refusing to give a 'yes' or 'no' answer to the question posed to him, as if both such direct and unequivocal responses had to be avoided.

the tax question. But it is, I think, a more natural reading of the text to take the 'us' as referring to a group of which Jesus is a vital part if not the recognized head.

113. I assume here, not unnaturally given how the two clauses of Jesus response seem to be adversative, that in the *Chreia* the activity of 'giving to Caesar Caesar's things' is presupposed as contrary to, and an abandonment of, 'giving God's things to God'.

With this before us, I return to the question of whether Mark was being theologically innovative, in explicitly casting his version of the tradition of the Tax Question as a 'temptation' story in which Jesus is put to the test over his faithfulness to the idea that loyalty to God means renouncing theocratically motivated violence. The answer seems to be *no*. The material upon which he based his version of the tradition already presented the Tax Question as something which involved Jesus in 'temptation'. Moreover, it assumed that the content of that temptation was basically that which confronts Jesus in Mk 12.13-17. However innovative Mark was in handling the form and substance of the material which underlies his version of the Tax Question story, when he took up and dealt with the *theme* of that material, the Second Evangelist acted conservatively and remained a traditionalist.

Chapter 11

SUMMARY, CONCLUSIONS AND SPECULATIONS

My efforts in the previous pages have been devoted to an analysis of eight of the eleven 'primary' versions of the Synoptic Tradition's twenty-one 'temptation of Jesus' accounts.[1] In carrying out this analysis, I have been concerned with determining several things. The first and foremost of these was what each of the eight 'primary' versions of these accounts presents as the nature and content of the particular temptation of which it speaks. But along with this I have also sought to know:

- whether and to what extent, if any, these versions as they now appear to us in their present form are either *'new' traditions or secondary expansions of existing ones,* that is, whether *as narratives* they are late and wholly *original* compositions of the evangelist in whose Gospel they appear, or whether they are derived from, and owe their shape and basic substance to, more primitive, traditional stories;

- whether or not, in the cases of those versions which *are* indeed secondary expansions, the primitive narrative upon which respectively they are based was also a 'temptation' tradition;

- whether, in the cases of those versions that are secondary expansions and whose *Vorlage was* a 'temptation tradition', any of these versions differs in what it presents as the nature and content of the temptation it recounts from what is presented in the particular traditional story from which it is derived;

- whether there is any unity of conception among the different 'primary' 'temptation traditions' and their sources regarding the *way* Jesus was tempted and the *issue* which formed the basis of his experiences with temptation.

---

1. For the list of these accounts, see above in the Introduction, pp. 21-22.

My findings regarding the question of what the investigated 'primary' versions present as the nature and content of the temptations which they each recount have been stated above. There is no need to repeat them here. But what has been determined with respect to the other things I sought to know? My findings are these:

- Three of the eight investigated 'primary' versions—the Q account of Jesus' Wilderness temptation (Mt. 4.1-11//Lk. 4.1-13); Mark's account of Jesus' Divorce Question Temptation (Mk 10.1-12) and Mark's account of Jesus' temptation at Gethsemane (Mk 14.32-42)—are 'new', that is, they are not derived or built up from a more primitive *story*. Rather, their existence *as narratives* is due to the evangelist's hand (or, in the case of the Q version of the Wilderness temptation, a tradent's hand).

- The remaining five of these eight 'primary' versions, namely, Mark's accounts of Jesus' Wilderness temptation (Mk 1.9-13), the temptation over the Demand for a 'sign' (Mk 8.1-13), the temptation at Caesarea Philippi (Mk 8.27-33), and the temptation over the question of the κῆνσος (Mk 12.13-17), as well as the Q account of Jesus' 'sign' demand temptation (Mt. 12.38-42//Lk. 11.16, 29-32), are secondary expansions, each having been based upon, and/or built up from, more primitive narrative tradition.

- All of the five traditional narratives underlying the secondary expansions were each originally 'temptation traditions'.

- There is not a single instance in which a 'primary' version, analysed as a secondary expansion of a 'temptation tradition' *Vorlage differs* in its presentation of the nature and content of the particular temptation it recounts from what is presented in the traditional story from which it is derived. The assumptions concerning the nature and content of Jesus' temptation contained in Mk 1.9-13; Mk 8.11-13; Mt. 12.38-42//Lk. 11.16, 29-32; Mk 8.27-33; and Mk 12.13-17 are the same as those contained in the traditions from which these secondary stories were respectively derived. There is, then, within at least the first two of the three stages of what has been outlined as the synoptic trajectories of each of these traditions, a *vertical* unity of conception regarding the nature and content of certain temptations that Jesus was thought to have experienced.

• There is also a *horizontal* unity of conception among the different primary 'temptation traditions' that I have examined with respect to the matter both of the *way* Jesus was tempted and the *issue* which formed the basis of his experiences with temptation. What is reported in Mark's story of Jesus' Wilderness temptation regarding the nature and content of that temptation is the same as what is reported in this regard *in all other Markan temptation stories* (i.e. his stories of the 'Sign' Demand, Caesarea Philippi, Gethsemane, Divorce, and Tax Question temptations) *and in the Q version of the 'Sign' Demand temptation as well.*

At the outset of this study I raised the question of whether there was any evidence that the early Church held a unified view of the nature and content of the temptations of Jesus that its various canonical traditionists recounted him undergoing. We can see now that there is. To the extent that we have not seen or determined what is said in this regard in other synoptic temptation traditions contemporaneous with the ones I have examined (e.g. the Lukan account of Jesus' experience of being 'tempted' when confronted with a question on the requirements of inheriting eternal life, Lk. 10.25-26), let alone in those which I have deemed 'secondary',[2] the evidence is, to be sure, only partial. But it is there, nonetheless, and it is highly suggestive: *What is presented as the nature and content of Jesus' temptation in the 'primary' versions of the respective traditions of Jesus temptations will be maintained (if not*

2.   That is, the Matthean version of the tradition of Jesus' temptation in the wilderness (Mt. 4.1-11); the Lukan version of Jesus' temptation in the wilderness (Lk. 4.1-13); the Matthean and Lukan versions of the tradition of Jesus' temptation in the demand for a '"sign" from heaven' (Mt. 16.1-4; Mt. 12.28-42; Lk. 11.16, 29-32); the Matthean version of the tradition of Jesus' temptation when faced with Peter's 'confession' at Caesarea Philippi (Mt. 16.13-23); the Matthean version of the tradition of Jesus tempted by the question on the legitimacy of divorce (Mt. 19.1-12); the Matthean and Lukan accounts of Jesus' temptation by the question concerning the legitimacy of paying taxes to Caesar (Mt. 22.15-22; Lk. 20.20-26 A D); the Matthean account of Jesus' being tempted when confronted with the question of the 'greatest commandment' (Mt. 23.34-40); the Matthean and Lukan versions of the tradition of Jesus' temptation in Gethsemane (Mt. 26.36-46; Lk. 22.40-46).

underscored) in these traditions' 'secondary' versions.[3] This conclusion, it should be noted, is sound not only because it is a reasonable inference given what we have seen is the solid 'trajectory' of thought that moves from the first to the second stage in the tradition history of each of the examined 'primary versions' which are secondary expansions of more primitive material. It is also the upshot of the fact, demonstrated in my examination of the Q version of the Wilderness temptation tradition and Mk 10.1-12, that when a 'new' narrative 'temptation tradition' has been *created*, the view of the nature and the content of the temptation of which this 'new' tradition speaks turns out to be cast fully in accord with the views set out in the 'older', traditional temptation narratives. Why should this be so if there was not within the early church a fundamental and constraining belief that the fabric of Jesus' temptations was always woven from the same material?

As I did in opening this study, I close it with a question, namely, What would be indicated if, as the evidence adduced here suggests, both the remaining 'primary' versions and *all* of the 'secondary' versions of the canonical gospel 'temptation of Jesus' traditions *are* of a piece with our investigated 'primary' versions as to the business of the nature and content of Jesus' temptations and if, therefore, there *was indeed* a unified view of this matter within the early church? It is beyond my purpose to answer this question here, at least with any degree of thoroughness. But four implications can be mentioned:

First, the mission and ministry of Jesus was viewed throughout the development of early Christianity as *intensely political*, centering primarily in raising questions not of individual piety and ethics but of the proper way of life for the Jewish *nation*. The church saw Jesus as involved in calling and constraining Israel, as he himself in his commissioning as Messiah, King of Israel, had been called and constrained, to make a particular choice between two conceptions of how Israel was to

---

3. This is, for instance, as even a cursory glance at the evidence shows, certainly the case in the Matthean and Lukan versions of Jesus' Wilderness and 'Sign' Demand temptations, in Matthew's version of Jesus' Caesarea Philippi temptation, and in the Matthean and Lukan versions of the traditions of Jesus' Tax Question and Gethsemane temptations. It is, admittedly, not so apparent in the Matthean versions of Jesus' Divorce Question and Greatest Commandment Question temptations. I believe, however, that it is nevertheless still the case even there, and I hope to show this in another study.

flesh out its appointment to be the Chosen People of God and thereby achieve its divinely promised destiny of becoming the nation through which God would become manifest to all peoples.[4]

Secondly, as a number of other New Testament traditions state or imply,[5] great weight was attached to the issue of the renunciation of violence and of abusive power, of war and killing, and to the necessity or appropriateness of love of enemies. This was not only a significant confessional and ethical issue in early Christianity, but one which was 'genuinely privileged',[6] and served more distinctively than any other as the primary touchstone against which one's full acceptance of the Gospel and the extent of one's faithfulness to the way of Jesus was measured.[7]

Thirdly, Mark's Gospel has as its background and occasion the outbreak and initial stages of the war of the Jews with Rome and all that it portended, and it dates from slightly before 70 CE. A continuing, powerful and concentrated emphasis within the Gospel, exemplified particularly in the temptation stories, is that the principal stumbling block for those following along 'on the way' which God has ordained for his elect is to think that suffering service and inclusive compassion, even for the enemies of Israel, are to be repudiated as the means by which God's purposes are implemented in the world. The essence of temptation, according to Mark, is to be faced with the option of choosing the 'things of men', that is, embracing the mindset taken up with violence, domination, and the destruction of 'the wicked'. Mark's urgency on this issue *may* be explained as a reminiscence of what the historical Jesus actually faced in his lifetime and taught his disciples. But it surely must

4. On the early church's (as well as Jesus' own) view of the message, mission and ministry of Jesus as political, that is, as having to do with the life and ordering of the *polis* and centering in questions of national as opposed to purely individual policy, see G.B. Caird, *Jesus and the Jewish Nation* (London: The University of London, The Athlore Press, 1965), and now especially M.J. Borg, *Conflict, Holiness and Politics in the Teaching of Jesus* (New York: Edwin Mellen Press, 1984).

5. Cf., e.g., Mt. 5.7, 38-41, 43-48; Lk. 14.27-33; 1 Cor. 1.23; 1 Pet. 2.20-21.

6. On this, see J.H. Yoder, 'The Unique Role of the Historic Peace Churches', *Brethren Life and Thought* 15 (1969), pp. 132-49. See also Yoder's 'Jesus and Power', *Ecumenical Review* 25 (1973), pp. 447-54.

7. On this see not only J.H.Yoder, *The Politics of Jesus* (Grand Rapids: Eerdmans, 1972), pp. 115-34, but also H.J. Schoeps, 'Von der Imitatio Dei zur Nachfolge Christi', in his *Aus Frühchristlicher Zeit: Religionsgeschictliche untersuchungen* (Tübingen: Mohr, 1950), pp. 286-301, esp. pp. 286-87.

also reflect the fact that Mark's readers were in special and immediate need of admonition on this point. And this in turn means that the community for which Mark wrote was embroiled in a situation the nature of which was such so as to convince them of three things: (1) that the 'Day of the Lord' was upon them and Kingdom of God was finally about to arrive, (2) that they would be untrue to their calling as God's elect if they did not give themselves over to the service of establishing God's sovereignty on earth, and (3) that the 'things of men'—especially with respect to the treatment of God's enemies and those who had harmed God's people—were the necessary, appropriate, and only means of achieving this end, having been sanctioned by God as the 'Way' he now wished his faithful to tread. But of all the situations occurring early in the latter half of the first century CE, and affecting Christians, what one *other than the outbreak and early prosecution of the war of the Jews with Rome* was capable of doing this?[8]

Finally, just as my first foray as an undergraduate student into the

---

8.   The persecutions in Rome of Christians by Nero (in 64 CE), held by the majority of Markan scholars to be the occasion of Mark's Gospel, does not, in my opinion, qualify as a plausible 'candidate' here. While it certainly explains and provides a viable context for Mark's well-known interest in, and persistent emphasis upon, the fact that Christians are bound to suffer for the Gospel, it does not fully account for the Markan theme of the necessity that his readers avoid both 'being led astray'—especially by pseudo-Messiahs and 'false prophets'—and falling into step with 'those outside' and with 'this generation', by becoming 'minded' to τὰ τοῦ ἀνθρώπου with respect to the enemies of Israel. To be sure, those who suffered under Nero might have been 'radicalized', that is, moved, as, say, various members of the Student Nonviolent Coordinating Committee were in the 1960's in the American South after being brutalized by certain state government officials and defenders of the status quo, (1) to renounce their initial acceptance of suffering as God's way in the world and (2) to see those who had persecuted them as those who deserved (and who would receive) God's destructive judgment and not, as they once believed, his mercy. But it is only during the Jewish War against Rome, and in active service within or in support of that war, that the activity envisaged (if only indirectly) in the temptation stories (the people of God actually acting like 'the great ones of the Gentiles who lord it over their subjects', cf. Mk 10.42, and engaging in an apparently divinely led vanquishment and subjugation of God's enemies) ever became for Christians and Jews a live option and a real possibility. For an extended defense of the idea of the outbreak of the Jewish War as the cause and occasion of the Gospel of Mark, see now J. Marcus, 'The Jewish War and the *Sitz im Leben* of Mark', *JBL* 111 (1992), pp. 441-62.

jungle of the epistle to the Hebrews made me suppose to be the case,[9] the fourth thing indicated is that, as with Mark's Gospel, so also in Hebrews it is the outbreak of the Jewish revolt against Rome, and more specifically, the author's perception of the certainty of his readers being caught up in the revolt's allure and all it seemed to promise for God's elect, that stands as the occasion which prompted him to take pen in hand.

9. See the Preface of this work for my account of this.

Appendix

INSTANCES OF THE VERB πειράξω IN CLASSICAL AND HELLENISTIC GREEK

Moving diachronically from the fifth century BCE forward, πειράζω is to be found employed first by Herodotus (*History* 6.86.3), Aesop (*Fabulae* 234, ed. Hausrath) and by Aristophanes of Athens (*The Wasps* 1129), then in the 4th century BCE by the Athenian comic playwright Menander (*Fragments* 42.319; cp. *Mono.* 1.573) and by his compatriot Epicurus (*Deperditorum librorum reliquiae* 29.15.15), but then not again until the third century BCE by Apollonius Rhodius (*Argon.* 1.495; 2.46; 3.10), the technological writer Philon of Byzantium (Philo Mechanichus) (*Belopoecia* 50.34; 51.9), and by the author (Pseudo-Callisthenes) of the *Historia Alexandri Magni* (1.23.13; 1.33.32 recension β [ed. L. Bergson, *Der griesche Alexander-roman: Recension* β [Stockholm: Almqvist & Wiksell, 1965], pp. 1-192; cp. also 1.23.17 and 1.26.78 of Recension γ [ed. U. von Lauenstein, *Der griechische Alexan-derroman: Recension γ. Buch 1* [Beitrage zur klassichen Philologie, 4; Meisenheim am Glan: Hain, 1962], pp. 2-150), where the text of 1.23.13 Recension β (the primary text of the *Historia*) is reduplicated albeit in a different narrative setting, as well as 2.35a, 17.6; 35a, 28.10 of Recension γ. It has been noted, however, that these latter passages are not by the author of the *Historia*. Rather, they have been taken over from *On the Brahmans*, a work by the fourth-century CE author Palladius].

The verb is used subsequently by the Macedonian historian Polybius (*Histories* 2.6.9; 5.69.5; 8.4.7; 21.4.7; 30.23.2; *Fragments* 195 [three times]) and the Alexandrian grammarian Aristophanes Byzantinus (*Epigrammata demonstrativa* 2.1.6) in the second century BCE, then by the mythographer Ps. Apollodorus (*The Library* 2.5.1; 3.8.9; 3.14.6), the Roman based Epicurean writer Philodemus (*On Methods of Inference* 32), the historians Diodorus Siculus (*Bibliotheca historica* 2.58.5) and Dionysius Halicarnassensis (*Antiquitates Romanae* 7.12.3; 10.1.5; 10.12.6; 13.4.3), the historian and geographer Strabo of Pontus (*Geography* 16.4.24), the Roman satirist Lucilius (Book 11, Epigram 183 in *The Greek Anthology*, IV, trans. W.H. Patton), and the Alexandrian Jewish theologian and philosopher Philo (*On Dreams* 1.194; *The Preliminary Studies* 163.10) in the first century BCE, then by Plutarch (*Cleomenes* 7.3; *Moralia* 230a; 508.A.1; 784.B.10), Josephus (*War* 1.654; 4.340; *Ant* 6.210; *Apion* 2.215), the Ephesian medical writer and physician Soranus (*Gynaeciorum* 2.43.1), and the authors/compilers of *The Anacreontea* (28.12; 33.24), and the *Vita Aesopi* (Vita G 64.2) in the first century CE, and then by the Samosataean essayist and critic Lucian (*Merc. Cond.* 39.13; *Podagra* 149; 165; 279), the Roman physician Sextus Empiricus (*Adversus Mathmaticos* 1.40), the Alexandrian grammarian Aelius Herodianus (*Schematismi Homerici* 114.2, ed. P. Egenolff, 'Zu Herodianos', *Jahrbuch für classischen Philologie* 149 [1894], pp. 338-45), the medical writer Galen (*De sectis ad eos qui introductor* 1.67.1; *De simplicium medicamentorum temperamentis ac facultatibus libri* 11.861.16; 12.8.3; *De antidotis libri* 2.14.2.6), the Bythinian historian and Stoic philosopher Arrian (*The Discourses* 1.9.29), and the astrologer Vettius Valens (*Anthologiarum* 1.39; *Additamenta* 4.24 [enumeration according to the edition of D. Pingree, *Vettii Valentis Antiocheni: Anthologiarum Libri Novem* [Leipzig: B.S.B. B.G. Teubner Verlagsgesellschaft, 1986]) in the second century CE.

πειράζω also appears five times in two works by Alexander Aphrodisiensis (*Problematica* 2.54; *In Aristotelis sophisticos enlenchos commentarium* 89.4; 96.28; 96.30; 97.27.2), a second to third century CE peripatetic philosopher, twice in the Papyri (*PSI* 927.25; Πειραζόμενη Fragmentum [P. Brit. Mus. 2208]), and once in the *Scholia* on Aristophanes (*Plutus* 575).

BIBLIOGRAPHY

Abel, F.M., *Géographie de la Palestine* (2 vols.; Paris: Gabalda, 1933–38).

Achtemeier, P.J., *Mark* (Philadelphia: Fortress Press, 1975).

—'An Exposition of Mark 9.30-37', *Int* 30 (1976), pp. 174-78.

—'He Taught them Many Things: Reflections on Markan Christology', *CBQ* 42 (1980), pp. 465-81.

Aland, K., *Synopsis Quattour Evangeliorum* (Stuttgart: Württembergische Bibelanstalt, 7th edn, 1971).

Albertz, M., *Die Synoptischen Streigesprache: Ein Beitrag zur Formengeschichte des Urchristentums* (Berlin: Trowitzche & Sohn, 1921).

Allen, L.C., *The Books of Joel, Obadiah, Jonah, and Micah* (Grand Rapids: Eerdmans, 1976).

Allen, W.C., *A Critical and Exegetical Commentary on the Gospel according to St Matthew* (Edinburgh: T. & T. Clark, 1909).

—'The Book of Sayings Used by the Editor of the First Gospel', in W. Sanday (ed.), *Oxford Studies in the Synoptic Problem* (Oxford: Clarendon Press, 1911), pp. 245-86.

—*The Gospel according to Saint Mark* (London: Macmillan, 1915).

Ambrozic, A., *The Hidden Kingdom* (Washington, DC: Catholic Biblical Association, 1972).

—'New Teaching with Power (Mk. 1.27)', in J. Plevnick (ed.), *Word and Spirit: Essays in Honor of David Michael Stanley, SJ on his 60th Birthday* (Willowdale, Ont.: Regis College Press, 1975), pp. 113-49.

Anderson, H., *The Gospel of Mark* (London: Oliphants, 1975).

Andrews, M.E., 'PEIRASMOS—A Study in Form Criticism', *ATR* 24 (1942), pp. 229-44.

Argyle, A., 'Scriptural Quotations in Q Material', *ExpTim* 65 (1953–54), p. 125.

Aufhauser, J., *Buddha und Jesus in ihren Paralleltexten* (Kl. Texte, 157; Bonn: A. Marcus & E. Weber, 1926).

Bacon, B.W., *The Sermon on the Mount* (London: Macmillan, 1902).

—*The Beginning of the Gospel Story* (New Haven: Yale University Press, 1909).

—*The Gospel of Mark: Its Composition and Date* (New Haven: Yale University Press, 1925).

—*Studies in Matthew* (London: Constable, 1930).

Balforth, H., *The Gospel according to Saint Luke* (Oxford: Clarendon Press, 1930).

Baljon, J.M.S., *Novum Testamentum Graece* (Gronigen: J.B. Woltes, 1898).

Baltensweiler, H., *Die Ehe im Neuen Testament* (Zurich: Zwingli Verlag, 1967).

Balz, H., 'τεσσεράκοντα, κτλ.', *TDNT*, VIII, p. 137.

Bammel, E., 'Markus 10.11f. und das judische Eherecht', *ZNW* 61 (1970), pp. 95-101.

Banks, R., *Jesus and the Law in the Synoptic Tradition* (Cambridge: Cambridge University Press, 1975).

Barbour, R.S., 'Gethsemane in the Tradition of the Passion', *NTS* 16 (1970), pp. 231-51.

—*Traditio-Historical Criticism of the Gospels* (London: SPCK, 1972).

Barclay, W., *The Gospel of Mark* (Philadelphia: Westminster Press, 1975).

Barnett, P.W., 'The Jewish Sign Prophets—AD 40–70—Their Intentions and Origin', *NTS* 27 (1981), pp. 679-97.

Barrett, C.K., *The Holy Spirit in the Gospel Tradition* (London: SPCK, 1947).

—'The Background to Mark 10.45', in A.J.B. Higgins (ed.), *New Testament Essays* (London: SPCK, 1959), pp. 1-18.

—*Jesus and the Gospel Tradition* (Philadelphia: Fortress Press, 1968).

—*A Commentary on the First Epistle to the Corinthians* (London: A. &. C. Black, 1968).

Bartlet, J.V., *St Mark* (Edinburgh: T.C. & E.C. Jack, 1922).

Bauer, J., 'De conigali foedere quid edixerit Matthaeus (Mt 5, 31; 19, 3-9)', *VD* (1966), pp. 74-78.

Beare, F.W., *The Earliest Records of Jesus* (Nashville: Abingdon, 1962).

Beasley-Murray, G.R., *A Commentary on Mark Thirteen* (London: Macmillan, 1957).

—*Jesus and the Kingdom of God* (Grand Rapids: Eerdmans, 1986).

Bennett, W.J. Jr, 'The Son of Man Must...', *NovT* 17 (1975), pp. 113-29.

Bell, H.I. and T.C. Skeat, *The New Gospel Fragments* (London: Trustees of the British Museum and Oxford University Press, 1935).

—*Fragments of an Unknown Gospel and other Early Christian Papyri* (London: Trustees of the British Museum and Oxford University Press, 1935).

Berger, K., 'Hartherzigkeit und Gottes Geretz: Die Vorgeschichte des antijüdischen Vorworfs in Mk. 10.5', *ZNW* 61 (1970), pp. 1-47.

—*Die Gesetzsaulegung Jesu*, I (Neukirchen: Neukirchen Verlag, 1972).

Bergson, L., *Der griesche Alexanderroman: Recension β* (Stockholm: Almqvist & Wiksell, 1965).

Bertram, G., 'θάμβος, κτλ.', *TDNT*, II, pp. 4-7.

E. Best, *The Temptation and the Passion: The Markan Soteriology* (Cambridge: Cambridge University Press, 1965).

—'Mark's Preservation of the Tradition' in M. Sabbe (ed.), *L'Evangile selon Marc: Tradition et Redaction* (Gembloux: Leuven University Press, 1974), pp. 21-34; repr. in Best, *Disciples and Discipleship: Studies in the Gospel according to Mark* (Edinburgh: T. & T. Clark, 1986), pp. 31-48.

—*Following Jesus: Discipleship in the Gospel of Mark* (Sheffield: Sheffield University Press, 1981).

—*Mark: The Gospel as Story* (Edinburgh: T. & T. Clark, 1983).

—'Peter in the Gospel according to Mark', in *Disciples and Discipleship: Studies in the Gospel according to Mark* (Edinburgh: T. & T. Clark, 1986), pp. 162-76.

Betz, O., 'Miracles in the Writings of Josephus', in L.H. Feldman and G. Hata (eds.), *Josephus, Judaism, and Christianity* (Detroit: Wayne State University Press, 1987), pp. 212-35.

Beyer, H.W., 'διακονέω', *TDNT*, II, p. 81-93.

Bientenhard, H., 'ὄνομα', *TDNT*, V, pp. 242-83.

Black, M., 'The Cup Metaphor in Mark xiv. 36', *ExpTim* 49 (1947–1948), p. 195.

—*An Aramaic Approach to the Gospels and Acts* (Oxford: Oxford University Press, 3rd edn, 1967).

Blackwell, J. *The Passion as Story: The Plot of Mark* (Philadelphia: Fortress Press, 1986).

Blunt, A.F.W., *The Gospel according to Saint Mark* (Oxford: Clarendon Press, 1929).

Bonnard, P., 'La Signification du désert selon le Noveau Testament. Essai sur l'interprétation théologique, par l'Eglise primitive, d'un concept historico-géographique', in J.-J. von Allmen (ed.), *Hommage et Reconnaissance: Receil de Travaux publiés à l'occasion du soixantiéme anniversaire de Karl Barth* (Paris: Neuchâtel & Niestlé, 1946), pp. 9-18.

Boobyer, G.H., 'The Miracles of the Loaves and the Gentiles in Mark's Gospel', *SJT* 6 (1953), pp. 77-87.

—'Mark II,10a and the Interpretation of the Healing of the Parayltic', *HTR* 47 (1954), pp. 115-20.

Borg, M.J., *Conflict, Politics and Holiness in the Teaching of Jesus* (New York: Edwin Mellen Press, 1984).

Bornkamm, G., *Jesus of Nazareth* (New York: Harper & Row, 1960).

Boucher, M., *The Mysterious Parable: A Literary Study* (Washington, DC: Catholic Biblical Association, 1977).

Bousset, W., *Kyrios Christos: A History of Belief in Christ from the Beginnings of Christianity to Irenaeus* (Nashville: Abingdon, 1970).

Bowman, J.W., *The Gospel of Mark* (Leiden: Brill, 1965).

Box, G.H., and C. Gore, *Divorce in the New Testament* (London: SPCK, 1921).

Brandon, S.G.F., *Jesus and the Zealots* (New York: Charles Scribner & Sons, 1967).

Brandt, W., *Die jüdische Baptismen* (Geissen: Töpelmann, 1910).

Branscomb, B.H., *The Gospel of Mark* (London: Hodder & Stoughton, 1937).

Bretcher, P.G., *The Temptation of Jesus in Matthew* (DTh Thesis, Concordia Seminary, St Louis, 1966).

Breymayer, R., 'Zur Pragmatik des Bildes. Semiotische Beobachtungen zum Streitgespräch Mk 12,13-17 ("Der Zinsgroschen") unter Berücksichtigung der Spieltheorie', *LingBib* 13-14 (1972), pp. 19-51.

Brown, R.E., 'Incidents that are Units in the Synoptic Gospels but Dispersed in St John', *CBQ* 23 (1961), pp. 143-60.

—*The Gospel according to John (i–xii)* (Garden City: Doubleday, 1966).

Brown, R.E., K.P. Donfried, and J. Reumann (eds.), *Peter in the New Testament* (Minneapolis: Augsburg, 1973).

Brown, S., 'Deliverance from the Crucible: Some Further Reflections on 1 QH III.1-18', *NTS* 14 (1967–68), pp. 247-59.

—*Apostasy and Perseverance in the Theology of Luke* (Rome: Pontifical Biblical Institute, 1969).

Bruce, A.B., 'The Synoptic Gospels', in *The Expositor's Greek Testament*, I (London: Hodder & Stoughton, 1897).

Bruce, F.F., 'Render to Caesar', in E. Bammel and C.F.D. Moule (eds.), *Jesus and the Politics of his Day* (Cambridge: Cambridge University Press, 1984), pp. 249-63.

Buchanan, G.W., 'Mark 11,15-19: Brigands in the Temple', *HUCA* 30 (1959), pp. 169-77.

—'Some Vow and Oath Formulas in the New Testament', *HTR* 58 (1965), pp. 319-26.

Bultmann, R., *Form Criticism* (Chicago: Willitt, Clark & Co., 1934).

—*The History of the Synoptic Tradition* (Oxford: Basil Blackwell, 1963).

—'λύπη, κτλ.', *TDNT*, IV, pp. 313-24.

Burkill, T.A., *Mysterious Revelation: An Examination of the Philosophy of St Mark's Gospel* (Ithaca, NY: Cornell University Press, 1963).

—*New Light on the Earliest Gospel* (Ithaca, NY: Cornell University Press, 1972).

Burkitt, F.C., 'Jesus and Divorce', *JTS* 5 (1904), pp. 628-29.

Buttrick, G.A., 'The Gospel according to St Matthew: Exposition', *IB*, VII (New York: Abingdon, 1951), pp. 250-625.

Butts, J.R., 'The Chreia in the Synoptic Gospels', *BTB* 16 (1986), pp. 132-38.

Cadbury, H.J., *The Style and Literary Method of Luke* (Cambridge: Harvard University Press, 1920).

Cadoux, C.J, 'The Imperitival Use of ἵνα in the New Testament', *JTS* 42 (1941), pp. 165-73.

Cailixt, G., *Quator Evangelicorum Scriptorum Concordia et Explicicatio* (Helmstadt: Henningus Mullerus, 1663).

Caird, G.B., *Principalities and Powers: A Study in Pauline Theology* (Oxford: Clarendon Press, 1956).

—*The Gospel of St Luke* (Baltimore: Penguin, 1963).

—*Jesus and the Jewish Nation* (London: University of London, The Athlore Press, 1965).

Carpenter, J.E., *The First Three Gospels: Their Origin and Relations* (London: Philip Green, 4th edn, 1906).

Carrington, P., *According to Mark* (Cambridge: Cambridge University Press, 1960).

Casey, M., *Son of Man: The Interpretation of Daniel 7* (London: SCM Press, 1979).

Cassidy, R.J., *Jesus, Politics, and Society: A Study of Luke's Gospel* (Maryknoll: Orbis, 1978).

Castor, G.D., 'The Relation of Mark to the Source Q', *JBL* 31 (1912), pp. 82-91.

Catchpole, D.R., 'The Synoptic Divorce Material as a Traditio-Historical Problem', *BJRL* 57 (1974), pp. 92-127.

—'The "Triumphal" Entry', in E. Bammel and C.F.D. Moule (eds.), *Jesus and the Politics of his Day* (Cambridge: Cambridge University Press, 1984), pp. 319-34.

—'The Beginning of Q', *NTS* 38 (1992), pp. 205-21.

Cerfaux, L., 'Les sources scripturaires de Mt.', *ETL* 31 (1955), pp. 335-36.

Ceroke, C.P., 'Is Mk. 2,10a Saying of Jesus?', *CBQ* 22 (1960), pp. 369-90.

Charles, R.H., *The Teaching of the New Testament on Marriage and Divorce* (London: Williams & Norgate, 1921).

Chase, F.H., *What did Christ Teach about Divorce?* (London: SPCK, 1921).

Chase, K.W., *The Synoptic* Πειρασμοί *of Jesus: Their Christological Significance* (ThD Dissertation, New Orleans Baptist Theological Seminary, 1989).

Cheyne, T.K., and J.S. Black, *Encyclopedia Biblica: A Critical Dictionary of the Literary, Political, and Religious History, the Archeology, Geography, and Natural History of the Bible* (4 vols.; London: A. & C. Black, 1899–1903).

Chilton, B.D., *A Galiean Rabbi and his Bible* (Wilmington, DE: Michael Glazier, 1984).

Clark, K.W., 'The Meaning of (Kata)Kurieuein', in J.K. Elliot (ed.), *Studies in the New Testament Language and Text* (NovTSup, 44; Leiden: Brill, 1976), pp. 100-105.

Cohen, B., 'Divorce in Jewish and Roman Law', in *Jewish and Roman Law: A Comparative Study* (2 vols.; New York: Jewish Theological Seminary, 1966), I, pp. 377-408.

Colpe, C., 'Υἱὸς τοῦ ἀνθρώπου', *TDNT*, VIII, pp. 400-87.

Colson, F.H. and G.H. Whitaker, *Philo* (LCL; Cambridge, MA: Harvard University Press, 1929–1962).

Colwell, E.C., 'A Definite Rule for the Use of the Article in the Greek New Testament', *JBL* 52 (1933), pp. 12-21.

Conzelmann, H., 'Geschichte und Eschaton nach Mc xiii', *ZNW* 50 (1959), pp. 210-21.

—*The First Epistle to the Corinthians* (Philadelphia: Fortress Press, 1975).

Corbett, P.E., *The Roman Law of Marriage* (Oxford: Clarendon Press, 1930).

Couchoud, P.L., 'Notes de critique verbale sur St Marc et St Matthieu', *JTS* 34 (1933), pp. 113-38.

—'Notes sur le texte de St Marc dans le codex Chester Beatty', *JTS* 35 (O.S. 1934), pp. 9-22.

Coutts, J., '"Those Outside" (Mark 4,10-12)', *SE*, II (1964), pp. 155-57.

—'The Messianic Secret and the Enemies of Jesus', *Studia Biblica*, II (1978), pp. 37-46.

Cranfield, C.E.B., *The Gospel according to St Mark* (Cambridge: Cambridge University Press, 1959).

Creed, J.M., *The Gospel according to Luke* (London: Macmillan, 1930).

Crossan, J.D., *In Fragments: The Aphorisms of Jesus* (San Francisco: Harper & Row, 1983).

—'Mark 12.13-17', *Int* 37 (1983), pp. 379-401.

—*Four Other Gospels: Shadows on the Contours of Canon* (Minneapolis: Winston Press, 1985).

Cullmann, O., *Baptism in the New Testament* (London: SCM Press, 1950).

—*Peter: Apostle, Disciple, Martyr* (London: SCM Press, 1953).

—*The State in the New Testament* (New York: Charles Scribner & Sons, 1956).

—'The Gospel of Thomas and the Problem of the Age of the Tradition Contained Therein', *Int* 16 (1962), pp. 418-38.

—*The Christology of the New Testament* (Philadelphia: Westminster Press, 1963).

Dalman, G., *The Words of Jesus Considered in the Light of Post-Biblical Jewish Writings and the Aramaic Language* (Edinburgh: T. & T. Clark, 1902).

Danker, F.W., 'The Demonic Secret in Mark: A Re-Examination of the Cry of Dereliction (Mk. 15.34)', *ZNW* 61 (1970), pp. 48-69.

—*Jesus and the New Age: A Commentary on St Luke's Gospel* (Philadelphia: Fortress Press, 1988).

Daube, D., *Studies in Biblical Law* (Cambridge: Cambridge University Press, 1947).

—'Terms for Divorce', in *The New Testament and Rabbinic Judaism* (London: Athlone Press, 1956), pp. 362-72.

—'The Abomination of Desolation', in *The New Testament and Rabbinic Judaism* (*q.v.*), pp. 418-37.

—'The "I AM" of the Messianic Presence', in *The New Testament and Rabbinic Judaism* (*q.v.*), pp. 325-29.

—*The New Testament and Rabbinic Judaism* (*q.v.*).

—*The Sudden in the Scripture* (Leiden: Brill, 1964).

Davies, W.D., *The Gospel and the Land* (Berkeley: University of California Press, 1974).

Davies, W.D., and D.C. Allinson, *Matthew*, I (Edinburgh: T. & T. Clark, 1988).

Delling, G., 'Das Logion Mark 10.11 (und seine Abwandlungen) im Neuen Testament', *NovT* 1 (1956), pp. 263-74.

—'BAPTISMA, BAPTISTHENAI', *NovT* 2 (1957), pp. 92-115.

—'Botschaft und Wunder im Wirken Jesus', in H. Rostow and K. Matthiae (eds.), *Der historische Jesus und der kerygmatische Christus* (Berlin: Evangelische Verlaganstalt, 1960), pp. 389-402.

Derrett, J.D.M., 'The Teaching of Jesus on Marriage and Divorce', in *Law and the New Testament* (London: Darton, Longmans & Todd, 1970), p. 363-88.

—'Render to Caesar', in *Law in the New Testament* (London: Darton, Longmans & Todd, 1970), pp. 329-33, pp. 313-38.

—' "Eating Up the Houses of Widows": Jesus' Comment on Lawyers?', *NovT* 14 (1972), pp. 1-9.

Di Lella, A., *The Wisdom of Ben Sira* (Garden City: Doubleday, 1966).

Dibelius, M., *From Tradition to Gospel* (New York: Charles Scribner & Sons, 1933).

—'Gethsemane', *Crozier Quarterly* 12 (1953), pp. 254-65.

Dinkler, E., 'Peter's Confession and the "Satan" Saying: The Problem of Jesus' Messiahship', in J.M. Robinson (ed.), *The Future of our Religious Past* (New York: Harper & Row, 1971), pp. 176-89.

Doble, P., 'The Temptations', *ExpTim* 72 (1961–62), pp. 91-93.

Dodd, C.H., 'A New Gospel', in *New Testament Studies* (Manchester: Manchester University Press, 1953), pp. 12-52.

Donaldson, T.R., *Jesus on the Mountain: A Study in Matthean Theology* (Sheffield: JSOT Press, 1985).

Doughty, D.J., 'The Authority of the Son of Man (Mk 2.1–3.6)', *ZNW* 74 (1983), pp. 161-81.

Driver, S.R., *Deuteronomy* (Edinburgh: T. & T. Clark, 1895).

Dungan, D.L., *The Sayings of Jesus in the Churches of Paul* (Philadelphia: Fortress Press, 1971).

Dunn, J.D.G., *Jesus and the Spirit* (London: SCM Press, 1975).

Duplacy, J., 'Marc II, 10, note de syntax', in *Mélanges bibliques ridigos en l'honneur de A. Robert* (Paris: Bloud & Gay, 1957), pp. 421-27.

Dupont, J., 'L'arrière-fond biblique du récit des tentations de Jesus', *NTS* 3 (1956–57), pp. 287-304.

Dupont-Sommer, A., *The Essene Writings from Qumran* (Oxford: Oxford University Press, 1961).

Easton, B.S., *The Gospel according to St Luke* (New York: Charles Scribner & Sons, 1926).

Edersheim, A., *The Life and Times of Jesus Messiah*, I (London: Longmans & Green, 1883).

R.A. Edwards, *The Sign of Jonah in the Theology of the Evangelists and Q* (STB, 18, 2nd Ser.; London: SCM Press, 1971).

Egenolff, P., 'Zu Herodianos', *Jahrbuch für classischen Philologie* 149 (1894), pp. 338-45.

Farmer, W.R., *Maccabees, Zealots, and Josephus* (New York: Charles Scribner & Sons, 1956).

—'A "Skeleton in the Closet" of Gospel Research', *BR* 9 (1961), pp. 18-42.

—*The Synoptic Problem: A Critical Analysis* (Macon: Mercer University Press, 1964).

Farrer, A., *The Triple Victory: Christ's Temptations according to Matthew* (London: Faith Press, 1965).

Fascher, E., *Jesus und der Satan* (Halle: Max Niemeyer Verlag, 1949).

—'Jesus und die Tiere', *TLZ* 90 (1965), cols. 561-70.

Fenton, J.C., *St Matthew* (Baltimore: Pelican, 1963).

Feuilett, A., 'Le baptême de Jesus d'apres l'évangile selon Saint Marc (1,9-11)', *CBQ* 21 (1959), pp. 468-90.

—'L'episode de la tentation d'apres l'évangile selon Saint Marc (1,12-13)', *EstBib* 19 (1960), pp. 49-73.

—'La coupe et le baptême de la passion (Mc, x,35-40; cf. Mt, xx,20-23; Lc, xii,50)', *RB* 74 (1967), pp. 363-88.

Filson, F., *The Gospel according to St Matthew* (New York: Harper & Brothers, 1960).

Finnegan, J., *Die Überlieferung der Leidens- und Auferstehungseschichte Jesu* (Geissen: Töpelmann, 1934).

Fitzmyer, J.A., 'The Priority of Mark and the "Q" Source in Luke', in D.G. Miller (ed.), *Jesus and Man's Hope* (2 vols.; Pittsburgh: Pickwick Press, 1971), I, pp. 131-70.

—'The Matthean Divorce Texts and some New Palestinian Evidence', *TS* 37 (1976), pp. 213-23.

—*To Advance the Gospel* (New York: Crossroad, 1981).

—*The Gospel according to Luke I–IX* (Garden City: Doubleday, 1981).

—*The Gospel according to Luke X–XXIV* (Garden City: Doubleday, 1985).

Fleddermann, H., 'The Discipleship Discourse (Mark 9.33-50)', *CBQ* 43 (1981), pp. 57-75.

—'A Warning about the Scribes (Mark 12.37b-40)', *CBQ* 44 (1982), pp. 52-67.

Floyd-Honey, T.E., 'Did Mark Use Q?', *JBL* 62 (1943), pp. 319-31.

Foerster, W., 'ἔξεστιν, κτλ.', *TDNT*, II, pp. 560-75.

—'κατεξουσιάζω', *TDNT*, II, p. 575.

—'κατακυριεύω', *TDNT*, III, p. 1098.

—'Σατανᾶς', *TDNT*, VII, pp. 151-63.

Foerster W., and G. von Rad, 'διάβολος', *TDNT*, II, pp. 69-81.

Fowler, R.M., *Loaves and Fishes* (Chico, CA: Scholars Press, 1981).

Foxell, W.J., *The Temptations of Jesus: A Study* (London: SPCK, 1920).

Freese, N., 'Die Versuchung Jesus nach den Synoptiker' (Dissertation, Halle, 1922).

Fretheim, T.E., *The Message of Jonah* (Minneapolis: Augsburg, 1977).

Fridrichsen, A., *The Problem of Miracle in Primitive Christianity* (Minneapolis: Augsburg, 1972).

Friedrich, G., 'Beobachtungen zur messianischen Hohepriesterwartung in den Synoptikern', *ZTK* 53 (1956), pp. 265-311.

Fuller, R.H., *The Mission and Achievement of Jesus* (London: SCM Press, 1954).

—*The Foundations of New Testament Christology* (New York: Charles Scribner & Sons, 1965).

Funk, R.W., 'The Wilderness', *JBL* 78 (1959), pp. 205-14.

Gabour, A., 'Deux fils uniques: Isaac et Jesus; Connexions vetero testamentaries de Mc 1,11', *StEv* 4 (1968), pp. 198-204.

Gage, L., 'La théologie de la victorie imperiale', *Rev. Hist.* 171 (1933), pp. 1-44.

Gaster, T.H., 'Satan', *IDB*, IV, pp. 224-28.

Gaston, L., *Horae Synopticae Electronicae: Word Statistics of the Synoptic Gospels* (Missoula: Scholars Press, 1973).

Gerhard, J., *Annotationes Posthumae in Evangelium Matthaei* (Jena: Georg Sengenwald, 1663).

Gerhardsson, B., *The Testing of God's Son (Matt. 4.1-11 and Par.)* (Lund: Gleerup, 1966).

Gerleman, G., '*nsh*, *versuchen*', *THAT*, V, pp. 69-71.

Giblin, C.H., 'The Things of God in the Question concerning Tribute to Caesar (Lk 20.25; Mk 12.17; Mt 22.21)', *CBQ* 33 (1971), pp. 510-27.

Gibson, J.B., 'The Rebuke of the Disciples in Mark 8.14-21', *JSNT* 27 (1986), pp. 31-47.

—'Mk 8.12a. Why Does Jesus "Sigh Deeply"?', *BTr* 38 (1987), pp. 122-25.

Gleuck, N., *Deities and Dolphins: The Story of the Nabateans* (London: Farrer, Straus & Giroux, 1966).

Gnilka, J., *Das Evangelium nach Markus*, I *(Mk. 1–8.26)* (Zürich: Benzinger; Neukirchen–Vluyn: Neukirchener Verlag, 1978).

—*Das Evangelium nach Markus*, II *(Mk. 8:27–16.8)* (Zürich: Benzinger; Neukirchen–Vluyn: Neukirchener Verlag, 1979).

Goguel, M., *L'Evangile de Marc* (Paris: E. Leroux, 1909).

Goldstein, J., *II Maccabees* (Garden City: Doubleday, 1983).

Goppelt, L., *Theology of the New Testament*, I (Grand Rapids: Eerdmans, 1981).

Gould, E.P., *A Critical and Exegetical Commentary on the Gospel according to St Mark* (Edinburgh: T. & T. Clark, 1896).

Goulder, M.D., *Luke: A New Paradigm* (2 Vols.; Sheffield: Sheffield Academic Press, 1989; repr. in 1 vol., 1995).

Grant, F.C., *The Economic Background to the Gospels* (Oxford: Clarendon Press, 1926).

—*The Earliest Gospel* (Nashville: Abingdon, 1943).

—*An Introduction to New Testament Thought* (New York: Abingdon Press, 1950).

—'The Gospel according to St Mark: Introduction and Exegesis', *IB*, VII, pp. 627-47.

Grant, M., *Jesus: An Historian's Review of the Gospels* (New York: Charles Scribner & Sons, 1977).

Grant, R.M, *The Secret Sayings of Jesus: The Gnostic Gospel of Thomas* (Garden City: Doubleday, 1960).

Green, F.W., *The Gospel according to Saint Matthew* (Oxford: Clarendon Press, 1936).

Grundmann, W., *Das Evangelium nach Markus* (Berlin: Evangelische Verlagsanstalt, 1965).

—*Das Evangelium nach Lukas* (Berlin: Evangelische Verlagsanstalt, 2nd edn, 1961).

—*Das Evangelium nach Lukas* (Berlin: Evangelische Verlagsanstalt, 10th edn, 1984).

—'δόκιμος, κτλ.', *TDNT*, II, pp. 255-60.

—'μέγας', *TDNT*, IV, pp. 529-54.

Guelich, R.A., *The Sermon on the Mount: A Foundation for Understanding* (Waco, TX: Word, 1982).

—*Mark 1–8.26* (Dallas: Word, 1989).

Gundry, R.H., *The Use of the Old Testament in St Matthew's Gospel* (Leiden: Brill, 1967).

—*Matthew: A Commentary on his Literary and Theological Art* (Grand Rapids: Eerdmans, 1982).

Gunkel, H., *The Psalms: A Form Critical Introduction* (Philadelphia: Fortress Press, 1967).

Haenchen, E., 'Die Komposition von Mk VIII 27–IX 1 und Par', *NovT* 6 (1963), pp. 81-109.

—*Der Weg Jesu: Eine Erklärung des Markus-Evangeliums und der kanonischen Parallelen* (Berlin: Töpelmann, 1966).

Hahn, F., *The Titles of Jesus in Christology* (London: Lutterworth, 1969).

Hall, A.C.A., *Christ's Temptations and ours* (New York: Longmans, Green & Co., 1897).

Harder, G., 'πονηρός', *TDNT*, VI, pp. 546-66.

Hardy, E.R., *The First Apology of Justin Martyr*, in *The Library of Christian Classics*. I. *Early Christian Fathers* (London: SCM Press, 1953).

Hargreaves, J., *A Guide to St Mark's Gospel* (London: SPCK, 1965)

Harnack, A., *The Sayings of Jesus: The Second Source of St Matthew and St Luke* (London: Williams & Norgate, 1908).

Harrington, W.H., *Mark* (Wilmington: Michael Glazier, 1979).

Hart, H.St-J., 'The Coin of "Render unto Caesar..." (A Note on some Aspects of Mark 12.13-17; Matt. 22.15-22; Luke 20.20-26)', in E. Bammel and C.F.D. Moule (eds.), *Jesus and the Politics of his Day* (Cambridge: Cambridge University Press, 1984), pp. 241-48.

Hatch, E., and H.A. Redpath, *Concordance to the Septuagint* (Oxford: Clarendon Press, 1906).

Hauck, F., 'μοιχεύω', *TDNT*, IV, pp. 729-35.

Hawkins, J.C., *Horae Synopticae: Contributions to the Study of the Synoptic Problem* (Oxford: Clarendon Press, 1909).

Hay, L.S., 'The Son of Man in Mk. 2.10 and 2.28', *JBL* 89 (1970), pp. 69-75.

—'The Son of God Christology in Mark', *JBR* 32 (1964), pp. 106-14.

Heitmuller, W., *'Im Namen Jesu'* (Göttingen: Vandenhoeck & Ruprecht, 1903).

Helfmeyer, A., *'nissah, massot, massah'*, *ThWAT*, V, pp. 473-87.

Hengel, M., *Was Jesus a Revolutionist?* (Philadelphia: Fortress Press, 1971).

—*Christ and Power* (London: SCM Press, 1977).

—*The Zealots* (Edinburgh: T. & T. Clark, 1989).

Héring, J., 'Zwei exegetische Probleme in der Perikope von Jesus in Gethsemane', in A.N. Wilder *et al.* (eds.), *Neotestamentica und patristica: Eine Freundesgabe, Hernn Professor Dr Oscar Cullmann zu seinem 60. Geburtstag überreicht* (Leiden: Brill, 1962), pp. 64-69.

Herron, R.W., Jr, 'Mark's Jesus on Divorce: Mk. 10.12 Reconsidered', *JETS* 25 (1982), pp. 273-81.

Hester, D.C., 'Luke 4.1-13', *Int* 31 (1977), pp. 53-59.

Hiers, R.H., 'Satan, Demons, and the Kingdom of God', *SJT* 27 (1974), pp. 35-47.

Higgins, A.J.B., *Jesus and the Son of Man* (Philadelphia: Fortress Press, 1964).

Hill, D., 'The Request of Zebedee's Sons and the Johannine ΔΟΞΑ Theme', *NTS* 13 (1967), pp. 281-85.

—*The Gospel of Matthew* (London: Oliphants, 1972).

—'Jesus and Josephus' "Messianic" Prophets', in E. Best and R.McL. Wilson (eds.), *Text and Interpretation: Studies in the New Testament Presented to Matthew Black* (Cambridge, Cambridge University Press, 1979), pp. 143-54.

Hobbs, T.R., *2 Kings* (Dallas: Word, 1985).

Hoerner, H.W., *Herod Antipas: A Contemporary of Jesus Christ* (Cambridge: Cambridge University Press, 1972).

Hoffmann, P., 'Die Versuchungsgeschichte in der Logienquelle: Zur Auseinandersetzung der Judenchristen mit dem politischen Messianismus', *BZ* 13 (1969), pp. 207-23.

—'Jesus' Sayings on Divorce in the New Testament', *Concilium* 55 (1970), pp. 51-66.

—*Studien zur Theologie der Logienquelle* (Münster: Aschendorf, 1975)

Holmeister, U., '"Jesus lebte mit den wilden Tieren", Mk. 1.13', in N. Adler (ed.), *Vom Wörte des Lebens, Festschrift für M. Meinertz* (Münster: Aschendorff, 1951), pp. 85-92.

Holst, R., 'The Temptation of Jesus: If thou art the Son of God', *ExpTim* 82 (1971), pp. 334-44.

Hooker, M.D., *Jesus and the Servant* (London: SPCK, 1959).

—*The Son of Man in Mark* (London: SPCK, 1967).

—'Trial and Tribulation in Mark XIII', *BJRL* 65 (1982), pp. 78-89.

—*The Gospel according to Mark* (London: A. & C. Black, 1991).

Horsley, R.A., *Jesus and the Spiral of Violence* (San Francisco: Harper, 1987).

Horstmann, M., *Studien zur markinischen Christologie* [Münster: Aschendorff, 1969).

Hort, F.J.A., *The Epistle of St James* (London: Macmillan, 1909).

Houghton, H.P., 'On the Temptations of Christ and Zarathustra', *ATR* 26 (1944–45), pp. 166-75.

Howard, W.F., 'Appendix on Semitisms in the New Testament', in J.H. Moulton and J.H. Howard, *A Grammar of New Testament Greek*, II (Edinburgh: T. & T. Clark, 1929).

Howton, J., 'The Sign of Jonah', *SJT* 15 (1962), pp. 288-304.

Hultgren, A., *Jesus and his Adversaries: The Form and Function of the Conflict Stories in the Synoptic Tradition* (Minneapolis: Augsburg, 1979).

Hummel, R., *Die Auseinandersetzung zwischen Kirche und Judentum im Matthäusevangelium* (Munich: Kaiser, 1963).

Hunter, A.M., *The Gospel according to St Mark* (London: SCM Press, 1948).

—*The Works and Words of Jesus* (London: SCM Press, 1950).

Hurtado, L.W., *Mark* (San Francisco: Harper & Row, 1983).

Hyldahl, N., 'Der Versuchung auf der Zinne des Tempels', *STL* 14/15 (1960–61), pp. 113-19.

Isaksson, A., *Marriage and Ministry in the New Temple* (Lund: Gleerup, 1965).

Jeremias, J., *Jesus' Promise to the Nations* (London: SCM Press, 1958).

—'An Unknown Gospel with Johannine Elements', in E. Hennecke, *New Testament Apocrypha*, I (Philadelphia: Westminster Press, 1963), pp. 94-97.

—*The Parables of Jesus* (New York: Charles Scribner & Sons, 1963).

—'Ἀδάμ', *TDNT*, I , pp. 141-43.

—'Nachwort zum Artikel von H.-G. Leder', *ZNW* 54 (1963), pp. 278-89.

—'Ἰωνᾶς', *TDNT*, III , pp. 406-10.

—*Abba: Studien zur neutestamentlichen Theologie und Zeitgeschichte* (Göttingen: Vandenhoeck & Ruprecht, 1966).

—'Μωϋσῆς', *TDNT*, IV, pp. 848-73.

—'Die Älteste Schicht der Menschensohn-Logion', *ZNW* 58 (1967), pp. 159-72.

—*New Testament Theology: The Proclamation of Jesus* (New York: Charles Scribner & Sons, 1971).

Jernstedt, V., and P. Nikition (eds.), *The Syntipas*, in *Memories de l'Academie Imperiale des Sciences de St Petersbourg* (8me Ser., Classe des Sciences historico-philologique, XI.1, 1912).

Johnson S.E., 'The Gospel according to St Matthew: Introduction and Exegesis', *IB*, VII, pp. 231-625.

—'The Temptations of Christ', *BibSac* 123 (1966), pp. 346-47.

—*The Gospel according to St Mark* (London: A.C. Black. 1969).

Jones, E.S., 'The Temptation Narrative', *RevExp* 53 (1956), pp. 303-13.

Joüon, P., *Grammaire de l'Hebreu biblique* (Paris: Pontifical Biblical Institute, 1923).

Kahler, M., 'Temptation', in *The New Schaff–Herzog Religious Encyclopedia*, XI (New York: Funk & Wagnalls, 1913), pp. 297-99.

Käsemann, E., 'Sentences of Holy Law in the New Testament', in *New Testament Questions of Today* (London: SCM Press, 1969).

Kautzch, E. (ed.), *Gesenius' Hebrew Grammar* (Oxford: Clarendon Press, 1910).

Kazmierski, C.R., *Jesus, The Son of God: A Study of the Markan Tradition and its Redaction by the Evangelist* (Würzburg: Echter Verlag, 1979).

Keck, L.J., 'The Introduction to Mark's Gospel', *NTS* 12 (1966), pp. 352-70.

Kee, H.C., *Community of the New Age* (London: SCM Press, 1977).

Kelber, W.H., *The Kingdom in Mark: A New Time and a New Place* (Philadelphia: Fortress Press, 1974).

—'Mark 14.32-42: Gethsemane', *ZNW* 63 (1972), pp. 166-87.

—'The Hour of the Son of Man and the Sparing of the Hour', in W.H. Kelber (ed.), *The Passion in Mark* (Philadelphia: Fortress Press, 1976), pp. 41-60.

—*Mark's Story of Jesus* (Philadelphia: Fortress Press, 1979).

Kelly, H.A., 'The Devil in the Desert', *CBQ* 26 (1964), pp. 190-220.

Kelly, B.H., 'An Exposition of Matthew 4.1-11', *Int* 29 (1975), pp. 57-62.

Kennard, J.S., 'Judaism and Images', *Crozier Quarterly* 23 (1946), pp. 259-65.

—*Render to Caesar* (New York: Charles Scribner & Sons, 1950).

Kertlege, K., *Die Wunder Jesus im Markusevangelium* (Munich: Kösel-Verlag, 1970).

Ketter, P., *Die Versuchung Jesu nach dem Berichte der Synoptiker* (Münster: Aschendorff, 1918).

Kilpatrick, G.D., *The Origins of the Gospel according to St Matthew* (Oxford: Clarendon Press, 1946).

—'The Order of some Noun and Adjective Phrases in the New Testament', *NovT* 5 (1962), pp. 111-14.

Kingsbury, J.D., *Jesus Christ in Matthew, Mark, and Luke* (Philadelphia: Fortress Press, 1981).

—*The Christology of Mark's Gospel* (Philadelphia: Fortress Press, 1983).

Kirk, J.A., 'The Messianic Role of Jesus and the Temptation Narrative: A Contemporary Perspective,' *EvQ* 44 (1972), pp. 11-21, 91-102.

Kittel, R., 'ἔρημος', *TDNT*, II, pp. 657-60.

—'ἔσχατος', *TDNT*, II, pp. 697-98.

Kloppenborg, J.S., *The Formation of Q: Trajectories in Ancient Wisdom Collections* (Philadelphia: Fortress Press, 1987).

—'Q 11.14-26: Work Sheets for Reconstruction', *SBLSP 1983*, pp. 133-51.

Klostermann, E., *Das Markusevangelium* (Tübingen: Mohr–Siebeck, 1950).

—*Das Lukasevangelium* (Tübingen: Mohr–Siebeck, 1975).

Knox, W.L., *The Sources of the Synoptic Gospels* (2 vols.; Cambridge, Cambridge University Press, 1957).

Koester, H., *Ancient Christian Gospels* (Philadelphia: Trinity International Press, 1990).

Köppen, K.P., *Die Auslegung der Versuchungsgerichte unter besonderer Berücksichtigung der Alten Kirche* (Tübingen: J.C.B. Mohr, 1961).

Korn, J.H., *ΠΕΙΡΑΣΜΟΣ: Die Versuchung des Glaubigen in der greichischen Bible* (Stuttgart: W. Kohlhammer, 1937).

Kraeling, C.H., *John the Baptist* (New York: Charles Scribner & Sons, 1951).

Kuhn, K.G., 'Jesus in Gethsemane', *EvTh* 12 (1952–53), pp. 260-85.

—'New Light on Temptation, Sin, and Flesh in the New Testament', in K. Stendahl (ed.), *The Scrolls and the New Testament* (New York: Charles Scribner & Sons, 1957), pp. 94-113.

Kümmel, W.G., *Promise and Fulfillment* (London: SCM Press, 1957).

—*Introduction to the New Testament* (London: SCM Press, 1975).

Kuschke, A., 'Das Idiom der "relativen Negation" im NT', *ZNW* 43 (1950–51), p. 263.

Kyne, W.L., *A Christology of Solidarity: Jesus as the Representative of his People in Matthew* (Lanham, MD: University Press of America, 1991).

Lagrange, M.J., *L'Evangile selon Saint Marc* (Paris: Gabalda, 1929).

—*The Gospel according to Saint Mark* (London: Burns, Oates, & Washbourne, 1930).

—*L'Evangile selon Saint Luc* (Paris: Gabalda, 8th edn, 1948).

—*L'Evangile selon Saint Matthieu* (Paris: Gabalda, 1948).

Lake, K., *The Beginnings of Christianity*, I: *The Acts. I. Prolegomena* (London: Macmillan, 1920).

Lane, W.L., *The Gospel according to Mark* (Grand Rapids: Eerdmans, 1974).

Laub, F., *Bekenntnis und Auslegung: die Paranetische Funktion der Christologie im Hebräerbrief* (Regensburg: F. Pustet, 1980).

Lauenstein, U. von, *Der griechische Alexanderroman: Recension γ. Buch 1* (Beiträge zur klassichen Philologie 4; Meisenheim am Glan: Hain, 1962), pp. 2-150.

Leaney, A.R.C., *The Gospel according to St Luke* (London: A. & C. Black, 1958).

Leder, H.-G., 'Sünderfallerzählung und Versuchungsgeschichte: zur Interpretation von Mc. 1.12-13', *ZNW* 54 (1963), pp. 188-216.

Lemcio, E.E., 'External Evidence for the Structure and Function of Mark iv.1-20, vii.13-23, and viii.14-21', *JTS* 29 (1978), pp. 323-38.

Lentzen-Deis. F., *Die Taufe Jesu nach den Synoptikern: Literarkritische und gattungs-geschichtliche Untersuchungen* (Frankfort am Main: Knecht, 1970).

Lescow, T., 'Jesus in Gethsemane', *EvT* 26 (1966), pp. 141-59.

—'Jesus in Gethsemane bei Lukas und im Hebräerbrief', *ZNW* 58 (1967), pp. 215-39.

Levi, I., *The Hebrew Text of Ben Sirah* (Oxford: Clarendon Press, 1904)

Liberty, S., *The Political Relations of Christ's Ministry* (London: Humphrey Milford, Oxford University Press, 1916).

Lightfoot, R.H., *Locality and Doctrine in the Gospels* (New York: Harper & Bros., 1938).

—*The Gospel Message of St Mark* (Oxford: Clarendon Press, 1950).

Lindars, B., 'Mark 10.45: A Ransom for Many', *ExpTim* 92 (1981–82), pp. 292-95.

—*Jesus, Son of Man* (Grand Rapids: Eerdmans, 1982).

Ling, T., *The Significance of Satan: New Testament Demonology and its Contemporary Significance* (London: SPCK, 1961).

Linnemann, E., *Studien zur Passionsgeschichte* (Göttingen: Vandenhoeck & Ruprecht, 1970).

Linton, O., 'The Demand for a Sign from Heaven (Mk 8,11-12 and Parallels', *StEv* 19 (1965), pp. 112-29.

Loftus, F., 'The Anti-Roman Revolts of the Jews and the Galileans', *JQR* 68 (1978), pp. 78-98.

Lohmeyer, E., *Galiläa und Jerusalem* (Göttingen: Vandenhoeck & Ruprecht, 1936).

—'Die Versuchung Jesu', *ZST* 14 (1937), pp. 619-50 repr. in *Urchristliche Mystic* (Darmstadt: Wissenschaftliche Buchgesellschaft, 1958) pp. 83-122.

—*Das Evangelium des Matthäus* (Göttingen: Vandenhoeck & Ruprecht, 1956).

—*Das Evangelium des Markus* (Göttingen: Vandenhoeck & Ruprecht, 1963).

Lohse, E., *History of the Suffering and Death of Jesus Christ* (Philadelphia: Fortress Press, 1964).

Loisy, A., *L'Evangile selon Marc* (Paris: E. Nourry, 1912).

—*L'Evangile selon Luc* (Paris: E. Nourry, 1924).

Lovestram, E., *Son and Saviour: A Study of Acts 13,32-37: With an Appendix: Son of God in the Synoptic Gospels* (Lund: Gleerup, 1961).

Lowe, H., *'Render to Caesar' Religious and Political Loyalty in Palestine* (Cambridge: Cambridge University Press, 1940).

Lowrie, W., *Jesus according to St Mark* (London: Longmanns, Green, 1929).

Lowther-Clarke, W.K., 'The Gospel according to Mark', in *Concise Bible Commentary* (London: SPCK, 1952).

Luccock, H.E., 'The Gospel according to St Mark: Exposition', *IB*, VII.

Luckock, H.R., *Footprints of the Son of Man as Traced by Saint Mark* (New York: Thomas Whittaker, 1886).

Lürhmann, D., *Das Markusevangelium* (HNT, 3; Tübingen: Mohr, 1987).

Luz, U., 'The Secrecy Motif and the Markan Christology', in C. Tuckett (ed.), *The Messianic Secret* (London: SCM Press, 1983), pp. 75-96.

—'Q4', *SBLSP 1984*, pp. 346-73.

—*Matthew 1-7: A Commentary* (Minneapolis: Augsburg, 1989).

Mackinnon, D.M., 'Sacrament and Common Meal', in D.E Nineham (ed.), *Studies in the Gospels* (Oxford: Oxford University Press, 1955), pp. 201-207.

Mahnke, H., *Die Versuchungsgeschichte im Rahmen der Synoptischen Evangelien* (Frankfurt: Lang, 1978).

Mally, E.J., 'The Gospel according to Mark', in R.E. Brown, J.A. Fitzmyer and R. Murphy (eds.), *The Jerome Biblical Commentary*, II (Englewood Cliffs, NJ: Prentice-Hall, 1968).

Maloney, E.J., *Semitic Interference in Marcan Syntax* (Chico: Scholar's Press, 1981).

Mann, C.S., *Mark* (Garden City: Doubleday, 1988).

Manson, W., *The Sayings of Jesus* (London: SCM Press, 1937).

—'The Cleansing of the Temple', *BJRL* 33 (1951), pp. 271-82.

—*The Servant Messiah* (Cambridge: Cambridge University Press, 1953).

—*The Teaching of Jesus: Studies of its Form and Content* (Cambridge: Cambridge University Press, 1967).

Manson, W., 'ΕΓΩ EIMI of the Messianic Presence in the New Testament', *JTS* 48 (1947), pp. 137-45.

Marcus, J., 'The Jewish War and the *Sitz im Leben* of Mark', *JBL* 111 (1992), pp. 441-62.

Marshall, I.H., 'Son of God or Servant of Yahweh?—A Reconsideration of Mark 1.11', *NTS* 15 (1968/69), pp. 326-36.
—*Commentary on Luke* (Grand Rapids: Eerdmans, 1978).
Martin, R.P., *Mark: Evangelist and Theologian* (Exeter: Paternoster, 1972).
Marxsen, W., 'Redactiongeschictliche Erklärung der songennanten Parabel-Theorie des Markus', *ZTW* 52 (1955), pp. 262, 255-71.
—*Mark the Evangelist* (Nashville: Abingdon, 1969).
Masuda, S., 'The Good News of the Miracle of the Bread: The Tradition and its Markan Redaction', *NTS* 28 (1982), pp. 191-219.
Matera, F.J., *The Kingship of Jesus* (Chico, CA: Scholars Press, 1982).
—*Passion Narratives and Gospel Theologies* (Mahwah: Paulist Press, 1986).
Maurer, C., 'Knecht Gottes und Sohn Gottes im Passionsbericht des Markusevangeliums', *ZTK* 50 (1953), pp. 1-38.
Mauser, U., *Christ in the Wilderness* (London: SCM Press, 1963)
Mays, J.L., 'An Exposition of Mk. 8.27–9.1', *Int* 30 (1976), pp. 174-78.
McCasland, S.V., 'Signs and Wonders', *JBL* 76 (1957), pp. 149-52.
McKenzie, J.L., 'Behold the Virgin', in *The New Testament without Illusion* (New York: Crossroad, 1982), pp. 103-13.
McKinnis, R., 'An Analysis of Mark X 32-34', *NovT* 18 (1976), pp. 81-100.
McNeil, A.H., *The Gospel according to St Matthew* (London: Macmillan, 1915).
Mealand, D.L., *Poverty and Expectation in the Gospels* (London: SPCK, 1980).
Meecham, H.G, 'The Imperative Use of ἵνα in the New Testament', *JTS* 43 (1942), pp. 179-80.
Meier, J.P., *Law and History in Matthew's Gospel: A Redactional Study of Mt. 5.17-48* (Rome: Biblical Institute Press, 1976).
—*The Vision of Matthew: Christ, Church, and Morality in the First Gospel* (New York: Paulist Press, 1978).
Meinertz, M., 'Dieses Geschlecht im Neuen Testament', *BZ* 1 (1957), pp. 283-89.
Mely, F. de, and C.-E Ruelle, *Les lapidaires de l'antiquité et du moyen age*. II. *Les lapidaires grecs* (Paris: Ernest Leroux, 1898).
Menzies, A., *The Earliest Gospel* (London: Macmillan, 1901).
Merk, A., *Novum Testamentum Graece et Latine* (Rome: Pontifical Biblical Institute, 1951).
Merrill, E.H., 'The Sign of Jonah', *JETS* 23 (1980), pp. 23-30.
Merx, A., *Die vier Evangelein nach ihrem ältesten bekannten Texte*. II/2. *Das Evangelien des Markus und Lukas* (Berlin: G. Reimer, 1905).
Metzger, B.M., *A Textual Commentary on the Greek New Testament* (New York: United Bible Societies, 1971).
Meyer, A., 'Die evangelischen Berichte über die Versuchung Christi', in *Festgabe H. Blümner übericht zum 9, August 1914 von Freunden und Schülern* (Zürich, 1914), pp. 434-68.
—'Die Enstehung des Markusevangeliums', in R. Bultman and H. von Soden (eds.), *Festgabe fur Adolf Jülicher* (Tübingen: Mohr, 1927), pp. 35-60.
Meyer, P.D, 'The Gentile Mission in Q', *JBL* 89 (1970), pp. 405-17.
Meyer, R., 'προφήτης', *TDNT*, VI, pp. 812-28.
Michael, J.H., 'The Sign of John', *JTS* 21 (1919–1920), pp. 146-59.
Michaelis, W., 'ὁδός', *TDNT*, V, pp. 42-96.

Moffatt, J., *Introduction to the Literature of the New Testament* (Edinburgh: T. & T. Clark, 3rd edn, 1918).

Mommsen, T., *Römisches Geschichte*, V (Berlin: Weidmann, 1933).

Montefiore, C.G., *The Synoptic Gospels*, I (London: Macmillan, 1927).

Morganthaler, R., *Statistik des neutestamentlichen Wörtschatzes* (Zürich: Gotthelf Verlag, 1958).

—'Roma—Sedes Satanae', *TZ* 12 (1956), pp. 289-304.

Moule, C.F.D., *An Idiom-Book of New Testament Greek* (Cambridge: Cambridge University Press, 2nd edn, 1959).

—*The Gospel according to Mark* (Cambridge: Cambridge University Press, 1965).

—'An Unresolved Problem in the Temptation Clause in the Lord's Prayer', *RTR* 33 (1974), pp. 65-75.

Moulton J.H., and W.F. Howard, *Grammar of New Testament Greek*, II (Edinburgh: T. & T. Clark, 1929).

Moulton, J.H., *A Grammar of New Testament Greek*, III (Edinburgh: T. & T. Clark, 1963).

Mowinckel, S., *He That Cometh* (Oxford: Blackwell, 1965).

—*The Psalms in Israel's Worship* (Oxford: Blackwell, 1967).

Moxon, C., 'Τὸ σημεῖον 'Ἰωνᾶ', *ExpTim* 22 (1911), pp. 566-67.

Muddiman, J., 'The Glory of Jesus, Mark 10.37', in L.D. Hurst and N.T. Wright (eds.), *The Glory of Christ in the New Testament: Studies in Christology in Memory of George Bradford Caird* (Oxford: Clarendon Press, 1987), pp. 51-58.

Müller, U.B., 'Die Christologische absicht des Markusevangeliums und die Verklärungsgeschichte', *ZNW* 64 (1973), pp. 159-93.

Murphy-O'Connor, J., 'Péché et communauté dans le Nouveau Testament', *RB* 74 (1967), pp. 181-85.

Mussner, F., 'Gottesherrschaft und Sendung Jesu nach Markus 1,14-15', in F. Mussner (ed.), *Präsentia Salutis* (Düsseldorf: Patmos, 1967), pp. 81-98.

Myers, C., *Binding the Strong Man: A Political Reading of Mark's Story of Jesus* (Maryknoll, NY: Orbis, 1988).

Nairne, A., *The Epistle of Priesthood* (Edinburgh: T. & T. Clark, 1913).

—*The Epistle to the Hebrews* (Cambridge: Cambridge University Press, 1921).

Neirynck, F., 'The Tradition of the Sayings of Jesus', *Concilium* 20 (1967), pp. 63-74.

—*Duality in Mark: Contributions to the Study of Markan Redaction* (Leuven: Leuven University Press, 1972).

—'The Redactional Text of Mark', *ETL* 57 (1981), pp. 144-62.

Neyrey, J.H., *The Passion according to Luke* (New York: Paulist Press, 1985).

Nineham, D.E., *St Mark* (Baltimore: Pelican, 1963).

Noack, B., *Satanas und Soteria: Untersuchungen zur neutestamentlichen Dämonologie* (Copenhagen: G.E.C. Gads, 1948).

Norden, E., *Agnostos Theos* (Leipzig: Teubner, 1913).

North, C.R., *The Suffering Servant in Deutero-Isaiah* (Oxford: Oxford University Press, 1948).

O'Neill, J.C., 'The Six Amen Sayings in Luke', *JTS* 10 (N.S. 1959), pp. 1-9.

Oepke, A., 'ἀποκαθίστημι, ἀποκατάστασις', *TDNT*, I, pp. 387-89.

Patterson, S.J., *The Gospel of Thomas and Jesus* (Sonoma, CA: Polebridge Press, 1991).

Percy, E., *Die Botschaft Jesu* (Lund: Gleerup, 1953).

Perkins, P., 'Prounouncement Stories in the Gospel of Thomas', *Semeia* 20 (1981), pp. 121-32.

Perrin, N., 'The Christology of Mark: A Study in Methodology', in *A Modern Pilgrimage in New Testament Christology* (Philadelphia: Fortress Press, 1974), pp. 104-21.

—*Rediscovering the Teaching of Jesus* (New York: Charles Scribner & Sons, 1967).

—'The Creative Use of the Son of Man Traditions by Mark', *USQR* 23 (1967/68), pp. 357-61, repr. in *A Modern Pilgrimage in Christology* (Philadelphia: Fortress Press, 1974), pp. 84-93.

—*Christology and a Modern Pilgrimage* (ed. H.D. Betz; Missoula: Scholars Press, 1974).

Pesch, R., *Näherwartungen: Tradition und Redaction in Mk 13* (Düsseldorf: Patmos Verlag, 1968).

—'Das Messiahbekenntnis des Petrus (Mk. 8,27-30)', *BZ* 17 (1973), pp. 178-95.

—*Das Markusevangelium* (2 vols; Freiburg: Herder, 1977).

Peterson, N.R., 'When is the End not the End? Literary Reflections on the Ending of Mark's Narrative', *Int* 34 (1980), pp. 151-66.

Pingree, D., *Vettii Valentis Antiocheni: Anthologiarum Libri Novem* (Leipzig: Teubner, 1986).

Piper, O., *Love your Enemies: Jesus' Love Command in the Synoptic Gospels and in the Early Christian Paraenesis* [Cambridge: Cambridge University Press, 1979).

Plummer, A., *The Gospel according to St Luke* (Edinburgh: T. & T. Clark, 1896).

Pokorny, P., 'The Temptation Stories and their Intention', *NTS* 20 (1973/74), pp. 115-127.

Polag, A., *Fragmenta Q: Textheft zur Logienquelle* (Neukirchen–Vluyn: Neukirchener Verlag, 1979).

Powell, W., 'The Temptations', *ExpTim* 72 (1961), p. 248.

Pryke, E.J., *Redactional Style in the Markan Gospel* (Cambridge: Cambridge University Press, 1978).

Quispel, Q., 'The Gospel of Thomas and the New Testament', *VC* 11 (1957), pp. 189-207.

Rawlinson, A.E.J., *The Gospel of Mark* (London: Methuen, 1925), p. 257.

Rehkopf, F., *Die lukanische Sonderquelle: Ihr Umfang und Sprachgebrauch* (Tübingen: Mohr–Siebeck, 1959).

Rengstorf, K.H., *Das Evangelium nach Lukas* (Göttingen: Vandenhoeck & Ruprecht, 1937).

—'σημεῖον', *TDNT*, VII, pp. 200-61.

—'Old and New Testament Traces of a Formula of the Judean Royal Ritual', *NovT* 5 (1963), pp. 229-44.

Reploh, K.G., *Markus—Lehrer der Gemeinde: Ein Redaktionsgeschichtliche Studie zu den Jüngerperikopen des Markus-Evangeliums* (Stuttgart: Katholisches Bibelwerke, 1969).

Reuman, J., *Jesus in the Church's Gospels* (Philadelphia: Fortress Press, 1968).

Rhoads, D.M., *Israel in Revolution 6–74 CE* (Philadelphia: Fortress Press, 1976).

Richardson, A., *The Miracle Stories of the Gospels* (London: SCM Press, 1941).

—*The Theology of the New Testament* (London: SCM Press, 1958).

Riesenfeld H., 'The Messianic Character of Jesus' Temptations', in *The Gospel Tradition: Essays by Harald Riesenfeld* (Philadelphia: Fortress Press, 1970).

Rigaux, B., 'ΒΔΕΔΥΓΜΑ ΤΗΣ ΕΡΕΜΟΣΕΟΣΥ (Mc 13,14; Mt 24,15)', *Bib* 40 (1959), pp. 675-83.

Rist, M., 'Caesar or God (Mark 12.13-17)? A Study in *Formgeschichte*', *JR* 16 (1936), pp. 317-31.

Robbins, V.K., '*Dynameis* and *Semeia* in Mark', *BibRes* 18 (1973), pp. 5-20.

Robertson, A.T., *A Grammar of the Greek New Testament in the Light of Historical Research* (Nashville: Broadman Press, 1917).

Robinson, J.A.T., 'The Temptations' in *Twelve New Testament Studies* (London: SCM Press, 1962) pp. 53-60.

Robinson, J.M., *The Problem of History in Mark* (London: SCM Press, 1957).

Robinson T.H., *The Gospel of Matthew* (New York: Harper & Brothers, 1927).

Rostovtzeff, M., *Social and Economic History of the Roman Empire* (Oxford: Clarendon Press, 1926).

Roth, C., 'The Cleansing of the Temple and Zechariah 14.21', *NovT* 4 (1960), pp. 174-81.

Sabbe, M., 'De tentatione in deserto', *ColBG* 50 (1954), pp. 459-66.

Sabourin, L., *The Gospel according to St Matthew*, I (Bombay: St Paul Publications, 1982).

Safrai S., and M. Stern, *Compendia Rerum Iudaicarum as Novum Testamentum*, I (Philadelphia: Fortress Press, 1974).

Sanders, E.P., *The Tendencies of the Synoptic Tradition* (Cambridge: Cambridge University Press, 1969).

—*Jesus and Judaism* (Philadelphia: Fortress Press, 1985).

Sanders E.P., and M. Davies, *Studying the Synoptic Gospels* (London: SCM Press, 1989)

Scheneke, H., *Studien zur Passionsgeschichte des Markus: Tradition und Redaction in Markus 14,1-42* (Würzburg: Echter Verlag, 1971).

Schenk, W., *Synopse zur Redenquelle der Evangelisten: Q Synopse und Reconstruction in deutscher Übersetzung mit kurzen Erlauterungen* (Düsseldorf: Patmos Verlag, 1981).

Schlatter, A., *Der Evangelist Matthäeus* (Stuttgart: Calwer, 1929).

—*Das Evangelium des Lukas: Aus seinen Quellen erklärt* (Stuttgart: Calwer, 2nd edn, 1960).

Schleiermacher, F., *Über den Schriften des Lukas: Kritischer Versuch* (Berlin: George Reimer, 8th edn, 1817).

Schlier, H., 'κέρδος, κερδαίνω', *TDNT*, III, pp. 672-73.

Schmauch, W., 'In der Wuste: Beobachtungen zur Raumbeziehung des Glaubens im NT', in *Memoriam Ernst Lohmeyer* (Stuttgart: Evangelischesverlag, 1951), pp. 19-50.

Schmid, J., *Das Evangelium nach Lukas* (Regensburg: Pustet, 4th edn, 1960).

—*Das Evangelium nach Markus* (Regensburg: Pustet, 1963).

Schmidt, D., 'LXX *Gattung* "Prophetic Correlative"', *JBL* 96 (1977), pp. 517-22.

Schmidt, K.L., *Der Rahmen der Geschichte Jesu* (Berlin: Trowitzch & Sohn, 1919).

Schmithals, W., *Das Evangelium nach Markus: Kapitel 1-9*, I (Gütersloh: Mohn; Würzburg: Echter Verlag, 1979).

—*Das Evangelium nach Lukas* (Zürich: Theologischer Verlag, 1980).

Schneider, G., *Das Evangelium nach Lukas*, II (Gütersloh: G. Mohn, 1977).

Schnackenburg, R., 'Der Sinn der Versuchung Jesu bei den Synoptikern', *TQ* 132 (1952), pp. 297-326.

—'Mk. 9,33-50', in J. Schmid and A. Vögtle (eds.), *Synoptische Studien: Alfred Wikenhauser zum siebzigsten Geburtstag am 22 Februar 1953 dargebracht von Freundenen, Kollegen und Schulern* (Munich: Zink, 1953), pp. 184-206.

—*The Gospel according to Mark* (New York: Herder & Herder, 1971).

Schneider, G., *Das Evangelium nach Lukas*, II (Gutersloh: G. Mohn, 1977).

Schniewind, J., *Das Evangelium nach Markus* (Göttingen: Vandenhoeck & Ruprecht, 1963).

—*Das Evangelium nach Matthäus* (Göttingen: Vandenhoeck & Ruprecht, 1964).

Schoeps, H.J., 'Restitutio Principii as the Basis for the Nova Lex Jesu', *JBL* 66 (1947), pp. 456-64.

—'Von der Imitatio Dei zur Nachfolge Christi', in *Aus Frühchristlicher Zeit: religionsgeschictliche untersuchungen* (Tübingen: Mohr, 1950), pp. 286-301.

Schrage, W., *Das Verhältnis des Thomas-Evangeliums zur synoptischen Tradition* (Berlin: Alfred Töpelmann, 1964).

Schrenk, G., 'εὐδοκέω, εὐδοκία', *TDNT*, II, pp. 738-51.

Schulze, W.A., 'Der Heilige und die wilden Tiere. Zur Exegese von Mc. 1,13b', *ZNW* 46 (1955), pp. 280-83.

Schürer, E., *The History of the Jewish People in the Age of Jesus Christ* (2 vols., ed. G. Vermes and F. Millar; Edinburgh: T. & T. Clark, 1973, 1979).

Schurmann, H., 'Die Sprache des Christus: Sprächliche Beobachtungen an den synoptischen Herrenworten', *BZ* 21 (1958), pp. 54-84.

—*Das Lukasevangelium* (Freiburg: Herder & Herder, 1969).

Schweizer, E., 'Der Menschensohn', *ZNW* 50 (1959), pp. 185-209.

—'πνεῦμα', *TDNT*, VI, pp. 389-455.

—*The Good News according to Mark* (Richmond, VA: John Knox Press, 1970).

—'σάρξ, κτλ.', *TDNT*, VII, pp. 119-51.

—'υἱός', *TDNT*, VIII, pp. 340-99.

—*The Good News according to Matthew* (Richmond, VA: John Knox Press, 1975).

Scramm, T., *Der Markus-Stoff bei Lukas* (Cambridge: Cambridge University Press, 1971).

Scrivener, F.H.A., *Novum Testamentum* (New York: Henry Holt, 1887).

Seesemann, H., 'πεῖρα, κτλ.', *TDNT*, VI, pp. 23-36.

Senior, D., *The Passion of Jesus in the Gospel of Mark* (Wilmington, DE: Michael Glazier, 1984).

Sharp, D.S., 'Mk. 2.10', *ExpTim* 38 (1927), pp. 428-29.

Shulz, S., *Q—Die Spruchquelle der Evangelisten* (Zürich: Theologischer Verlag, 1972).

Snodgrass, K., 'Western Non-Interpolations', *JBL* 91 (1972), pp. 369-79.

Spitta, F., 'Betrage zur Erklärung der Synoptiker', *ZNW* 5 (1904), pp. 325-26.

Stanley, D.M., *Jesus in Gethsemane* (New York: Paulist Press, 1980).

Stanton, G.S., 'On the Christology of Q', in B. Lindars and S. Smalley (eds.), *Christ and the Spirit: Essays in Honour of C.F.D. Moule* (Cambridge: Cambridge University Press, 1973), pp. 27-42.

Stauffer, E., *Christ and the Caesars* (London: SCM Press, 1955).

Stegner, W.R., 'Wilderness and Testing in the Scrolls and in Matthew 4.1-11', *BR* 12 (1967) pp. 18-27.

Stein, R.H., 'The "Redactionsgeschichtlich" Investigation of a Markan Seam (Mc 1.21-22)', *ZNW* 61 (1970), pp. 70-83.

—'Is it Lawful for a Man to Divorce his Wife?', *JETS* 22 (1979), pp. 115-21.

Steiner, M., *La tentation de Jésus dans l'inteprétation patristique de Saint Justin à Origine* (Paris: Gabalda, 1962).

Stendahl, K., 'Matthew', in M. Black and H.H. Rowley (eds.), *Peake's Commentary on the Bible* (London: Nelson & Sons, 1962).

Stenger, W.R., 'The Baptism of Jesus: A Story Modeled on the Binding of Isaac', *BR* (1985), pp. 36-46.

Stevenson, G.H., 'The Provinces and their Government', in *The Cambridge Ancient History*, IX (Cambridge: Cambridge University Press, 1932), pp. 437-74.

—'The Imperial Administration', in *The Cambridge Ancient History* X (Cambridge: Cambridge University Press, 1934), pp. 182-217.

Stock, A., 'Matthean Divorce Texts', *BTB* 8 (1978), pp. 24-33.

—*The Method and Message of Mark* (Wilmington: Michael Glazier, 1989).

Stonehouse, N.B., *Origins of the Synoptic Gospels* (Grand Rapids: Eerdmans, 1963).

Strauss, D.F., *Das Leben Jesu, kritisch bearbeitet*, I (Berlin: Osiander, 1835–36).

Strecker, G., 'The Passion and Resurrection Predictions in Mark's Gospel (Mark 8.31, 9.31, 10.32-34)', *Int* 22 (1968), pp. 421-43.

Streeter, B.H., 'St. Mark's Knowledge of Q', in W. Sanday (ed.), *Oxford Studies in the Synoptic Problem* (Oxford: Clarendon Press, 1911), pp. 165-80.

—'The Original Extent of Q', in W. Sanday (ed.), *Oxford Studies in the Synoptic Problem* (Oxford: Clarendon Press, 1911), pp. 184-208.

—*The Four Gospels* (London: Macmillan, 1924).

Suhl, A., *Die Function der alttestamenliche Zitate und Anspielungen im Markusevangelium* (Gütersloh: Gerd Mohn, 1965).

Sundwall, J., *Die Zusammensetzung des Markusevangeliums* (Acta Academiae Abensis, Humanitaniora, 9; Åbo: Åbo Akadamie, 1934), pp. 1-86.

Swartley, W.M., 'The Structural Function of the term "Way" (*hodos*) in Mark's Gospel', in W. Klassen (ed.), *The New Way of Jesus* (Grand Rapids: Eerdmans, 1980), pp. 73-86.

Sweetland, D.M., *Our Journey with Jesus: Discipleship according to Mark* (Wilmington, DE: Michael Glazier, 1987).

Swete, H.B., *The Gospel according to St Mark* (London: Macmillan, 1905).

Swetnam J., 'No Sign of Jonah', *Bib* 66 (1985), pp. 126-30.

Taber, C.R., 'Semantics', *IDB*, V, pp. ??.

Tagawa, K., *Miracles et évangile: Le pensée personelle de l'évangeliste Marc* (Paris: Presses universitaries de France, 1966).

Tannehill, R.C., *The Sword of his Mouth* (Philadelphia: Fortress Press, 1975).

—'The Gospel of Mark as Narrative Christology', *Semeia* 16 (1979), pp. 57-98.

Taylor, A.B., 'Decision in the Desert: The Temptation of Jesus in the Light of Deuteronomy', *Int* 15 (1960) pp. 300-309.

Taylor, V., *The Formation of the Gospel Tradition* (London: Macmillan, 1949).

—*The Gospel according to St Mark* (London: Macmillan, 1955).

— *The Passion Narrative of St Luke: A Critical and Historical Investigation* (Cambridge: Cambridge University Press, 1972).

Tcherikover, V.A., *Corpus Papyrorum Judaicarum*, I (Cambridge, MA: Harvard University Press).

Telford, W., *The Interpretation of Mark* (Philadelphia: Fortress Press, 1985).

Thackeray, H.St-J., *Josephus* (New York: Putnam, 1926-65).

Theissen, G., *The Miracle Stories of the Gospel Tradition* (Philadelphia: Fortress Press, 1983).

Thiering, B.E., '"Breaking of Bread" and "Harvest" in Mark's Gospel', *NovT* 12 (1970), pp. 1-12.

Thompson, J.M., *Jesus according to St Mark* (London: Methuen, 1910).

Thompson, G.P., 'Called—Proved—Obedient: A Study in the Baptism and Temptation Narratives of Matthew and Luke', *JTS* 11 (NS 1960), pp. 1-12.

Throckmorton, B.H., 'Did Mark Know Q?', *JBL* 67 (1948), pp. 319-29.

Tödt, H.E., *The Son of Man in the Synoptic Tradition* (London: SCM Press, 1965).

Torrey, C.C., *The Lives of the Prophets: Greek Text and Translation* (JBLMS, 1; Philadelphia: Society of Biblical Literature and Exegesis, 1946).

Traub, H., 'οὐρανός', *TDNT*, V, pp. 497-538.

Trench, R.C., *Studies in the Gospels* (London: Macmillan & Co., 3rd edn, 1874).

—*Synonyms of the New Testament* (London: Macmillan, 12th edn, 1894).

Trocmé, E., *The Formation of the Gospel according to Mark* (Philadelphia: Westminster Press, 1963).

Tuckett C.M., 'The Present Son of Man', *JSNT* 14 (1982), pp. 58-81.

—'The Temptation Narrative in Q', in F. Van Segbroeck, C.M. Tuckett, G. Van Belle and J. Verheyden (eds.), *The Four Gospels 1992: Festschrift Frans Neieynck* (3 vols.; Leuven: Leuven University Press, 1992), I, pp. 479-507.

—'Mark and Q', in C. Focant (ed.), *The Synoptic Gospels: Source Criticism and the New Literary Criticism* (Leuven: Leuven University Press, 1993), pp. 149-75.

Turner, C.H., 'Markan Usage: Notes Critical and Exegetical on the Second Gospel', *JTS* 26 (1924/25), pp. 12-20.

—'HO HUIOS MOU HO AGAPETOS', *JTS* 27 (1926), pp. 113-29.

—'Marcan Usage: Notes, Critical and Exegetical, on the Second Gospel', *JTS* 29 (1928), pp. 346-61.

—'Western Readings in the Second Half of St Mark's Gospel', *JTS* (1928), pp. 1-18.

—'The Gospel according to St Mark', in C. Gore and H.L. Gouge (eds.), part 3 of *A New Commentary on Holy Scripture* (London: SPCK, 1928), pp. 42-104.

—*The Gospel according to St Mark* (London: Macmillan, 1928).

Turner, N., *Grammatical Insights into the New Testament* (Edinburgh: T.& T. Clark, 1965).

Tyson, J.B., 'The Blindness of the Disciples in Mark', *JBL* 80 (1961), pp. 261-68.

van Iersel, B., *The Bible on the Temptations of Man* (DePere, WI: St Norbert Abbey Press, 1966).

—'Jesus' Way of Obedience according to Mark's Gospel', *Concilium* 30 (1981), pp. 25-33.

Vassiliadis, P., 'The Nature and Extent of the Q Document', *NovT* 20 (1978), pp. 49-73.

Vawter, B., 'Divorce and the New Testament', *CBQ* 39 (1977), pp. 528-42.

Vermes, G., 'Sectarian Matrimonial Halakhah in the Damascus Rule', *JJS* 25 (1974), pp. 197-202.

—'Redemption and Genesis XXII', in *Scripture and Tradition in Judaism* (Leiden: Brill, 1961), pp. 193-227.

Vielhauller, P., 'The Gospel to the Hebrews', in E. Hennecke, *New Testament Apocrypha*, I (ed. W. Schneemelcher; Philadelphia: Westminster Press, 1963), pp. 158-65.

Vögtle, A., 'Das Spruch des Jonaszeichen', in J.A. Schmid and A. Vögtle (eds.), *Synoptische Studien: Alfred Wikenhauser zum siebzigsten Geburtstag am 22 Februar 1953 dargebracht von Freunden, Kollegen und Schulern* (Munich: Zink, 1953), pp. 230-77.

—'Messiasbekenntnis und Petrusverheissung. Zur Komposition von Mt. 16,13-23 par.', *BZ* 1 (1957), pp. 252-72; *BZ* 2 (1958), pp. 85-103.

Wansbrough, H., 'St Mark', in R.G. Fuller, L. Johnson and C. Kearnes (eds.), *A New Catholic Commentary on Holy Scripture* (London: Nelson, 1969).

Waty, W.W., 'Jesus and the Temple—Cleansing or Cursing?', *ExpTim* 93 (1981–82), pp. 235-39.

Weber, J.C., Jr, 'Jesus' Opponents in the Gospel of Mark', *JBR* 34 (1966), pp. 214-22.

Weeden, T.J. Jr, 'The Heresy That Necessitated Mark's Gospel', *ZNW* 59 (1968), pp. 145-58.

—*Mark: Traditions in Conflict* (Philadelphia: Fortress Press, 1971).

Weiffenbach, W., *Wiederkunftsgedanke Jesu nach den Synoptikern* (Leipzig: Druck & Verlag, 1873).

Weinel, H., *Biblische Theologie des Neuen Testaments* (Tübingen: Mohr, 1928).

Weiss, B., *Das Markusevangelium und seine Synoptischen Parallelen* (Berlin: Wilheim Hertz, 1872).

—*Die Quellen des Lukasevangeliums* (Stuttgart: J.G. Cotta, 1907).

Weiss, J., *Das alteste Evangelium* [Göttingen: Vandenhoeck & Ruprecht, 1903).

—*Das Markusevangelium* (Göttingen: Vandenhoeck & Ruprecht, 1912).

—'ΕΥΘΥΣ bei Markus', *ZNW* 2 (1910), pp. 124-33.

Weizer, A., *The Psalms* (London: SCM Press, 1962).

Wellhausen, J., *Einleitung in die drie ersten Evangelisten* (Berlin: George Reimer, 1905).

—*Das Evangelium Marci* (Berlin: George Reimer, 1909).

—*Das Evangelium Matthai* (Berlin: George Reimer, 1914).

Wendling, E., *Die Enstehung des Mk-Evangeliums* (Tübingen: Mohr, 1908).

Wessel, W.W., 'Mark', in F.E. Gaebelein (ed.), *The Expositor's Bible Commentary*, VI (Grand Rapids: Zondervan, 1984).

Whittaker, M., '"Signs and Wonders": The Pagan Background', *Studia Evangelica* 5 (1965), pp. 155-58.

Wilkens, U., 'ὑποκρίνομαι, κτλ.', *TDNT*, VIII, pp. 559-70.

Williams, A.L., and B.C. Caffin, *St Matthew* (2 vols.; The Pulpit Commentary; New York: Funk & Wagnalls, 1892).

Williams, G.O., 'The Baptism in Luke's Gospel', *JTS* 45 (1944), pp. 31-38.

Williamson, L., *Mark* (Atlanta: John Knox, 1983).

—'Matthew 4.1-11', *Int* 38 (1984), pp. 51-59.

Wilson, R. McL., *Studies in the Gospel of Thomas* (London: SCM Press, 1960).

—'Thomas and the Synoptic Gospels', *ExpTim* 72 (1960–61), pp. 36-39.

—'Mark', in M. Black and H.H. Rowley (eds.), *Peake's Commentary on the Bible* (London: Nelson & Sons, 1962).

—' "Thomas" and the Growth of the Gospels', *HTR* 53 (1969), pp. 231-50.

Windisch, H., 'Friedensbringer—Gottessöhn', *ZNW* 24 (1925), pp. 240-60.

Wink, W., *John the Baptist in the Gospel Tradition* (Cambridge: Cambridge University Press, 1968).

—'Mark 2.1-12', *Int* 38 (1984), pp. 58-63.

Wood, J.E., 'Isaac Typology in the New Testament', *NTS* 14 (1967–68), pp. 583-89.

Wordsworth, C., *The New Testament of our Lord and Saviour Jesus Christ in the Original Greek* (London: Rivingtons, 1881).

Wrede, W., *The Messianic Secret* (Cambridge: James Clarke, 1971).

Yoder, J.H., 'The Unique Role of the Historic Peace Churches', *Brethren Life and Thought* 14 (1969), pp. 132-49.

—*The Original Revolution* (Scotsdale, PA: Herald Press, 1972).

—*The Politics of Jesus* (Grand Rapids: Eerdmans, 1972).

—'Jesus and Power', *Ecumenical Review* 25 (1973), pp. 447-54.

Zeller, D., 'Redaktionsprozesse und weckselnder "Sitz im Leben" beim Q-Material', in J. Delobel (ed.), *Logia: Les Paroles de Jésus—The Sayings of Jesus* (Leuven: Leuven University Press, 1982), pp. 395-409.

Zerwick, M., *Untersuchungen sum Markus-Stil: Ein Beitrag zur stilistichen Durcharbeitung des Neuen Testaments* (Rome: Pontifical Biblical Institute, 1937).

Zimmermann, H., 'μὴ ἐπὶ πορνεία (Mt. 19:9)—Ein literarisches Problem. Zur Komposition vom Mt. 19:3-12', *Cath.* 16 (1960), pp. 293-99.

INDEXES

INDEX OF REFERENCES

OLD TESTAMENT

NEW TESTAMENT

RABBINIC LITERATURE

Mishnah		89	29, 59, 108,	*Mek. Pisha*	
Abod. Zar.			113-16	1.103-105	201
1.8	308	89	201	1.112-113	201
Giṭ.				1.80-82	204
9.10	280	*j. 'Abod. Zar.*		1.80	201
		3.1	308	1.82	201
Sanh.					
7.4	287	*t. Sanh.*		*Midr. Qoh.*	
		89	84	1.9	102
Talmuds					
b. Giṭ.		Midrash		*PRE*	
90	280	*Gen R.*		10	201
		20.1	307	43	201
b. Pes.		56.4	84		
104	308			*Pes. R.*	
		Lam. R.		126	102, 107
b. Sanh.		(Proem 31)	201	13	61
67	188			36	102, 107
				55	61

JOSEPHUS

Ant.		20.97-99	162, 163,	2.258	162
1.1.4	307		188, 193	2.259	61, 163
2.286	188	20.97	187	2.261-63	163
2.327	187, 188	20.99	193	2.261	187, 188,
4.8.23 (253)	280	20.167-68	187, 188		193
5.1.21	303	20.167	61, 163	2.262	187
6.11.9	231	20.168	162	2.622	61
6.210	325	20.169-70	187	4.340	325
8.347	162	20.169	188, 189,	6	191
9.10.2	201		193	6.201-19	191
10.28	162	20.188	61, 163,	6.258	258
15.7.10 (259)	280		187, 188	6.284-86	188, 193
15.259	263	118.19	287	6.285-86	106
17.1.1	311			6.288-315	191
17.188.317-		*Apion*		6.288	162, 191,
18	286	2.215	325		192
18.1	311			6.351	61
18.1.1	309, 310	*War*		7.6.1-4	310, 311
18.1.6	309, 310	1.654	325	7.8.1	309
18.25	310	1.664	286	7.438	61
18.100-25	286	2.8.1	310	6.258	162
18.110	286	2.118	310, 312	6.288	162
18.136	263, 286	2.258-59	188		

CHRISTIAN AUTHORS

CLASSICAL

Aeschylus
Ag.
1355   161

Aesop
Fabulae
234   325

Alexander Aphrodisiensis
In Arist.
89.4   326
96.28   326
96.30   326
97.27.2   326

Problematica
2.54   326

Apollonius Rhodius
Argon.
1.495   325
2.46   325
3.10   325

Appollodorus
Library
2.5.1   325
3.8.9   325
3.14.6   325

Aristophanes Byzantinus
Epigrammata
2.1.6   325

Aristophanes
The Wasps
1129   325

Plutus
575   326

Ra.
933   161

Arrian
Discourses
1.9.29   326

Cod. Iust.
5.17.5-6   259
8.38.2   259

Diogenes Laertius
8.32   161

Dionysius
Ant. Rom.
7.12.3   325
10.1.5   325
10.12.6   325
13.4.3   325

Dioscorides
Mat. Med. Praef.
5.12   245, 246

Epicurus
Dep. lib. rel.
29.15.15   325

Galen
De antidotis
2.14.2.6   326

De sectis
1.67.1   326

De simplicium
11.861.16   326
12.8.3   326

Herodianus
Partitiones
110.5   245

Schematismi
114.2   326

Herodotus
2.38   161
6.86.3   325

8.92   161
7.128   161

Homer
Od.
9.281   54
16.319   54
23.114   54

Lucian
Merc. Cond.
39.13   326

Podagra
149   326
165   326
279   326

Menander
Fragments
42.319   325

Mono.
1.573   325

Philo of Alexandria
Congr.
163.10   325

Somn.
1.194   325

Spec. Leg.
3.5   280

Philodemus
Inference
32   325

Philon
Belopoecia
50.34   325
51.9   325

INDEX OF AUTHORS

JOURNAL FOR THE STUDY OF THE NEW TESTAMENT

Supplement Series

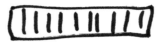

DATE DUE